The Hypothetical Government

by Elliot Lord

©2011 All rights reserved

The Hypotheti

Table of

Section 2: Policies

Section 3: Laws

Section 4: Forming a Government

Acknowledgements

Along with my friends with whom I have discussed my ideas and received valuable feedback from, my special thanks go to Ana Pinho Silva for her input into matters of the economy.

I am indebted to the work and experience of Buddha, Gandhi, Thomas Paine, Rob Hopkins, and Michael Moore (whose research into uncovering the problems has often been the starting point for formulating the proposed solutions).

Introduction

There are a few basic principles which form the foundations of a government. As a government is for the purpose of governing the people of a country, the well-being of its citizens is central. What this encompasses is vast and all its aspects will be addressed throughout the book. Secondly, the well-being of the environment is fundamental, too and thirdly, the well-being of all other life within a nation is of equal importance to the overall equilibrium.

It is imperative that these foundations are the basis on which all rules, regulations and freedoms are made and any law must fulfil the above requirements for it to be implemented.

In the financial world, the stability of the economy is important to the point of being beneficial to every single citizen. Economic growth is only necessary to keep on top of inevitable inflation but it must not under any circumstances grow through of any type of exploitation of people, animals and the environment.

There are various types of government which have been constructed. Those which do not favour total equality of people and are arranged in a hierarchical fashion are a monarchy, where a ruler is not democratically elected and the role is passed onto the heir to the throne, a despotism, where the single ruler considers every one of its citizens to be the slaves, a dictatorship, where an individual has complete power over the country, an oligarchy, where a small group of individuals with similar interests share the rule over everyone, a plutocracy, where the rulers are formed by the wealthy citizens, a theocracy, where the religious elite control its people and an anarchy, where there is no government and the society is highly liable to descend into chaos, hatred and war.

The other type is a democracy, where the people as a whole have the collective power and their beliefs and opinions are conveyed by them or through an elected representative.

A true and pure democracy will allow the majority to succeed in forming the laws either through direct democracy (citizens actively involved in the decision making) or representative democracy (government officials who are spokespersons for the citizens). However, there are criticisms of democracy. For example, with representative democracy, those elected officials have the right to use their own judgement with regard to how they will decide to act. They also have the potential to abuse their power and exploit the workers for their own and their peers' gains. With either form of democracy, a majority verdict will never be to the agreement of every individual concerned. 51% of people in favour of passing a certain law would be enough to enforce it but if the other 49% were strongly opposed to it, there are likely to be conflicts between the two parties and therefore a generally unsettled feeling in the society. Ways to minimise the disagreements and abuse of power will be discussed later in the book.

Forming this hypothetical government could be seen as another attempt to form a utopia or ideal society. The term, originally used by Sir Thomas More in his 1516 book, is intended to create an ideal society which generally considered as impossible to achieve. With the main goals of equality, pacifism, the removal of poverty and misery, More's book can be seen as an outline for an ideal society but it can be seen as a satirical work which exposes the failures of a real society. Economically speaking, a utopia is in opposition to commercialism and capitalism with the aim of equally distributing wealth and goods but no agreement has so far been reached to create an economy which attains these aims in a utopian form.

The concept of utopia would never be realisable because the concepts of good and bad or right and wrong can only remain as concepts or opinions and never as facts or truths. So the question is – how can we form a society where everyone believes in the same opinions of good, bad, right and wrong? Previous and present governments have attempted this via propaganda; the deliberate, systematic attempt to shape perceptions, manipulate cognitions, and direct behaviour to achieve a response that furthers the desired intent of the propagandist (Garth S. Jowett and Victoria O'Donnell, Propaganda and Persuasion). The most famous attempts at propaganda in recent times have been by Hitler, Stalin and Mao Zedong (Mao Tse Tung) and have, of course, been heavily criticised due to the messages being sent out to and forced onto their respective citizens to achieve what those leaders themselves wanted for their countries. Therefore, their tactics of enforced persuasion (and intolerance to anyone who did not accept the messages) are of a hierarchical nature and without the involvement of the citizens further down the hierarchy. Lying has also been a form of propaganda from the above mentioned leaders and at some point by every political leader to try to achieve social tranquillity and support for the political parties involved. For example, Iraqi ministers, during the Iraq war, claimed that their military had been winning every battle which then culminated in an undeniable defeat for the Iraqi government. Likewise, the US administration has continuously claimed that it is winning the war in Iraq despite (at the time of writing) there being no notable progress in the level of peace in the country.

In the hypothetical government, there would be no place for propaganda but there must be an attempt to educate the people so that opposing opinions can reach a peaceful compromise. This cannot be done with a hierarchical system functioning in a 'top-down' method where ministers propose issues to resolve as there would always be ulterior motives for their words and actions but with a more purely democratic method involving free speech to convey opinions that must be justified only in moral ways.

Morals can be described as guidelines for human behaviour to reduce suffering between people and to establish appropriate and inappropriate behaviour. This is also a contentious issue as morals do not exist universally but are defined by groups or individuals of religion, philosophy, culture and individual or societal conscience. Whereas the basis for defining morals would generally be thought of as more acceptable than propaganda, we have to take into account the reasons for putting them forward. Words are chosen carefully so that as many people as possible will accept them but this is a form of persuasion and, due to the stubbornness and defiance of some individuals or groups, have to be considered tentatively in case of possible hidden agendas.

Noam Chomsky states that there is a principal of universality, meaning that if any action is right or wrong for others then it must be right or wrong for ourselves. Those who do not follow this principle cannot be taken seriously when speaking of appropriateness or of right and wrong, good or evil.

Following on from these introductory notes, to form a hypothetical government we need to take account of these basic principles when forming each and every policy and law. It will be firmly based on morality, democracy and equality. To establish such principles in a society is not easy, however, and the root of all of them is in a society's education.

This book is not a critique of previous methods but a forming of a new government where it needs to be relevant to the issues of modern times with the plan of forming ideals that are intended to be continued way into the future.

It would be impossible to form a realistic system without evaluating existing or previous governmental models, therefore, we can form a model by taking into account laws and policies that have worked for the majority in a moral sense, have failed for the majority or have failed for the minority. It is a bringing together of the best points of existing models and putting forward new ideas to address issues that have not been resolved by any political system.

Whereas this book is intended to be a model that can be applied to any country, the reader has to take into account that I am from England and spent my formative years there until I lived and worked in western and central Europe. This means that many of the observations and ideas in this book reflect my own experiences and are more relevant to this part of the world.

However, having lived mostly in western Europe certainly doesn't mean that I have experienced what it is like living in some of the most developed places in the world. Everywhere falls short of stability, safety and life satisfaction in different ways and for different people. The ways that people don't feel fulfilled are similar from one country to the next as well as in every other country in the world.

Elliot Lord, 2011

Section 1: Shaping a Society

Before we can begin looking at how a government should work and how effective it can be, we need to identify the basis of what makes a successful society. It is more than simply stating that the government will spend X on health, Y on education, follow this policy or implement that law. Any government coming into power will have underlying issues that need to be addressed if it is going to have a significant effect.

There is no country that can be said to be free of problems. Even the most developed countries can have problems on a huge scale. The misconstrued term 'developed country' does not imply the development of the society in general in terms of their level of knowledge, mental and physical skills, or relationships with people living in their community. Instead, the main criteria are the gross domestic product (GDP) and level of industrialisation. Whereas these factors may be important for economic stability so that the country is producing new technologies and has enough money for purchasing power on a national scale, this is only of real concern to politicians and business people and it has little relevance to the happiness and satisfaction of the lives of the general public.

Kofi Annan, the former Secretary General of the United Nations, in 2000, defined a developed country as "One that allows all its citizens to enjoy a free and healthy life in a safe environment."[1] These are also invaluable factors to consider, rather than proudly stating how well one's businesses are exploiting the poor for enormous and superfluous profits. But to really create a developed country, we need to identify the problems that the general population has, understand them on a personal level, find out why these problems are in place and how they developed, and from this, work on how these problems can be overcome.

For example, if the society suffers from problems of unemployment on any notable scale, e.g. more than 2%, then it needs to find the cause of the problem. If crime levels are high, then the government needs to find out what is causing the crime to happen, not just how they are going to punish the offenders; it needs to look at the whole picture in terms of the real truth behind the issue (not the 'truth' that they tell to the people) and implement a strategy to reduce or even eliminate the problem, which has a good reason to justify why it could work. By looking at the latest statistics and comparing them to those of a few years ago is not going to tell us anything about the lives of the people whom the problems affect.

Crime

Generally speaking, any underlying problem that is connected with low income or poverty is due to the fault of previous governments, regarding how they either ignored the problem or claimed to attempt to tackle it in a way that never really had any chance of being successful. Crime usually happens in its many guises because of the individuals involved earning little or no money and having few or no opportunities available for them to better their lives. In some ways crime is committed simply to be able to feed, clothe and provide shelter for oneself and one's family when they have no practical means to achieve such an objective. Whereas the excuse in this type of case is more legitimate, a criminal activity such as shoplifting is still not acceptable. We can sympathise with such people if their motive is unselfish and they feel they have no opportunities to rise above such circumstances, but they are still committing crimes which go against the principles that we should desire in society. It is not just that the supermarket or private business owner will lose a little money from the lack of the item's sale but the because of the principal of unethically taking from others something that it not yours, or that the owner would not want you to take for free because their business depends on sales.

Unfortunately, most of the reasons for crime are not unselfish but are an act of rebellion. But against what? Some people may argue that these able-bodied individuals should go out and get a job and work like the rest of us but the argument is nowhere near as simple as that. It is down to marginalisation, rejection and scorn by others including the government. It is about never being given the opportunities to succeed or achieve and never being given support to try to make a better life for themselves. It is about knowing that other people who are considered as honest, working people will view them with prejudice and will always view them in this way. This is how stereotypes are created and enforced and people are seen as belonging to one class or another in the class system. In this case, crime happens because there is a notable divide between so-called classes and this creates conflicts when it is seen that some people have everything they want and others have almost nothing. Those who have very little are understandably going to feel frustrated if they think they will never be able to legitimately have what the well-off have. Jealousy occurs and this is because of the capitalist mentality of believing that wanting more and having more is the way to succeed in life. We will come back to this delusion later.

So what is the result of these stereotypes and the denial of opportunities and support? Birds of a feather stick together... It is human nature to feel identification with a group where we feel we belong, where we share beliefs, opinions, circumstances and so on. Therefore, people who are seen as at the lowest level in society bond with others with similar situations, they consequently have children that grow up within the group of 'rejected by mass society' who in turn learn to turn against the society that scorns them and against the government that seeks to battle hard against crime. Thus, the initially involuntarily formed sub-group becomes manifest, develops an identity, grows and becomes a sub-group that 'flourishes' under its own weight and, with each generation, stays resolutely rebellious to mass society and the government simply because it has its roots in the parents that shaped and maintained the overall group identity of each subsequent child to be born to them.

But why do people in this 'group' commit crimes against people who are said to be in a class above them? In Deepak Chopra's book "Buddha", he tells the story of when Buddha was in the presence of a murderer. To be able to help him, Buddha needed to understand him profoundly: "You share the same fate as everyone. You wanted to find a way out of suffering... You imagined that if you caused enormous suffering, you would be immune to it."[2]

Buddha taught that people who commit crime are suffering in their lives and to try to raise their own self-esteem, they feel that making other people, who are better off than themselves, suffer, they will have risen above their suffering. Of course, this is not actually the truth of the matter, but to those who do suffer and have a desperate need to gain more than their basic means, it gives a moment of gratification. But as it is not a real answer to the problem of suffering, this moment soon fades and the compulsion to raise themselves out of their suffering continues and crimes will be committed again in a similar manner.

When we have the realisation that this is how humans behave, we can start to empathise with those who we may have always viewed with contempt. People are not genetically predetermined to steal, or to be charitable. This behaviour and mindset is something that comes about for a reason.

Only when we can understand and empathise with people who cause anti-social behaviour can we begin to help them. Punishing them, in the light of this knowledge, is not going to make the problem stop and to believe that it will, as governments have done when reacting to rising crime rates, is a pure delusion. Making the punishment harsher will not deter the behaviour. Otherwise, we would have no crime now.

The first step to helping those who commit crimes is to give them a feeling of inclusion in the general society (note how I don't use the word 'criminals' here as this is a label that implies that that is the definition of the people in question). They need to feel that they are accepted like everyone else. To achieve this, the other people must treat them with decency, politeness and not react unfavourably to any action that is done with the intention of upsetting the 'more comfortable' people.

This can be illustrated with The Sermon On The Mount from the Bible's New Testament (Matthew, chapters 5-7). It is included here for the reasons of morality and empathy:

"If anyone hits you on the right cheek, let him slap your left cheek also. And if someone takes you to court to sue your for your shirt, let him have your coat as well."

By offering passivity, the adversary will soon question their actions. The intention is that they may feel that taking your possessions doesn't give them a feeling of 'your loss is my gain' if they see you are not affected by it. If you are not seen to be suffering, they are not achieving what they set out to achieve. Instead, you are seen to be offering them more than they set out to take.

"Love your enemies and pray for those who persecute you" (Matthew 5:44). It is not the person that is wrong but the ideas that they have that cause you an injustice. By accepting them as people, you will be more likely to help them to change their ways when they see that their aggression does not get them the results that they expect. It may be difficult for most people to forgive those who commit anti-social acts but we need to realise that there is always a reason behind them and it doesn't mean that that person is beyond help or beyond hope.

When we understand the people and their reasons for their undesirable actions, we can really begin to work on solving the problem. We need to earn their trust and show that we are going to create projects whereby they feel that their issues are being taken seriously, their opportunities are being developed and supported if we are going to create a society where crime only has a small likelihood that it will occur. If people don't have the reason to commit crime, they won't. Prevention is better than punishment.

Identity – The Class System

Other stereotypical social groups form in fundamentally the same ways as those who are marginalised for their anti-social behaviour; people flock to be seen as part of the group that they feel an identity with, based on such aspects as income, car, type of house, level of education, family status, type of employment, etc. or in its discriminative term - class. Sub-groups of societies are labelled depending on which criteria they meet, explicitly in the case of the class system of the United Kingdom or implicitly in countries which don't use class labels but where people still identify with specific types of people and not others.

The problems with class systems, explicit or otherwise, is that labels stick and they are hard to remove. If the general public judges someone as being working, middle or upper class, they will usually find it difficult to be able to transfer to another class unless their circumstances and assets change dramatically. Similarly, if the person is from such a discriminative society, they will probably view themselves as belonging to the class that they were labelled with from birth unless they strive to improve their life situation and succeed. Generally, this doesn't come about as opportunities are more easily available to those who either already have money or connections with known names (nepotism). Those who come into large sums of money from artificial means (e.g. winning the lottery, fame and fortune via a manufactured identity like pop stars) may also claim that they now belong to another group but if they have not worked to achieve it sincerely, they will be deceiving themselves (as well as the public) by laying claim to an identity that they want just because they have more money. As a person, the chances are slim that they will have earned the label they desire through sincere means, i.e. that of hard work.

But are any of these labels deserved or appropriate? Those who claim to be middle or upper class will unquestionably argue that their status is deserved. Such class labels imply certain things, most notably an air of superiority over supposed lower classes which, in some cases, is believed where the perceived criteria of belonging to a class are primarily the amount of money and assets owned. Those who are given the label of working or lower class will, in the end, reluctantly live with it and sometimes go along with it throughout their lives. This is because the effects of time making the label stick more firmly will leave them believing that they are part of this class and that it is just a fact of life. This can also lead to people who are labelled as such to feel that they will never be able to achieve much and that it is their role simply to continue in life by the rules pertaining to their given class. In truth, the working class people are the ones upon whom the upper classes depend entirely; either through their work for big companies, for which they are usually paid a minimal amount) or as consumers who are encouraged to buy the products of those same big companies. People who have little are often inclined to want more so that they feel they are not so left behind in society but the reality is very different; the desire to own items that the richer people own leaves them with unnecessary possessions and less money – i.e. no improvement in the level of their true happiness and satisfaction with their lives.

So, a people's behaviour tends to be largely governed by something that is an abstract concept that, even if it is rarely spoken about, will be subconsciously felt to be a part of them. This is part of their identity, even if it is reluctantly taken on board. It is not, however, something that they chose to be labelled as, therefore this part of their identity was given involuntarily.

Of course, other abstract labels can be given out that become so rooted in a society's subconscious beliefs that even when they are addressed, they are hard to really break down and eliminate: gender, skin colour, nationality, sexual orientation, etc. One may argue that these labels are not abstract at all but they are defined by the characteristics that people have - Caucasians have white skin and Africans have black skin, right? Well, in both cases, no. Nobody is white or black per se but this and other discriminative labels will be discussed later on.

Currently, society is shaped by discrimination. Sub-groups of all kinds are formed by whatever labels people can think of and justifiably apply to a large number of people and thus, through the domino effect of propaganda, embed into the subconsciousness of a society (or even societies on an international level) to make people almost involuntarily believe they are true.

Materialism and False Identities

In the Western world, people rely heavily on material objects to try to form their identities as well as notions fed to them by the mass media and marketing companies. This has been prevalent for many decades on a smaller scale, such as women being told that certain kitchen appliances, skirts, hairdos and so on are what they 'need' to please their man/ look after their home better/ be accepted as a 'proper' woman by society. Advertisements for such things were abundant in the 1950s and 1960s and can be easily analysed to see how shamelessly explicit they were; there was very little in the messages that had to be discovered implicitly. But eventually, people got wise to these direct techniques and would not respond to them as much as the corporations wanted (or they began to protest against them, e.g. the feminist movement) and a new plan had to be formulated to make the public do what they were told. Over the following decades, advertising became more implicit and sought ways to appeal to the public so that the public would not realise they were being fooled into believing what the marketing strategies were telling them. Advertising techniques became more subliminal and they aimed to imply feelings and emotions that the customers would believe the products would give them and the belief that the product was going to make them more attractive, more confident, part of a cool group or generally make them feel more like people that would be happy deep down when they had these products.

In the current times, corporations create and force identities onto people so that they will become rich off those who subscribe to them. As long as the advertising is powerful enough on a subconscious level, their target audience would believe what they were told, see other people looking cool by wearing certain clothes and want to be a part of that 'culture' (which in reality is about the least correct term for this concept). This propaganda which gets under the skin and into the subconsciousness does, after enough sensory bombardment through adverts, become believed by the masses and especially by the impressionable emerging generation of adolescents before they are experienced enough to investigate how they want to develop their own identity on a personal level. Individual identities don't sell. Mass-production companies can't tailor identities for everyone individually so they must be prevented from forming their own at the earliest opportunity. The younger, the better.

TV shows, pop 'music' acts and associated merchandise are becoming more and more aimed at younger audiences, even those as young as 4 and 5 years old. The reason being that if the tiny, developing minds of these children, that can already respond to and express a liking for certain products, can be captured, the identity-manufacturing corporations will have them for life and will saturate their minds so much that they will eventually have no way of being able to form their own identities. They will need to look to the advertisements to find out what they need to buy for the next season so that their pre-packaged identity will be the 'right' one that their peers will accept them for.

A deeper analysis and a proposal to tackle this problem of deception can be found in the chapter on Advertising.

Recent action in the popular media has been the categorisation of men. Men have, until more recently, been more on the fringes of corporate control and are less likely to buy whatever is said to be fashionable. Men have been less likely to care about what they wear or about what their friends wear and they have been more in control of what they personally choose to wear. But the marketable concept of false identity has taken off more towards the end of the 20th and beginning of the 21st centuries. We hear more questions of "Do you belong to this group (like these celebrities) or that group?" (like those celebrities). Many terms have sprung up to which men are deciding which group they fit into more - am I metrosexual or ubersexual? "Well, to be one of them means I use these beauty products and own this brand of mp3 player but the other one means I use this and own this electronic device. I think I'm more like this group." These categories do not actually exist; they have been dreamed up with the sole aim of controlling men. More recently, adverts have appeared that say it's now fine for men to care about their skin or companies claim to be delivering what men want even though it's highly unlikely that men have, in general, been consulted on this issue.

It has to be said that women have been successfully brought under control by the capitalist system due to the historical inequality that have been subjected to. For an analysis of this, see the section on gender roles later.

But as long as men question which group they identify with, the chances are they will have succumbed to the control of the corporations who have commissioned such labels and who will effectively supply the demand that such categorisation creates. This is a disturbing level of propaganda whereby, somehow, everybody will be controlled by the dictating groups at the top of the free market. If they create identities for the people and the people go along with them because it doesn't appear that they are going to suffer (that's how it works, very cunningly) then their lives will essentially not be their own. They will merely belong to the dictators who 'recommend' which accessories they should own as members of the group they 'decided' to be in. "We told you which groups are available, you choose which one you want to be controlled and defined by."

It should be noted that not everyone is sucked into this idea of manufactured identity. The more educated and more philosophical people continue to see through it (or at least to some degree) and will not be affected by the advertising campaigns but considering the amount of TV advertisements for beauty products, cars and so on, the majority of the public, due to the excessive exposure to these products, are fooled to some extent. What it has resulted in is that there are only so many things that we can buy to entertain ourselves and even if we do not agree with how much we are controlled by them, this is all we have and we end up buying these things because we know so much about them.

Morally speaking, this idea of freedom to choose is an oxymoron as we are free to choose what we are provided with and deceived by and the prevalence of these products keeps of from exploring our own interests and viewing life in a profound way. A system of regulations needs to be brought in to limit the amount that we are influenced by corporations. Again, see the chapter on Advertising for more on this issue.

Another aspect of following false identities is the notion of status symbols. This is when people buy certain items to make others notice them with the intention of making them think that the owner is of a higher social and economic status simply because they own them. This is nothing short of being severely misguided. Common status symbols include certain cars for their design or their engine power, jewellery such as gold and diamonds, big houses and a significant amount of land and expensive 'designer' clothes. By buying them, people want to say to others that they are superior; that they have lots of money and therefore are at the pinnacle of society.

But when we think about this, is that really the case? Does it make someone superior to others because they have an expensive car with one of the 'elite' logos? How does it make anyone superior just because they own something like this? The fact of it is that the person in question may have more money but they use it to attempt to further themselves. This is where the misguided aspect comes in. How can a person be furthered by owning something that basically just gets them from A to B? Yes, it may look nice, it may have a lot of horse power but these are characteristics of the car, not of the owner. It is an example of self-serving extravagance, and what is the point of that? The owner is showing that they'd rather spend their money on themselves rather than use their money constructively, i.e. in a way that other people would 'really' respect or admire them for.

The same goes for the other examples of status symbols given above. All it shows is that one has wasted their money on such things. And for what purpose? What does it really mean to own a gold necklace or diamond earrings? It means that they own them. They serve no purpose whatsoever. They don't mean that the owners are now more developed people, that they know more, that they are more respectable, that they are more charitable.

In short, status symbols are more like symbols of being disconnected with reality or living in a fantasy world. Such symbols are not going to do anything meaningful for anyone, except of course, the companies that sell them at inflated prices.

So what should be the methods of forming one's own identity? First of all, a truly individual identity is not something that can be formed in a way that is unique to everyone else. It is a common misconception to say that everyone is unique. Absolutely nobody is, neither on a biological level or a mental level. We live together as people, we are influenced by each other and cannot live in isolation as a unique self. We can only be part of an elaborately woven tapestry of people that influence and react to one another. It is also human nature to want to be part of some group(s). This is the feeling of contentment that can be achieved through a kind of brother/sisterhood and knowing that you can relate to other people well and have similar interests. This means that to attempt to be entirely different is not going to work as we all have something in common with someone else. It would be more unsettling for us as individuals if we felt we couldn't relate to anyone or have anyone who understands us, regarding interests or problems that we may want to talk about.

However, we can form identities that will be accepted by many people but are not the result of becoming as manufactured as the pop idols that are purely artificial, lacking in any substance or real talent but are forced upon anyone who watches commercial television and listens to commercial music. The types of programmes, films and musical acts that fall into these categories are deliberately created to gain control over people's minds and, equally importantly, money through the merchandise that they saturate our minds with.

If we are going to make any progress with developing ourselves in terms of our positive influence on the life that we manage, the lives of others we communicate with and the world in which we play a part in whatever aspect, we need to know who we are and how we became like this.

As babies, we are all fundamentally the same. We are very limited in terms of what we can do and how we can communicate with others (whom we don't even realise are not an extension of ourselves). We are all equal and regarding what we amount to, we are effectively all the same in our first few weeks of life. But we change and we develop in fairly specific ways because of how we learn to make mental relations between how things happen and noticing the consequences of actions and their consistency. So, slowly, we begin to be pro-active beings that start to make sense of the world we are in. As we begin to put two and two together, we develop mentally and of course, after a few months we begin to understand the connections between what older people say to us and what these sounds refer to, due to the repetition and, again, consistency of what they are linked to. People react to us in different ways, depending on how they are and how much interest they have in us and so on. They begin to influence us in many ways. They can show us certain things that can act as stimuli to our development, tell us things that when we can understand what they mean, generally believe them because we don't know any better. We are still purely impressionable within the first few years of our lives and make the connection that because someone bigger than us its telling us something, it is simply true. We don't have the capacity to contemplate if it is right or if maybe they are telling us lies for some other reason that they will get some benefit from. We are effectively like empty containers to be filled with knowledge and truth and the only way we can be filled is from external sources unless we can work out things for ourselves. But these things have to be simple so that we can understand them, such as that wooden bricks can be built up but will fall down if they get knocked.

So in terms of understanding who we are, all our information is given to us. We learn that we are members of families and how we are related to the others. We make friends with other children and play together or fall out with them for various reasons but we also find out that we are either a boy or a girl and that boys do some things and girls do other things. But, when we are, for example, two or three years old, we don't have a great deal knowledge of gender roles; to us, they are just other children about the same size as us but they all look a bit different. However, we don't pay attention to that because their appearance has little consequence for us other than that we can recognise who they are. As I have found out through a study I did for my psychology degree at university, children younger than about four see no difference between putting a dress on a girl doll or a boy doll. To them, it's meaningless even though they will probably be dressed in 'gender appropriate' clothing themselves. It is at this point that we start to need to question things. Who is right and who is wrong in how they dress others, the parents dressing their children or the children when asked to put clothes on dolls? If parents put a dress on their son and a shirt and trousers on their daughter, is this wrong? It is seen as wrong when we think about how other people would react to seeing them. A boy coming to school in a dress would be laughed at (by those old enough to know what's 'wrong' with it) and the parents would be looked at or spoken to with scorn for doing such a thing. Why is this so? A five year old child might know what is wrong about it, but do they really *know* that? Society has established that it's not right for boys to wear dresses (although these days, of course, it is all right for girls to wear shirts and trousers!) But to say that *society* has established it is a little misleading because society is not an independent, authoritative being; it is merely made up of people and their decisions and agreements on such things determine what we see as right or wrong to do, even in such trivial matters as what types of clothes boys and girls can wear.

What this shows is that we end up growing up thinking that we should do this and not that because we are boys or because we are girls and that's what our families and friends say. We don't actually make the decisions ourselves about whether we are going to receive a baby doll or a toy race car for our birthdays. The decisions come from outside and we unquestioningly go along with playing with what we are given because, well, that's just how it is. Or as we get a little older, as boys we might want a football kit or a robot because our (male) friends have got them or as girls we might want necklaces or toy ponies because our (female) friends have got them. Or, of course, because our role models have got them. This is where we start to move into more controversial territory.

Role models. How do they work? We are always at the mercy of others' likes and opinions when we are young. If most of our friends like some football team or some pop singer, we generally like them, too. It's a question of group identity which is just as important as personal identity. We are already aware from the age of five that we see mostly the same people a lot of the time and that we spend time with our friends as much as we can. We also know that we need to act or respond in certain ways so that we will maintain our friendships. This often means doing what they like to do, playing with what they like to play with and owning the kind of things that they own. Deep down, we probably don't even realise that we don't actually care for these things. We have been persuaded to like certain things and we simply believe that we do because we don't want to be cast out by our friends who are manically enthusiastic about a certain sports star, for example.

As we grow up, the same pattern continues and our identities become more concretely formed but actually, most of it will not have been done of our own free will. We become made by other people for a large part of it. Sometimes, if we are seen to be influential enough, we might suggest something to the group of friends that we like and they might agree to like it, too. In this case, we are helping to shape their identities but if they don't like what we suggest, it will probably be dismissed and you will just carry on as you had been doing.

As we get older and move into the teenage years, we start to think more about things from our own perspectives. We may like a certain singer, though our friends don't, but it doesn't matter as we can still listen to them anyway because we are more confident with making our own choices (sometimes). But we probably still support the football team that our friends got us into all those years ago, we may follow the religion that our parents told us that we followed from a young age or we may still play the piano because our parents effectively forced us to learn it against our will from the age of seven.

So, whereas we might be making more of our own choices without any concern for whether our friends like the same things or not, we will still be defined by some things that have an enduring influence on us. But there remains the chance of alienation from our friends if our likes and interests start to differ to the point of incompatibility. The power of the mass media is there to save the day and we can rely on it to shape our likes and make our choices for us. Certain music channels on television play mostly the same genre of music throughout the day and it has had a considerable influence on those who have not felt confident enough to make their own choices about what they listen to. It's seen as cool to like musicians X & Y and all the cool kids at school listen to it and dress like the performers. They are the ones with lots of friends and are getting more relationship experience so maybe we should also get into it, too. Everyone's talking about this TV show, so we should watch it and talk about it, too, to be in there with the cool crowd. Whether we actually like these things or not is irrelevant. In fact, with the rise in popularity of certain types of music, it is likely that a significant percentage of the buying public don't actually like it at all but they've become so convinced by the mass media that they just don't know what they really like any more.

The mass media has, of course, been used more increasingly over the last few decades by marketing people to sell meaningless and superficial merchandise to those who have had their identities created for them. It is basically a Big Brother/ dictatorial technique where the influenced masses (the percentage of which is rapidly increasing) are left stranded until they wait to be told what the next big thing to come along is and what they should listen to, watch, like and buy. The identities become more and more impersonal and more and more defined by those who seek to make money from the susceptible public. To attempt to make this clearer, we should look at how the gender roles of men and women have been developed.

Identity – Gender Roles

Men and women, boys and girls are seen as being very different on more than just a biological level. Historically, we have been divided in terms of what is expected of both sexes which originated from the difference in the general level of strength and physical size.

There are generally accepted stereotypes of how men and women behave in the western world and they are not too different from country to country. There are concepts of masculinity and femininity and it is very easy to think what they consist of and if a person is considered to be either one; we have a clear idea of what they refer to. But where do these concepts originate from? Like any concept of such a type, they are humanly constructed and at this point in time, they have become so engrained in our collective mind that we don't even realise that they are not factual concepts. To be brief, masculinity entails being strong, courageous, dominant, unlikely to cry or show any sensitive emotion and possibly even aggressive and violent when the time requires it. Femininity, on the other hand, refers to being emotional, sensitive, caring, perhaps mentally weaker and more submissive. If asked to explain why the two (opposing) characters are like that, one might simply say that it's genetic or that's just how it is. However, this doesn't mean that all men have the apparent masculine characteristics and all women have the feminine characteristics. Some people may be described as being the opposite to what they are 'supposed' to be like, in which case the two concepts are invalid. Unless for reasons of excessive neurotransmitter levels that involuntarily influence someone's behaviour, e.g. too much testosterone leading to almost uncontrollable violence, we are not born to be masculine or feminine, only male and female. These concepts have developed from the fact that generally, men are physically bigger and stronger than women, thus gender roles of men being the warriors and women being the home-keepers have developed throughout history. Even though these ideas have been addressed, attacked and adapted in the last few decades to, primarily, enable women to have more rights, it has been hard to shake the concepts of masculinity and femininity completely because of the status they have had for millennia.

Real men don't cry? Who says? And why not? Men are just as capable of experiencing emotion as women, therefore they are allowed to and they should when it feels right. Women don't go around with unshaven legs, but why? I'll bet that the vast majority of western women would never entertain the idea of appearing in public with hairy legs but why has this 'rule' come about? Why do women feel they also have to shave under their arms, wear make-up and wear specific clothes? Even though many women at this time would say it's because they care more about what other women think rather than what men think, up until recently, it has been for the acceptance and approval of men, to make them happy and to hopefully seem attractive to them. Whether women care not what men think is irrelevant though; they still do what society's rules tell them to do and unfortunately don't question the rules. Their identities were partially defined before they were born and they don't contemplate it, they just go along with it.

The same can be said for men to a certain extent. The boyish, laddish mentality that is prevalent in the western world has been demanded of them from various sources: school, older boys, men's magazines, action films, etc.. A lot of boys or men don't want to appear 'girlish' or effeminate for fear of being laughed at and shunned by their peers. It's seen as the thing to do, in some cultures, to get drunk, be loud, be disrespectful and domineering to women and fight with other men. All of these behaviours have either been forced upon them or willingly assimilated if, for example, they have the physique to pass it off (as well as the mentality to be unable to reject them). There are certain behaviours to take on board and other behaviours which are definitely to be avoided, at least when with friends.

What this all amounts to is that many people develop identities which have not been ones that they would have chosen if they had been free to do so or more confident to do what *they* want. Obviously, there are those that have been more 'individual' and shaped their identities due to what they like and how they have no qualms with being, but the reason for this can be attributed to one main reason: education. In this sense, education means how people have learned to be, not just what subjects they have learned in school. Those who are less self-confident will take on a persona that has already been moulded and that they can practise to be like. And once it's been practised for long enough, it's difficult to shake off or even realise that it's not really 'you'. Also, with the hindrance of capitalist ideology, such concepts have been exacerbated because where there are specific identities, there are ways that they can be enforced, encouraged and most importantly, used as a source to make money from. To create a set of 'personality moulds' means the people who fit in certain categories will want to buy the products that fit with the pre-defined characteristics that the marketing directors maintain vehemently.

National Identity

So should a government seek to shape the identities of its population? Yes and no. No in terms of attempting to classify people according to the certain groups described above, nor what has been enforced by various dictatorships – that of political or social conformity, past and present. Notable examples would be those of Hitler and Stalin who practically forced the people to strongly support their regimes, for which failure to do so would result in severe punishments such as ten years or more in forced labour camps, torture and death. They greatly wanted to have a nation that believed the same things, worked very hard and served their nation but it was at a great cost: people who weren't sincere supporters of the leaders would do what was expected for fear of death and those who wanted to stand up for their rights would be removed from society in various ways.

This isn't to say that this is the only way to form a national identity but to have the ideology of trying to do so simply wouldn't work. In the present time, some governments advocate national identities based on a set of principles but these are usually decided without the general consensus of the population. Such principles can be encouraged among the general populace but in practically every case this is a form of propaganda. Governments want the people to support them and they want the people to believe that the government is in tune with them. This is a very important point to make and to think about. Governments want to protect their positions of power and they will sometimes deceive people to gain support.

Governments acting in this manner have ulterior motives, no matter how democratic they claim to be. One of the underlying principles of a government is to keep the population quiet and believe they are happy. Unfortunately for the governments, people have learned to be sceptical through history and experience of ruling parties. There have been enough scandals, instances of corruption, false allegations and deceptions to leave any population suspecting that things are being kept a secret from us all, irrespective of the country, although the penalties for speaking up in some countries render any opposition detrimental to those who want to speak out. The type of corruption can be so deceptive that governments are even willing to sacrifice their own citizens to serve their own interests.

Peter Joseph of The Zeitgeist Movement stated in the first Zeitgeist documentary that:

In the documented conversation between Colonel House,

Wilson's adviser and Sir Edward Grey, the Foreign Secretary of England regarding how to get America into the war, Grey inquired:

"What will Americans do if Germans sink an ocean liner with American passengers on board?"

(The) house responded:

"I believe that a flame of indignation would sweep the United States and that by itself would be sufficient to carry us into war."

So, on May 7th 1915 on essentially the suggestion of Sir Edward Grey, the ship called the Lusitania was deliberately sent into German controlled waters where German military vessels were known to be. And as expected, German U-boats torpedoed the ship, exploding stored ammunition, killing 1200 people.

From this point, the American people were behind the government to enter the war. This is a despicable act of how to get the people on your side and falsely create a sense of patriotism. The people came together but it was entirely choreographed by the government and the military.

From this, we need to examine what national identity actually means.

National identity is the idea that people living in a certain country, or region within a country, can be affiliated to a shared identity with certain values and cultural aspects relevant to that place. Whereas on a superficial level, this is an acceptable idea, exploring it more deeply to define what it means to come from a certain place can lead to divisions between people who either feel they are different to the norms, don't want to conform to the norms or are viewed by others as not conforming to the norms of a group identity of this kind and this can lead to conflicts of interest which have no real merit. People's opinions of what it means to belong to a particular country or region will differ depending on their own views which leaves it open to debate. It would be fruitless to try to search for indisputable definitions of what constitutes a national identity due to the diversity of regional groups, religious groups as well as the beliefs and opinions of people living within any defined group, no matter how small and particular it may be.

People within a given community can believe they belong to a certain group yet have differing levels of agreement as to how resolutely they believe that, for example, other people should be allowed to join the group, how strongly the identity should be defended in any way, or how people should behave with respect to the perceived identity.

In the modern world, every country and probably every specific region which has its own ideas of its specific identities has inhabitants that originate from a number of other places whose group identity may not conform to those of their place of residence. There are arguments about the loss of national identity when there is a large number of immigrants, for example, whom the indigenous residents feel are a threat to their model of the identity. This is a useless argument, however, due to the fact that certain immigrants may be more than willing to fit in with the identity of the country or region and also that some indigenous inhabitants may not feel that they themselves belong to the prescribed identity due to differing viewpoints in an open-minded sense, yet they are accepted by the community because they happen to come from the place in question.

Furthermore, what is the national identity of someone who has, say, parents from Greece and Poland who had both lived in France from the age of five, grew up and got married there, then moved to England and had a child there, then moved with the child to Australia when the child was two years old? Is that child English because he or she was born there? Australian because that's where they subsequently grew up? Half-Greek, half-Polish because of the parents nationalities (even though they had a cultural upbringing in France)? This may be an extreme example but it shows that it is difficult to say what their national identity is. More realistically speaking, the most appropriate would be to say that the child is Australian because that is where they grew up and this is the culture which was very influential in the formation of their character.

Therefore, anyone who is born in a certain country or has lived there since they were a small child will adapt to the culture of that country, regardless of where their parents are from (unless, somehow, the parents manage to keep them from being influenced in any way by the country in which they live. This is unlikely as the child would need to be isolated from seeing any television or any people who are not connected with their family). To be racist towards someone who has Indian parents but has never even been to India is completely unacceptable. Yes, they will probably have some influence of their parents' culture but when they have grown up completely in England, they are practically English.

So national identity cannot be limited by factors such as the colour of someone's skin, their parental background or anything that doesn't have a significant influence on the development of their character regarding the cultural influences.

What would be more recommended is that people should not view their identity as belonging to a specific group but should be open to cultural variety from other perceived groups that they may enjoy and maybe prefer to those that they are currently seen as belonging to their own culture. This doesn't mean that people should reject parts of their cultural identity but accept that cultures are always adaptable with the times and are refined and can be morally improved with influences that come from what may be seen as an outside source. This can be illustrated by the fact that people in what they may see as a very specific society don't give thought or opposition to eating food that comes from different cultures. Asian foods are very popular in the UK as well as Italian pizzas and pasta dishes, along with other international foods that are too numerable to mention. The same can be said for other products that have their developmental origins in other countries, such as computers, stereos, cars, clothes, etc. The full list of such things would be very long indeed.

Those people who would consider themselves to be more nationalistic, racist or xenophobic might argue that such things as products or food have nothing to do with cultural beliefs or behaviours and that they could enjoy such things but still justifiably defend their prejudices. They should consider things like music, sports and arts in general. If you like a certain genre of music and consider it to be 'white' music, for example, you would need to investigate its evolution. Pretty much all modern music derives from African and Afro-American music. Rock 'n' roll developed from the blues, pop music such as dance developed from soul, heavy metal was influenced significantly by Jimi Hendrix, who also became an influence for punk. So most, if not all 'white' music has its origins in 'black' music. Similarly, sports have originated in specific countries which have then been gladly taken on by other countries to the point where they are called the national sports even though the country that embraced them had practically no influence on the evolution of the sports themselves.

What this shows is that due to the improved levels of communication between countries, the world has sometimes unknowingly open its arms and opened its mind to other cultures and the whole concept of a national identity is therefore rendered pretty much meaningless. We share interests and likes and it would be more correct to think of it as a global identity, which for the intentions would be a lot more peaceful in principle.

Taking pride in coming from a country is something that should be discouraged for the following reason: Pride, being considered a sin (which we'll come to later), is more than likely to encourage divisions between people who think of their country being superior to another. This is such a big generalisation that has no basis for argument as it's highly likely that you have friends from other countries, other regions, other cities or that their families come from other places. You will also dislike certain people who come from the same street as you, have the same skin colour as you, like the same music as you and so on. Judging someone by their nationality is as worthless as judging someone by their height. It's not going to give an indication as to what they are like when you get to know them. This level of ignorance and intolerance will always show you as being someone who needs to contemplate who you are and whether your opinions are valid and worth maintaining. Upon investigation of yourself, you will find that such ignorance needs to be addressed as it will show hypocrisy that has no place if you are to develop your level of happiness. Deciding that you don't like people from a particular country before you even get to know them means you will have a sense of dislike or even hatred for no actual reason and you will have negative feelings that have absolutely no justification. This will never make you an all-round happy person.

Also, the country in which you live has had its borders decided by other people, many years ago who have probably tried to define an identity for their own purposes. Land borders don't actually exist and being prejudiced against someone who lives over these imaginary but political borders is absurd. We come from the countries that we do because that's where we were born. And that's it. We had no choice in where we were born so how can we think that we are better (or worse) than someone who was born within some other historically and politically defined borders?

An example of this can be seen in Slovakia, where the borders (of the former Czechoslovakia) changed in the aftermath of World War One, following the breakup of the Habsburg Dynasty of Austria-Hungary. As it stands now, Slovakia has a large number of Hungarian residents within its borders as Czechoslovakia's expanded. There is still ongoing xenophobia between the Slovaks and these Hungarians as the Slovaks tend to feel that people living in their country should speak Slovak and the Hungarians feel that where they live is still Hungarian. This situation is a difficult one to resolve because of the stubbornness from both sides. But the reason for this dilemma is simply because some other people decided the borders were now somewhere else. It didn't actually change the people who found themselves living in another country. Historically speaking they were Hungarian but now are they Slovak or still Hungarian? It doesn't even make sense to argue about it. It is irrelevant where they might have entered the world. The citizens should be more supportive of each other, show compassion and try to find a peaceful resolution by asking those who refuse to speak Slovak to learn it as well as maintain the Hungarian language. And the Slovaks should understand their dilemma and let them have their culture and language as well. It was not their fault that the borders changed but they should have been accommodated better to achieve integration and acceptance by the Czechoslovaks, now Slovaks.

And there's another dilemma – Czechoslovakia ceased to be on 1 January 1993. Many of the citizens didn't want the split (which was done peacefully, known as the Velvet Divorce) but their passports now show them as divided, when before they came from the same place. This example shows that the label of nationality has very little to define the people in terms of their real identity.

Thomas Paine in "Rights of Man" hoped that "as the barbarism of the old present governments expires, the moral condition of nations with respect to each other will be changed. Man will not be brought up with the savage idea of considering his species as his enemy, because the accident of birth gave the individuals existence in countries distinguished by different names." (p.143) However, this book was written in 1791 and although Paine is seen as someone who pioneered a lot of the thinking that influenced growth and development in the USA and Britain, we can clearly see that more than 200 years later, his vision still hasn't been achieved.

So should we support our countries at all? Of course, but not xenophobically. That is the important distinction. When backing your country in a sports competition, for example, be supportive, but don't see your country as being superior to another and don't view other nationalities as bad in any way. In this example, your sports team is not made up of your country, it's only made up of the people who have been chosen to represent your country's team. It is likely that you don't know any of the players personally. If you did know your team's players and those of the opposition, you are just as likely to find that you would actually prefer to be friends with the opposition players as with those of your country's team. Know your limits, be prudent. If your country's team doesn't win, then that's all there is to it. It's not that your country didn't win. Just the group of people who went out there to play a game. The other country cannot claim superiority over your country, either.

In terms of those who feel their country's culture is being compromised by the influence of other cultures, then, by all means encourage the cultural events and practices that are traditional to your country or region. Organise events that will not only bring your traditions to the forefront but that will also encourage non-indigenous people to learn about them and join in. Organise multi-cultural events that will bring relevant cultures together or even aspects of cultures that no-one in your community can claim to be their own. Being open-minded will do wonders for our collective sense of happiness, understanding and awareness. If there is no moral problem with any practices, there is no problem at all.

The lesson that can be learned from analysing the pros and cons of national identity is that generalisations cannot be made and that we need to emphasise the fact that we all come from one planet and there are no true boundaries between us. We can't be defined as people of one type or another. We have far more in common with each other than we differ from each other. Keep an open mind and embrace other cultures, they might show you something that you like greatly that your culture never showed you.

Learning from this knowledge, it is important not to falsely lead the population in any way as it probably will be found out sooner or later. Heads of state are not immune to the law (nor should they be) and the greedier and more megalomanic they become, the greater the chances are that they will pay the price one way or another - in a court of law, through imprisonment, exile, execution or assassination, but in a Hypothetical Government, such proceedings would have to be done ethically and this would involve prosecution in a court of law with the penalties of imprisonment and freezing of assets being more moral.

Therefore, what a government must not be is also what it should encourage its people not to be: controlling, megalomanic, deceitful, greedy and corrupt. These qualities are undesirable for any individual or group as they will be implemented at the expense of other people, animals or the environment.

So, without wanting to form a nation of identically-thinking copies of each other (as is advocated by the marketing people), we should look at the kind of values that would shape a society for the benefit of every citizen.

Mutual Trust and Respect

A government should want its people to be respectful to all other people. Whereas this could be viewed as unrealistic, it should be emphasised that we should treat others in the way that we would like and expect to be treated. This is, by no means, a new concept, in fact it dates back in history to Confucius and almost everyone has heard a phrase of this nature, which is now known as The Golden Rule. However, it is fundamental to the success of a society. There are many arguments between people about particular actions, behaviours and beliefs but, even though one person may not agree with what another does, people need to be reminded that we should all have the freedom to practise what we choose to as long as it always corresponds to this condition: that it, in no way whatsoever, causes any distress, either psychologically, physically or monetarily, to any other human being, group of human beings, other living creatures or the natural environment. If you have a particular interest in something that is, in general, viewed negatively by society but it doesn't harm anyone else, be sensible and perform it away from the awareness of others. If it will actually harm anyone else but you still want to do it, think about how you should try to change your behaviour so that you can overcome this fault that you have. People with this kind of problem should feel free to seek help where they won't be looked down upon but treated equally to help them overcome their problem. Consequently, the government should encourage and support groups whose aims are to help people address their difficulties.

We will see, later in the book, the many circumstances in which this fundamental principle for a society (treat others how you would like to be treated) can and should be applied. With respect to governmental policies and national laws which have been seen as controversial in various societies, to establish what can not be argued against concerning the benefit and comfort of everyone, we have to approach each issue from this same starting point.

The concept of "Respect for others and the natural world" would need to be taught in every school in a non-discriminative way, which favours no system of thought, either religious, philosophical or scientific. It would need to be the underlying principle for every business and company where it would be the foundation of the laws which would apply to them. If a product or service was in any way exploitative, discriminatory, damaging, deceitful or created primarily to extort money from the general public, it would either be illegal to sell the product or provide the service or it would be subject to significant taxes to create a deterrent for its continued production. If a company's goal was to attempt to deceive people by convincing them that their product is beneficial to them when it is actually of no sincere benefit or even harmful, the company would be forced to remove the product from sale and banned from ever manufacturing it again as well as facing a severe monetary fine.

Even though this sounds like a very strict rule which could potentially change the products available to the public on a very large scale, it would be for one specific reason: to improve the well-being of society and the inner well-being of every citizen. This simple concept is of paramount importance if a society is going to have any chance of functioning smoothly; with as few conflicts as possible and with as much community spirit as possible.

To give some tangible examples to illustrate this rule, let's look at some types of products which are exploitative and deceitful to the public: hair-care products are advertised in their hundreds with the aim to convince people that it will make their hair stronger, shinier and generally make them a more attractive person (and even increase their confidence). The reality of these claims is very different: strength of hair is an empty point- nobody needs their hair to be strong for any reason, it simply grows from the scalp and performs no function for which strength is needed.

Incidentally, Channel 4 News did a study to examine whether hair could be made stronger by applying certain shampoos. Fructis products were shown to make hair shinier but not stronger. Pantene products were shown to actually make the hair weaker. The Advertising Standards Agency (ASA) confronted Pantene for its adverts purporting to make hair 10 times stronger. Pantene was "surprised and disappointed" with the decision... The overall verdict was that there is no publicly available evidence to back up claims that it makes it stronger.[3]

To make hair shinier, artificially manufactured chemicals are added to the product which become fixed to the hair providing an artificial shine, which after long-term and consistent use could damage both the hair and the skin from which there is no available solution. Why? Because these companies don't care about what will happen after a number of years. As long as the unsuspecting public keep buying it, they extort their money in vast quantities. What is someone really going to gain from having shiny hair anyway? Is it going to make your life more fulfilling? Your job more satisfying? Your personal relationships more solid? Regarding how attractive it could make someone appear is the kind of ideology that the Hypothetical

Government would want to discourage. No person is defined by their appearance. Only their appearance is. The actual value of a person in a meaningful sense is never apparent on their exterior, physical side. What a country should be concerned with is how to make the character of a person attractive and likeable to other people. One can only connect positively with a person who is respectful, sympathetic, empathic, moral, generous and generally polite. No hair-care product can provide any of this, therefore they are of no value other than to clean the hair without leaving any artificial chemicals behind. And no, you are not going to become more confident, either. The same argument is also applicable to all forms of clothes and shoes. As Ben Goldacre rightly points out in his "Bad Science" book, there needs to be independent scientific evidence to support the claims made by the companies. Otherwise, the products should not be allowed on sale for reasons of deception.

Other types of products which are manufactured for the above reasons are electrical products such as mobile phones, music players and huge plasma televisions. The rate at which they are being produced in different styles and with different specifications provides the public with effectively no escape from the promotion that accompanies them. However, to have a mobile phone that makes and receives calls and messages and has a few accessories like a calendar or a calculator is sufficient. They are marketed in such a way that, for a period, certain functions will be available on the phones and after a few months, the next set will be released which have a few more functions, most of which are actually unnecessary or pointless. Then, of course, there are the almost infinite designs which are for aesthetic reasons only and some people will buy simply because they like how they look. In a word, all of this is exploitation. It is the business of practically *making* people keep spending their money to keep this frankly worthless market alive and profitable. Business practices such as these would make the tax payable by the manufacturers relative to the number of models they release over a certain period of time, i.e. the more released, the higher their tax level goes. If a mobile phone manufacturer released 10 models in a year, the tax would be relatively low but if they released 50 or more models in a year, the tax payable from all sales would increase significantly so that it would be in the company's interests to limit the number of models of phones they release. The very same principle would apply to makers of any electrical equipment which is seen to exploit the public through false claims that their lives would benefit greatly from buying them and updating them regularly. Peter Joseph of The Zeitgeist Movement also points out in his Orientation Guide that the 'cyclical consumption' market of churning out products that are designed to break down in about 3 years also causes an environmental problem of poisonous chemicals that leak from their components infiltrating the soil as well as killing wildlife because the amount of products that get thrown away every day is simply an unacceptable and totally avoidable burden on the world.

Advertising works on a large scale by deceiving people so cunningly that they not only don't realise they are being conned but actually believe that the advertisers' claims are true. Thus, the general public is willingly dragged into a world where they lose sense of their own likes and dislikes and are contentedly taken through life having their choices made for them as to what they (think they) will get satisfaction from.

But we could also see this as not being something that is particularly bad. What if people really do feel happy with following the adverts and buying what seems to be something that they have apparently been waiting for? Is it so bad to let these people continue in their rose-tinted way? On a surface level maybe not, but on a deeper level, yes. What we have to be aware of is that true happiness is never going to be found through buying a succession of 'newer and better' versions of material goods that if they hadn't been invented or developed, we wouldn't have even thought about wanting such a product. It is very unlikely that anyone ever feels that something is missing from their life because of some material thing that doesn't yet exist but when it does come along and we have its apparent merits thrown at us so much through advertising, we then have the potential to feel that we do need it.

Also, the general public is giving up its money in massive quantities to the corporations that enough power to be seen as the producers of the 'best' products, which is, of course, what those corporations are working on.

The fundamental issue in this argument is that people are at a point where they don't make their decisions themselves but simply do what they are told. The term 'fashion victim' is already well-known and can be used to clarify this point: a fashion victim is considered to be someone who buys whatever clothes are said to be in fashion in a particular season. They aim to strive for 'perfection' through what they buy and possibly end up spending most of their money or more money than they actually have (and get into serious debt with credit cards) on what they are told is in fashion at the time. What this leads to is an accumulation of clothes over time that would not be worn again when they are considered to be no longer in fashion. This can be analysed to illustrate the issue of lacking personal identity.

First of all, how can something be said to be in fashion or not at any time? Surely it would make more sense for people to just buy and wear whatever they like and leave it at that. Philosophically speaking, maybe, but there is no real money to be made from philosophy alone. The fashion industry is extremely influential, controlling, deceitful and exploitative and it is in its best interests to control and determine the purchases and thoughts of the mass public for them. They are seen to have the ultimate say on what we are supposed to wear, regardless of whether we would ordinarily wear something of a certain colour or style. Many people unquestioningly accept what they are told they will look good in and then, after a few months, they would no longer look good in it and 'must buy this' to keep up with fashion or, in real terms, finance the fashion industry because they demand it for their own interests which are, of course, making profit. This is another example of cyclical consumption.

Another exploitative and selfish aspect of the fashion industry is their tendency to label each of their items with the names or logos of their company because apparently it is 'cool' to show that you spend more money than you probably should on such and such an item. Such logos are used as status symbols. What each person is doing by wearing or carrying such items is providing free advertising for the company by walking around and displaying the name to everyone else. The people spend unjustified amounts of money on these items, advertise the company and get no reward for it. 'Fashion victim' is not quite a strong enough term for this, maybe 'marketing slave' would be more precise.

So, in the end, people are willingly giving up vast amounts of their money or even more than they have (through credit) to support and promote their own exploitation and for having their own identities stripped from them to the extent that they are unaware that they never make their own choices. Even more importantly, the consumers, by spending more money than they actually have to try to look 'good' and to impress other people, end up making themselves poorer financially and no better off on any real level. Their actual status is no better than it was before because showing that you have acquired clothing with certain brand names does not actually change anything about your circumstances. It is the difference between reality and fantasy. Some people would like to think that they look like a 'star' but this is not a true reflection of themselves and could be seen as dangerous to one's sense of who they really are. The more trapped in this fantasy world one becomes, the more difficult it will be to be in touch with the reality of one's own life. They would keep pretending they are effectively someone else and lose their own identity, which is something that is very sad to think about.

As an example, imagine some people who are on the poverty line. They don't like the fact that they are poor and they don't have as much access to the same clothes that richer people have. They have a low-self esteem because of this dilemma. In order to try to rectify this, they either save up their money or borrow it, thus going into debt, so that they can buy a certain brand of trainers, thinking that doing so will up their status and make their peers think they have achieved something. On the personal level they have made themselves poorer for no good reason as their lives will be as unfulfilled as they were before the purchase. But on the other side of it, the company who sold the product earned that money and if you multiply that by the number of people who made similar purchases from the same company, then one company got richer while thousands of people became worse off.

Considering that this type of behaviour happens regularly on a large scale, most people are unaware that they are dragging themselves further down the slope into poverty and, at the same time, are pushing the richer people further up it. Therefore, the consumers are the ones who are actively increasing the rich-poor divide and their own level of dissatisfaction with life.

The same consumers complain about certain people exploiting their wealth by attempting to show their own fictional status as highly successful individuals. If the general public turned around and rejected the products from the big companies on a large scale, they would not be so poor and the heads of the corporations would not be so rich. It is a simple and achievable situation as the whole process depends on the people who buy the products. We mistakenly feel that we will be more accepted by our peers if we have certain trainers or bags, etc. which display a certain brand name that is supposedly in fashion but it is a pure delusion which most people don't seem to realise as being detrimental to themselves.

As a result, many people in the western world have trouble ascertaining what they really want from life. They are being taken along on a roller-coaster ride where they have no time to stop and reflect "Why am I buying this?", "Do I really want it?", "Is this really going to make me feel more complete as a person?"

The Hypothetical Government would encourage people to reflect on what they really want, what would bring them deep satisfaction, what they should be aiming for in life. It would want people to seek their own identity, by exploring their true desires and how to take the steps that would help them to reach their true goals. It would want people to question what they do and for what reason; to be more adventurous to improve their own life, not just in terms of their job and income but to form stronger relationships with other people and become happier with being a part of society. Such goals are never going to be obtained through artificial means such as clothes, hairstyles, mobile phones, etc. People who rely on material goods to try to appear better than others ought to be looked at as needing help to find their own liberation from the endless wheel of slavery to the capitalist system. People who try to use their wealth to gain superiority over others should be informed of how their actions are immoral and more importantly, how they can be supported to change their business practices so that they are not exploiting people but actively helping the general public to regain their own interests and choices. In an ideal society, such exploitative people would not even be seen as acceptable but instead their status should sink to the level of undesirable people. Why? Because what we should try to establish is a system whereby people are judged on what they can contribute in a positive way. People who are friendly, helpful, caring and avoid using an artificial identity would be and should be the kinds of people that are held with the highest regard. Those people who have unjustifiably large amounts of money ought to be judged on how much they contribute to society in a meaningful way, not on how much they spend on lavish clothes and smile inanely for the cameras at elite events. If they are known to use their money for the development of the world they should be treated with respect, but only if they don't counteract their good deeds with selfishness and greed.

But, you may ask, shouldn't we try to avoid judgements altogether? Shouldn't we treat everyone equally regardless of what they have or haven't got? It's an understandable point but this is, at least at this point in time, just idealistic. In reality, to hope everyone would become non-judgemental is a dream that would currently be seen as impossible but as something we need to at least try to work towards. People judge others; it's how we make sense of the world and how we relate to or don't relate to other people. Therefore, we should be encouraging more appropriate kinds of judgement. We should be opening people's minds to what really makes a person worthwhile. Designer clothes and expensive (and environment-destroying) cars do not and never will define someone as being an admirable person.

So what should we look for when trying to define what is 'good' in terms of our characters? Whether someone is selfish or more altruistic is a key distinction. Although it has to be noted that it is not exclusively the case that all rich people are selfish, there is more of a tendency towards that than there is towards altruism. Fame, for example, or being cursed with the status of a 'celebrity' nurtures greed and selfishness to a shameful level. Unfortunately, what many members of the general public see in celebrities is only what they see and not what they know about them as people. Posing for magazine photos and being used as the face of some worthless product is often seen as meaning that the person is some kind of role model. "Never judge a book by its cover" is of course a famous phrase. We should not be encouraged to aspire to be like these types of celebrities but instead to pay no attention to those people whose image is used to try to extort money from us or distort our notion of reality. These deceitful techniques should be treated with rejection and the people being used to exploit us should only be judged fairly if they really prove that they contribute to the development of society. Whereas it would be better for all concerned not to have to introduce laws to prevent such mind control, if the support that was given to improve their practice was ignored on a large scale by many companies, laws would need to come into place to prohibit such deceptions.

It is very important to look at what would be a more positive and desirable way for people to behave, but before we can address this, we need to look at why, at least in the western world, we have such a selfish desire to obtain more and how it has come about.

The Self and the Capitalist System

Concern for the self is an issue which is fundamental to addressing the problems, not only of the western world, but eventually of the whole world. The self is a concept that has been nurtured and encouraged by the capitalist system for one underlying reason: to ensure that people keep spending their money and propagating the businessman's desires, that of getting richer and more powerful. This has been achieved by making people like they are in competition with one another, to have more than one's neighbour, to obtain status symbols and generally aim to make as much money as possible.

The idea of self is the one that has been the fuel for the expanding system of greed, which has, of 2008-2009, potentially reached its bursting point, as the most powerful, the richest and therefore the greediest have caused an economic meltdown of the western world, particularly of the richest and greediest countries. Those who had money and power were addicted to having more to a point where nobody was going to be allowed to stand in their way. People with less fortune have been tricked into giving away their money in the false hope that the scheme they entered into was going to bring them more riches, but those who were organising the schemes had no intention of making anyone rich but themselves.

But how have they managed to ensure that people keep spending their money? By feeding them propaganda that it is ultimately desirable to possess every product that they can think of and find a way by which to convince the general public that they want them and that they need them. This has been done by sensationalising and keeping in the forefront of many people's minds the idea that certain celebrities are the most desirable, the happiest and the most successful people in the world and that the general public has a duty to emulate them. By manipulating our minds in this way, people have been force-fed this for so long and with such intensity that now, this is all they know and therefore it must be true. Television and magazines in particular have been on a non-stop mission to make sure that people are never satisfied with how they look and that they should follow the perpetual cycles of changing fashions and trying new ways to lose weight and to "combat the signs of ageing". The value of these operations in the business world is amazingly high and they keep a lot of people rich. However, the richer people get, the more they want which makes it clear that greed is a very active trait in humans, although it cannot be seen as genetic or a part of human nature, for it is not present in everyone and it can be overcome. Humans have the potential to be greedy but it is not something that everyone is guilty of.

But is there any reason to overcome it? Shouldn't we all try to get as much as we can, in terms of money, possessions and desirable appearance? Don't these things make us happy? We need to look at what this all means and how everything is linked together by it.

Business plans are worked out so that the businesses will last as long as possible and hopefully will grow and gain the largest sector of its respective market. To do this, a business needs to make sure that their products are going to continue selling for many years. For such products as food and drink, the plan doesn't need to develop very much as certain soft drinks and fast foods continue to sell without any drastic changes to the products available. But in the electronics and fashion industries people are not so satisfied with using and wearing the same products indefinitely. Why? Because of cyclical consumption. Things aren't made to last. Products are designed to have a short shelf-life. It is not that the buyers get dissatisfied quickly, it is that they are 'instructed' to be dissatisfied by the time the next model becomes available. This, in itself, makes for a great market. If people are never satisfied with something, the companies can make sure that the people remain dissatisfied indefinitely. By continually 'enhancing' the products within carefully decided time frames, people won't have to keep updating things too often but they won't have to wait for too long to be able to get the 'new model with improved features'. As a result, people have become attuned to the idea that their electrical products will always get better and they have to buy them so that their friends and/ or other people won't mock them for having such an antiquated model as one from as little as two years ago.

The same kind of strategy is firmly in place for the fashion industry, which controls the minds of those who desire their products. They can dictate things as they want and change styles and colours as quickly as they want because they know they have a substantial market already in place and they can keep these people buying items that have no value to the development of the human need for satisfaction or the development of the human mind. The fashion industry has made people believe that certain styles are only appropriate for a few months and that they will not want to wear them again the following year or hopefully never again in their lives. The fashion industry is like a reservoir that releases an enormous amount of water and then when it has all been soaked up by the sponges, will release a new 'style' of water which is apparently better than the last one (when of course it is no better as that is only opinion and can never be fact but the consumers who have successfully been deluded will never question it) and when the sponges have dried out, they will return to soak up as much as they can hold again.

The cosmetics industry is similarly manipulative but is even more guilty of misleading and lying to the public so that it can maintain its profits. It continually gives out false information that, for example, the ageing process can be reversed. They never refer to any scientific research into time travel, so quite how they intend to support this claim is quite unfathomable. In recent years, it has developed this strategy and forced it upon the susceptible public with such repeated propaganda that many people have now been sucked into the whole delusion that they can slow the signs of ageing. Well, you can apply as much make-up as you want but it will always and only be a cover (i.e. an illusion). Even if you go for the surgical procedures to remove wrinkles, etc. you are still actually getting older and you will die some day. The truth hurts? Only when you are convinced that the truth can be reversed. It can't. Seek the truth and accept it. You can't accept what is not true and never will be true.

So, such industries are dedicated to manipulating as many human minds as possible, convincing them that they have to believe them and that they have to buy what they are told to otherwise their lives will not be satisfied. All of this idea of satisfaction through material gain is pure illusion and not a single word of it is true in any way. Yet these industries thrive and continue to grow because they have severely distorted the views of those that they enslave into their systems. The fact that the number of people who fall into this category is in the millions is depressing.

Spain has already started to tackle this issue by putting a ban on adverts for products that promote a "cult of the body" ideal, such as slimming pills, or adverts which claim that success is based on weight or looks. It has put restrictions on others, such as those advertising cosmetic surgery or beauty treatments by not allowing them to be broadcast before 10pm so that youngsters will be less likely to be put under pressure and influenced by them.[4]

The obsession with the self has been one that has taken over the majority of the western world, yet the obsession would not have come about of its own accord. It was forced onto the public and every effort is being made to make sure that its vice-like grip will never slip. "Think about yourself all the time, treat yourself by buying our product, you will feel like a new person, everyone else is doing it so don't get left behind" all has the underlying meaning of "We want your money and we want so much of it that we will never stop until we have as much as possible."

This sounds quite like the idea of evil. In fact it is, in its purest sense. The capitalist system is founded on greed and making everyone feel like they have to have more than everyone else to be happy.

So, if this is a good system, then why isn't the western world happy? You can have as big a television as you can get or a mobile phone with as many applications as the companies can think of, but deep down inside, people won't be happy just because they have them. Why not? Because this kind of happiness is just an delusion. It is false happiness that can only remain in the mind for a very short time until we don't feel satisfied any more. Westerners keep trying to overcome the disappointment by buying more and more but it will always lead to indifference and disappointment because such products will never make us feel like we have developed as people. It means nothing to know that you have something that thousands or millions of others do. In the end you won't care, but westerners have been conditioned not to realise that they don't care but that they should combat the feeling of not feeling good by updating and replacing their possessions. And so the cycle of delusion goes on without an end.

All this has happened by convincing people that their 'self' is what matters the most in life. To be better than the rest, to have more than your neighbour. This can only result in conflicts, jealousy and bitterness, which ultimately perpetuates the myth of self and individuality by making people see themselves as different from other people when in fact, because they are trying to obtain, in essence, the same products, makes them all the same. Now there's a largely unseen paradox; "We're competing against the other people even though we're all fundamentally aiming for the same things."

Living in such a high-pressure society as in the western world causes tension where it shouldn't exist. It causes friction between people for no valid reason. In the end, this all points to a system of perpetuating an immoral society that metaphorically (and sometimes even literally) fights against itself by continually chasing an illusion (or the end of the rainbow where the mythical pot of gold lies).

On the business side of it, companies have competed with each other to try to gain the majority of the market. Why? What is the point of wanting to gain control over more than 50% of the market compared to your competitors? Why can't they be content that they have 20% of the market and their business is still making a substantial profit? Why don't they agree to restrict their production so that all existing companies in the same market area can remain stable and continue in a non-competitive way? The answer is not even slightly difficult or complicated to explain: greed. On the business level, it is comparable to on the individual level but obviously on a much larger scale. The bigger a company gets, the more it wants and the redder its eyes get. As its market share goes up, the level of mental development goes down. They will not stop until they have got as much as they can and have forced their competitors out of business. Can anyone really feel properly content with knowing they have caused such things?

What it has resulted in is that companies have resorted to borrowing money to expand their evil empires and gamble with it on risky deals whereby they have lost billions of dollars of other people's money. The capitalist system moving towards a point of collapse due to its extremely immoral practices and it's time to devise a new system that protects itself against such immorality and greed. People are getting more and more dissatisfied with how politics and life are going. People want and need a new system. They are starting to realise that things are not working. In fact, things have never been working but people are getting wiser to it at this point in time.

The Self and Others

This section draws influences from Buddhism and Confucianism which are both quite difficult to understand, especially from a western viewpoint so I have tried to apply their philosophies to the modern world and present them in a way which is easier to follow.

The self is like a container that can be filled with the characteristics of what makes someone a person. For reasons of making this easier to visualise, I'll label the good things as blue and the bad things as red. The good things that can fill up the vessel that is the person are things that would come in the categories of the virtues, e.g. acts of humility, charity, selflessness, honesty and so on. The bad things would be acts of rudeness, conceit, deceit, lying, greed, etc. We can justify the allocation of such attributes by saying if we would like or dislike, approve or disapprove of them in someone close to us, whether they are a friend, relation or colleague. No-one could honestly claim to like a colleague if they were seen to be conceited or dishonest, but it would be hard or almost impossible to see them in a bad light if they were polite, helpful and compassionate. However, they can't achieve any of these attributes that may be given by other people in their life circle without having some kind of relations with other people. We can't exist in a vacuum, we live in the vicinity of other people whether we want to or not. Even people who may be literal hermits had to be created by their parents and would have reacted to and had their own behaviour shaped by those whom they have encountered in their lives before they lived in a solitary manner.

So, to visualise the whole system by how we are who we are, we can imagine ourselves as the container in the middle, other people whom we relate to in our lives as essentially identical containers that surround us and the relations we have to them as arteries and veins going to and from us and them. These connectors cannot be removed unless another person is no longer in contact with us in any way; for example, if they live away from us and we don't see or hear from them again. Otherwise, every person that we communicate with in some way is meaningfully linked to us and therefore they are a part of our lives as we are a part of theirs.

Of course, we have control over what goes into what we consist of in terms of characteristics. To follow on from the earlier categorisations, it would be preferable to be filled with more blue parts than red parts. The bluer we are, the stronger the links will be to the others in our midst because they will like us more and we will be more favourable and popular with them. The redder we become, the weaker the links get and the more likely the chance is that the links will break, either by them not wanting to have contact with us any more or with us shunning them due to the level of redness we have. But is this true? Does it all work like this? Well, our level of happiness depends on how well we relate to other people. If we know that people like us and we get on well with them, we feel good, there's nothing we can do about that. But if we know that we have weak, tense and conflictive relationships with people in general, we cannot be content and satisfied with our lives, even if other aspects, such as how well we are doing with our jobs, how much money we have, etc. are thought of as being at a good level. Even those people who claim to be happy when they know they've annoyed many people, e.g. the 'internet haters', delude themselves into thinking they've achieved something, but deep down inside, if they honestly analyse things, they cannot be happy and satisfied with their lives. They feel the need for attention and get it, even by negative means but fundamentally, they know they are not really happy people.

This shows that we all have an inextricable link with other people that we come into contact with, even if we only speak to them once. The fact that we can communicate with them means we cannot exist totally independently. So, going back to the blue versus red characteristics, if we are mostly with blue aspects or if we are, one day, feeling in a particularly blue mood, we will pass on the blueness to others through the connectors. The same thing goes for the red mood. It doesn't mean that our red mood will be caught by someone else but that our redness has been transferred to the other person as they will feel annoyed or upset with our behaviour and the connection has been weakened. This, in turn, can increase the level of redness or blueness that we feel if we have had a pleasant or unpleasant experience with someone else.

The nest question is to ask how we can make ourselves bluer and less red. To feel happy, we need to be as blue as possible, which will cause stronger blue connections with other people who, in turn, become a little bit bluer themselves. This is where we turn to the virtues and contrast them with the sins, or faults, which will be looked at in more detail later.

To begin with, I need to state how we should look at the various opposites so that we can reduce or hopefully eliminate any arguments as to their validities. Hence, place yourself in the position of someone who is viewing another person who you adjudge to have the following characteristics. You will be more likely to judge someone else objectively than yourself as people try to justify their own actions in as positive a way as possible, even if they know deep down inside that they are inappropriate. Incidentally, people are far more likely to try to con themselves about their own behaviour to believe that a less than moral act was actually justifiable than to judge someone else favourably in the light of a negative act.

For example, you are likely to approve of someone who you see is acting rationally and reasonably rather than someone who you think is acting for their own self-serving reasons, even if it is not for monetary gain or at the noticeable detriment of others. If someone is not being prudent, we don't think of it as a good way to be. Therefore, being prudent would earn you a blue point and other people would respect you for it, making all people involved happier than someone who was acting unreasonably. Now, we will look at virtues and faults (or sins) that, again, will be explained in greater detail later.

Regarding justice, you would treat someone positively if they were seen to do a good deed, either to you or to someone else and if someone did something that was not seen as just, depending on the severity of their actions, you are likely to view them with contempt (although, morally speaking, it would be best in your case to act justly; that is to either inform the appropriate authorities or try to help them to see why they should have acted differently).

Temperance is about people acting with moderation and restraint. If someone reacts to something responsibly and calmly, you would respect them more than someone who starts throwing a tantrum and lashing out with their fists, for example.

Having courage to take risks (within reason) and stand up to difficult situations is an admirable characteristic. Those who shirk at challenges may not necessarily be seen as weak but may be less confident than others and in this sense, lacking courage cannot be seen as a 'red' behaviour. However, defecting responsibility to others because someone doesn't want to face the possible outcomes is a red act, and bosses, this redness will be sent through your red arteries straight to your workers who will give some more redness back to you.

Charity, kindness and friendship are unquestionably blue. Show this to other people and blue will flow back to you in great quantities. But beware those who may try to take advantage of your charity for their own gain. Better to sever the connector completely if that person won't respond to reasoning about their behaviour.

Humility versus pride is one that needs more illustration. People like to feel good about themselves, it gives us a feeling of satisfaction and worth. However, in the western world, pride is encouraged by those who seek to make money out of doing so. The powerful company bosses are practically insistent that you, as consumers, are proud of how you look and what you own, for their own personal benefits. They don't actually care about you at all as they are unlikely to know you personally or even see you to approve of your appearance. Warmongering presidents demand that you feel pride for your country so that in the face of (their own) enemies, you will support them "because it's what the country needs." Don't comply with their underhand tactics. The country doesn't need you to suddenly hate people that yesterday, you knew basically nothing about. The president needs your support so that you will not demand that he is removed from power.

Pride in one's own appearance leads to boasting, conceit, a superiority complex and an incorrect and morally unacceptable feeling of self-importance. No-one can be more important or more attractive because of what they wear, whether it's make-up, jewellery, clothes or shoes. I will be as bold to say that this is a fact. Do you have respect and admiration for people who are conceited and snobbish? Or do you have respect for people who are humble and accept praise for their actions with a simple smile and a thank you? Pride and selfishness fill a person with a huge quantity of redness that will sever connections abruptly.

Diligence, or hard work, is viewed with a lot of respect, as long as it is done for charitable reasons and not exploitative or otherwise dishonest reasons. We all respect those who work hard to support their families. In fact, such people deserve more recognition and praise when they work really hard to ensure that their children or other family members are well looked after. We don't think the same about those people who refuse to work and instead live off the state, or those who sit pretty on top of a huge pile of money that was immorally gained while they command others to slavishly do their work for very little in return.

And finally, greed. People who want more and more things for themselves may not always be viewed unfavourably. In fact, it is quite common to be told that it is great that some 'celebrity' now owns a number of expensive cars and homes and hundreds of pairs of shoes, etc. and that we should revere them because they are so successful. Wrong. Magazines and television programmes that advocate such shameless wantonness actually help to instil a sense of envy into their readers and viewers with the intention that they will want to achieve the same, at least to a certain degree. "You can look like X cheaply by buying this similar dress" and all the rest of it. But what is the point, really? At the very most, it is temporary happiness as long as the feeling of novelty prevails for owning a certain garment of having a certain hairstyle. However, one's life is not going to improve in any long-term way because of it. If you have a similar dress, then what? Has it actually changed anything about your personal circumstances, your job, your relationships? It will have done absolutely nothing to develop your life at all. All that greed will leave you with is the addictive desire to possess more to keep up with the fashions. And it is very addictive, for no worthwhile reason. It can be, and very often is, a form of escapism from the mundaneness or the hardship of life that your average person might be suffering. So is there a justification for such greedy acts? No. Like many drugs and medicines, greed only covers the symptoms as long as you are partaking in it. It will never get to the root of why one's life may not be fulfilling. It is a mask that covers the surface while surrounding a potentially rotten core. Without getting to the root of the problems, it serves no useful purpose and should be avoided, not just until a real level of happiness and stability has been achieved, but way beyond the attainment of such a level. It needs to be maintained until it feels like it is a part of who we are. Otherwise it would be like overcoming an alcohol addiction and celebrating by getting drunk. Back to square one.

Additionally, those so-called celebrities whom we are, in effect, instructed to admire and aspire to are people we will never know personally and they are treated by the staring public as not real people, just puppets who don't have real lives. In a way, they are just that, but deep down, they are real people and we have no right to intrude into their personal lives without their permission. Put yourself in their shoes and ask yourself if you would like it. When it comes down to people who we really do know, do we like those who fill their lives with endless wantonness? Do we like those who waste a large amount of money on flashy items of all descriptions? Or do we actually find it hard to relate to them as well as finding it unpleasant to 'have' to relate to them? Greed, along with pride and extravagance, leads to self-obsession and essentially, a very deep, staining tone of red that is as hard to remove as red wine from a white rug. Greed leaves frayed blue connectors between people and poisonous red connectors as long as we have to remain connected in some way to the greedy people.

So, if we can agree on the division of the virtues from the sins and honestly see these differences between red and blue attributes, we can have a starting point from which to work towards reconstructing an actually valuable sense of self with powerful and stable connectors to other people that have a direct influence on our selves. To some degree, most people would have to admit to being guilty of at least a small amount of sins or vices. Even the friendliest, most peaceful and charitable people might be guilty of buying lottery tickets each week. I'm sorry but gambling is an act of greed. The lure of millions of pounds, dollars, Euros or whatever is tempting for a huge number of people. How many of those people actually stop and think whether their lives will actually improve in terms of human relations by having, for example, a million pounds? Wasting money on superficial goods will never help to improve your deep-down level of happiness and nor does anyone need so much money. A motto that I think would be a more respectable and prudent way of living one's life is: You get what you deserve and you deserve what you work for. If someone you knew but weren't well-acquainted with won a prize of a million pounds, you would not think it was fair. You would think they hadn't earned it, especially if you didn't think very highly of the person to begin with. And you would be quite right. They didn't earn it and they don't deserve it, just like you wouldn't deserve it if you hadn't worked for it.

Of course, what we should aim for are more blue attributes as, after analysis, I hope you would find it very difficult to argue against the points I have put forward here. And luckily, none of them are difficult to achieve. It costs nothing to develop a stronger sense of charity, humility, temperance, etc.. For some, it may require more work than others but that's where we have to be realistic and set ourselves targets. We should write up lists of the virtues, faults and sins (along with any others that you think should be included in them; please don't think of the lists provided below as absolute or exhaustive) and honestly question yourself as to how well you possess the virtues or how badly you are guilty of the faults and sins. Don't feel that you have to admit anything to anyone else if you don't wish to but above all, be honest with yourself. If you find there are a number of red aspects to your current behaviour, set yourself goals to reach. Think about what you do that leaves you guilty of something and aim to be more aware of your actions, then more aware and more so that you are practically always conscious of your undesirable behaviours. By being so very aware of what you do, you will have a much greater chance of eliminating your bad actions.

Along with this, what you should not do is worry about what other people might think about you. This can lead to neurotic and even paranoid thoughts which can lead to a mental breakdown in the worst case. All you need to worry about is how you think of yourself. From this, what other people will then think of you will come naturally. If you feel you are improving, people will notice it without any words needing to be spoken and their impression of you will improve.

You can, of course, be supportive of those who would like you to know what they are working on improving, but it would never require anyone else's input into what you should do for yourself. As in Buddhism, you have to look for your own truth and only you will find it. Don't be tricked by anyone who claims to be able to guide you, especially if it is for any monetary gain to them. They do not want to help you, they want to trick you and exploit you.

Be realistic and be persistent. Another saying goes: Teachers can open many doors, but only you can enter. A sense of inner strength is very valuable in order to reach goals that you may find difficult to attain. Even if, at the beginning, you feel that you don't have the strength to work through some aspect, believe that you have the potential as much as anybody else, for this is true. Step by step, little by little, your actions will not only pay off for you but they will pay off for other people whom you are in contact with and as is in human nature, your actions will be reciprocated, whether they are positive or negative. Every cause has an effect as Buddhism states in the rule of karma. You will find that your self is not a unique self at all but it is linked to everyone that plays a part in your life and the more you rid yourself of the red characteristics and increase the blue ones, the more you will improve other people's lives and vice versa.

At this point, we should examine what kinds of actions we should be looking at in terms of those that we should regard more highly and what kind of jobs deserve respect.

Those people who actively work for charities, voluntarily, part-time or otherwise should be seen in the group of society's finest. The same would go for professionals like doctors, nurses, teachers, veterinarians and those whose job it is to devote their careers to the care, well-being and development of those they work with. It would be preferable to avoid giving labels, like classes, to any groups of people, but to view them with respect would justifiably mean a significant amount to them.

People involved in business, marketing and general financial gain for the sake of it would be less respected in general. Again, it is important to note that we can't tar everyone with the same brush; if they show that they do not make money simply to get richer at the expense of other people, animals or the environment but are still responsible and caring people and use their money productively, then they should be viewed as such. If, however, they do not care for anyone or anything except for themselves, then they should be viewed negatively as this is one of the lowest forms of being that there can be in a society. A person's value will never be determined by the amount of money they earn.

Aside from professions, people will be treated with respect if they are known to be respectful to others. This means to show empathy to others, to be accepting of people whose views differ from their own, be them politically, religiously or on many other levels, such as sexuality. People should be made to feel welcome and part of a social group if they are accepting of others and not conducive to discriminatory remarks about those whose actions or beliefs have no consequence on themselves or other people. If they are not respectful in these ways, they should (politely) be made to realise that they are not welcome while their views are so inclined.

The overall aim of a person should be to be someone who is not destructive in any way, either on a verbal, psychological or personal level. If someone has a negative belief, like being racist, then other people that they know should try to help them examine this way of thinking and help them to understand that it is not beneficial or morally correct in any way. It is also important to not simply reject a person because they are negatively discriminatory. To be discriminatory is purely psychological and it has a solution. It is a learned opinion that will have been influenced by other people and is something that can be changed in a positive way. There are some opinions which will always remain opinions, for example, whether a song is good or not, but opinions such as thinking someone is better or worse because of the shade of their skin can never be justified. People can only be judged on what they do and whether it is for the benefit or detriment of anyone or anything else.

As the western world is becoming more and more lost in terms of who we are and what we are looking to achieve in life, it is important to look at different attributes of human behaviour. Over the millennia, there has been much discussion about what makes a person good or bad and there have been many different attempts to guide people onto a better path so that they can live more fulfilling lives.

The next sections will analyse these philosophies to attempt to give an unbiased guide to how we should try to develop ourselves.

Parenting

Parenting might not usually be considered a governmental issue but as it is of a great importance for shaping a positive society, it should be addressed and supported by a government. Advice needs to be given as to how to raise children effectively and appropriately so that they will grow up as well developed people.

First of all, from birth, it is important to look after your children well and give them love and affection. However, it is not as simple as just that. Babies have an incredible skill from a very young age of how to manipulate parents and grandparents. They learn very quickly that crying will get them attention and help them to get what they want in a selfish manner. As they are still very young, social skills and appropriate behaviour is not part of their capacity. Even though parents often want to make their children as happy as possible, bowing down to their every desire is actually going to make the child become a more badly developed person. The development of manipulative skills is going to lead to tension between the children and the parents. The child will be more prone to tantrums and more selfish behaviour in general and if the parents let them have their own way most of the time and buy them the sweets and toys that they demand, the child will effectively become the authority of the family, in their eyes. They will learn that they only need to turn on the waterworks to get what they want and as they grow older, this undesirable behaviour will get worse and lead to tenser human relations between them and their peers, teachers and people in general. Additionally, spoiling the children and treating them like they are 'special' people will cause more upsets when they get older and can lead to arrogance.

There is a fine line between caring and spoiling. Children should be supported and loved but they have to learn that society is not a place where they will always be able to get everything they want. They need to be taught that they can't have their own way all the time and that sometimes, something can't be given to them. In this case it is very important to explain clearly *why* they can't be allowed to have or to do something. I have heard parents, on a number of occasions, tell their children "because I said so." This is totally inappropriate as the child is not given a reason as to why they can't have their own way. They need to be able to understand the rational reasons for why they can't do certain things at certain times. Parents need to learn how to calmly and sensibly take a minute to explain they can't have their own way for whatever reason. It would make a huge difference in the overall character of the new generation.

Parents need to be aware that children's minds are very primitive compared to their own. By the time we are adults, we have enough experience to understand how we function, physically and socially, but young children are at the beginning of their social development and do not yet understand people in the way that adults do. Parents need to realise that their children are in the process of learning and that they will make what we would often think of as mistakes. It is the way of learning. Sometimes they may behave in what seems an irresponsible or anti-social way but we must use understanding to remember that there is the possibility that the child is not aware of the social rules that most adults live by. The world is still a very new place for 3 year olds; they are still discovering and have plenty to uncover. Unfortunately, they dig in what turn out to be the wrong places. It is their way of learning. Don't shout at them, don't hit them. Explain to them why it is not a good idea to do what they might have done. They will respect you and listen to you if you treat them with empathy, but they won't if you are aggressive with them.

For birthdays and Christmases children shouldn't be showered with a huge number of presents from all the family, for two reasons. Firstly, because the child will continue to feel that they can have whatever they want, in huge quantities, which leads to a very materialistic state of mind and they will think that happiness can be achieved simply by obtaining more. Secondly, having too many toys and games will diminish the attention span of the child. If they know they have a mountain of toys, they will not learn to dedicate their time to any certain activity. If they get bored of playing something or they find something too hard, they can simply switch to another toy which leaves them with a short attention span and the inability to learn how to devote more time to improving their skills in an area. This will subsequently mean that the child develops boredom and frustration quickly and that they are harder to satisfy which, of course, will also come back on the parents, in that their child will be creating more tension in the home and with the family with their continuous demands.

It is important to help the child develop as many practical, creative skills as is possible (and practical). This means learning to swim, to ride a bike, hopefully developing an interest in sport and other such physical activities. Why? Because these are very common skills and ones that will prove to be very useful as they grow up as well as being skills that help to keep them active, fit and healthy instead of filling their time with being in front of the television or computer. But again, one needs to be careful as to how one encourages such skills and interests. Thought should be given to activities that child shows a genuine interest in. If, for example, the father is a big football fan but the child doesn't really care for it, don't make them join a football club and expect them to like it. Parents need to think about what the child appears to be interested in. Note what they like to do. If they like building things from construction sets, maybe they would develop a future interest in mechanics and engineering. If they like to sing or dance, support them with their interests and look for ways that they can develop them. It must be emphasised that they child must not, for example, attend piano lessons just because the parents want them to do so. If they do want to learn to play a musical instrument then certainly encourage it but don't push them too far so that they feel they are being forced to do it. This will never lead to happiness for the child if they really don't care for such an activity or they are being expected to give more time to it than they feel comfortable with. They will also feel that their parents are not sensitive to their own desires and they will in turn resent their parents.

This also leads on to what kind of toys and other stimuli the children should be given. It is very common in western society to give cars to the boys and dolls to the girls. There are many toys which are stereotypically 'girls' toys' and 'boys' toys'. The main problem with this is that the more we enforce the stereotypes that boys should be fighting with one another with their cars, robots and pretend guns, the more they will grow up in that mould. Similarly, the more we give the girls baby dolls in pushchairs and dolls to dress up in nice clothes, the more they will grow up thinking that their main aim in life is to have their own children and be trapped inside the cycle of materialism and superficiality. It is quite shocking to see two year old girls pushing a baby doll in a pushchair as they are being taught from a very young age that their role in life is to have their own children. Of course, this is something that they may eventually do (have children) but we shouldn't be forcing the idea on them when they are still young themselves. There is the positive aspect that they may develop their compassion for others by caring for their dolls but historically speaking, this act comes from the expectation of women to primarily conform to the role of the carer.

Reading is a very positive interest to foster. There are innumerable books that children can be interested in and if they are guided to the kind of books they will enjoy, their imagination will increase along with their knowledge and understanding of the world. It is also a much more valuable pastime than being given a hand-held games console to keep them quiet.

Activities which promote social skills are very important in terms of their ability to relate to other people and to show compassion and if the child is interested in something that the parents can share, this will strengthen the relationships that they have with them. Even if the parents don't share an interest that the child has, take part anyway and support them. The child will get a lot of enjoyment and a feeling of bonding from knowing that their parents are happy to engage in activities that they enjoy.

When parents have more than one child, it is very important not to treat the younger one like the baby of the family and not to lose interest in the older child or children. Obviously this will lead to sibling rivalries and if the youngest child is constantly wrapped up in cotton wool, they are going to develop badly as a person for the reasons outlined above. From personal experience as a teacher, I have seen diminished responsibility in children who are the 'baby' of the family even beyond 8 years of age who think they can everything their own way. They are usually the ones who have to be spoken to more regularly about their inappropriate behaviour.

In terms of twins, triplets, etc., it is also important not to treat them like they are just copies of one another. This means don't dress them in identical clothing just because they were born at the same time. They are still individual beings who need to be able to form their own identities separately from their siblings. If they don't, they are more likely to grow up being very dependent on one another and in some cases being unable to function if their siblings are not there.

Finally, a skill that is highly important to foster in a child is that of responsibility. At a young age, children are not really aware of their actions and they will often act selfishly and without compassion for others. Time needs to be taken to try to show the child that actions have consequences and that they need to be aware of the feelings of others if they are going to develop as happy, fulfilled people. A child who is often left out of games because of their behaviour is going to be unhappy and this can lead to jealousy and in the end, undesirable behaviour.

Another point worth noting is being aware how much sleep children need. A newborn child requires 18 hours of sleep per day, gradually decreasing as they get older to 9 to 11 hours for 5 to 12 year olds, to around 8 hours for adults. The reason that this is mentioned is because of the number of young children that are seen out late at night with their parents, especially in countries in southern Europe. This is a sign of irresponsibility from those parents who need to be less selfish and consider the needs of their children. One way is to make this information known to everyone and ask them to put their children first. If the parents want to go out late, they should find someone to look after their children and if they can't, they should be selfless and stay at home.

To help enforce this point, there could be a law introduced that makes it prohibited for children under 12 to be in a private place like a restaurant later than 9pm, or 7pm for children younger than 3 years.

To summarise, support your children, care for them, show interest in what they like but always keep an eye on making sure that what they do isn't going to be detrimental to anyone else. Find out what they are interested in and help them to develop their interests.

So what should be the government's position regarding parenting? It would be a question of providing enough support for parents so that they can understand how to become more effective at doing what is the hardest job in the world and the one which has the most responsibility. Information in the form of television programmes, books, parental discussion groups both on the internet and in person should be encouraged and monitored to make sure that it is appropriate and effective. Considering that raising children well is the foundation of the success of humanity, it is one that would need to be treated seriously and supported wholeheartedly. The government doesn't need to be the institution that makes these things happen but it should be in a position to make sure that the most effective strategies can be offered to everyone, everywhere.

Virtues and Faults

After looking at the problems that current societies have and how they have come about, the obvious next step is to think about how we are going to attempt to rectify these issues. In the preceding section, individual issues were addressed regarding how they could be turned around, but we also need to have an overall set of principles that should be encouraged and taught in a society on the whole so that we can attempt to develop the way of life of the citizens.

Note that these suggestions should not in any way be seen as a set of rules that are effectively law; the failure to heed them resulting in some kind of punishment, either physically or spiritually (in the present or in 'the next world'). It would be morally inappropriate and possibly even seen as dictatorial or dogmatic to expect everyone to act according to such rules. Instead, what needs to be established are a set of principles that everyone (or at least the majority of the population) can agree on. In the beginning, we should be patient with people's undertaking of them as, of course, to change a firmly embedded mindset can be very difficult. But with enough exposure to the principles and the reasons for proposing them, along with discussion groups and debates so that people can contemplate and understand the reasons for them.

The only way that any principles can be agreed upon by the majority is when there are no better alternatives and when they have a strong moral basis. If any principle is seen to be more in favour of a particular group of people, there will never be an agreement on it being included in what could become a kind of guide book for how to live productively, compassionately, morally and peacefully.

This quest is, by no means, a new one. Of course, such principles have been considered throughout history by religious believers and philosophers alike. First of all, let's take the most commonly used principles that have been largely agreed on over time.

Whether a believer of any religion or a non-believer, it is very difficult to argue against the case for the justification of the seven virtues versus the seven (deadly) sins. The word 'deadly' has been put in brackets as, although this is how they are commonly known, 'deadly' is an unnecessarily strong term to be used; it comes from the church's intention of convincing its followers that they will go to hell if the sins are committed. In order to contemplate what we should be looking for in order to develop a more all-round, psychologically and philosophically sound society, we can do well to start with looking at these two sets of characteristics and seeing how useful and relevant they can be.

Firstly, the seven virtues were originally chosen by Plato and Aristotle before they were taken up by the church as a guide for how to live well with others.

1. Prudence – This refers to making reasonable judgements and actions with regard to appropriateness. It is particularly relevant to The Hypothetical Government as it is based on morals and ethics. Prudence is generally seen as the father of all virtues as it sets the scene for how to begin with approaching all situations in life. In order to instil this and all other virtues in a society, they must form the basis of education, especially from the youngest age of schooling to stand any chance of succeeding. Being prudent would mean to follow Confucius' Golden Rule of "Don't do to others what you would not like to have done to you." It would also mean to promote conscientiousness, acceptance, respect and care for others which would undoubtedly be the building blocks for developing a cohesive and happy society.

2. Justice – This also refers to being appropriate in terms of what people should receive as a result of their actions. We should remember that it doesn't only refer to a 'punishment that fits the crime' but also reciprocal rewards that fit sociable behaviours. Firstly, in terms of the punishment type of justice, it needs to be made explicit that this should not mean that if someone commits murder, they ought to be given the death penalty as this is just as immoral as the crime of murder itself. From the guilty party's point of view, their death would mean that they wouldn't have to endure the rest of their life behind bars with very limited opportunities – the lack of freedom to mix with other people or live in a comfortable manner. It is actually an easy way out for them, which some of them would welcome. We need to look at the morally appropriate punishments - those that would actually be likely to improve the guilty person's attitude and outlook on life. Of course, in the case of murder, the murderer would need to be incarcerated in prison due to the potential danger to kill again, but simply treating the murderer with vengeance would never do anything to improve any aspect of life on either a personal or societal level. To find out more about this issue, please see the section on Prison. Secondly, it should be emphasised that acting appropriately to a person's sociable behaviour would be equally as important to

strengthen the relationships between people in general. It is usually very difficult to snub someone who acts politely to you as it almost automatically gives you a sense of respect and liking for that person but it should be encouraged and explicitly taught to make sure that people don't take too little notice of a polite act but act reciprocally to show that the other person deserves at least an equal amount of politeness and respect in return. It would be recommended to show even more respect in return to someone who has treated you well.

3. Temperance – This is the practice of moderation and restraint. It can refer to many types of actions, such as drinking alcohol, sexual practice and behaviour in general. In order to get the concept of temperance into perspective, we need to make our own analyses to judge whether we are being responsible to ourselves and to others, e.g. is the amount of alcohol that we drink causing problems for us and other people? If so, it would be more responsible to look at drinking in moderation for the additional reason that others would view us more favourably, which again would lead to stronger relationships between the people that may be involved in any interactions, whether they are friends, family or just strangers in the vicinity at the time. It also refers to reacting responsibly to any negative behaviours that we may receive from other people. Starting a fight with someone because we don't like what they are doing or saying is never going to lead to resolution of the problem. The practice of non-violence, as advocated by probably the greatest, most moral leader in history, Gandhi, is what should be investigated on a large scale model. We should try, at all times, to quell any arguments through words and even if the other person uses physical force to attack, self-defence should be the only way of reacting, and methods of which should also be taught in schools from a young age – never fight fire with fire, only fight it with water. Regarding moderation with sexual practice, it would be suggested that people should be responsible and sensible with their behaviour so that sexual desire does not gain too strong an influence in their lives. As long as they are involved in a truly consenting relationship, there is no problem but regarding meeting people and trying to attain sexual gratification, decency and respect would be advised and encouraged to attempt to avoid the occurrence of conflicts and assaults.

3. Courage – This does not simply refer to being brave in the face

of attack, but more to the ability to face adverse factors in one's life such as fear, pain, danger, intimidation and uncertainty. Without being aggressively courageous, people should be encouraged to believe in their own strengths to be able to overcome difficult situations. Strength of character can be used to help those who may not have such strength in times of illness, bereavement or loss of a job. Ways of developing these skills would be very beneficial for people to feel a sense of inner strength but again, not in a way that would cause any detriment to others as this would be seen as bullying or violence and certainly not courage. People need to be supported so that they feel that they can look after themselves well and are not too dependent on others. As mentioned earlier, we all depend on other people to some degree but to be able to have our destiny in our own hands is something that everyone needs to achieve.

3. Faith – This virtue needs a lot more analysis as, in the 21st century, it is quite controversial. Faith refers to belief in a god and often one that ought not to be questioned. It is the only virtue in this list of seven which needs to be treated with a lot of caution. Whereas religions can be a source of comfort and peace for those who are in need of salvation, an unquestioning belief in something that has never been proved to exist is not a recommended way to approach life. In a truly moral society, we should be looking at how to develop our understanding of how to live in harmony with each other and with the planet but to make progress in this area, analysis needs to be made and proof needs to be ascertained for any theory put forward if it is going to be regarded as real knowledge or Truth. Human knowledge and theory can only be advanced with the viewpoint of "Question Everything". Only when you reach a point where you can be sure that something must be true or when you have analysed abstract ideas to a point of morality that cannot be argued against, should you have faith in it. Religion, being a very difficult topic to reach a compromise with, requires its own chapter and will be discussed further there. Hence, the virtue of Faith would be more appropriate if it was altered to the quest for knowledge, or Intellectualism, which in the Wordsworth dictionary is defined as: the doctrine that derives all knowledge from pure reason.

4. Hope – Hope is a theological virtue in Christianity. It is therefore more religious based, regarding the hope for divine

union and eternal happiness, which should also be treated with caution. However, hope can also be used in a non-religious way to give people a positive outlook with which to approach life. People should have a sense of hope that what they truly want can be achieved, but only through moral actions and they should be given practical advice on how to move towards their goals which will lead to happiness, satisfaction and peace. The opposite to hope, despair, is obviously one that would never benefit any person and the feeling of despair is one that should be guarded against so that it could be preventable by everyone.

5. Charity – Not really one that needs much justification, charity means loving kindness to others. People would usually think of charity in terms of giving money to those without, but it is much more than that. Charity also refers to giving support to people who may be going through difficult times by being there to talk and listen to them. It can mean simply being polite to strangers, opening a door for someone (male or female!), smiling at someone or helping them to pick up something they have dropped. An idea that I have taken with me for a few years is that if you have made someone smile, you have had a good day. Like receiving an act of politeness from someone, it is almost impossible not to feel content if you know you have made someone else happy.

There could be other possible contenders for the list of virtues when reflecting on the current state of societies. Companionship would be up for contention to try to promote the idea of living together peacefully and with acceptance of differences of opinion and lifestyle rather than mere tolerance, the difference being that tolerance implies that one begrudgingly accepts another's actions or beliefs while still having misgivings about the said action or belief. Acceptance is about being more open-minded so that the action or belief really has no negative influences on your way of thinking and you have no qualms with the person for their differences.

Diligence, or a strong work ethic, is a virtue to be emphasised and praised to help give people a sense of worth and achievement with what they do. It needs to be made very clear that the value that should be given to work is due to what it means for other people and the stability of the world in general and certainly not about how much money can be made from it. The value of a street cleaner's work is far greater than that of a bank executive who exploits people through deceit to make financial gains for themselves and their partners, in terms of their contribution to society.

Humility is a favourable trait as opposed to pride. As it is noted in Buddhism, one shouldn't be incited to perform actions by the hope of their reward as this gives an ulterior (and ultimately selfish) motive for performing the act. Working from the mindset of what it might provide for yourself is an act of selfishness and feeling proud of how you might feel from carrying out an act is arrogance. The perfect act is, in Buddhism, one that has no result. That means that what it may give to you is irrelevant and instead, one should perform acts simply because the acts need to be performed. Nobody deserves respect for selfish acts of charity as they are not done primarily for charitable reasons, but for the desire to get recognition and admiration. Respect those who do what needs to be done and who expect nothing in return.

Self control is a virtue that is highly honourable. Many people today find it difficult to control their desires in many ways: eating too much food, eating what is tasty but unhealthy, getting emotionally involved with someone when one of them is already in a relationship, etc. Being guilty of these kinds of behaviours is generally agreed upon as being a weakness yet a lot of the time people don't really worry about them too much.

This is due to the capitalist model, which takes advantage of people's weaknesses. It is a lot easier to give in to something that you like, e.g. eating chocolate that it may be difficult to stop yourself eating too much, too often. Given that the amount of chocolate products that are on sale and are advertised in a way that makes people crave it because it looks so delicious is exploitation of our weaknesses.

It is undeniably true that this is one of the ways that the capitalist system not only survives, but thrives. It is easy to convince people to give in to their desires, no matter how damaging they may be. As it is more difficult to overcome cravings, this aspect unsurprisingly features a lot less as there is no money to be made from convincing people that eating chocolate is not a good idea.

Similarly, in television and cinema, people's weaknesses feature prominently. People are seen to be seduced by adulterers very frequently, i.e. giving in to their weaknesses of sexual desire. The problem that this type of storyline has is that when seen repeatedly, the viewers have the potential to do likewise as it can give them the idea that if everyone else is doing it, then I can, too.

The United States, probably the most devoutly Christian country in the western world also has the highest divorce rate of any sizeable country in the western world (just under 50% of marriages ended in divorce as of 2008.[5] Coincidentally, it is also the largest producer of such television programmes and films as described above.

It ought to be emphasised that having the value of self control is what we should all be aiming for. It might be easy to get away with losing self control but that doesn't make us better, more respectable people. There will always be consequences to giving in to weaknesses. Having an affair is nothing short of a personal fault. How would you like it if you found out your partner had been cheating on you? If you eat too much unhealthy food and you become fat or even obese, are you going to be satisfied with yourself? Self control is not actually a difficult thing to address. It cannot be bought but it can be consciously worked on. When you realise you might be guilty of losing it, it is not too difficult to stop and think about whether it would be a fault to give in to temptation. Of course, it is an area that needs a great deal of support and there are already many support groups in place, at least in the western world.

The Hypothetical Government should do everything that it can to promote and encourage morality on all levels, even if this means more restrictions have to be brought into place. The promotion of positivity is imperative in any society and when help is needed, it should be freely available.

After showing the positives of life and discussing how they can (and really should be) emphasised from as early as possible in a person's life, it is almost a shame to turn to the seven sins. However, as western society, as well as many other world societies that fail their people, is generally guilty of most of these, they require analysis to be able to be aware of what we need to address to improve the general level of stability of a society. Another point of note is that the implication of 'sin' and 'sinning' is quite an aggressive way of confronting people who may be thought of as being guilty of one of these behaviours. As aggressive tactics are more likely to lead to spite and rebellion if the person is viewed as being a 'sinner', it would be more appropriate to warn against such actions and instead try to encourage people to analyse their own actions with the aim of improving their behaviour for their own and others' well-being. It can also be seen to be cool, by some people, to be a sinner. Some adolescents (and sometimes still even some adults) like to think of themselves as people who commit sins. Being against society or against the system is viewed among some groups of people as being cool. Even though such people might justify their behaviour as being their form of protest against the system, it is actually destructive and not offering a a constructive alternative solution to what they don't agree with. It is also a weakness and a sign of being too incompetent to rise above detrimental behaviours that other people don't like to see. The power is in being able to strengthen relationships with other people in positive ways and to show your worth as a person in the community in which you live.

When something negative is committed, it is important to be aware of yourself as the guilty party and take the blame personally. This is the ability to be honest with yourself, which everyone needs to be but some people are not.

Whereas the opposite to virtue is 'vice', as we shall see, some of the characteristics are too strong to lose their status as a 'sin'. Otherwise, the concept of 'fault' would be a more appropriate term as viewing oneself as having a fault is something that can be taken personally and something that people would not like to think of themselves as having.

1. Lust/ Luxury/ Extravagance – As, historically, there have been different versions of the lists of sins, there may be more than one term used in this section for each one. Each of these refer to acts of excess in terms of personal gain, for example of material goods and sexual gratification. The capitalist society is encouraged to be excessive in terms of personal possessions and for what reason? To answer this, we need to look at how it works from the business perspective. Many businesses, especially large corporations persistently encourage 'consumers' to want more so that they themselves will gain more revenue. Therefore, they advocate extravagance and luxury for their own lustful gains. The main problem with this is that the vice of lust and luxury is like a wheel where it is difficult to get off and there is no end to be reached. As people have more, they want more and when they get more, they still want more, ad infinitum. The problem that results from this is that happiness and fulfilment will never be attained if one always wants more. It is a futile exercise that will only end in disappointment, as most material goods have very little personal value and effectively no way of bringing inner reward that one can use to develop as a person. Therefore, this is something to be warned against as it not a virtue for either the individual or the society. Regarding lust in a sexual manner, the status of sexual behaviour and the taboos that have been linked with it historically mean that it is a very different issue to discuss now compared to hundreds of years ago. Rather than

go into it here, it will be discussed in detail in the section on Sexuality.

2. Gluttony – A very specific entry in the list of sins, gluttony is especially relevant in the 21st century with increasing levels of obesity on a worldwide scale. It is to be warned against to eat too frivolously and eating foods that lead to excessive weight gain. Fast food restaurants, chocolate manufacturers and soft drinks companies, etc. simply use the knowledge that people like eating certain things, especially those which have addictive qualities (due to the deliberately added addictive chemicals to ensure that people will want the product again and again) regardless of the fact that such products are causing harm to the human body. As this is purely an immoral practice, it will be discussed in more detail in the section on The Economy.

3. Greed – Arguably the worst of the seven sins and the one that the capitalist model has advocated and based itself on the most. Humans are susceptible to greed as we are creatures that feel that obtaining more of what we like is going to lead to happiness. Buddhism states that this idea is incorrect and as stated above in Lust, it can quite easily be seen to be untrue. Capitalist propaganda thrives on convincing people that they want more material products, yet even with the extreme saturation of pointless products in the western world, it can be argued that its society is becoming unhappier, more dangerous and more fragmented in terms of human relations. Again, greed is like a never ending circle and not only is it never going to lead to true happiness, it can also be the cause of recessions, notably seen in the global recession which was confirmed in 2008. Companies and individuals became greedy in their lust for power and material gain and the banks, blindly and irresponsibly, lent money to everyone who wanted it because they expected to get it back along with the interest they charged on it. As it got to cataclysmic proportions, the whole spiral of greed caused the greedy people and companies, as well as the banks, to collapse as they didn't know when to stop. The result of the recession was that the workers (the poorer servants in the whole capitalist model) were the ones to suffer the most as their jobs were cut away like corn at harvest time and the most irresponsible of banks deceitfully used the 'ordinary citizens" money to lend to the greedy, who likewise were deceitful and gambled it all away or simply wasted it on feeding their own greed. Greed is the sin (and it would be right

to retain the word 'sin' in this case) that can cause worldwide damage to many innocent citizens. It would be necessary to teach at school the terrors of greed and why it should be avoided at all costs, as well as, of course, how we should live instead and why.

4. Sloth – The idea of being lazy to a wasteful level should be discouraged, not because it is necessarily as bad for humankind as the ways that the previous three can be but because it can be argued to be a result of greed and extravagance in the western world. While susceptible people may choose to dedicate their lives to more and more material gains, they are at risk of losing sight of what they could 'really' be attaining in their lives. In schools in the most liberal democratic societies, students lose interest in their studies, thereby wasting skills that they may have, but have never even realised that they have, and becoming apathetic to properly developing their lives and opportunities because they are too preoccupied with getting the latest gadgets and clothes that the shameful corporations insist that they want and need. (This is due to the failure of the education system which advocates teaching subjects in isolation, which will be covered in the chapter on Education). Instead, creativity and productivity should be encouraged along with the search for people's skills that they may not yet have found. The feeling of satisfaction gained when one knows that they have done something well can not be marketed, cannot be taken away and costs nothing as it is far more valuable than any material possession.

5. Wrath – Anger or rage is defined as uncontrolled feelings of hatred or as extreme displeasure of someone, a group of people or of certain rules or laws. On the worst scale, genocide can be a result of wrath as well as religious extremism regarding unreasonable reactions to things that one does not agree with. It can be seen as a total bypassing of all morality due to poor education which leads to such warped views. Many civil wars in Africa are caused by wrath towards particular groups of people whom the governments see as being the 'wrong type of people' or opponents to their appallingly blinkered ideals, whereby most of the population suffers from poverty and famine due to the greed of some military dictatorships. Wrath is also a common cause of war against other nations and the total non-acceptance of any opposition. Again, Gandhi was one of the (sadly) few leaders who called for total acceptance of

everyone in India, no matter what their religion was and even in the face of the disgraceful British Imperialists (including Winston Churchill who didn't want to give independence back to India), he demanded that the Indian people show non-violence in their protests towards their system of a hugely divisive class system whereby the 'whites' were the superior, ruling section and the natives to the land were effectively the slaves to their occupying rulers. Gandhi's long struggle to reclaim India for the Indians through non-violence and non-compliance to the imposed laws seriously embarrassed the Imperialists who implemented violent reactions to the Indians' non-compliance but in the end, Gandhi won independence for India in what can only be described as probably the most moral and admirable 'battle' against an unjust system in history. He showed no anger and no hatred towards his oppressors and won independence through the strength of his ethics and his words.

6. Envy – The selfish principles set in place by the capitalist system have been responsible for the rise of levels of envy in the western world. It has promoted the ideal of idolatry of the rich and famous with the goal of making people strive to mimic their valueless and largely talentless heroes. Obviously, if you can make people want something, you can then produce it and make money from them. As the class system has also created bigger divides between people in western societies, poorer people have, in their attempts to have what the richer people have, become more involved in crime to attain material goods in the hope that it will make them feel better as people. However, as their actual life situations largely remain the same and they continue to have very few opportunities, the envy remains, crime levels rise and wrath and greed are exacerbated. False worship of those who are purported by the commercial media to be successful only adds to this ever-increasing problem and, very sadly, the ever-increasing bank balances of those at the top of the hierarchical pyramid of power and control. In Buddhism and Islam, idol worship is not recommended or forbidden, respectively, as it is taught that it is not the teacher or the prophet that should be worshipped but their words and philosophies that should be used to guide us on the right path through life so as to develop inner awareness and not to be distracted by those who falsely claim to be enlightened or worthy of our attention. Such people are seen as fraudulent and should be ignored.

7. Pride – The desire to be more attractive or important than others is, to be blunt, one of the most pathetic things to be guilty of. Pride has been considered to be the most serious of the seven sins and I would put it up there, very closely, with Greed. The excessive love of oneself and the failure to acknowledge the good work of others is something to be seriously discouraged. As this is another of capitalism's failures, whereby it is advocated that people create a false version of themselves with clothes, make-up and status symbols, it needs to be addressed very strongly to try to dissuade people to act and appear so dishonestly and falsely. As mentioned earlier, those who feel the need to fill their lives with innumerable material possessions and to appear unnaturally in the vain attempt to be theoretically more attractive are more likely to pay little attention to their value as a human being in terms of the good that they do to help further the society that they are a part of. This is something that is never promoted by the companies that make their money through superficiality, simply because it can't be bought or sold. This marginalisation of values is at a dangerously low level that society needs to become very aware of so that we can begin to resolve the fact that most westerners have no idea and may not even contemplate how to develop their own lives and the state of society. For any happiness, peace and stability to be evident in a society, this is what needs to be addressed first of all.

Faults and Sins in Capitalism

At this point, we should consider how the virtues, faults and sins relate to capitalism. Which of them are prevalent in this system, which ones don't appear and why this is the case.

Looking through the list of virtues, there aren't any that could be considered apparent or relevant to capitalism. Prudence is not encouraged as making decisions (for example, those in business) based on morality is certainly not part of the general ideology. Instead, decisions are made so as to make oneself benefit as much as possible, without any regard for the well-being of others or the environment.

Justice is not particularly relevant to capitalism in the sense of law as, again, decisions aren't usually made with respect to whether they are justified, only to whether the actions will generate more money or not.

Temperance, or moderation and restraint certainly don't feature in the capitalist system; quite the opposite. People are encouraged to exercise a egotistic attitude so that they will keep buying products that they falsely believe will make them happy. We are recommended to treat ourselves frequently with jewellery, clothes, fine foods and wines, etc. so that the masses feel that they are valuing themselves, when in fact as they spend their money frivolously, their money keeps transferring to the people who already have far more money than they could ever possibly need but manage to convince the general public that they ought to do what the adverts tell them.

Courage isn't relevant to this discussion but faith can be interpreted to be. Having faith in capitalism could be referred to as believing that it is the best system and not questioning it. To consider this, it would be pitted against other existing systems like communism, dictatorships, religious states and so on, with the easy task of coming out on top with all points considered. That is a fair point but when you think of the negative points to capitalism, it doesn't mean that it is the best possible system. It's more like the best of a bad bunch.

Charity is really not a concept that has any place in this system. Generosity in capitalism? It does not in any way nurture the idea that having lots of money means you should therefore help society to develop in some way. Think of the American Dream, whereby James Truslow Adams, in 1931, famously stated that all citizens of every rank should feel that they can achieve "a better, richer and happier life." As the American Dream is now generally taken as meaning the ownership of one's own home, with it being seen as a status symbol as opposed to those people who can't afford their own home, this concept is firmly rooted in the idea that money brings success and happiness. Note the word "richer" in the above quote sandwiched between the words "better" and "happier". To own your own home you need enough money, it's as simple as that. You can't own your own home by being charitable. As we have seen, however, money does not guarantee happiness. In Scotland in 2010, lottery winner Stuart Donnelly committed suicide at the age of 29 due to the misery that his fortune brought him. He was so sick of the publicity that he inevitably got that he preferred not to leave the house and even had people camping outside his home. He had won just under £2 million when he was 17.

Let's move on to the relevance of the faults and sins in the capitalist system.

It heartily promotes lust, luxury and extravagance in all its forms, no doubt about it. Using jewellery and such decorations as an example, people are considered to have a high status if they wear diamonds and gold and other so-called precious stones and metals. The reason being that such items cost a lot of money so one can show-off their wealth or try to appear well-off or posh if they can at least acquire one diamond ring or a gold necklace. In the Bible, it is said that if you have gold or jewels, so what? What does that mean to how valuable you are as a person? Why do these items cost so much money? It is not because they are actually valuable, but because they are scarce. All they really are are natural materials found in rock in certain places. They have not been created by anyone through years of hard work, they are just minerals that happen to have pretty colours. More to the point, we don't really hear too much about the people who mine for these minerals in war-zones in Africa. The film "Blood Diamonds" was made in 2006 to illustrate how the process works. Diamond companies around the world use countries such as Angola, Liberia, Sierra Leone and Côte D'Ivoire to supply them with diamonds, in return of course for amounts of money which in these countries would be substantial. However, being war-zones, the money is used for insurgencies or warlord activities, therefore resulting in the deaths of many more people because they have the money to buy weapons and ammunition.

Obviously, this is kept quiet in the oblivious and ignorant west because such knowledge could damage the jewellery industry.

Gluttony is also there in the capitalist model, in the confectionery industry especially, not to mention the fast food industry; the success of which go hand in hand with the rise in levels of obesity in the west. People are encouraged to eat delicious chocolates and children are very much targeted by the funny, colourful characters that adorn the adverts for products which have absolutely no health benefits whatsoever. Advertising restrictions are definitely needed there.

Greed is unquestionably there. What is probably the worst sin in the list is the one that is basically the foundation of the system. I would like to hear someone try to argue the opposite.

Sloth is there, too. "Why learn how to do something by yourself when you can buy this machine that does it for you?" Well, because I'd have some skills then. "You don't need to get off the sofa to lose weight, just attach these electrical pads that will induce muscle spasms and the pounds will drop off." No they won't, that is not exercise. To make any significant changes to the amount of fat in your body, you need to increase your heart rate, break into a sweat and actually move. It's not difficult to understand but it is difficult to make some people realise.

Wrath? Not surprisingly enough, that is there, too. The arms industry thrives on keeping people hating each other so much that they want to kill each other. Very profitable. As long as wars can be maintained, weapons can be sold. In 2007, the USA made $7454 million from arms exports, compared to China's $355 million. Why would they want to damage such a profitable industry?

As long as the general public are allowed to have weapons, other people in the same community will feel threatened or scared and think they need weapons to defend themselves. Profit. Wrath is promoted a great deal in the USA for this very reason. Interestingly enough, some other countries in the west also maintain the legality of owning firearms but the homicide rates are staggeringly lower. The USA, as of the statistics for 2008, has the highest homicide rate of any western country at 5.4 per 100,000 whereas the next highest western country is Portugal with a rate of 2.5.

Michael Moore, in the documentary "Bowling For Columbine", showed the difference between the USA and Canada in terms of homicide rates. It is legal in both countries to own a gun but in Canada (with a homicide rate of 1.83) the people don't actually feel that they depend on them to survive. Why not? It's all about the mentality. Fear is not promoted in Canada so the people don't generally feel that they could be attacked at any point but in the USA, it's a very different story. For example, when Barack Obama won the election in 2008, the rise in the number of firearms sales was incredible as the people thought that the new president would change the law, banning the ownership of guns.

In Wikipedia, in the list of modern armament manufacturers, Russia has 4 companies, China has 1, Iran has 3, Iraq has none and the USA has 46. The UK also has 11 which is comparable to the USA relative to population. In some countries, the arms industry is so big that the people that control the governments will basically not let any change happen in the law or the constitution.

Finally, do envy and pride feature at all in the capitalist system? They have already been discussed and there is no more that needs to be said.

In conclusion, we can see that capitalism is based very much on what has traditionally been known as the seven deadly sins. Or to be more exact, on exploiting those sins. It thrives by coaxing people into committing sins as much as is humanly possible, in every aspect of their lives. Is this really the best system to be living under? It sounds shocking to know that this is the case but again, it would be interesting to hear someone argue for the other side. For any religious believers reading this, can you really agree that this is how life should be? I can't see how it can be accepted in any way, or that it can continue to be implemented when we are aware of how it is really formulated.

Michael Moore again, in his documentary film of 2009, "Capitalism, A Love Affair", exposes the disgraceful exploitation that occurs in this system, from people having their homes repossessed when they have been conned into re-mortgaging them for no good reason, to companies that have secret life insurance policies on their employees, hoping that they will die so the company can reap the rewards of the payouts, which have been in the millions for just one deceased worker.

It is a system that has to come to an end. Now, people are becoming more aware of its evils (and evil is not too strong a word), through the work of Michael Moore, Noam Chomsky, Naomi Klein and many others. The difficulty that people have is thinking of what we can replace it with. There is nothing that has been used before in history that can be argued as being better so that leaves us with a dilemma. We have to devise something different. We need to help people to change their mindsets; not through force or any other kind of propaganda but by awareness and education that will lead to liberation from this awful system; by telling people the truth and not hiding inconvenient facts that go against proposals put forward by politicians; and not withholding information that the people may not approve of if they knew about it. We need to involve everybody to make them feel that they are a part of it, that their concerns are listened to and acted upon in the most moral way possible; that the people are not the ones that are instructed to act as they are told and accept what the government decides for them. This type of ideology is a failure and even now, it seems like a very primitive form of civilization.

Corporate Exploitation

Whereas this book is not intended to be a critique or an attack on particular companies (for one reason because of legal repercussions and for another because of inadvertently giving publicity to brands), to illustrate my point of how capitalism is allowed the freedom to enslave people into parting with their money for no valid reasons, I would like to discuss the enormous merchandising brand of Hello Kitty.

In 2004, this company introduced a way of exploiting children even more than it does by stamping their brand onto effectively anything that it can, by creating the Hello Kitty Debit MasterCard. They enthusiastically announced this on their website with the slogan ""Freedom! You can use the Hello Kitty Debit MasterCard to shop till you drop."

First of all, it is worth drawing attention to the use of the word 'freedom'. Making available a new debit card to spend one's money without thinking about the consequences is not really an accurate way of defining freedom. Instead, it should be seen as a way of tricking people into giving away their hard-earned money with nothing useful to show for it while the company gets even richer. The concept of 'shop till you drop' is worded to make the idea of wasting your money on useless items a fun thing to do.

Now, it is interesting to find out what their target audience was. Ordinarily, debit cards would only be available to adults, for obvious reasons – one needs to understand the responsibility of taking care of one's own money that has been earned through employment and to be of a legal age to have the independence to do so. However, Bruce Giuliano, senior vice president of licensing for Sanrio Inc., which owns the brand, was more than willing to make clear, as reported in The Washington Post that "We think our target age group will be from 10 to 14, although it could certainly go younger." He added that it's a great way for adults to "help teach their children how to manage their finances." [6]

I don't think that giving children a debit card that can really be used in shops is the best way to *teach* children how to manage their finances. First, lessons in school need to be taught about the dangers of being let loose with a card where you have no indication of how much money you have at your disposal. Joline Godfrey, author of "Raising Financially Fit Kids" and chief executive of Independent Means Inc., a California financial-education firm, was wary of this freedom that financial institutions have, saying that the cards become a "great educational tool . . . to say to kids, 'Spend, spend, spend, buy, buy,

buy.' "

Unsurprisingly, officials at MasterCard and Visa defended their idea. "We think it's a good way to teach teens good money management early on," said Rhonda Bentz, spokeswoman for Visa USA. But when you look at the terms and conditions, namely that the activation fee for the card is $14.95 (and another $14.95 if you renew after a year), there is a $2.95 monthly maintenance fee, a $1.50 ATM-withdrawal fee and a $1-per-minute fee to talk to a customer service agent, I can't see that anyone with a milligram of human decency would argue that this is a morally acceptable way of dealing with children. Robert McKinley, chief executive of CardWeb.com Inc., a Frederick firm that tracks the credit card industry, said the fees are "probably the worst I've run across."

Children younger than 14 simply do not have the life experience to realise how important it is to be prudent with money, even more so those younger than 10. Giving them the freedom to spend money that can't be seen is a despicable abuse of childhood innocence and morality as well as a way of turning them into mindless consumers to fuel those who already have far more money than they can personally use in their own lifetimes. As, in the United States, children are not legally allowed to be employed at such a young age, the capital would have to come from the parents and if parents agreed to obtain this debit card for their little ones, then even more questions of responsibility need to be asked.

But what would be the reason for children wanting to even bother with having a debit card? Well, Visa's promotions, after they had introduced a Hilary Duff gift card in five denominations from $25 to $200, urged girls to "shop like a star."

This is a blatant example of how children can easily be exploited for their (parents') money. Shop like a star? This would give innocent children the idea that, to be someone, they should try to be like their Disney Channel idols (whom Hilary Duff is; I'd never heard of her until I read this article), and they therefore have to spend lots of money to be as extravagant as possible to aim to reach the dizzying, materialistic heights of a marketing puppet.

Duff, who was around 17 at the time, promoted the gift cards by stating that it was "the perfect way to shop for school and beyond. . . . Now I can easily buy stuff online without having to borrow my parents' credit card." Great, but more importantly, without having to think about the consequences of being frivolous and frittering away money that 'normal people' more than likely don't have, especially children.

The exploitation involved in these products is frankly disgusting. It is all about tapping into the market of pre-teenagers so that more money can be made at their own and their parents' expense, without having any consideration for the consequences that will result from this way of living. The Washington Post pointed out that the Hello Kitty debit card showed how the corporations aggressively court the $30 billion-a-year youth market. Well, when we see how much the youth market is potentially worth, the free market will go for the throat of any child they want and provide them with absolutely nothing worthwhile in return. This has to be stopped if we want to live in a truly developed world.

Especially when parents had been calling in to complain that they couldn't top up the Duff cards and that they wanted 'boy-friendly' products as well. The Hello Kitty card beat this 'problem' by allowing parents to top it up whenever they wanted. Well, if they are willing to practically burn their own money whenever their children demand it, we can't even rely on certain parents to educate their own children in a system that advocates the practice of "spend, spend, spend".

It doesn't stop there. Toy manufacturers have been immoral enough to team up with MasterCard and produce games where children as young as 3 can practice swiping their MasterCards on toy supermarkets, promising that it provides "hours of non-stop fun . . . to enhance social skills". Debatable? I'll leave you to think about that.

For slightly older girls, 9 and up, there is a board game, where the goal is to "find the steals and deals." The winner is the first shopper to make six purchases and get to the right destination. To do that, girls can swipe their cash card or get money at the ATM. As the blurb on the box says: "Hey girls! Don't miss the next big sale." Because, apparently, this is more important than retaining your childhood innocence and devoting your time to creative activities that will help to build your self-esteem and your own identity and not leave you feeling dependent on trying to cover up your perceived failures because you don't look like the manufactured role models. Apparently.

Fortunately, a few years after this sickening marketing scheme of Hello Kitty was introduced, US senator Byron L. Dorgan criticised the marketing pitch by saying "I'd just love to know the person who thought this up and to say, 'Are you nuts? What on earth are credit companies doing soliciting young kids to get a credit card?' "

ConsumerReports spoke to Peter Klamka, president of Legend Credit, the company that developed the Hello Kitty card, about the marketing logic behind the card. "If one teenager gets the card, then others see it and want one too," he said. "There's a whole Hello Kitty culture that's kind of like Nascar for young women."[7]

At this point I am exhausted from the amount of unbelievable quotes from these people. They want people to follow each other like sheep and think that they have to do what everyone else does. By demanding adults and children to want and buy everything that really serves no useful function, these people want the general public to dig themselves into serious debt for their own extremely selfish purposes. There is no question that they don't care about anyone but themselves and their like-minded friends. Yet, I will always fail to see why anyone thinks they need so much money and power. We don't live forever. Even if someone has something like $1 million at their disposal, why would they need more? Especially when they are already over 60 years old. What are they going to spend it all on before they die? Mansions? sports cars? Why? What is that ever going to achieve?

However, to finish on a more positive note, the version of credit card reform legislation approved in 2009 aims to protect consumers under the age of 21 from getting deluged with unsolicited credit card offers. Barack Obama has publicly called for an end to card practices. It's a shame that it took until he came into power before anything was done to address this issue.

Fame

It is a typical human characteristic to want to be noticed. The concept of attention seeking has been studied by various researchers over the years and there have been four styles of attention seeking identified:

Extroverted positive overt style – this is when people boast about themselves or try to be controversial with types of exhibitionist behaviour.

Extroverted positive subdued style – such as dominating conversations or wearing designer clothes simply so that people will look at them.

Extroverted negative overt style – looking for pity or reassurance.

Extroverted negative subdued style – making negative statements to the world like dressing as a punk or in other non-conformist styles, or by making spiteful comments as in the case of 'internet haters' (those people who deliberately make offensive comments on the web, anonymously, to incite arguments).

All of these four styles of attention seeking have negative connotations and are usually the result of the people concerned feeling low self-esteem and that otherwise nobody would notice them. It is understandable that if someone feels that nobody notices them, they can be driven to seek attention in some way. Unfortunately, if the person feels 'lost' as to how to be noticed for something that they can offer positively, like in the case of a certain skill or talent, they often choose the easy way which is negative behaviour reinforcement. This is when someone gets attention for doing something controversial or criminal because they know that they will at least get noticed. This is because the people who do notice such attention seeking activities often find it difficult to ignore the perpetrator but instead respond, just as negatively, thereby giving the required result to the person who began the act.

Obviously, this kind of behaviour is not what should be encouraged. Instead, people should be supported to find ways that they can feel valued by society and feel they are respected and positive members of the community. This is very closely linked to the ideas of 'losing the self' and Creativity in the Community, which we will come to later. By aiming to bring people together in positive, constructive ways, we can help to reduce both the frequency and the apparent need to seek attention.

Being famous is of course another way that people think they will achieve success. Being a celebrity has, over the last 20 years especially, become exacerbated to the point where we now have something called Celebrity Worship Syndrome (CWS). This is when someone becomes obsessed with the personal life of someone who is famous. There are three grades of obsession on the scale of CWS, devised by psychologists in the UK and the USA, ranging from liking to hear about and talk about their favourite celebrity to believing that their favourite celebrity will be there to rescue them when they need help.

CWS has undoubtedly been enhanced by celebrity magazines that have really taken off in the previous twenty or so years that have the aim of glorifying certain people, even if they have no specific talent or skill. This used to be a precursor for becoming famous but these days many people are famous for being famous and simply being dressed in expensive clothes at exclusive events with vacuous grins on their faces for the tabloid photographers. These celebrity magazines like to publish photos and stories of pop stars and soap opera stars, showing how extravagantly they decorate their homes, their spouses and their children and for some reason, the public lap all of this up as though these marketing puppets are actually useful to society in some way. Flaunting one's wealth in a selfish way really can't be argued as a display of one's worth. If the same person instead showed how they give their millions to projects for developing society and the world, and bringing about equality, that would be something worthy of attention. These kinds of magazines would be in a higher band of corporate tax to aim to make them think about their business practices. (See the tax section later for more details on this.)

The idea of celebrity as a mass media phenomenon has also increased over the last few decades. Being famous has been pushed as something that everyone should try to attain with the advent of reality TV shows where people become famous just for being there rather than for doing anything of any value. With the immoral practices of the tabloid press digging into the private lives of such people as well as people who are famous for a reason such as actors, the public become more willing to find out about such people without their consent. To apply the Golden Rule again, let's have a quick think about this. The general public often see no problem with seeing paparazzi photos of celebrities where they are going about their daily lives but being photographed and commented on depending on whether they look fat or are wearing clothes are are not considered to be stylish. But turn the situation around – imagine that it was you who kept having photos printed without your consent and the reporters were pointing out that they could see cellulite on your thighs or evidence of a belly, for example. Imagine that this kind of thing kept happening regularly over the years. How would you like it? Or how would you like reporters and consequently the general public commenting on rumours about your private behaviours and what has happened in your relationship?

I would doubt that you would like that at all but if you are guilty of gossiping about so-called celebrities in the same way, you should question your level of morality and try to get your principles into perspective.

We, as the general public, don't tend to hear so much about the effect that our voyeuristic behaviour has on the celebrities. They are viewed as not being real people and that we are allowed to stare at them because they have lots of money. Again, turn it around and think about whether you would like it. They may be rich but they are still real people with real lives and they can be psychologically affected, disturbed and even destroyed by the amount of attention they get. The pop singer Britney Spears may have been manufactured solely to make huge quantities of money for her management team but she is still a person and she has been through a huge amount of stress and personal abuse from both the media and the public which has led to alcohol and drug problems as well as having the custody of her children taken away from her. Imagine if it was you that millions of people were constantly scrutinising and criticising even though none of those people know you personally.

Fame is not a measure of success. It is extremely destructive, especially if it comes to someone who is not prudent and modest, and likes the idea of receiving attention. The chances are, in the end, they will wish that they were not famous and never had been when they see that their private life has all but disappeared.

Just like other conclusions made thus far in this book, people should be made aware that aiming for the highest is both unrealistic and pointless. Keep things in perspective. If people who know you personally appreciate what you do, then why should you need more? What does it matter if people you will never meet approve or disapprove of you? That is irrelevant to your personal development.

Focus on becoming more respected and valued by the people in your family, by your friends and by the people with whom you share the community. It may sound familiar by now to read such things but in this time of so many people being lost in their own lives, I feel it can't be emphasised and illustrated enough.

So, the next question is how to promote the application of virtues and how to help people steer clear of vices, faults and sins. As has been mentioned, teaching children about these issues from a young age is fundamental for the fastest reform of society. It should be compulsory to begin exploring virtues in the first two years of school as well as, where applicable, how to avoid the opposites in the list of faults and sins.

I have not separated the list into these two sections of faults and sins as there could be debate about which ones to put into the relevant sections, although my suggestion would be to at least keep Greed and Pride in Sins. Lust, Gluttony, Sloth, Wrath and Envy would be more appropriate in the list of Faults though Wrath, depending on its severity could have a place in Sins.

Of course, to be consistent in schooling, these characteristics would need to be evaluated by school children throughout their years of education as we are at a point in time where values need to be emphasised. It ought to be made clear that even though the lists of virtues and sins have a lot of historical origins in religion, they can be equally applicable in a secular society and hopefully would be seen to be valid regardless of belief or non-belief.

Additionally, it would be recommended to provide information for adults to use to evaluate their own lives as we simply cannot neglect those who have already finished their formal education. Attempting to bring up children in a more virtuous way while they are faced with the vices and sins of the established society would make it a very shaky project in which to achieve good results, so consistency is essential if people are going to understand, accept and value each other. Information can be provided in discussions on TV, the internet and in the press to help guide people on a more positive path. Again, it must also be made explicit that people should not be *expected* to follow the paths suggested, but they should make their own informed decisions. The choice has to be left with the people. We have to discover our own truth to be sure that it is truth, rather than rely on supposed intellectuals (or politicians) to provide the answers for us and form rules based on their conclusions which may not have taken general opinions into account. This is something that politicians are very guilty of. Quite often, the public is not consulted before laws are brought into effect, but in The Hypothetical Government, it is imperative that the public is encouraged to participate in offering ideas for improving our lives and that their ideas will be listened to and used to adapt or add to the notions which we use to guide us through life. This is what Socrates called Democracy, an idea that is much lauded in the west but too often only stays theoretical. The politicians are the ones who make the laws with very little or no consultation with the public, then kindly inform them of what they have to do or cannot do.

Buddhist principles for life

Following on from historically significant principles on how to live life, it is very useful, from a moral perspective, to examine, more deeply, Buddhist principles to give us more of a background with which we can develop society for the better of everyone.

One of the most fundamental teachings (or Dharma) in Buddhism is the Four Noble Truths. This is how life can be analysed in four simple truths:

1. Life is suffering. The aspects that contribute to suffering are such things as birth, illness, ageing, sorrow, grief, pain, death and not getting what we want. Obviously, suffering can occur in any of these ways as well as others and can occur regularly and repeatedly in 'normal' life.
2. The Origin of Suffering. Craving is what leads to suffering, craving to have more, to feel younger, to be more attractive, to be richer, etc.. As long as we crave things, we will suffer as attaining things brings pleasure (on a shallow and temporary level) and we want it again, thus leaving people in an eternal cycle of craving and therefore suffering.
3. Overcoming Suffering. This is the truth that if we no longer crave for things, we will no longer suffer. We must be content with keeping life simple and paying no attention to pointless items that will do nothing for us.
4. The Way. How we can overcome suffering, which is the most important of the Four Noble Truths. We need to have guidelines so that we can achieve liberation from materialism, dogmas and delusions so that we can find ourselves on the path to enlightenment.

From The Way, comes the Noble Eightfold Path, which are the methods by which we can achieve happiness in a truthful, profound sense. They are often depicted on a wheel to indicate that they are not necessarily steps to be taken one after the other but to be taken in conjunction with all the others.

However, the first two are essential for people to be able to take the Dharma seriously. The Noble Eightfold Path is as follows:

1. Right View. Before we begin, we know that life involves

suffering and change (Buddha taught that nothing is constant, everything is changing at all times; as we get older, as flowers die, etc.). We must understand that the Dharma shows us a way to overcome suffering and be happy.

2. Right Intention. Having the right views is all well and good but if we do not act with those views, we will not achieve much.
3. Right Speech. We must speak the truth and only speak positively and helpfully.
4. Right Action. Be kind to all living things, be generous, be honest and keep your mind clear.
5. Right Livelihood. We must earn a living in a way that follows all the values on this wheel. We must not exploit anyone or anything, or cause any suffering to anyone or anything.
6. Right Effort. Don't think harmful thoughts and try to give goodwill to everyone.
7. Right Mindfulness. Become more aware of those around you and of your own feeling. See things as they really are and not in a way that is delusional.
8. Right Contemplation. By training your mind, you will be able to get rid of hatred, greed and ignorance and therefore experience happiness and peace.

Even though this path of eight points can be described briefly and simply, to truthfully follow them is an exercise that continues for your entire life. Of course, all the points are unquestionably moral as is the true nature of Buddhism.

The Noble Eightfold Path is not easy to stick to at all but requires a great deal of dedication and commitment. After the first two points can be achieved, the next three give us practical advice about how to think and act. The last three train one's mind to think and feel in a positive way.

It has many similarities with the list of virtues but is more structured so that people can use it to organise their progress along the Path. A structured guide is something that people in this modern age need as it is common for people to think that life is just how it is and we have to try to support ourselves through it until we die even if we have no idea of what we are aiming for. This is why so many people leave school and try to get any kind of job so that they can pay the bills without any thought for what they should be trying to achieve. They don't know what they really want but they have probably never been asked or encouraged to explore their real interests. Living hand to mouth in this way is completely unfulfilling and should not be accepted as a way to live life as people will gain no benefit from it and no long-term happiness, which is what everyone strives for yet many people feel they will never achieve.

The Buddhist notion of community (Sangha) is one that can be assimilated perfectly into the society that a moral government would want to attain. Before becoming the Buddha (the enlightened one), Siddhartha Gautama followed the Hindu religion, which is organised into castes; very similar to the class system. The caste system operates on the belief that it is entirely hereditary – you are born into the same caste as your parents and your opportunities are limited by that label.

Siddhartha did not agree with this system and thought that everyone in the community should be treated equally and could improve themselves by following the Noble Eightfold Path.

Going for refuge is another Buddhist thought that can be used to understand our current situations. When people are suffering, they take refuge in many ways – they can go to their friends, to work or to some kind of distraction so they can forget about their suffering. This is considered to be a bad idea in Buddhism as all of these things can let you down and fail to save you from suffering. Instead, to go for refuge in the Buddhist sense, we should go back to the teachings of the Buddha, which is going for refuge *to* life with the intention of understanding it better and not escaping from life by buying clothes or getting drunk.

The Buddhist way of life is suggested through guidelines and not through rules. Therefore, it is not a dogma or something that is claimed is necessary for everyone to work on. They are recommendations and by offering them so, they are more likely to be met with interest and serious contention than when they are demanded or expected.

There are five main precepts that all Buddhists should try to follow:

1. Avoid killing – As well as not killing people, most Buddhists are vegetarian unless their remote settlement prevents this from being possible. Every living creature belongs in this world, otherwise it wouldn't be here. Show kindness to all creatures instead.

2. Avoid taking what is not given – As well as being like the Bible's 'Thou shalt not steal', we should not try to get more than our fair share or to get something at the expense of others. We ought to share the extra that we have but don't need with those

who have less than they need.

3. Avoid harmful sexual activity – Any kind of sexual harassment should not take place in one's life.
4. Always tell the truth – Don't lie or try to distort the truth and equally importantly, be honest with yourself.
5. Avoid intoxicants – Do not use drugs (including alcohol) as they can alter your mind in adverse ways. This also includes not doing anything that will cloud your mind – addictions like gambling or certain computer games. We should always aim to keep our minds clear of bad judgements and false hopes.

Buddhism may be seen in the west as a way of life that wouldn't suit our modern world as its simplicity is not conducive to our complicated lifestyles. This, however, is the very problem that the western world has – it is far too complicated to be able to make real sense of and there are far too many things happening that we are supposed to be paying attention to. We have to pay the bills, pay the rent or mortgage, do the shopping, get the computer fixed, etc.. We simply do not have enough time to stop and contemplate the things that really matter. By working through all this suffering, we would be able to simplify our lives, notice what's going on and share our time with other people, whereby we can come together and enjoy each other's company without getting stressed by things that we shouldn't have to worry about.

The Four Noble Truths and the Noble Eightfold Path can be used with the virtues list to begin forming the basis of how a society and how a governmental system should work.

From both of these reference points, we can construct a set of moral guidelines with the intention of total agreement from everyone. In principle, this sounds like a ridiculous idea but all you have to do is remember the Golden Rule. This can't be argued against, as explained above. We can base other principles accordingly but in the context of this book, they cannot be taken as universally agreed upon as I have had to write them first so that you can discuss them. Therefore, all I can do is propose a set of principles that can be used as a starting point. They should be analysed, adapted and improved until we have a set that is agreed on by the majority of people. The hope would then be that, over time, people who didn't agree with them to begin with would realise the reasons for aiming to achieve them and give up their selfish desires to stick to their faults and sins.

In terms of their application, they should be implemented in all aspects of life including work so that in some contexts they are actually laws that companies have to adhere to for the well-being of its employees.

The basic criteria that we should focus on are those which really have the potential to bring people together to create a society that feels like the people want to work together and that they feel happy.

We need to propose guidelines that people are willing to take on so that they can improve their own and other people's lives. By this, I am not referring to becoming richer or convincing people that they should believe in something that someone suggests. Again, people do not like this aggressive approach and it is against human rights to try to change someone's beliefs to match your own. We need to help people achieve liberation from the delusions that they have about life and happiness that have been put into effect as the truth by the capitalist system.

People need to feel that they have a purpose and that they are in control of their own destinies. It is not correct to educate children so that they will be able to get jobs in the market that is currently in place as this severely limits their possibilities and also dictates to them what is available. Their own desires and interests may not be able to be pursued because there is not a big enough job market for them to work in the field of their choice. The big problem with this is that this sector comprises many artistic and creative interests. It is very difficult to get a job as an artist; be it as a painter, sculptor, actor, singer, dancer, comedian or in other personally constructive ways as sports people.

Instead, the service industry is currently very big on the job market, where it used to be manufacturing and agriculture. This is due to the mechanisation of much industry and the outsourcing of jobs to countries where companies can pay much lower wages and maintenance costs. Service jobs cannot be outsourced or mechanised so easily; being a shop assistant, bank clerk, bar staff, etc.. These are huge areas of employment but on the large scale, such jobs are unfulfilling and bring no real reward to the workers in terms of personal development.

Other jobs that are part of the service industry include hospital staff and teaching, which in theory can give job satisfaction and a feeling of purpose, although many teachers and hospital staff in current western societies would argue that their jobs are becoming less satisfying as the years go by, due to the increasing pressure that they find themselves under.

So we need to try to change the way we live so that people can almost create their own jobs so that they can follow their own interests. To do this, we need to start with less of a reliance on money. With the amount of personal loans available and the number of ways that people can try to increase their capital through stocks and shares, bonds and investments that try their hardest, and succeed in many cases, to ensnare the unsuspecting public by convincing them that putting their money into some scheme will very probably benefit them in the future through financial gain, the amount of debt that is created is phenomenal and seriously evil.

People, particularly those who don't have a surplus of money are encouraged to borrow money from banks and loan companies so that they can buy the things that apparently everybody has and wants, therefore so should they. In both Judaism and Islam, it is forbidden to make interest on loaned money. The Qu'ran states that it is despicable to capitalise on another person's misfortune or need because of the obvious moral reasons – charging interest makes rich people richer and poor people poorer. This is an excellent principle which would certainly be taken into account when performing the massive reform to the banking sector that is needed in the capitalist west.

What might be considered as an acceptable Annual Percentage Rate (APR) of 8% on loans between £7000 and £25,000 in the current set-up would not be legal in the Hypothetical Government. The only reason that such a loan system is in place is so that the banks can make money out of the poorer people by welcoming them with open arms to borrow as much money as they can lend them, then repossess their house when they can't pay it back.

The banks would certainly not be so willing to lend people money if the APR was not allowed to be any more than the interest rate set by the central bank for the whole country. Then, there would be fewer enticing adverts trying to pull the general public in, leaving a state where loaning and borrowing money is no longer such a typical thing to do.

However, if people needed to borrow money to start a business or for something like essential repair work on their house, banks wouldn't be able to reject applications that meet the conditions, which would of course be standard for all banks and out of their control to change them. This issue is discussed in detail in The Economy section.

If we can reduce or even remove the desire for wanting to gain more money than anyone needs to live comfortably, we would be on the right first step. If people feel free from cravings, they won't buy so many things. But to reduce the desire to have more money, we need to be able to distribute the wealth more evenly. This can be done by emphasising cooperativeness. This is illustrated in depth in the section on The Economy, so I will briefly outline it here:

Cooperativism means the movement away from supporting the

large, private national and multinational companies, such as the regular high street shops that form clone towns across countries and giving the incentive to the people to run their own shops and companies that work on a local level, i.e. are there for the needs of the local people. This would stabilise people's lives more effectively as they wouldn't be so reliant on the big companies to secure employment and then be at the mercy of them in a recession when they decide to close a number of their stores. The cooperation side of it is that smaller businesses work together as a union to ensure that they all survive and thrive in the long-term, thereby removing competition which seriously jeopardises overall stability.

To start to organise a set of principles with which it would be encouraged to live by, we should divide them into different areas depending on their relevance and application.

Although the concept of self has been argued against above, while it is still a way that people construct their understanding of the world, it would be useful to give the public a starting point that they can use personally.

Problems with Personal Development

The main principle for people to address is losing the desire of craving. But to have any chance of success, we need to suggest alternatives so that one's own life can become happier on a smaller scale. As we have seen, craving is escapism; that is, to try to escape from the real world, or as in Buddhism, to take refuge in distractions. There are many types of distractions, some of which have been illustrated above but for reasons of conciseness it would be useful to summarise them in a list here. Note that, of course, this list is not exhaustive as distractions can take so many forms so here are some that are very common.

Shopping – Taking refuge in buying new clothes, new shoes, handbags, accessories, the latest gadgets, mobile phones, etc. will not bring fulfilment to our lives. The cyclical nature of their production mean that to cling to this desire to own more will only result in being stuck on the wheel of buy it, use it for a short time, discard it, buy the next one. The happiness that such a practice can bring is only temporary, which means that it is not true happiness and it will fade after a short time leading to the craving to attain the same feeling again. Additionally, the buying public gives away their money to corporate monopolies who then have the fuel to keep the wheel in motion, thus the control over the general public's lives. Obviously, this means that taking refuge in this kind of way is going to keep people in a state of stagnation and suffering, whereby they are constantly trying to find something that will bring them happiness but which fails them every time.

Addictions – Drinking alcohol, smoking, taking drugs, dependency on medicines, gambling, eating junk foods and, again, shopping are all forms of addiction. They are stronger forms of escapism. Even if you don't drink every day but you regularly go binge drinking, you are addicted. It is a routine that you feel you always have to return to to help you forget about the real world. Taking tablets or illegal drugs is a bad idea, they will often only cover up the symptoms and once their effects wear off, you need to go back to them. If it is for a medical reason, it could be that it is only because your body is weak due to an unhealthy lifestyle. The more you take the drugs, the more you become dependent on them. You are not going to improve from it, but you will be kept in the cycle of dependency which helps to create a large profit for the pharmaceutical industry who like to provide you with chemical solutions to the problems that they claim you have.

False Identity – Getting new haircuts/ hairdos, using make-up, wearing what our friends/ other apparently cool people wear. By taking in part of these kinds of activities, people deceive themselves and deceive others by trying to come across as someone that they are actually not. This results in people who follow the trends becoming lost as to knowing who they really are. They merely become just another clone that has come off the production line, looking like all the others who follow the same rules and pay no attention to their own interests and what they would really do if they made their own choices.

Financial Gain – The quest to become rich is futile. Having a lot of money will only mean that you have a lot of money. As long as you are comfortable financially and can afford to live without relying on credit, loans and other kinds of debt, then you don't need to have more. The banking sector and independent lenders do not have the public's interests at heart. They want you to get into debt for the sole purpose of making them richer. We are being force-fed propaganda to convince us that we need more money but in the attempt to get more money by any other means than working for it, we will inevitably become poorer.

Competition with others – We are not in a race with everyone else to be successful or to be the most successful. Any attempt to out-do someone else is, again, futile. It is not going to bring about anything other than contempt. We do not live to be better than other people. We are of the same species and we depend on each other to maintain and develop all of our lives. Our common aim is to achieve happiness and being jealous of someone or feeling superior to someone will never help us to live in harmony. It will only result in a very divided society as we currently have under the capitalist system.

Television - As stated in the 1976 film "Network", television is there largely to escape from boredom. It delivers series and game shows that make you think that the life of which you are not a part is wonderful. Everyone is beautiful, rich and has exciting lives. It is fantasy, but a form of escapism that many people are ore than willing to take refuge in. You can forget about your own life and imagine living like those characters. The problem is, when the programme finishes, you have to confront reality again. Some people cling to this form of 'entertainment' as much as possible to avoid having to think about reality but it will never help them as they can't actually escape into the fantasy worlds that are created for them.

Incidentally, there are other types of TV series that aim to show us the reality of life. Eastenders, a UK show based in London, has been consistently popular since it began in the 1980s because it looks like real life and portrays the issues that many people go through. However, it has consistently used themes of violence, arguments, murder, other crimes, drugs, etc., which have come to be seen as exciting for the viewers. It leaves people thinking that their own lives might be bad but at least they are not as bad as those of the characters. The problem with this is that it doesn't give the viewers hope, it just makes their lives seem not quite so bad instead of showing them how they could actively rise above their problems. I have my suspicions that Eastenders is government-approved to help keep the less-developed public from revolting by saying that it's not only them that have problems, this is just what life is like. This type of television promotes acceptance of stagnation when people need to have constructive help to develop their lives.

Suggestions for Personal Development

It is easy to point out where things are going wrong but without alternatives, it is a waste of time. People need help to be guided onto the right path, that is, for a more satisfying way of living.

Strengthen Your Relationships

If we are going to lose our cravings, what are we going to do instead? We need to look at things that are going to bring about true happiness that is long-term. It is like developing a routine that becomes a natural part of our lives. Forget about buying things that you find on the wheel of disappointment, forget about trying to pretend you are someone that you really aren't. Forget about being in competition with other people because where is it going to end?

Instead, work on strengthening your friendships and other connections with other people. Start by aiming to smile at people more and appreciating what they do. Get together with friends and family and do things together – play cards or board games, agree on a day each week where you will get together and have simple, inexpensive fun. There are many board games that have been around for decades and are still enjoyable. The best part of it is that you don't need to keep paying for them once you have them.

Organise a regular date where you will have a meal with a group of people. Make it communal, too. Don't just expect to turn up at someone's house and to eat what they have prepared for you. Do it so that each person needs to bring some ingredients and you all take part in the preparation of the food. It will be a lot less stressful for the people whose house is the venue, it will be more fun to prepare the food together and it will strengthen your bonds with all involved.

Spend less time watching the TV. As the rap musicians The Disposable Heroes of Hiphoprisy informed us, television is "The drug of the nation, breeding ignorance and feeding radiation." It is just another way of escaping from reality by watching programmes abut fictional characters leading fictional lives. So what? Don't concern yourselves with what happens in your favourite soap operas and having discussions with your friends about what happened, it's not real. You need to focus on your own lives. Get out and do some exercise, join a gym, go for a run and do it with friends and family. Read books that aren't just trashy distractions from real life. Those kind are just the same as trash TV. Learn about the world, find out about other cultures, study something that you have always wondered about. You will feel that you grow a lot more and that you feel better for having increased your knowledge and awareness and that you can tell other people about the amazing things you have discovered.

Explore who you are. Be honest with yourself and think what you would really like to do. Even if your friends might look at you askance for taking up a new activity, as long as it is constructive and no-one is coming to harm, what's the problem? You might even inspire them to explore themselves and discover things that they never knew they enjoyed doing.

Become healthier

People in the west are probably the unhealthiest that have ever been in history. This is because it is easy to succumb to eating foods that are tasty but do nothing good for your body. They are freely available and cheap enough to keep buying. Often, this is because they are very low quality products with enough artificial ingredients that are going to make them taste better. It is also easier to succumb to them because people don't need to have any skills to prepare their own foods any more. Do you see how this all works? That is part of the whole plan – encourage people to be lazy and less knowledgeable about making their own meals and at the same time fill the shelves with things that they can buy cheaply and put in the microwave for 5 minutes. Problem solved. Well, from the marketing perspective but not for the well-being of humans. It is far more satisfying to know that you can cook things for yourself that taste good, are made from natural ingredients like fresh vegetables and that you know exactly what is in them. In this way, you are not having the truth hidden from you as in the case of pre-packaged foods where the additives mean nothing to the lay-person.

More can be read on this topic in the section on Health and Healthcare.

Be creative

In this way, a very important thing to keep in mind is that if you are going to develop yourself in some way, keep it positive and creative. There can be no greater feeling of personal development than knowing that your skills in some area are improving. In terms of creativity, there are so many areas that can be explored: music, writing, acting, dance, comedy, cooking, sewing, construction, gardening, archaeology, mechanics, science, engineering, design, etc.. Creativity is so broad and can bring so much satisfaction on a deep level that there can't be any doubt that exploring our creativity can only benefit us. As long as it is not to anyone else's disadvantage or is destructive in any way.

There is also what is probably the most fulfilling: being charitable. Remember, knowing that someone's or something's life has improved because of what you have done to help is a wonderful feeling. Volunteer at an animal centre, at a homeless organisation, at an orphanage, at an old people's home. When you really become involved with others' lives and see that you can have a positive effect, you will find that you don't want to stop. As you develop the responsibility that means that they need you and they want you to come back because what you do, it means a lot to them and it will automatically mean a lot to you. This is a good example of the Buddhist saying "The perfect act has no reward." You don't need to be paid for your help, you don't need to receive a gift. You will go home feeling fulfilled with what you have done and that is all the reward you need. This is true happiness. Even if someone gave you £500 for what you have done, the feeling of achievement in terms of the real meaning renders the money as useful but not anywhere near as important.

We need to find out what is going to make us content with life. There are many people whose job is to work for charities. Their salaries will be minimal, enough to live on, but because the main outcome of their work is satisfaction, they know that this is sufficient. This is an example of when life is good.

Creativity in the Community

After focusing on how it could be suggested that people try to improve their personal lives, if we don't have fulfilling jobs we are still not going to be able to achieve true happiness.

There are plenty of jobs or ways of progressing through life which do provide satisfaction and inspiration, e.g. being a teacher, doctor, engineer, musician, sports player, etc. There can also be jobs which fewer people would agree with regarding how fulfilling they are. The point is that it's different for everyone; some teachers are fulfilled with their jobs, others aren't. Some people would feel happy to be a gardener, others wouldn't. The problem is that there are far too many people who do a job that they really don't care about and only do it to earn money. And, as has been documented throughout history by people like Confucius, Buddha and Gandhi, as well as the holy books, money isn't going to bring satisfaction to one's life. In fact Gandhi summed it up well when he said that the question is not 'to have', it is 'to be'. It is the experiences that we have that will define if we are happy, not what we own. For example, if you have a flashy sports car but your job is filing someone else's documents all day, merely owning your favourite car is not going to leave you feeling fulfilled. You will probably leave the leave the office each day thinking "I hate my job."

Many people do find their vocation and secure a job that they are passionate about doing because it brings them happiness and a sense of value to their lives. Others don't and they are the people that need to be supported more in terms of helping them to find ways in which they can get fulfilment from their lives.

For some people it is difficult to work out what they would really like to do with their lives and what they would happily devote their lives to doing. People need to be encouraged to look inside themselves and find out what it is that they would like to do the most. Sometimes, this thing might be something that is very difficult to do as a job, e.g. acting, singing, painting. In these cases, there are ways that the person can do a variation of their desire as their job and as their real desire in their free time, for example, being a singing coach, a piano teacher or joining an art group that could lead to exhibiting and selling paintings on a small scale.

The important thing to remember is that it really doesn't matter if you are not making lots of money from doing it, as long as you are enjoying the experience and have enough money to be comfortable with. If you were just earning enough to have a few simple luxuries like eating out with friends once a month but you were feeling that you control your own destiny by doing what you want to do in some way, you are going to feel happier and more inspired.

Another reason why the general public may not feel content with life is because they feel that they are doing jobs which have no meaning to them but they are merely working as a kind of servant to a rich boss or company whom they feel nothing for. This notion, which is common in the so-called developed world, is an indication that the system that we live under is a failure. If the workers are not happy with their work and they don't care about it as long as they get paid every month, the system simply is not good enough for a society. It is great for the people at the top, who are getting richer, more influential and more powerful to be able to control the masses, but these people are few and far between (luckily, as they are generally those people with fewer morals as they hoard their wealth and distance themselves from their workers even though they depend on them for their own personal livelihoods) but it is far from good for those workers who feel they are simply doing something for other people to benefit from even if they don't truly deserve it. The menial, meaningless work is not part of the workers' lives, it is not something that they own and get any pleasure from.

This problem is very much related to economic globalisation and ever-expanding multinational companies which leave less and less scope for small businesses to function and for individuals to do what they want in their own ways. Many people might work for a large supermarket chain or retail store because there are more jobs available than if they wanted to work in their own shop or the family business due to the fact that the big businesses have all but eliminated the 'need' for such small businesses to exist. And the people that have to work for the big corporations have no personal connection with what they do. They have no ownership of their work and feel no purpose to what they do other than to earn a fixed sum of money which is just about enough to survive on.

This leaves communities in more of a state of alienation where the people don't feel like they are all part of their own group that works together to provide for other members of the community. They mostly work for someone whose face they have never seen and will probably never see and they sell products that were made by people in another country that they've never been to. The personal touch is lost in what they do and it leads to feelings of 'what's the point?'

Communities need to be rebuilt so that people feel they are doing work that benefits the people that they live amongst. They need to be able to feel to solidarity and that they are doing something because the family down the road needs it or the children in the area would like it. Despondency has become a familiar part of life in this modern era where there are fewer and fewer connections between people in communities. The government needs to give incentives to the people so that they can do things more as they want to. A sense of belonging to a community, personal responsibility and ownership of actions needs to be given to the people.

We need to give people the chance to use and develop their skills and interests, especially those who are unemployed because the big businesses use workers in poorer countries to do the work now. In every town, city and village, there should be opportunities for people, unemployed or not, to be able to make something more of themselves. Those people who feel that their skills or talents are wasted because they never get an opportunity to use them should be allowed to use a community building or room where they can, for example, teach other people in the community how to do what they can already do well (languages, cooking, sports, dancing, etc.) To do this, the people who could offer an activity would not have to pay tax, but would only have to register it at the council to ensure that it is something positive and not hateful or dangerous in any way. The criteria would need to state that it must be something positive and creative. Those people who became the students would be asked to pay a minimum fee and at the end of the lesson they could pay a little extra if they think the 'teacher' deserved it. This would help strengthen the community spirit in many ways: the unemployed would feel they have more value in the community, members of the community would be brought together more in positive ways, there would be the sense of ownership of the skills, increased self-esteem and sharing of skills with people that they know. People would have more of a reason to do things when they can see the results.

A similar idea can be used for more artistic talents that are generally more difficult to find work for. Community shows can be put together for very little money for people to sing, play musical instruments, dance, tell jokes, etc., so that people who wanted a chance to perform can get the chance. Even though it would be on a small scale to begin with, it could always lead to bigger things. Again, there would need to be a small entrance fee for the audience to see a show that would go to the performers on each particular night. The community spirit can be brought into it even more by getting other people to make food and drinks to sell during the show. The ownership of the event and the reason for doing it would be more personally fulfilling and help to build a group identity that has real meaning and value.

It would also help to build the local economy as the money that changes hands completely remains in the community. This idea of a local economy is one that will be explained fully later.

To give another suggestion that could inspire creativity on a small scale, at this time, it is much easier to obtain a device for recording video but to make it in the world of cinema is extremely difficult because one would need either a lot of money, the right contacts, the chance to study cinema and other media-related subjects at university or college and so on, but not everybody has these opportunities. However, if we scaled it down and organised a project to get people together who like the idea of making films and supported them to create a simple studio in an otherwise disused building, they could take on the ownership of editing and producing by themselves.

Like-minded people who have an interest in making films and animations should recognise that they are in the same boat and not feel that they are in competition with each other, rather, they should work together to share ideas and further their collective development. But what are they going to do with the finished product? They are very unlikely to be able to sell it to a cinema chain or have it seen at a major film festival. But again, by down-sizing things, they could use another building as their cinema. Other members of the community could help out with refurbishing it, decorating it and together they could raise the funds needed to buy a large TV screen instead of a projector. Put in some tables and chairs and organise local film festivals, where people can come along to watch locally produced material (that has been independently approved so as not to be controversial in any way). It could then raise funds for the project to continue and flourish as well as provide employment for other people who could be involved in the festivals or simply cinema evenings, like making and serving food and drinks in the earlier example.

Not only would this kind of project help people to be able to make use of their artistic dreams and put them into practice but it would also help to bring the community together to support each other. A small entrance fee would soon cover the costs of the electronic equipment and the refurbishment/ decoration costs. Imagine each region of each town having its own film festival, to celebrate small achievements, create its own entertainment and finance itself.

If these kind of projects became the norm, people would understand that life should not be about trying to become rich or famous, as only a few people can achieve this pointless exercise anyway, but about really being able to achieve satisfaction and ownership of one's actions through working with basic resources, local support and good organisation.

In Louis Fischer's biography "The Life of Mahatma Gandhi", he writes about the time that Gandhi read John Ruskin's book "Unto This Last". Gandhi took note of the idea that:

"Men should not 'seek greater wealth, but simpler pleasure; not higher fortune but deeper felicity; making the first of possessions, self-possession; and honouring themselves in the harmless pride and calm pursuits of peace.'"[8]

Fischer states that Gandhi took this to mean "only that economy is good which conduces to the good of all."

Giving people more of the power over their own destiny would result in a feeling of worth for the people. Finding one's own path for self development and that of the community would leave people with the idea that there is a point to doing what they do; it is for their benefit and the benefit of their families, friends and neighbours. It is real and on their level.

Regarding the governmental involvement with CITC, there would need to be very little action needed. Such projects could be devised and brought to fruition by the communities themselves. Obviously, the government would need to support such initiatives but giving people their ownership and encouraging it, we would certainly begin to see more stable and constantly developing communities.

The local film-making project could be adapted and used as a template for many other similar projects that encourage creativity. Being an artist that wants to paint, sculpt and design is an area where it is usually very difficult to find work. They could, however, form a community group for the reasons of improving the surroundings, such as refurbishing dilapidated areas by redesigning them to be more attractive. They could submit proposals for the people of the local community to approve of or select through voting, which would then lead to people becoming involved in the realisation of the selected project.

Similarly, graffiti artists who might ordinarily be disliked for their apparent vandalism could instead be asked to join such projects so that they find a valid means for their interests and they would be less likely to feel shunned by the community but respected and praised for what they contribute.

By developing these kinds of projects to bring creativity out of the people, the community spirit would grow as a direct result. People would see how interdependent they are and how great things can be achieved without needing to have vast capital or resources. People would also feel less of a need to escape from reality as the jobs that many people have wouldn't feel like jobs any more, instead they would feel like their roles in society and in their lives. It is possible to find ways to inspire creativity and to realise it. And when people feel inspired, they feel happier and more fulfilled and such feelings drive people to keep going in their area of work and think about what they can do next. They will go home at the end of the day not thinking that at least they have made more money to pay the bills but that they have done something really worthwhile,that their ideas have been appreciated and their input has made a positive difference to themselves and the people with whom they share the community.

The area of arts and entertainment is one in which it has been difficult to realise one's dreams but it can happen. Of course, not everyone has interests in this area but that means that it should be even easier to develop projects in other areas. Take science and technology. People have ideas all the time but without the right contacts or the necessary qualifications, often their ideas get shelved indefinitely. However, if such developments happened on a smaller scale, ideas could be delivered on the same day that the person has them. If someone had an idea for how something local could be improved, they could walk into the office and share their ideas, or submit them to the institution's website. As it would be on a smaller scale, there is a far greater chance that they could become involved in the project if the idea was viable. Most people probably wouldn't bother trying to submit their ideas if it had to go to a government ministry or they had to try to sell it to a huge multinational company but they would if they could just walk down the road and speak to someone who is not so busy trying to manage all the aspects of a national business.

Again, imagine this kind of thing happening in every town across every country. People would feel a purpose to life and they would want to be active in the development of something that they could see happen in their own community. As long as such projects are working along agreed principles and constantly evolving guidelines where ideas could be shared all across the country, if one community comes up with someone really special, a country would eventually be managing itself; developing constantly based on the principles of solidarity and collaboration instead of competition and the selfish quest for power and domination in any area.

This idea of Creativity in the Community is one that would also be fundamental to the education system and so it will be brought up again in that chapter in the *Policies* section.

The Meaning of Life

"I'm not young enough to know everything."
J.M. Barrie

The question of the meaning of life is one that has intrigued people over the millennia without reaching an agreement. People have mulled over the subject wanting to work out why we are here. Sometimes, life seems so unfair for us for a variety of reasons and it leads us to think "What's the point of it all?" or "What's it all about?" The question has been addressed by philosophers and religious leaders which, even though we might think we can rely on them to give us the answer, have actually provided varied answers. Before attempting to answer this perpetually difficult question, let's have a look at previously proposed explanations.

Firstly, let's consider the proposals that have come from philosophers over the years. Back in Ancient Greece, Plato answered that the meaning of life was to attain the highest form of knowledge. An interesting thought as, of course, at that time, philosophy was just beginning to develop in Europe and the people wanted to know as much as possible about the world and their respective societies.

However, in another Hellenistic school of philosophy, the Cynics said that it was to live a life of virtue in agreement with nature. A different perspective but one that comes across in a peaceful and positive way. Another Greek philosopher, Epicurus, claimed that the meaning of life was to seek modest pleasures in order to attain a state of tranquillity and freedom from fear. Once again, this is a nice, simplistic way of proposing what we should be looking to work towards in our lives.

In the 19th century, Jeremy Bentham was a Utilitarian philosopher, which derived from the Epicurean school of thought. The Rule of Utility that was put forward was that "The good is whatever brings the greatest happiness to the greatest number of people." This later became adapted to simply "Whatever brings the greatest happiness." Unfortunately, this Rule is extremely vague and ambiguous and it is open to all sorts of interpretations. Just because something brings happiness to someone doesn't make it good; look at the actions of hunters who kill for entertainment. There is nothing moral about that, yet they would adamantly state that it brings them happiness.

Pragmatism evolved in the 19th century, concerning itself only with 'truth' and therefore the pragmatists stated that it would need to be practically verifiable to have any real substance. Therefore, whereas the question could not lead to a definitive answer, "the meaning of an individual's life can be discovered only through experience and the purposes which cause you to value it."

Moving into the 20th century, philosophy was coming more to terms with the idea that this question isn't one that can really be answered in a way that would be true to everyone, and the Existentialists proposed that "Individuals create the meaning and essence of their lives, as opposed to deities or authorities creating it for them." Therefore, moving away from a possible universal answer, meaning was only relevant to the individual and could only be defined for ourselves, by ourselves, and it would be as true as anyone else's definition of the meaning of *their* lives.

Humanism offered a less egocentric way of looking at the reason for our being here and preferred to propose that it is "Our ability and responsibility to lead ethical lives of personal fulfilment that aspires to the greater good of humanity." This approach wants to make a bond between the individual and the society so that everyone would want to work towards helping other people and therefore strengthen the society. It is a moral perspective which is more like what we should be looking to achieve within any society but is a humanly-constructed concept and can't be seen as one which everyone would unquestioningly agree with (i.e. the instinctual *meaning* that we all possess).

For logical positivists, such as Wittgenstein, the question is meaningless as things in a person's life can have meaning (importance), but a meaning of life itself, i.e., apart from those things, cannot be discerned. Therefore, already we can see that there have been many conflicting views in the last two and a half millennia from philosophers, even though their intentions can be seen as positive and ethical.

In religion, the focus is of course a deity and there is more of a general agreement to the question of the meaning of life in various major religions.

In Judaism, the purpose of life is to serve God and to prepare for the world to come. In Christianity, loving God is the meaning of life, and in order to achieve this one would ask for forgiveness of sins and receive God into their heart. In Islam, the ultimate objective of man is to seek the pleasure of Allah by living in accordance with the Divine guidelines as stated in the Qur'an and the Tradition of the Prophet. In Buddhism, the meaning is to become enlightened as to the nature and oneness of the universe.

Other religions give more complicated views on the subject, which we won't go into here, but ultimately they do not differ too much from the above mentioned ideas. Religious views generally state that it is not down to us to define the meaning of life but to the respective deity that has already stated what we should work towards as written in the holy books.

Nowadays, we live in a world where there are many conflicting views of religions as well as a large number of people who do not follow any religion or believe in a deity that could have prescribed any meaning of life to us. Without wanting to undermine the meaning given by the above-stated religions, they are rather ambiguous and on their own do not give a clear indication of where we should be heading within our lives, although of course, the holy books themselves are dedicated to spelling out the paths of life that the followers should be taking.

So, many ways of interpreting the question and many answers given by those deemed to be in a position of offering divine truths and theories. But where does that leave us? From these historical perspectives, we cannot reach a conclusion, nor have the various theories followed the same path that has gradually become more specific or more correct. The other way of interpreting the question is to look at it from the "Why are we here?" angle. This is more of a scientific question and without wanting to offend any religious views, it can quite summed up fairly simply in terms of evolution, the conditions necessary for sustainable life on Earth given that it is at a good distance from the Sun to be able to support the ingredients upon which life thrives. We can give a clinical answer to show how it has all progressed and evolved regarding the interaction of animals, plants and minerals and provide enough evidence to prove many of the theories to date. However, answering the question in this way does not give any philosophical or personal reason as to why we are here or more to the point, what we are all aiming for from life. It may give us all the scientific answers, but that doesn't 'mean' anything to us personally.

The problem that we have when trying to answer the question in this way is "are we aiming for the same thing?" You could ask any number of people what they want to attain in life and you will get as many answers as the number of people you ask, which will all vary depending on the cultures and societies that they live in as well as what their beliefs are, religiously or philosophically.

Also, should we be aiming for the same things? Materialistically speaking, we are not aiming to obtain the same possessions, no matter how hard the marketing companies try to define our desires for us.

The main hurdle when trying to arrive at a compromise like this is people use language to think about it and answer it. Plato based it on knowledge. But what is knowledge? Aristotle argued that it is not certain knowledge like epistemology or metaphysics, but general knowledge. He thought a person acts to strive to be good.

However, 'goodness' is not a universal concept either and can mean many things to many different people. Shakespeare later said that "nothing is either good or bad but only thinking makes it so." The whole problem is that we rely on what our concepts mean to us and most concepts of this kind cannot be agreed upon by everyone. They are humanly constructed and not things that were part of the world before we came along.

Similar problems come up when we look at the other philosophers' ideas stated above. "To live... in agreement with nature" – who can say if someone is or isn't living like that? There is no universal way that this can be ascertained, which reduces the validity of the statement. "To seek modest pleasures" – how many people would completely agree on what a modest pleasure is? Again, we are limited by we believe such concepts to mean.

Wittgenstein, who studied the limits of language came closer to addressing the problem by saying that the "meaning of x" is a term *in* life usually conveying something regarding the consequences of x, or the significance of x, or that which should be noted regarding x, etc. So when "life" is used as "x" in the term "meaning of x", the statement becomes recursive and therefore nonsensical, or would simply refer to the obvious fact that the condition of life is essential for having meaning (in life).[9]

Whereas this was a profound way of saying that the question is unanswerable, even if many people were aware of Wittgenstein's views, they wouldn't necessarily be happy with his way of explaining that it is nonsense to even think about it. We still want to have a meaning. We want to know what we should be aiming for.

Wittgenstein approaches the question in terms of "what is the reason that we are here?" or "what is the point of being alive?" In this way it is true to say that there can never be an answer; it is recursive and nonsensical. This is usually the way that most people address the question of the meaning of life. So are we stuck at this point or should we ask the question in a different way?

I pointed out above that a more useful question would be "what are we aiming for?" But to answer this via language is, as Wittgenstein correctly pointed out, inconclusive. So how can we answer it without using language?

What we need to do is analyse human behaviour to try to uncover the instinctual personal needs. Unfortunately, using adults as subjects for an analysis of this nature is ultimately fruitless. By the time we are adults, our behaviour has been shaped so much by reinforcements of all kinds that there appear to be too many things that people are aiming for. Our aims have mostly been defined by language, often the persuasive language of marketing and advertising that has penetrated our thinking so much that many of us are convinced that we want a certain car, a certain brand of clothing, a certain way of life that instinctively, we really have no profound use for.

How can we uncover our instinctual aims when we have been shaped by so many reactions to things, both material and emotional? We need to analyse people who are not shaped by language, who do not make sense of their world with words; people who do not even have a concept of language.

The answer, therefore, comes from babies.

We are not born with the concept of language. It is many months before we begin to learn that sounds are used to represent objects or people. When a baby starts to assimilate what to them is a specific sound (or to us, a word) with an object or a person, its way of perceiving the world is about to change forever and in most cases it is irreversible. Once we know that that big person is 'dad' and the other person who is not quite as big is 'mum' and that round, green thing is 'apple' then we are not starting to make sense of the world, we are merely copying what has been agreed on by speakers of the same language. We are making sense of it in a different way – by using labels.

So we need to look at what babies want from life before they learn to speak.

Babies need food and sleep but these are merely biological necessities that all animals have. We also have an instinctual desire to develop. Babies don't realise that they are going to get bigger and their brains are going to be more able to comprehend things, but without being able to express it, they like to know that if they do something, something else is going to result from it; that if someone does something that they like to sense in whatever way, they are going to smile or laugh because of it. Babies show us that they make sense of things by smiling and laughing. Their ability to react in these ways is not learnt (like language), it is instinctual. They can't help reacting like this, nor can they help crying if something hurts them or the light is too bright or they don't like their food. If their senses are overstimulated to the point of discomfort, they react in the only way they can in the first few months of their lives.

So obviously, whatever makes a baby cry is not what they are aiming for. Whatever makes them smile is what they want. And what they want is not material. They may like the touch of their soft toys or the colours of them but in the first few months of human life, objects and people are not seen as separate entities to the babies. They simply take pleasure in knowing that certain things usually respond in the same ways.

Babies feel the love of a parent, sibling, friend or whoever can make them smile. They feel calmed by being held by another person in a caring way. They also feel a sense of satisfaction when they know what will result if they perform a particular action. If they can stack three or four blocks on top of each other, they feel that they have achieved something. If they touch a certain object and it makes the sound that they expect it to make, they know they have learned something (they often do it repeatedly because they know what it will then do, which is the reward in itself). But is there underlying concept that unites all of these simple things in a baby's life?

There is something that brings all of these things together and we call it 'happiness'.

Babies feel happy when they feel the love of another person. They feel happy when they can stack blocks up or when their toy makes the sound that they like. You can think of numerous examples of what babies get satisfaction from before they can speak and basically, these things are the only things that they want to do. Of course, there is always the introduction of new toys or games that also make them happy. For example, babies often react positively to a game such as 'peek-a-boo' which can provide entertainment for many weeks or months of their lives.

But what about things that babies don't react favourably to? It's true that not everything will capture their attention and make them smile. This is simply down to certain things not stimulating their senses enough for some reason. Perhaps they don't care for the feel of it or the colours are not bright enough. Babies are able to judge for themselves based simply on what interests them. It is all totally egocentric in the first year of life. In the baby's head, there are no such concepts of politeness. They aren't going to smile at a new toy just because someone has bought it for them. But if it does fire the right neurotransmitters then it will make them happy.

But this way of being happy is only one way of achieving the goal. It is limited and as the baby grows and the brain develops and forms more synaptic connections, the more the baby will want to interact with objects and people in more depth.

As the baby becomes more articulate, he or she will naturally want to do things that will make him or her happy. The baby wants to play and whereas there has never been an agreed psychological definition of the concept of 'play', we can envisage it as the pursuit of happiness through actions that stimulate interest and enjoyment in a predominantly hedonistic way.

What this means is the baby, as previously stated, is a being that is not aware of itself as being separate to other people or objects. The baby has no notion of identity or individuality for the first few months. They see themselves as connected to everything that is at least in their field of vision. Studies have shown that if an object with which the baby is playing is placed behind it, it may quickly forget that it was there (out of sight, out of mind).(10) Sometimes it requires the baby to be distracted with something else but even if it was happily playing with it then it seemingly disappears, it will not regard the object as in existence until it sees it again. The baby does not have any concept of the feelings of others in the initial months (or even years – it depends how badly brought up the child is...) and only shows any interest in things that will bring positive stimulation to themselves. This will involve external sources (toys, people, sounds, etc.) as the baby is incapable of creating its own entertainment due to the lack of thought processes and kinaesthetic ability (control of its bodily movements).

As the baby grows and develops mentally and physically, it will develop its motor skills and seek and find pleasure in successfully interacting with objects or people.

With objects, the baby will turn its attention to activities where it knows it has some idea of what is necessary to provide successful results, whether this is fitting pieces of a game or puzzle or toy together or using pieces to construct various things in any way the baby sees fit. Obviously, there are more activities that a baby can obtain enjoyment from, but they are generally based around this principle of satisfaction with successful results.

Regarding interacting with other people (usually family members or those whom the baby remembers from repeated meetings which provide pleasurable feelings), happiness can be obtained in other ways, which are more psychological and emotional and can only be explained using the abstract concepts of love and contentment. To experience these, the baby does not need to manually interact in the same way as with objects but a feeling of contentment and love can be gained from such a simple act as being held carefully in a person's arms. Such interactions will usually produce an increase in the neurotransmitter dopamine, which has been defined as the the main neurotransmitter that results in the feelings of love and pleasure.

As the baby begins to learn how to speak, walk and develops its other skills, it retains the desire to play and hence, seek happiness. The only thing that changes is the way that he or she wants to play. They become more capable to partake in more complicated activities and as they realise their own potential to bring about the desired results of completion, improvement and general satisfaction, they want to keep developing step by step. Of course, as they become able to convey their desires through language, toddlers are more likely to state that they want or don't want to do something, which can lead to minor conflicts between the baby and the carer at the time. Due to their still hedonistic desire to do what they want, tantrums of the 'terrible twos' may appear and become more frequent unless calm reasoning and alternative stimuli are quickly provided by the carer (I use the term 'carer' here to denote any older person who is currently interacting with the child, whether it is a parent, sibling, grandparent, babysitter or significantly older friend or acquaintance). The toddler may develop resentment if he or she is not provided with appropriate reasoning for having to stop an activity or having to eat their dinner. There are many ways of responding to a toddler's tantrums in positive ways but they should not involve any kind of physical restraint or hitting, nor displays of anger or aggression from the carer. As a carer, as defined above for the purpose of this text, may not always be a philosophical and intuitive adult, unfortunately it would be an ideal world where the toddler grows up having every tantrum resolved swiftly and expertly.

Similar advancements and alternatives to the methods of play become manifest as the toddler becomes of primary school age. They (hopefully) begin to realise that there are other important things to attend to, as well as play, such as education and development of skills that they don't always see as personally relevant. However, even if they do finally accept that certain things need to be done, their main area of interest will still be play. Some children will also discover other interests which may not be strictly considered play, such as reading and drawing, but the reasons for engaging in such activities is to bring about the increase in dopamine and therefore the ultimate desire of finding happiness.

At this point in the child's life, they will realise that happiness in this sense may now be only obtained in shorter bursts (playtimes and after school). They will still seek it as often as they can but become aware that they can't act in their preferred ways whenever they want (of course, some children remain persistent with wanting to play and not do their school work but this is most likely to be due to undemanding parents and families who give their 'little angels' a free reign at home).

As they move through the primary school years, as long as the teachers have been good at their job and the parents have been sensible and responsible, the children will have been encouraged to partake in other activities that will bring them happiness. These can come in many forms, for example: playing musical instruments, developing artistic skills, developing an interest in sports, drama, dance, etc., but there is something very important to remember from the adults' point of view – if the child does not have an interest in a certain activity, don't make them learn it. You, as an adult, may want your child to do an activity that you like or did when you were young or that you think may raise their perceived status in society, but if they don't have the desire to do something, they will not find happiness from it. We should not pressure children into doing what we might want them to do, we must discover either what the child has already expressed a real interest in or we must look out to see what kind of activities they like and hence suggest something that they might like to try in order to develop their skills. For example, if they like drawing pictures in their spare time, even if they are not of a great quality or deep subject matter, help to channel their interest into doing some more specific types of art that they could be capable of. Knowing that they can try another aspect and find success with their results will help to give the child a feeling of self-esteem, satisfaction and mental strength. If they don't appear to have any specific interests and no-one guides them towards finding something that is personally constructive and rewarding, it will lead the child along a path of apathy, low self-esteem, a lack of identity and there is a good chance that they will become resentful, rebellious and destructive.

Why does this happen? Why do some children take what appears to pleasure from destroying things, such as something that another child in the vicinity has created? The anger comes from jealousy. If the child feels that he or she doesn't have the skills to do what another child can do, he or she will resent it, feel a personal void in what they think they are and can do and they don't like to see other children succeed when they think that they themselves can't.

But what tends to happen as a result of destructive behaviour by such a child is that the adult that is present will often punish the child, verbally, physically or using removal of privileges. These sorts of reactions do nothing to help the child develop or learn to behave more positively. The child needs to be spoken to calmly and rationally to get them firstly to understand that such behaviours are not going to be for the good of anyone, including themselves, and secondly to help them find something with which they can develop a skill so that they can find satisfaction with something that they can do.

Every child, no matter how negatively they may be viewed by adults in general will have some skill they they need encouragement with to be able to develop. When the child comes from an unstable home, this can be more difficult to achieve, as co-operation from the parents may be nigh on impossible to achieve in the more severe of cases but teachers have the responsibility to care for the children and the mental stability to help them find their strengths that they can use to work towards their own state of happiness. Social workers should also be approached to attempt to develop the weaknesses of the parents.

There is also the case of learning difficulties to discuss. There are too many types of impairments to list here and some of them may only affect one area of a child's development. In this case, extra help needs to be given to support the child's difficulty and depending of the severity of the impairment, support needs to be given psychologically to ensure that the child doesn't become too frustrated by their problem and to help them accept their difficulties if they are ones that will always remain in some way like medical problems or conditions such as dyslexia.

There may also be learning difficulties that cause more widespread problems and slow the progress of the child's general learning. In this case, there may be the potential problem that the child will end up with a low self-esteem and even depression. The actions mentioned above will, of course, be applicable in this case, but possibly on a larger scale, especially in terms of psychological support. The child may have learning difficulties in all areas of education but the aim of the adults who are in contact with the child must strive to identify a way of working that the child can have some success with.

Many teachers will know of this already and may have come across a child with general learning difficulties but not every reader of this book is a teacher and may not have been in a situation where they have have to consider such an issue.

I remember, when I was training to be a teacher, that I was with a class of four year olds. There was one boy who had already completed this school year but due to his general learning difficulties and attention deficit had to repeat the year. I found that, whereas he had difficulty with performing typical tasks along with the other children, he paid more attention when he was doing something manually rather than mentally. He would happily keep his concentration on building things and putting things together, so from this I knew that that was the avenue we needed to follow to help him develop his skills. The one episode that I will never forget was when the children went outside to play on the bikes and other big toys in the afternoons. He had never ridden a bike before but he wanted to try it. The first afternoon, he persisted with riding a bike with one stabiliser, riding up and down the playground with determination and not being distracted by what the rest of the class was doing for the thirty minutes that they were outside. The following afternoon, he went straight back to the bikes and tried one without any stabilisers. He wasn't going to give up and after this half-hour session, he had taught himself how to ride a bike.

As children grow up, their interests change or grow. They may, of course, retain interests in some things like sports or playing music but as they mature, they will develop new interests. For example, they may become more interested in reading, writing, painting or different sports. Some may develop deep interests in certain school subjects and may find their future path developing along the lines of science or history or whatever subject. Any of these things plus about a thousand more possible examples can bring happiness and satisfaction but it is certainly not always that simple. Human relationships, family stability – both emotional and financial – will play a huge part in the successful development of any individual. The biological changes of puberty will expand the range of possible interests – being attracted to other people and having success or failure in first relationships can play a significant role in establishing a level of self-esteem that could be hard to alter, whether for the better or for the worse.

Additionally, as they move into the teenage years, more pressure is placed upon them to start thinking about their future after school – what type of job do they want or will they study at university first? As most of us are aware, all of these factors combined can be stressful and difficult to deal with. Teenagers in general have rather selfish and cruel attitudes to their peers and may jump at the chance to hurt them emotionally and may maintain this cruelty for a long period of time which will have a profound effect on the individual as they move towards adulthood.

Also, in these times in particular, teenagers will be influenced by material goods that are proposed to be what they all want even though it is very unlikely that they would want them all if they made their own choices without thinking about whether it would make them look cool or be accepted.

I'm sure that many of us who have already been through the teenage years would say that they were not the happiest of times and certainly not the easiest. It's not just due to increasing responsibilities and having less time to play in a narcissistic manner but our attitudes to life have, by the age of thirteen, already been twisted and shaped in countless ways that make it more difficult to find our identities. Many attitudes begin to crop up during this stage of life which could have been better to have been missed entirely. Negative views towards certain 'groups' may rear their hideously ugly heads. Racist views may by now have developed to a point where there is little chance of them being rebuked. Sexism can be apparent in younger children, although to a milder and less offensive extent (boys who like to assert themselves as being stronger than girls or girls who generally make more progress in school subjects) but with the ever-malleable mind and the usual desire to be seen as a 'bigger person' who should now be viewed and listened to seriously (in the teenagers' own unspoken ideas about themselves), such views can be seen as a way to gain superficial power over the opposite sex in a vain and unconscious attempt to increase self-esteem.

Why is it that children can sometimes express sexist attitudes from such a young age as three or four years? Adults are of course to blame. Parents often willingly follow the rules of society and push their little ones along the 'male' or 'female' stereotype paths of life. Girls play with cuddly toys and dolls. They have to like sickeningly, mind-controlling commercial pop music and TV shows. Boys play with toy weapons and games consoles. They have to like the pantomime that is wrestling and stories about pirates. Thus, the boyish and girlish mindsets are rigorously followed. Are you a parent who is thinking that you didn't bring your children up in the stereotypical way? Do you have a boy who you dress(ed) in pink clothes? Do you have a girl who play-fights with toy guns? It would be difficult to find many children who do not, to some extent, act in the way that is expected of their gender.

Not that this in itself is bad or wrong. In truth, it is pretty much inescapable. Even if you tried to raise your children in a way that was as countertypical as possible, their identities have also been shaped by their school-friends. Boys play with boys, girls play with girls. Divides begin and they continue to divide. Differences between the sexes are more noticeable than the similarities, as seen by both the children and the adults.

What this leads to is not something that really shouldn't have happened, but due to a firmly established and unbreakable divide that has been there throughout history and even in these times where there has been a push to establish equality for both sexes, it is quite impossible for most of us to think of both sexes as being closer to 'similar' than to 'different'.

So what does this all mean in terms of the search for happiness? Basically that rifts can occur more easily because it is always easier to make your point of argument against the other sex in terms of the differences between men and women. We both use the differences as a crutch with which to make our points. As adults, I'm sure that most of us can criticize the other sex in general ways - "You women are so .....", "Men are all the same..." Does this help matters in any way? But can we get away from these generalisations? Now, it would be very difficult. But one can make a concerted effort.

Overcoming Prejudices

People should be encouraged to look for the positives in everyone. Judging someone whom you don't know on something like their appearance or religion is a sign of weakness. This kind of ignorance is something that people should be reminded of avoiding. Once a society has an agreed set of principles to follow, we should strive to remind ourselves and other people to work towards them, like maintaining temperance and prudence. A good proverb to use in this case is "Don't criticise someone until you have walked a mile in their shoes."

Aim to understand people and be careful of judging people prematurely. This is the first step to take with this aspect of personal development as when you are able to keep your prejudices under control and you remain aware that you have to examine a person's actions, it is important to point out that we should then set ourselves the aim of not judging anyone at all. To go back to a previous point, the sum of a person's behaviours does not equal a person. People act the way they do because of reasons, whether they are thought of as good or bad. These behaviours are all learnt and those which are detrimental to themselves or others can, with empathy and support, be reduced and potentially eliminated.

Judging people on things like their nationality is also without merit and without justification. We must act on how to bring people together in harmony as in through local festivals which emphasise the differences that people can bring and share for the enjoyment of everyone.

Get to know people in your street more, organise a street party where people are invited to make their own food and drinks to share for free. Such a thing doesn't require special permission, money or a lot of work and planning – it can be a simple event for the reason of bringing people together and strengthening the immediate community, to enhance trust between the people, developing communications and resulting in a more coherent and peaceful local environment.

As the world becomes more multicultural and integrated, there have been more cases of xenophobia and racism. They are still ongoing issues for the simple reason that they have not been addressed well enough. As was explained earlier in National Identity, there is a connection with the inappropriate and illogical way that some people judge others on the colour of their skin, which when we look at how it works, is completely illogical.

Racism

The main problem with racism is that it doesn't have any real valid meaning. To say that anyone belongs to a particular race implies that they have certain beliefs, behaviours and traits that are genetic to that race. Otherwise it would not even be attempted as an argument that race is a thing that exists. However, in terms of behaviours and beliefs, these are socially and culturally developed practices that are not exclusive to any specific group of people. For example, people practise the same religions in various countries regardless of their skin colour or other cultural behaviours. People follow the same sports regardless of religion so such things merge from one group of people to another. No defined group of people can be described as exclusive from another because there will always be things in common between them.

To say that white people definitely differ from black people because of their skin colour simply doesn't work. Just look at your average western football team and you will find that there are players from different countries, with different skin colours but they all play for the same team and depend on each other to meet their objectives. This shows that they are actually part of the *same* group, that is, people.

This also applies to any society in general. People will be alike in some way, different in others but to function as a well-adjusted society they all need to work together and they rely on each other for certain things such as the work they do. It would make no sense to reject your doctor on the grounds of their skin colour if you depended on their knowledge and expertise so that you can recover your health.

Those people who would prefer their country to consist of only those people who have the same skin colour is impractical because if there were not enough of those people to fulfil the roles needed in a society, it would be practical to bring in other people from abroad to be able to fill the gaps, as has been done to a large extent in countries such as the UK and the USA. If there was a shortage of doctors from the indigenous population but it was possible to employ people, who happen to have a different skin colour, to help improve and maintain the overall well-being of the population, it would be absurd not to do so.

There is the other argument that foreigners come to a country and take all the jobs of the native people. This has been heard so often that many people take this to be true, whereas on inspection of the dilemma, it is not even slightly true. For this to be true it would mean that, say 10,000 people come from country B to country A and step into the jobs that the people from country A already do, thus making 10,000 country A employees unemployed. This is, of course, not what happens. The people from country B come with qualifications and experience to do the jobs when there are not enough people from country A to fulfil specific positions of employment. As a result, theoretically, country A will have developed in terms of its provision for its inhabitants (human capital) but this is seen by people who suffer from being racist in a completely incorrect way. They, instead, see it as though country A has been 'polluted' by foreigners who have different coloured skin, speak a different language or practise different religions.

To analyse this, we need to think about what it means for person A when person B is living in their community. A person's skin colour does not have any effect on anyone else. Literally, that alone can not have any impact on anything. It does not mean that persons A and B cannot relate to one another for that only depends on the attitudes and actions between the two. If A and B get on fine and are polite and sociable to each other, there is no problem in that respect but if one of them is hostile towards the other for no personal reason but only because of their different skin colours, then this is a result of deluded prejudice. You simply cannot judge someone on how they look but only on how they are.

With this attitude, if person A is racist and hates anyone who does not appear to have the same skin colour as themselves, person A is assuming that all people indigenous to country A are good, superior or exactly what the country needs to maintain its identity. For a non-stereotypical example, let's say that people who are considered to be white are arrogant, selfish, exploitative, violent and narrow-minded. For this to be true, it would mean that *absolutely every one of them* would have to be so. Of course, it is not the case. Some of them are, some of them aren't. Some of them have one or two of these characteristics but still, they would not be true in every case.

Nor is it true that every white person is clever, altruistic, kind, peaceful and open-minded. Some people may be seen to have some of these attributes some of the time but it can never be argued that white people are the best when comparing them to people of another skin colour. A person like Bernie Madoff, who fraudulently extorted millions of dollars from people of all skin colours was white. Adolf Hitler, who sentenced white disabled people to death could not even be seen as always favouring those of his own idealistic racial group. White people steal from other white people. Black people murder other black people, and vice versa.

So from this, we can see that it is not valid to claim that all white people are great or all black people are great. As much as you strive to defend your own race, there will always be people who upset your theory. Robert Mugabe could never be considered a good role model for black people when his rule has led to the starvation, diseases and deaths of black people from Zimbabwe.

The term race is obsolete, especially in the modern world where we live in increasingly mixed societies as time goes by. It requires analysis from everyone who has prejudices towards people whom they perceive to be belonging to a particular group. These people require education and support to enable them to lose this fault and to be able to bring them up to a level where they will pay no attention to skin colour but will form good relationships with people depending on their merits, i.e. a more well-developed person.

In terms of cultural influence from immigrants from country B to country A, country A people often claim that their culture is being tainted or diminished. They claim that they live in their own little communities where they speak their own language, wear their own style of clothes and follow their own religions (or not). However, if the people from country A weren't so hostile and actually welcomed them, the people from country B would become more integrated and wouldn't feel the need to only mix with their own people, which is due to their marginalisation and prejudices from people A. Sub-groups and neighbourhoods of immigrants are actually created by the intolerant, racist people, therefore they make the problem even worse by keeping their minds closed and their attitudes primitive.

Country A can still celebrate its own culture actively which would mean that it wouldn't become saturated or lost. The cultural events could be as vibrant as ever but they could also benefit from people B by allowing them to join in, feel that they are a part of the country, learn the language more quickly because people A are happy to talk to them and support them. In turn they would learn about other cultural events, food and music, join in and become more knowledgeable and understanding of the world that we are all an equal part of. The same would be true for people B as they would be more willing to learn about the culture of country A because they feel that they are welcome and a part of the society. The blue veins and arteries would be flowing well and filling the containers with more blueness.

Moving on from the personal level to the community level, the above suggestions could all be applied to a society. Once people in the neighbourhood start to feel they are relating to each other well and getting to know more about each other, they can start to work on projects that develop the community more like forming local businesses with the purpose of benefiting the people who live in the immediate surroundings. With the development of capitalism and the big corporations that open a branch wherever they see an opportunity has left many towns and cities in a state of becoming more disorganised. For example, a neighbourhood would probably already be in a state of self-sufficiency with the local grocers, butchers, bakers and small convenience stores to take care of their essential needs. However, this doesn't stop a large national supermarket chain from opening a massive superstore there. Such companies will justify this to the public by stating that they can get everything they need in one place, which is true but it completely upsets the equilibrium of the community when people start going there instead of having to spend more time going to four or five local shops. But whereas this may seem like a nice idea for the general public, it is very bad news for the local businesses as their sales will drop and eventually they will probably have to close down. People in general don't give this any concern as the typical strength of community spirit in any sizeable metropolitan area means that people have no interest in anyone else unless they know the shopkeepers personally. There need to be regulations that limit the freedom of these companies from opening branches wherever they want. Their proposals should be discussed and either agreed upon or rejected by the people who live in the relevant area. If they feel it would be detrimental to their neighbourhood, then their desire to stop a new superstore from being built would be definitive through voting.

Even though it may sound like going back in time to suggest that we should try to organise things better so that every community is resilient to provide for themselves on a local level, it would benefit the community a great deal in terms of the amount of money that stays in the local area and the level of employment, where the people have control of their own destinies more. And also, people who lived during the 1920s to the 1950s would generally tell you that the community spirit was a lot stronger than in the 21st century where people either live in fear of their neighbours or they don't even know them despite living just a few doors away, along with the level of their local resilience.

This topic is discussed in more detail in the Economy section to illustrate how such ideas can be realised.

Sexuality

As sexuality has been through some controversial periods in the last few decades, it needs to be addressed and made clear as to what the moral positions are for the different categories of sexuality. These are heterosexuality, bisexuality and homosexuality. It is of course the latter group especially that has come under the hammer of criticism the most. Let's first of all look at what this refers to.

Homosexuality is when a person is attracted to members of the same sex and may wish to form a relationship with someone of their own gender. On a moral level, it isn't hurting anyone as yet... The question of acceptability has come up regarding what such partners may then do in the privacy of their own home. If they are in a stable relationship, it is likely that whatever they wish to do will be under the consent of both partners. Morally speaking, it's still all above board. The only thing that could be recommended is that they are careful to ensure that neither partner's health will be at risk and that they take precautions whenever necessary, just as in the case of heterosexual or bisexual partners who ought to put their own and their partner's safety first. This means, of course, to avoid spreading or contracting any sexually transmitted diseases.

So what we have found out so far is that there is no difference between what people belonging to any of the sexual groups should be responsible for. In that case, why has there been any reason for controversy or debate? This all comes down to the ruling classes. Throughout history, the conservative elite and the religious groups which have had significant influence and power have not agreed because they either don't like the sound of two men or two women getting together and performing acts of 'their choice', or they believe that a divine power forbids such activities. In the former case, where they simply don't like the idea and think it is horrible and wrong, it has probably been unheard of or at best, extremely rare that anyone has told those in power that they have to experience something before they pass a judgement on it. This has meant that the opinions of a select few have decided the laws that individuals of the same species have had to endure and suffer from. Now we are reaching questions of morals. Those people who control and pass laws, if they have been heterosexual, have not had to test the waters for themselves or examine the circumstances which the people in question are in before making their decisions on people whose feelings and beliefs they don't understand and more to the point are unwilling to even contemplate as being morally acceptable. Therefore, those individuals who have been moral enough to try to form and maintain relationships with other individuals, which have been consenting and not causing any direct problem to people who would regard themselves as heterosexuals, have been punished and the people who have stubbornly remained ignorant of a different notion of human relationships and who have acted very immorally, by passing judgement on what they refuse to consider could actually be of no consequence to heterosexuals, have come out on top and maintained their position of power and rule.

In the latter case, the religious perspective, it does say in the Bible (Leviticus 18:22) that "No man is to have sexual relations with another man; God hates that." It is also forbidden to be homosexual in the Qu'ran. Therefore, it is understandable that religious believers have a reason to believe that homosexuality is a sin. Which leads us to the next question: Why are there homosexuals in the world? There have been debates about whether it is a choice or whether is occurs naturally. The American Psychological Association, among others, have found that "Sexual orientation has proved to be generally impervious to interventions intended to change it, which are sometimes referred to as "reparative therapy." No scientifically adequate research has shown that such interventions are effective or safe. Moreover, because homosexuality is a normal variant of human sexuality, national mental health organizations do not encourage individuals to try to change their sexual orientation from homosexual to heterosexual."[11]

To be able to determine such answers, studies like these have to be done. It is not enough to make your own theories with no evidence to support them. From this, we can conclude that homosexuality is natural and not a choice made by people. But coming back to what it says in the Bible, there is no correlation. God is said to hate it yet homosexuals seem to develop their sexual orientation through no choice of their own. Therefore, considering that Christians believe that God made everything in the world, why did He make people whom he will hate? There can be endless attempts at answering this and justifying why God acted thus, however, the answer cannot be found because it is unacceptable from a religious point of view to claim that your theories are God's words if they have not been written in the Bible or any other holy book. Holy books should not be open to interpretation but in reality, they are and this dilemma will be left for the section on religion.

To further examine the debate of choice versus nature, we should examine the consequences of declaring one's homosexuality. Homosexuality has been something that, historically, has led to persecution, verbal and physical abuse, stigmatisation and disowning. Would anyone really choose to be something that they know they are likely to suffer all these prejudices for? If it was a choice, then under these circumstances, of such reactions from heterosexuals, nobody would choose to be gay. It would be absurd unless the person was a serious masochist. It is as unquestionable as it can be to say that homosexuality is not a choice, so therefore, how can you be prejudiced against someone who is who they are when they have had no choice in the matter? It is no different to being prejudiced against all people who are shorter than 1.50m. They had no say in the matter, it's just how it is.

From this, some homophobes may argue that homosexuals are likely to molest them and try to transfer their sexual feelings to them. I don't think it needs to be discussed very much that this is an absurd idea. It is as realistic as saying that your average heterosexual man or woman is likely to attempt sexual acts with every member of the opposite sex that they meet.

Whilst writing this in 2009, it makes me think whether in 20 years, people will be shocked to find out that human beings were treated differently and had laws imposed on them for no valid reason. If it is not going to harm you in any way and you are not going to see any acts that make you squirm, then what is the issue exactly? If heterosexual men were judged negatively on whether they had partners who were taller than them and were forbidden to be seen outside with them, would this be accepted as an appropriate law?

Hence, in a truly moral world, nobody would be subject to any rules or restrictions depending on their sexuality. There is not much more to say on the matter than that. The only thing that could be punishable by law is if anyone else treated someone differently because of their sexuality. For example, it would be illegal and open to investigation if someone was refused a job because they were of a sexuality that the employer did not agree with. This goes both ways, too – homosexual employers would not be allowed to refuse a heterosexual applicant based on their sexual persuasion and vice versa.

When looking at the issue of various sexualities from a religious perspective, it has been noted elsewhere that religious groups are not allowed to have any influence in politics. Nor are they allowed to on a social level where any perceived group is then seen to be inferior in any way. It always comes back to the same underlying principle: if you would not like to be treated as inferior by anyone, do not treat anyone else as though they are inferior to you.

Gay Marriage

The concept of gay marriage is one that has raised controversy. People who are opposed to it think that it is not right, for one reason or another, which is due either to their religious views, or their homophobic views that are unrelated to any religion. To say that it should not be allowed is a strange view because the relationship between the couple in question has no direct effect on anyone else. Just as the marriage between a man and a woman has no direct effect on anyone else.

If two homosexual people are in a relationship but are not married and certain other people who know them are not aware of it, there is no problem simply because the others don't know about it. Even if they do, what goes on the personal lives of the gay couple in their own privacy largely remains their own private relationship. It is only when someone raises an objection that there is a problem. A problem only arises when someone has a prejudice against the couple, otherwise everything would be fine. So when the couple gets married, nothing changes except that they are officially registered as being married. So what? Has it affected anyone when a heterosexual couple gets married? If two of your friends get married, it actually has no real impact on your life. All that is different is you know they are now married. So why should it be any different if two gay people are married?

Another issue that is possibly more difficult to accept or allow is the notion of a gay married couple adopting, or in some other way, having children. I would say that at this time, I would find it hard to say that it should be allowed because of the problems that could arise from this. What I mean is that this new family would likely be subjected to insults and abuse of some kind from those people who don't like the idea. If no-one had any objection, how could there be a problem? If the gay couple who had a child lived in isolation and cared for and brought up the child well, there would not be any room for any objection from anyone as there would be no-one to communicate with them. The same would go for if they lived in a community and the the fellow residents treated them the same as anyone else.

Therefore, there is only a problem when there are prejudiced people around.

We could talk of family values, which is an aspect that judgemental people raise. Well, what are family values? It certainly doesn't mean that the family should consist of a mother and a father and their children because this doesn't leave any room for the way that they bring up their children. People, quite rightly, wouldn't approve if these parents raised their children to be anti-social, aggressive and generally offensive to others. But does it mean that it is o.k. Just because the parents are a man and a woman?

Family values relate to how the parents treat the children. Parents should be caring, supportive, loving and there to help their children develop as well-educated and friendly people. Children who love and respect their parents would be an example of good family values.

So if a gay couple raised their children in such ways, what's the difference?

The difference is, again, those people who are opposed to it for no proper reason. Those who believe that gay married couples and gay parents should not be allowed. But just because they believe that doesn't mean it is correct. It is only their opinion and it is an opinion that will *cause* problems because they are the ones who express their negative views.

So this is why we can be reluctant to say that gay couples should be allowed to adopt. Because the problems will not necessarily come from the family itself (as long as they are raising the child well), but they come from the people who create the problems – the prejudiced ones.

In the end, what this means is that the people who disapprove and protest against gay marriages and gay parenting are actually protesting against their own opinions or beliefs. They are the ones who make the problems happen, so because they are prejudiced and the problems wouldn't exist if they weren't prejudiced, they are protesting against themselves.

From this reasoning, we can see that gay marriage has to be given an equal status to heterosexual marriage.

Personal Finances

Regarding finances and wealth, I have already discussed the need to control the ease of which people can get very high interest loans from private lenders and how people ought not to concern themselves with gaining more money, but even if this happened for some people, there would still be others who continue to earn unjustified salaries and bonuses. What we need to do as a society is encourage the rich to spread their wealth. It would be immoral to say that the richest people should be taxed something like 75% or that they should be obliged to give their money to charities. We simply cannot impose restrictions on anyone in this way as that would be hypocritical to the whole proposed system.

Instead we should be respectful to those who donate to charities and give exposure to those who deserve it and not to those who flaunt their wealth and bask in the glory of being photographed wearing stupidly expensive clothes in the mistaken belief that they have some value to society.

It should become an agreed perspective that the measure of someone's success is not the amount of assets they have but how much they contribute to society. We hear about the rich lists each year that show the chart of the richest people in the world, but how about a list to show the most generous donors to charities? It already exists but we don't tend to hear about it in the mass media. 'Business Week' magazine compiled a list of the 50 Most Generous Philanthropists.[12]

Bill Gates, the former head of Microsoft is well known for his charitable donations. As of 2007, Bill and Melinda Gates were the second most generous philanthropists in America, having given over $28,144 million to charity supporting global health, development and education (48% of the Bill and Melinda Gates Foundation's net worth).

People like Bill Gates and Warren Buffett, the Berkshire Hathaway CEO who has given over $40,780 million (or 78% of his wealth) to health, education and humanitarian causes, are ones who should be held up as role models, not just to the general public, but to the other company owners, elite sports stars, Hollywood actors and pop stars who are not known to use their wealth in such positive, constructive ways.

This idea of encouraging the rich to use their wealth productively is one that has been developed by the Institute For Philanthropy (IPF).[13] This is an institution whereby programmes are developed for wealthy individuals and families so that they can donate their money in a structured sense, so they can gain a full understanding of the project that they can be involved in. The IPF work with a number of wealthy people to help them understand how they can use their money effectively, often in a global sense, by providing workshops and by building programmes for future generations. Therefore, the long term aim of the IPF is to raise awareness among people, especially the younger generation so that they can become actively involved in charity work and the development of the community. This is an important difference from just giving money to charity and then carrying on with your daily business as the relations between the volunteers and those in need is fundamental to understanding suffering and developing empathy. This type of project can be very significant to the progress of humanity that is very much needed at this time.

Another major problem that capitalism has given us is the selfish desire to be rich. The main problem that this has resulted in is that some people have the capacity to be rich more than others, depending on their skills and their connections. The rich-poor divide has been to the detriment of far too many people, even in western societies. The poor have been left at the mercy of the multinational companies who, for a large part, determine whether jobs are available, depending on whether they are in a boom or bust period in the cycle of the free market economy. Many people are in the situation where they directly or indirectly rely on the biggest companies doing well (indirectly in the case of businesses that act as suppliers to bigger companies).

As these people (the majority) have little control over their personal destinies, they can be left in state of needing to borrow money to cover their everyday costs. This unfortunate situation has created a very immoral solution in that predatory lenders have moved into the arena to capitalise on it.

The BBC made a documentary called "The Money Trap", which documented the lives of some people who had been lured into debt by their high street banks. Inside information was given by a whistleblower who revealed that banks put their profit before customers at every opportunity.

These kinds of banks want to retain the type of customers who borrow money monthly and are likely to go over their credit limit. This means that they are then obliged to pay extra fees. They are the people that the banks value the most; those who make minimum payments and whose repayments are not even covering the interest are the ideal credit card customers.

Banks look to see which of its products their customers don't have and probably don't need, then they try to sell them to these people. It works because people who are in desperate situations financially feel better in knowing that the bank has allowed them a credit limit of several thousand pounds. What they don't realise, however, is that the banks are deliberately providing them with much more than they can afford to pay back so that their interest keeps on accruing.

Obviously, we can see that banks need to be very tightly regulated. This aspect will be saved for the Economy section in Policies, so here we will look at how we can help people to become aware of the need for money and how it differs from the desire for money.

As the current system works, people and businesses need money to survive. That, in itself, is a very sorry situation because people's level of stability and happiness depend largely on money. Peter Joseph (The Zeitgeist Movement) is looking to replace the monetary system with a resource-based system that effectively works from trading certain items and materials for others as well as for human skills, i.e. a piece of work can be traded for items that are assumed to be worth the same value. Whereas the work of TZM is similar in many ways to the ideas proposed in this book, it would take a very long transition period to phase out money entirely and at this moment cannot be seen as one we should be entertaining.

However, the selfish desire to attain more is one that can be addressed. It is difficult to sum up in a few sentences here as to how it can be done, as it would require the implementation of all the ideals and policies in this book together to be able to reach a state where people are not in such wildly different states of financial stability, and where they do not feel that their life's goal should be to gain as much as they can. Remember Gandhi's point where the question is not "to have", it is "to be". It is not the means to keep possessing more and better items, it is the means to keep improving our combined level of happiness that we need to focus on.

It is therefore the government's responsibility to help this situation arise and remain, through education, awareness, support for creativity and persevering so that the gap between the rich and the poor will decrease significantly.

What will follow in this book, particularly in the Policies section, will show you how we can practically and realistically change the course of humanity in ways that do not require unimaginable revolutionary ideas, but take pre-existing ones that are not effective and need to be reformed, as well as alternative practices that have already been implemented on a small scale and have been proved to work for the benefit of all concerned.

Should a government play a part in shaping a society by aiming to guide its people's beliefs? Understandably, this could be seen as controversial but that depends on the way that the government acts. To be in a position of governing the citizens, one has to take on the responsibility of shaping a society so that it is going to be as agreeable and uncontroversial as possible. Therefore, it is fundamental that a government acts to influence its people for the benefit of the society. To try to steer people away from the superficial and artificial world of things like fashion in its many guises there would need to be limits on advertising so that no product could be advertised in a way that is interpreted by a standards authority as being deceitful or exploitative.

This way of taking refuge in false identities and escape from the truths of one's life has been raised previously but deserves its own section to analyse it more profoundly.

Escapism

In terms of shaping a society, what the Hypothetical Government should aim to do regarding the influence it has on the people is how it can improve the level of overall happiness that the society has.

To be able to analyse this, we have to look at the kind of problems that are prevalent in the society on a large scale. The level of satisfaction that any person has can be measured in terms of how much they feel they need an 'escape from reality' to get any sense of fulfilment. There are many forms of this kind of escape – alcohol, drugs (both legal and illegal), superficial shopping (for clothes, shoes, anything that just 'makes me feel better', albeit temporarily), computer and console games (where people can lose themselves in the virtual world) and television programmes that have no more value than they are a distraction from everyday life (reality shows, soap operas, get-rich-quick game shows, etc.) to name the most common types in western societies. The more that people reach out to escape routes such as these reflects how unsatisfied the person is with the reality of their lives.

A good example of this is the Ecstasy phenomenon which came about around the early 1990s. This illegal drug became very popular with teenagers as well as adults in the music club scene. Despite there being warnings about its dangers (dehydration, detachment from reality and in a few cases death) it remained very popular for a number of years. The question is why? Why do so many people gladly reach out for a way of detaching themselves from reality? This is the question that a government needs to address rather than "How can we tell people to stop taking these drugs?" The latter is the typical approach from the average government. How to dissuade people from taking a mind-altering substance that is illegal (and therefore untaxable. Alcohol is taxable so that's fine. Many people, tens of thousands a year die from abusing alcohol but if there's money to be made, who cares? (See Bill Hicks, the late great philosophical comedian)) and how to punish them if they are found with it in their possession.

The main problem with this approach is that if people like to do something, even if it is illegal but it's not going to kill them as long as they are careful not to take too much, is that if they feel they are just being looked down on with scorn by the government, the people are not really going to care. Why not? Because they feel that the government doesn't care about the state of their lives anyway and one can feel happier when under the influence of such a drug.

This leaves us with the problem of the people not feeling a kinship of any kind with its government. They see the government as being the evil rulers who just try to stop anybody from doing anything that makes them feel good. When we have this kind of situation, government projects that try to warn us of the dangers and inform us of the penalties are going to make a lot of people rebel. They don't want to have their lives mapped out by the Big Brother that tells them how they have to behave. If they know that the chances of them getting caught are relatively slim, they will continue doing it, for they have no good reason to not do it. Life is otherwise bad, depressing, unfulfilling so they would happily turn to an escape of this kind.

A British film, "Human Traffic", was released in 1999 and focused on a group of teenagers and young adults who depended on taking mind-altering substances like alcohol and ecstasy. It contrasted the experiences with their daily lives such as being unemployed or working in a clothes shop. In the film there is a part where one of the characters is talking about how he feels when he is under the influence of ecstasy:

> The present has gone, fantasy is a part of reality...
> This feels right, we stop trying to control things...
> We forget all the pain and hurt in life, we want to go somewhere else.
> We're not threatened by people any more.
> All our insecurities have evaporated.
> We're in the clouds now, all wide open.
> We're spacemen, orbiting the earth.
> The world looks beautiful from here now.
> We're nympholeptics, desiring for the unobtainable.
> We risk sanity for moments of temporary enlightenment.
> So many ideas, so little memory.
> The last thought killed by anticipation of the next.
> We embrace an overwhelming feeling of love.
> We flow in unison, we're together.
> I wish this was real, we want a universal level of togetherness
> Where we're comfortable with everyone.
> We're in rhythm, part of a movement, a movement of escape.
> We wave goodbye.
>
> Ultimately, we just want to be happy. [14]

This is a good indication of why people feel they need a way of escaping. "We want a universal level of togetherness, where we're comfortable with everyone." To take such mind-altering substances helps people to forget about reality and lose their inhibitions. Depending on the drug taken, it can lead to feelings of togetherness and pure happiness. A similar sensation can be obtained with cocaine and alcohol (although the experience can, of course, go completely the other way depending on the circumstances) but people just want to be happy. It is an in-built desire, it is instinctual. If they have no job or a job which really doesn't inspire them and their future looks bleak, they can understandably look for a way to escape the mediocrity.

Again, governments view such people in a purely negative way and look for ways to control those who get drunk or they look to crack down on those who buy or sell illegal drugs. They never seem to ask why they are so in need of an escape and what can be done so that life is more enjoyable for people. This is the foundation of the problem and is what should concern a government the most if they are really going to tackle the issues of drugs, both legal and illegal.

Imagine how different the general public's opinions of the government would be if they said and showed that they weren't going to take the traditional tough stance on drugs but were going to show compassion to the people who take them and actively help them to find true fulfilment in their lives. Of course a government needs to work on stopping drugs being easily available to the public but if the demand wasn't there so much, neither would be the supply.

To have any hope of restructuring society in a positive way that is more likely to lead to fulfilment, we need to start with the problems that are the most fundamental. Poverty and lack of opportunities, lack of motivation to give something back to society is a sign of an underdeveloped world yet these things are very common in the so-called developed world. As we have already seen what the primary goal for everyone is - happiness, this is how development must be measured.

The United Nations Development Programme constructs a Human Development Report where it states very clearly that "People are the real wealth of nations" and that "Human Development is (...) about much more than the rise or fall of national incomes."[15]

Their Human Development Index (HDI) combines indicators such as life expectancy, educational attainment and income, which are then adjusted for gender inequality in each relevant country, the Gender Empowerment Measure which evaluates progress in advancing women's standing in political and economic forums. The fourth aspect is the Human Poverty Index which measures more than people's income, it evaluates the most basic dimensions of deprivation: a short life, lack of basic education and lack of access to public and private resources.

Given these criteria, the HDI report of 2009 shows Norway to have the highest level of human development, with Australia second, the

USA 13th and the UK 21st. Considering that governments stress the need for economic growth as a measure of the country's success, and that the USA is considered an economic superpower, that it is behind smaller countries such as Ireland (5th) and Iceland (3rd), this shows us that money does not equal human development. There is a lot more to it and we need to examine the factors that make society function badly, understand why they happen and what we can do to truly improve them.

Gambling

Gambling is a popular pastime on a global scale. It is the practice of betting one's own money on an event whose outcome in uncertain with the aim of accumulating more money. It is undertaken in many forms: casinos, horse racing and other sports events or lotteries as well as many others.

Some religions have quite liberal views on gambling. Catholicism and Judaism embrace it on a small scale but Islam either regulates it or imposes a ban on it in some countries.

It is an activity that is enjoyed by people when, for example, betting with their friends while playing card games or betting on a football match. However, on a large scale, like betting large sums of money in casinos or poker tournaments, it can cause the destruction of people's lives if they lose all their money and other possessions.

Lotteries are also large scale events, although in general, most people probably only spend a small amount on buying a single ticket. However, a substantial number of people obsessively spend large amounts each week on multiple tickets.

First of all, we need to look at why people partake in the practice of gambling. In the majority of cases it is to gain more money if the person has relatively little to live on. Understandable so far but some people put themselves and their families at risk by developing an addiction to gambling which can lead to breakdowns of families and big financial problems for relations who are not involved in the activity on any level.

Before I start addressing the regulation of gambling, the idea of feeling the need to gamble is an important issue to address. Gambling is constantly promoted as an attractive temptation with the chance of winning huge amounts of money. It focuses on the concept of greed and flaunts it to a massive extent. It preys on people who are in financial trouble and convinces them to part with even more of their money, even when the chances of them winning are incredibly small. It successfully convinces people that their lives would be so much better if they won millions of pounds, Euros, dollars, etc. It provides people with an escape mechanism to try to increase their bank balance with ease.

The problem with this is that the gambling industry very carefully devises systems, like lotteries, where the chances of winning are almost zero. This means that the institutions themselves will be the ones profiting on a massive scale each week, at the expense of the poor people who are desperate for a way out of their unfulfilling lives.

By fooling people into thinking they have a reasonable chance of winning, they can create false hope and desperation for their own gain.

Another problem with the gambling industry is that it encourages people to make gains that they haven't worked for. In this case it ought to be emphasised that you get what you work for and you deserve what you get. If people are unwilling to work for money, they don't deserve to have it. By encouraging people to look for easy ways out, a well-rounded society is not going to be attainable.

From this, we can start to look at regulating the industry. In terms of the corporations that make their profits from their customers gambling, there would be a deduction on their revenues that would go toward the state (i.e. the benefit of the country as a whole) so that the profits made will be a lot more reserved. They would still make enough money to live comfortably enough but not to any excessive extent. The prizes that could be won would be limited so that, for example, instead of there being €2 million available to win each week, the highest amount that could be won would be, say, €100,000. The reason for this is to try to reduce the level of greed in people as a whole to wean them off the idea that their lottery ticket could be the answer to their dreams. At present, €100,000 would not be so life changing – it would not be enough for someone to never have to work again and they wouldn't be able to live a life of misguided luxury but it is still a substantial amount.

The amount that people would be allowed to spend on their bets should also be regulated. For example, in a betting shop, which are prevalent in the UK, only bets of £1 or £2 would be able to be made. This could easily be enforced by automating the system so that each customer has their own betting card, individual in the same way as a debit card and the computer would only be able to register a bet of this much money. The same system could be in place for buying lottery tickets.

However, this is a potentially controversial issue and one that would need to be debated and agreed upon by the general population if it was going to be implemented.

There would be no laws in place for people betting at home with their friends. They would only be asked to maintain moderation for their own well-being; to prevent arguments and unjust losses taking place.

In terms of underground events like clandestine poker tournaments, these would need to be classed as illegal due to the large sums of money that tend to be up for stake as well as threats of physical violence and illegal gains of the subject's property. This would require strict policing to try to uncover and prosecute those who organise such events, again, for the benefits of people involved.

The aim over time would be to try to bring the practice of gambling to a point where people are just not interested in it any more and realise that if they want something, they must work for it.

This may seem like an unachievable goal but considering that this book is dedicated to the development of a society on the whole, it is something that should come about of its own accord if these principles were followed on the whole.

The Power of Truth

The philosophy and discoveries of Gandhi are some of the most useful and beneficial for the betterment of humanity and at this point it would be worth looking more into the ideas that he developed to try to provide valuable suggestions for how we should live our lives.

Satyagraha is the name of a principle which he held as being fundamental to a peaceful society. 'Satya' means truth and 'agraha' means force or firmness. In English, therefore, it can be taken as meaning 'the power of truth'. This principle points to the idea that truth should be adhered to completely and the establishment thereof should be the ultimate goal for everyone.

To illustrate this, Gandhi said that 'the vindication of truth (is) not by infliction of suffering on the opponent but on one's self.' This means that if one sees another's actions as corrupt or deceitful in some way, one should not try to rectify it through violence but through peaceful means. One should approach the opponent's unethical words or actions by attempting to persuade them otherwise; that their approach is incorrect. If this doesn't work, "humility and honesty will." The opponent must be 'weaned from error by patience and sympathy' not crushed, converted or annihilated (in Fischer's words).

If, in the case of a government putting a law into effect without the consultation of the people and the people don't agree in general with the law in principle, then violent protests are not going to lead to a peaceful resolution of the issue. Any form of violence or aggression will only lead to tension and often revenge through reciprocal force (the use of the police or the army). As a result, hatred, conflict and unhappiness will be the outcome. The people need to react in a peaceful way; make their voices heard; show that the people are not willing to tolerate the law and in Gandhi's philosophy offer passive resistance: simply ignore the law and be prepared to accept the punishments that are given out. If it means many people going to jail (as happened many times in Gandhi's life to him and his followers), then go along with it, repeatedly if necessary. What will happen is that one's passive and peaceful resistance will embarrass the powers that deal out the punishments and eventually their unjust laws or policies will collapse.

Suffering

This feeling that to raise oneself above one's own suffering by causing other people to suffer even more so is a good explanation for why people who are suffering inside themselves commit crimes. They don't want to feel so low. Their attempt to rise above it, they feel, must be done in a way that they can have mastery over someone else. If they directly cause suffering to other people, they feel that they have at least put other's circumstances below their own. It is true that this is a desperate measure but when being rejected by society, by the government and being trapped inside a life when there appears to be no alternative, things will get desperate.

As Buddha did, it is important to understand people's suffering. This means on a profound level. It is not enough to say that it must be difficult for them or that you honestly feel sorry for them, for this is only a superficial level of understanding. One needs to speak to those who suffer to be able to feel true empathy towards them. One needs to experience the problems that they live with to be able to get inside their situation. Only when you can do this can you make a connection with someone who suffers in some real way. From this, you can earn their trust and respect; note that it is not the other way around – they don't earn your trust and respect because whereas you are both equal, their needs are greater than yours and they are likely to be sceptical of other people with whom they don't usually associate. You need to be open, compassionate and supporting of them so that they can feel they are being accepted. This is the first step of helping to develop and strengthen human relations. Barriers between people need to be dissolved. People do not and cannot live in isolation. There are always other people to relate to in some way, whether we choose to or not. We are together in life and we belong together. We depend on each other and need each other to be able to work towards a state of true happiness that we can only achieve if we do it together.

Conquering False Beliefs

The main aim of this chapter is to make clear that in order to develop as a society should, we need to address certain long-held traditions and beliefs that do not stand up to scientific study or reason, and their rejection if they falsely interfere with our lives. For this reason, astrology will be used as a powerful example.

Astrology was first devised in the third millennium BC, when humans were still in a very naïve state of understanding the world and beyond. Having no way to make sense of the multitude of stars in the night sky, supposedly educated people noticed how the position of the stars appeared to change throughout the year with regard to the times that they would appear to rise above the horizon. As telescopes and other such scientific equipment had not been invented, no-one knew anything about such rudimentary things as the distance of the stars from Earth or even what stars actually were. All the stars appear to be equidistant from us and some appear to be brighter than others. As this was all they had to go on, the new astrologers begun to infer the significances of stars like assuming that those which were brighter were more significant and that the stars were related to each other in some way. This is where the idea of constellations came into being. We all have some idea of some of the more well known constellations such as the Ursa Major, Orion and the signs of the zodiac but it is interesting to understand how they were decided upon.

Certain stars were perceived to be set in groups depending on which stars were near to each other. From this, interpretations were made as to what the pattern might represent. Orion, for example, seemed to have a belt of three stars in a line and four stars that surrounded them. It is a very basic and self-fulfilling conclusion that if the three in a line were really a belt, judging by where the others were, they would be points of the shoulders and leg joints. Unfortunately, this is so far from a scientific conclusion that it can only seriously be seen as nonsense in the light of astronomical research to date. The same applies to all the other constellations. The groups that were decided on are all simply human inferences and what they are supposed to represent is as liberal an artistic licence as can be put into practice. There is no evidence that any of them are true celestial beings but as they were taught to people who were even more scientifically naïve at the time, it was accepted as a system and, of course, continued throughout history right up to this day.

Astrology, once it had developed its grip and authority on the public, had scope to be applied in even more nonsensical ways. The twelve established zodiac constellations were said to define how people were, depending on which one was in ascendency at the time of their birth. Astrology was also used to claim to predict the future of people's lives and world events, as well as having relevance to past ones. The prediction of the future became known as horoscopes and this practice is still widely in use today.

Before we go on to look at the impact on people's beliefs about horoscopes and signs of the zodiac, we need to make clear the relevance of stars to one another in scientific terms.

In Orion's belt, Alnitak is the easternmost star. It is 800 light years away from Earth. Alnilam, the middle of the three is 1300 light years away and Mintaka, the westernmost is 900 light years away. This means that between the nearest to us and furthest, there is a gap of 500 light years. As we now know, this is a phenomenal difference when it has been assumed that they were meant to be part of a hunter's belt. Therefore, when we speak about stars' relevance to each other on a three dimensional scale, the stars in any constellation have absolutely nothing to do with each other and for all intents and purposes function independently of most other stars. This is equally true of the signs of the zodiac and research over the last few centuries into astronomy has shown that our knowledge of the universe has increased dramatically and that astrology has been relegated to the annals of the history of human understanding.

Except that it still has a great deal of influence over many modern people's lives.

Horoscopes are still prevalent in daily newspapers, on the internet, in books and magazines and on television. How can it still have so much influence on people's lives at this point in history? Primarily because there is still money to be made from it. Anyone who writes horoscopes that are published in the press or shown on TV get paid for doing so. People buy, read and listen to them, thereby giving the institutions a reason to keep providing them. The believers, quite often, strongly believe that what they take in is true but non-believers reject them with ridicule as they are always so ambiguous that you can interpret them however you like to make them seem true.

There is no science in this whatsoever and astrology has never stood up to scientific investigation. There have, however, been psychological studies that have asked people to answer questions about their lives and from the results, have given them reports about themselves, either positively or negatively.

This is called the Forer Effect (also known as the Barnum Effect). Bertram Forer carried out a psychological experiment in 1948 where the subjects had to take a personality test. Afterwards they were given a so-called analysis of their scoring but they all received the same report, which, in an abbreviated form, was as follows:

"You have a great need for other people to like and admire you. You have a tendency to be critical of yourself. You have a great deal of unused capacity which you have not turned to your advantage. While you have some personality weaknesses, you are generally able to compensate for them. Disciplined and self-controlled outside, you tend to be worrisome and insecure inside. At times you have serious doubts as to whether you have made the right decision or done the right thing. You have found it unwise to be too frank in revealing yourself to others. At times you are extroverted, affable, sociable, while at other times you are introverted."

The subjects were asked to rate the accuracy of their 'personal report' from 0 to 5 where 5 was "completely agree" and 0 was "completely disagree". The average rating was 4.26. The subjects were then informed that the report had been made up of parts of horoscopes and not based on their personality tests in any way. If you re-read the above 'report' you can see that the statements could apply to practically anyone because even when they are critical, they are usually backed up by an counterbalancing statement that is positive.[16]

It shows that people are willing to believe anything they are told about themselves as long as it doesn't sound too bad. In fact, the more positive it is, the more likely they are to agree with it. This is to do with self-image. People in general like others to view them as good people with certain attributes that make us feel good about ourselves. If someone who knew you said they had done a psychological analysis on you and concluded that you were usually friendly but got upset when other people treated you unfairly, you would very probably agree with it. But if they said you were usually unfriendly and very often got upset with other people, you would reject their analysis. If the 'researcher' then told you that they had just said that off the top of their head without any analysis whatsoever, you would probably feel a bit gullible.

This is how horoscopes work. The only time that you will hear about negative things due to happen in your lives are when they come from outside sources, from your boss or your partner, for example. They are not based on any analysis or facts at all and everything you read in horoscopes is a lie.

This kind of delusion is unacceptable and should not be allowed to happen in a society that wants to truly develop. Such superstition would be banned from appearing in any medium where anyone had to pay to receive it. Whereas it would be a waste of time to say that it is illegal to ever write horoscopes, as on the internet it would be impossible to regulate, it would be important to ethically educate people that understand that astrology and horoscopes are not only untrue but are harmful to a person's sense of being and knowledge of the world. Delusions must be eradicated as they are ultimately only used for financial gain or social control at the expense of the naïvety and gullibility of the general public. This also goes for other occult practices like tarot cards and numerology. If there is no objective proof that they are true, the general public should be able to personally reject it once they feel that they have understood the truth of it.

But what about those people who like the idea of guidance from horoscopes and feel that it gives them a path to follow in life? Well, the very fact that they are all lies should be borne in mind and instead, people should be given honest and realistic ways that they should travel through life in order to truly develop their characters. They should be encouraged to analyse ideas and beliefs so that they can have either proof or refutation of what they think to be true to help them to stop believing whatever they are told just because it has been said to be true for millennia. Just because thousands or even millions of people throughout history have claimed something to be so doesn't mean that it is true, as in the incorrect belief that the world is flat. Until evidence came along that rejected this belief, people thought it was true and this shows with that a lack of real knowledge, theories must be treated with either scepticism or, in the case of ulterior motives like financial gain, must first be rejected until otherwise proven to be true.

After all the above discussions we can arrive at what this newly proposed system of government should be called, and it is simply Moralism.

This is not the first time the term has been used in history but the points where it differs from previous ideologies need to be clarified.

In the past, Moralism has been a vague, semi-structured concept which adheres to the idea that humans should not try to explain what they can't prove. It has been divisive between science and religion, which is not the aim of Moralism in the context of this book.

David Hume, an 18th century philosopher, historian and economist has been credited with laying the foundations for Moralism. He believed that humans are implemented with morals but didn't choose to explain where they come from, either from God or from society. I would suggest that more than two centuries later, we can agree that morals are humanly created through the power of reason and that they exist on an intrinsic level of both personal and societal.

For example, almost all humans would agree that it is immoral to commit murder but elsewhere in the animal kingdom murder is committed within the same species for reasons of survival and protection of territory. We, as humans, decided that these conditions are not conducive to the justification of murder within our species.

Regarding Moralism and government, the previous definition of it does not associate it with any government. It also favours heavy punishment but as you will have read, and as you will read in subsequent chapters, the Moralism described in this book does not agree with this idea.

It is thought to be likely that previous Moralism would favour a strict capitalist society, which is of course the complete opposite in its current sense.

Thus, with the principles of Moralism initially set in place (depending on the agreement of the general public after reading them), we can start to look at how policies would be formed in this respect.

1. www.unescap.org/unis/press/G_05_00.htm
2. Buddha: Deepak Chopra - HarperOne; First Edition (2007) p.236-237
3. www.channel4.com/news/articles/society/health/can a shampoo strengthen hair /168125
4. http://www.guardian.co.uk/media/2010/jan/18/spain-television-advertising
5. www.cdc.gov/nchs/fastats/divorce.htm
6. www.washingtonpost.com/wp-dyn/articles/A2959-2004Oct2.html
7. blogs.consumerreports.org/money/2009/05/credit-card-reform-bill-teenagers-teens-teen-hello-kitty-obama-children-prepaid-marketing-fees.html
8. The Life of Mahatma Gandhi, Louis Fischer. Harper Collins Publishers.
9. Wittgenstein (from) en.wikipedia.org/wiki/Meaning_of_life#20th_century_philosophy
10. Jean Piaget's The Study of Figurative Thought
11. www.courtinfo.ca.gov/courts/supreme/highprofile/documents/Amer_Psychological_Assn_Amicus_Curiae_Brief.pdf
12. bwnt.businessweek.com/interactive_reports/philanthropy_individual/

13. www.instituteforphilanthropy.org

14. Human Traffic, 1999. Written by Justin Kerrigan, Renaissance Films.

15. hdr.undp.org/en/humandev/

16. Forer, B.R. (1949). "The fallacy of personal validation: A classroom demonstration of gullibility". Journal of Abnormal and Social Psychology (American Psychological Association) 44 (1): 118–123.

Section 2: Policies

Religion

In a book about government, some people may think that religion should not have a place, others may think that it should be the foundations of a government. This section has to be included to aim to bring about compromise and reconciliation between people who have differing and opposing views.

It is probably the most difficult topic to address as throughout history, religion has been at the heart of so many disagreements, fights and wars and there has been no significant progression in terms of overcoming this seemingly eternal dilemma.

This is not the place to attempt to analyse religion-based battles over the millennia and decide who was right and who was wrong but what we need to look at is how religion came about and its legacy for subsequent religions and the general public, the validity of religion in general, the reasons why followers of different religions have come to blows and how we can move forward in these still troubled times in a way that always approaches it from a moral perspective.

Religion is something that came about in ancient times in all parts of the world with the development of human intellect. The earliest records we have of religious beliefs came with the advent of writing, 5000 years ago. Yet, at this time, there was of course, no way that people could communicate with each other in places as far away as separate continents or even just as near as 500km from their settlements. However, despite this scattering of communities and tribes that didn't have any knowledge of most others in the world, people started to think about life and what it all meant.

We have to understand that, back then, people had very little and rudimentary knowledge of the world. They could understand how they related to other people that they met on a daily basis and what they thought they ought to do if a foreign tribe came to their settlement (usually attack as they didn't know who the other people were and it is a human instinct of survival, as it is for other animals, to defend their territory and kin). But as to the grand scale of things, it was all a lot more mysterious. As farming developed, people began to learn that crops didn't always grow, even if they lived in a particularly stable climate that usually behaved in a fairly predictable way. But why did they sometimes fail? In primitive minds, it didn't make sense that they could grow food without any real mishaps one year but then they could be left with dry land that wouldn't provide crops the next year.

Understandably, this kind of inconsistency led people to start questioning what was happening in the world. What was the reason for this? Was there something else controlling the fate of their crops? Why were there sometimes flashes of light from the skies that sometimes destroyed a part of the land or even a person? Why did the ground rumble and split open with the capacity to destroy communities? When there had been no investigation into these kinds of things (storms and earthquakes), it was difficult to make sense of why they happened. Such natural disasters could happen on incredible scales, such as volcanic eruptions or hurricanes, and it must have been even scarier for people of 4000 to 5000 years ago than for us as we at least have more insight as to why such events happen. But they didn't know anything about tectonic plates or that weather systems built up in fairly regular patterns that provided them with more or less predictable climates like we now know.

Civilizations were the beginning of societal development and without any previous knowledge to read about, understanding the world from a human perspective was it its absolute start. So the challenge was on to try to explain what such large scale events were and why they happened, for they were not the result of human actions. They just seemed to happen on their own. Or was there something else that was setting them off? As Richard Dawkins stated in The God Delusion people tend to think that everything happens because there is an agent behind it with an intention to cause it to happen. We learnt to make sense of cause and effect and, because of our awareness of the world from our own perspective, we unconsciously think that there is always something that intentionally made the event happen. Blame is usually attributed to anything, particularly if it has a negative impact on ourselves. I've seen people trip on the pavement and then look round in disgust at it for doing such an rude thing to them! People curse at their shopping bag if it splits and their eggs break on the floor. But if you think about it, it is unlikely that the pavement or the shopping bag was having a quiet smirk to itself for successfully pulling a trick on you. However, attributing actions to agents is how we generally make sense of the world, we humanise events. So people started to philosophise from scratch and try to work out what it all means.

The problem is, when you have no points of reference to build a philosophy, you are pretty much feeling your way around in the dark. Primitive minds thought that something must be sending the sun around the earth every day because it always happened with astonishing regularity. The sea was always moving, sometimes violently, so something out there must have a reason for causing it to happen that way. Why, when voyagers set out on ships in large numbers, did they sometimes get tossed to sea and were never seen again? Surely, some greater spirit was angry about something and demanded that the people did something that was going to please it and make it content again.

Thus, people attributed reasons to things that must have been invisible because no-one ever saw anyone do these things. And they could happen in such amazing ways and on such a grand scale that no individual or group of people would be capable of something like causing the sea to move around so powerfully. Why did the crops fail? Humans had already worked out that plants need sunlight and water to ensure their growth so why was it that in certain times not enough water was sent to their land? Someone or something must be displeased about something.

This led to the idea that there was some kind of agent that was doing things that humans could not control and were sometimes at the mercy of. But it was no good if the crops failed year after year, whole communities could starve if this kept happening. The primitive mind, when attributing reason to something that they couldn't perceive, only really had the capacity to think of something that must be like some kind of giant human, but one that was actually invisible. It was an easy way to picture what this thing was if you were going to explain it to other people. Hence, these gods were decided upon for all manner of things that were not governed by humans: the sun god, the sea god, the rain god, etc.

When you have nothing else to go on, it does kind of make sense. At least you can accept that something is causing all of these events to happen even if it never communicates to you in words or appears before you. And you can then give them names and explain to everyone else what these gods do. Ancient Egyptians, Greeks and the pagans all worked along this theory and it made a lot of sense at the time. Reasons could be given to things like storms or droughts and the people would then, considering that they now believed that there were gods, think of ways to appease them if a catastrophe occurred. This led to the concept of sacrifice, whereby you had to offer something on a meaningful scale if the god was going to appreciate your offering and allow you to have enough water for the crops, etc. But if things got really bad, the level of sacrifice had to be stepped up, from simple gifts of fruit to shiny jewels to animal slaughter to human slaughter. If the lower level of offerings didn't have any effect, they had to try something that was more intense. The only way that depth of meaning could be gauged was to think of what would be more of a sacrifice from their own lives. The people wouldn't want to give up gold, nor would they want to give up their livestock. But if these didn't change the gods' minds, then the ultimate sacrifice of humans would be the highest level of offering and of desperation.

As humans all over the world were experiencing similar catastrophic events and had no other points of reference to try to explain them, it is easy to see why similar beliefs developed in all corners of the world. People had no instruments to record seismic activity or movements of high and low pressures in the atmosphere that caused variations in weather. They did however, have the enthusiasm to come up with explanations for things beyond their control for they weren't aware that we have always lived on a planet that is not just a ball of rock but a living object with many facets that is still in the process of its own evolution (shifting plates under its surface, ice ages, etc.). For humans who were trapped on the surface of the planet that could only see with their own eyes and hear with their own ears, very little could be explained scientifically and truthfully.

Such polytheistic religions continued to exist over thousands of years and I'll come to them again later but monotheistic religions also emerged. These types of religions (which worship one god rather than many) developed similarly out of a desire to make sense of how we got here and what we are supposed to be doing while we are here.

Whereas there were records from ancient cultures, such as the Egyptians, that recorded events such as battles and everyday life in hieroglyphic paintings, there was a point in human history where there were either no records of what had happened or very few and basic ones, such as cave paintings. So as the human mind developed and people were learning from their elders about the theories (or as they were then thought of – truths) about the world, what about how it all started?

There must have been a point when humans suddenly came into being because they had no evidence of civilizations that had been existing and leaving clear records for all of history. It all kind of faded away beyond a certain period so it must have been that the earliest records left by humans documenting their lives were the ones that showed when humans first came into being. Now they had something to go on and could begin thinking of stories that would make sense as to how it all began. Something must have put the sun and moon in the sky and sent them travelling around the earth like people have always seen happen. Probably the same thing made all the plants grow and the animals live. People knew that other animals didn't function in the same way as people, for buffalo and fish and so on led a very simple existence, mainly consisting of travelling aimlessly and eating so they must be less important creatures to humans who for all we know are the only ones that can communicate with each other and build things and make our own plants grow. Therefore, people are the highest level of life in the world and so must have control over everything else. But surely, someone must have decided for all this to happen in this way at some time. And so became the book of Genesis. And the people who heard it were enthralled. It all seemed to make perfect sense. The writers thought they had written something ground breaking and kept going through the generations.

This was also the advent of what we know as Abrahamic religions. Abraham was considered to have been born around 2000BC and lived for 175 years. His name appears in the Jewish, Christian and Muslim holy books which is the first of many connections between these three religions. Many names and stories of the Old Testament also appear in the Jewish holy book, The Tanakh, and in the Muslim holy book, the Qur'an.

At this point, I would like to suggest the first instance where we should think about the validity of the holy books. Abraham is believed to have lived for 175 years, which is by no means the oldest age recorded in the Bible – there is a long list of those who lived longer, up to Methuselah, who apparently lived to be 969. Now, at a time when there was no medicine, very limited sanitation and a much more basic diet than we have today, would it really have been feasible that people could live for so long?

This is one of many types of questions that I would like to ask but would not like to try to answer as doing so would be met with all types of agreement and disagreement that should be left to everybody who is interested in discussing such controversial subjects. I have no intention of trying to convince anyone that what I think is the right perspective and especially that what they think is wrong. We need to get as close to the truth as we can through research, debate and analysis. I wouldn't recommend that you take such words as truth as their ambiguity has been the reason for so much disagreement, bloodshed and death over the last 5000 years. Question everything until you reach a point where it can't be questioned any more. Thomas Paine, in his book "The Age of Reason", was brave enough to undertake a critical analysis of the entire Bible, which in 1794 was a huge risk. I will use this book as a reference many times in this chapter, abbreviated to AOR.

It's one thing to explain the history of the world and the hierarchy that all the living creatures have in relation to each other but what is the point of us being here? The animals can't talk and they just eat and reproduce but we can do a lot more, so there must be a special reason for our existence.

People had worked out by now that there is a god who made everything for us to use, so obviously we need to have utmost respect for him. Why is god always thought of as a 'he'? Historically, men have been considered to be the dominant gender and it wouldn't have made sense to think of god as a woman because women had a far lower status in society. He gave us food and water and wood and all the other things so that deserves even more than just respect, in fact absolute worship. Now we have a whole hierarchy in place so let's work out the rules of life.

The writers carried on working through the years but they found that people were not interested in hearing lists of rules for how they should live their lives so they had to make it more exciting so that they would pay attention. The process continued to develop over many years so that for each rule that they could think of, there was a story that would illustrate it. Genesis was a good story that people could believe really happened. It was a way of engaging the people and making it believable and interesting (Incidentally, it is said that Moses wrote the first five books of the Old Testament, a point which will be referred to shortly).

And over time, the writers developed their literary skills and because the people started to like the stories so much, they gained a prominent place in society and became a manual for how to live life. The only problem was that by this time, so many stories had been written and altered and by so many different people during their relatively short lives (due to a lack of medicine and therapy back then) that some stories had conflicts of interest with others. One story was giving out one message but another story later in the book was giving a contradictory message. The question at this point is - was it really the word of God or was it the word of men who attempted to write from what they thought would be God's perspective? Maybe it was that God didn't give his word at all and that the people of successive generations had different opinions about the truth of life and would say something in a different way. This is something to discuss.

Channel 4, a television channel in the UK, created a documentary in 2004 called "Who Wrote The Bible?" Robert Beckford, an academic theologian, went on a journey to discover who wrote the original stories and who then altered them. He began this quest as a Christian. He talks about how his religious upbringing was beneficial in terms of bringing about order to his own life, whereas if he hadn't believed the Bible as the word of God, he might have entered into a world of drug-dealing or basically uncivilised behaviour.

He recognises that the stories of the Bible can be interpreted as either symbolic or literal which again leads to a question – If God wanted his people to be clear about how to live our lives, wouldn't he have wanted to deliver his word so that it couldn't be up for debate and multiple interpretations?

The symbolism of the stories in the Bible leave them feeling wondrous and magical. They have probably been a great inspiration for subsequent story tellers who have used their imagination to tell fables and fairy tales but is it likely that those in the Bible really happened as they were told? Or are they more like fables, where they have a message to deliver but they are embedded in enchanting tales to give them a lasting beauty?

Beckford goes to Israel to examine the archaeological sites of places that were recorded in the Bible. He finds that the dates and sizes of places like the City of David and the kingdom of Israel don't match the chronology given in the Bible (there is a discrepancy of two centuries between the biblical and archaeological accounts of the City of David). This raises serious questions as to their authenticity and to the validity of the books on the whole.

If Moses was said to have written the first five books, why is it that he wrote about his own death in Deuteronomy chapter 34:5-6?

"So Moses, the Lord's servant, died there in the land of Moab, as the Lord had said he would. The Lord buried him in a valley in Moab, opposite the town of Bethpeor, but to this day no one knows the exact place of his burial."

Also, why the vagueness of his place of death? Was there a reason why it should be impossible for anyone to find? Moreover, how could Moses write about his own death?

Beckford concludes about this issue that there are four original sources of this particular text, each of which has its own style and agenda so that it unlikely that Moses wrote any of it. With this in mind, is it likely that Moses was a real person?

Paine points out that if Moses wrote these books, it was unusual but possible that he wrote of himself in the third person but "it cannot be admitted as a fact in those books that it is Moses who speaks, without rendering Moses truly ridiculous and absurd: for example, Numbers xii. 3, "Now the man Moses was very meek, above all the men which were on the face of the earth." If Moses said this of himself, instead of being the meekest of men, he was one of the most vain and arrogant coxcombs." (AOR, p.94)

Regarding his death, as noted above, Paine points out that if no-one knew where Moses was buried, how does the writer know he was buried in the land of Moab? (AOR, p.96)

There are other contradictions present, regarding the nature of God. In Exodus 3, God uses a burning bush an an intermediary with which to talk to Moses as he can't speak directly with him but there are countless other times when God speaks to Moses in different places as well as other people in a direct sense, i.e. not through an intermediary.

The same process of editing on a vast scale is evident in the Torah. It developed from four sources and was interweaved into one book to try to assimilate the ideas, opinions and stories. This, like with the Bible, is something that is openly admitted by religious leaders of the respective faiths without any problem but it still leaves us wondering: Is it really then the word of God?

It is clear that these books were written with a specific agenda: to affirm the monotheism of Jerusalem. Beckford likens it to the political dogma of Stalin. They were written with specific objectives to be reached through their application and that seems to be one of social order rather than wanting to enlighten people with the historical facts.

The Torah and the Bible, having many essential points in common, don't conclude with the same overall perspective as there are discrepancies between the actual recollections of events, hence leading them to exist as separate religions. However, the commonality of them is the most important issue here. They began with the intentions of proclaiming a monotheistic religion but differed along the way, splitting into two paths and disagreeing on the fundamental principles. To look at the differences is one thing. It is very easy to defend your own belief and argue that the other person's is wrong but this can only result in a state of stagnation. If, on the other hand, believers of different faiths took their time to explore how they could reach a common consensus and accept that one side prefers to interpret a story in one way and the other side another way but fundamentally they agree on the principles, then we would be making progress in terms of human relations.

Also, an interesting question to consider is that if God wanted people to worship him alone following the same rules and way of life, why did he develop so many religions that are in a constant state of stubborn disagreement? Why did he speak to Moses, either via the burning bush, the angel Gabriel or directly so that the first holy book could be completed, then hundreds of years later send the angel Gabriel to visit Muhammed to devise another holy book that is in conflict with the previous two yet mentions many of the same names and stories? It seems strange to think that if this happened, what was God's intention? Wouldn't he have preferred to have the whole world living peacefully with one another and having a very clear idea of how to live life so that everyone would be aiming for the same things and achieving them? The very idea that there can be different religions co-existing in conflict with one another doesn't really add up.

Beckford, when meeting with a Rabbi in Israel and asking him about the work of scholars who have dedicated their careers to understanding the truth of the holy books, raising the question of why there are four sources is given a response by the rabbi that these people are naïve "that they can't believe in the divinity of the Bible."

The rabbi refused to engage in any discussion about the questions of the validity of the books, preferring the belief that the words cannot be questioned or altered in any way and that what they say is the absolute divine truth.

Question everything.

The Old Testament can be seen as a book full of extremely violent stories and even brutal commands from God. Paine wrote "Whenever we read the obscene stories, the voluptuous debaucheries, the cruel and torturous executions, the unrelenting vindictiveness, which which more than half the Bible is filled, it would be more consistent that we called it the word of a demon, than the Word of God." (AOR, p.34)

When we move on to the New Testament, there are some very important issues to address regarding the first four books: those of Matthew, Mark, Luke and John. After investigating these texts, conclusions have been drawn that none of these people knew Jesus or even lived at the same time as him. These four books are four accounts of the life of Jesus, which have similarities in some parts, differences in others and recount different stories entirely, such as in Mark, there is no mention of the birth of Jesus, nor of his resurrection. There is a huge amount of plagiarism between the four books, which, as Beckford points out, is sometimes even word for word. Matthew seems to be the most guilty of this, trying to supplant Mark's gospel by adding to it the story of Jesus' birth, the sermon on the mount and the resurrection.

The question that comes to my mind the most about these four books is that if Jesus was the most important person to have ever lived, why are there four different stories of his life in the Bible instead of one unified story that accounts for everything of significance? Why were the stories of Jesus not written until decades and even centuries after his death? This, which has been established by scholars, makes us doubt the authenticity of the stories by people who weren't even there at the time. And why wasn't there editing, like in the Old Testament, so that all of the individual stories of Jesus' life could also be put together in one concise gospel?

Considering that biblical scholars have established the approximate times when these gospels were written, there are an enormous amount of quotes accredited to Jesus. How could such writers be so sure that these are the words that Jesus said? Given that there was no method of recording at that time, other than through writing, where did they get so many of Jesus's words from? Even if they were 'stories based on real events', who told the gospel writers about them so many decades after the life of Jesus?

It is interesting to recall that Jesus, the apparent son of God, never wrote a single word in his lifetime. This alone is very curious, considering that if he had so many speeches to make and laws to inform the people of, why wouldn't he have written them down for future generations to be sure that they wouldn't be altered over the years?

Beckford believes that the gospels are not in any way eye-witness accounts and that we can't take the stories of such things as the miracles performed by Jesus as being literal. Wouldn't it be more useful to take such stories symbolically, examining the morals of them rather than believing that they are true accounts even though they would have no evidence to back them up? We mustn't blindly believe such stories to be true when there are four distinctive gospels, but we can use them for guidance as long as they are morally acceptable. And by this, I mean even used by non-believers. It is not necessary to think that the stories come through a god. They can be universally agreed upon as principles by which we should act. They can form the beginning of a new progressive way of thinking and living.

Now, going back to the history and development of religions, let's address polytheistic religions. In what are now known as the continents of America, there were some well-known civilizations that flourished there for thousands of years. The Mayans, the Incas and the Aztecs, to name but a few of the most famous all ended quite abruptly. The Mayans were the first of these civilizations to collapse and whereas it is still a theory as to why, the evidence points to this - being a civilization that worshipped gods and used sacrificial rituals to appease them in the hope that their crops would always succeed, eventually, they learned that it never worked. Cities that had been constructed to be agriculturally self-supporting failed when the people lost faith in the gods. Cities were left abandoned with no evidence of war, conquest, natural disaster or fire, but simply because they realised that there were no gods who were ensuring that they could grow enough food to survive. It didn't matter how bloody or violent their sacrifices were or how many humans were used for one sacrifice, the droughts continued and the belief system fell apart. The people worked out over time that there was no supreme being that was always taking care of them. We can't be sure of what they then believed as so few written records survived and those that did tend to tell stories of rituals and gods and other practices but not why the people abandoned the cities.

The Aztecs and the Incas were civilizations that succeeded the Mayans up into the 16th century. Even though these two groups suffered similar crop failures and abandonments of cities, they generally moved to another site and started building again with the belief that the previous one was exhausted. The reason for their demise was the invasion of the Spanish conquistadors around the 1520s. Among other things, the Spanish brought with them their religion, with which they had every intention of putting into place over the traditional beliefs. Christianity in place of the culturally relevant religions was not proposed as an option. It was dictated that it would be practised. Fortunately for us now, the westerners had more of a reputation of keeping written records of events and we know that the natives had been tortured and killed for refusing to take on Christianity, instead continuing to follow their own beliefs. Such punishments that went along with the physical abuse was to burn all the written works of the Incas and Aztecs so that they had no record of their religious beliefs and thus, they have mostly been lost in history.

We can, of course, never know what would have been the fate of the Aztecs and Incas if the Spanish Christians had never invaded and dictated their beliefs to the natives but judging by what happened to the Mayan culture, they may have come to a similar end.

The fate of the Mayans is especially interesting as it showed us what happens to religions that are untarnished by rival religions or rival groups of people. They simply lost faith. They learned from experience that there were evidently no gods controlling their destiny. They were insightful enough to work out that the reason for their crop failures were not supernatural. They may not have been able to understand it in the scientific way that we do today but it demonstrates that people's knowledge and understanding evolves at a fairly rapid rate, compared to physical evolution, and that with enough evidence and enough reason to doubt beliefs when they can't be supported, it is possible to realise that traditional practices can be wrong and that there are reasons to change how we think. As we learn more, we have to be flexible enough to change our beliefs and move on. The sun does not go around the Earth. People used to suppose that because that's how it appears but since it has been proven by science without any shadow of a doubt, we have accepted it and moved on. There are not four corners of the earth as was believed in ancient times. Taking further steps in human exploration have shown that the belief that probably everyone had in general, only as recently as 800 years ago, was completely wrong. It has been proven that people didn't just get planted onto the Earth at a given point just because they took a while before they had the capacity to invent writing. In fact, millions of years of life went on long before we even started to walk upright. Subsequently, this proves that the Bible was written by a number of people who were trying to fathom it all out. In fact they had a good go considering the limitations of their knowledge.

One important thing that they realised they could do with it was to gain power. By convincing people that their words were actually God's words, the people could be made to fear doing what was warned against in the Bible and the Torah as well as later on in the Qur'an. Societies could be controlled much more effectively if they feared God's wrath. People could be oppressed and abused by those who held office and spoke 'God's word'.

This still happens very frequently today. People who are in some way representatives of God, selected either by voting, by their education or by self-appointment, claim to be delivering God's words. This happens probably most notably in the USA in major sects of Christianity where they comment on current affairs saying that something like Hurricane Katrina happened because it's God's way of punishing certain groups of people that they don't like. Quite obviously this event is not in the Bible so the question is where do they get this information from? At what point did God make it known that the hurricane happened for this reason? To claim to be the spokesperson for God has to be seen as extremely sinful, especially by the followers of that very religion or sect. Surely it is the equivalent of altering the words of the Bible which in its final paragraph (Revelation 22:18) is strongly warned against:

"I, John, solemnly warn everyone who hears the prophetic words of this book: if anyone adds anything to them, God will add to his punishment the plagues described in this book."

So by assuming this to be the Truth, claiming that God is punishing us with a natural catastrophe (that can be explained entirely through science) is adding to God's words and committing a sin against their own religion.

Paine also points out that "Revelation when applied to religion, means something communicated immediately from God to man." (AOR; p.23) It is only a revelation to the first person told. As soon as that person tells another, it is no longer a revelation, but instead, hearsay. "it cannot be incumbent on me to believe it in the same manner, for it was not a revelation made to 'me', and I have only his word for it that it was made to 'him'." (p.24)

Christmas Humphreys, in "Exploring Buddhism", uses the teachings of Buddha to warn in a similar way:

"Among those who claim to be masters are, unfortunately frauds of all degrees, from self-deluded men who, on the strength of a small experience truly believe themselves to be enlightened and teach accordingly, to evil men who consciously attempt to gain power over their fellows to their own advantage."

These are wise words indeed and should be taken on by the general public to be wary of those who vociferously claim to be able to show you the way to salvation (which, if it is exclaimed loud enough will also usually demand that you hand over your money).

Never trust anyone who says that you will be saved if you give them your money and/ or possessions.

In fact, to preach in such ways would be illegal under a Hypothetical Government. Religion is not to be funded by the state. The government cannot have any authority over what its citizens should or shouldn't believe as this is also against human rights. In order to maintain or build religious buildings of any kind, the followers must raise their own money to do so and they are not allowed to secretly divert any funds from any external sources as this would be an example of corruption and the funds would be returned to any source which has not given its written permission to use the money for such purposes.

People can be asked to donate but not in any forceful way. If anyone suspects a religious group to be doing this, they would be asked to contact the authorities so that it can be investigated. It is extremely important to put limits on religion so that immoral practice is strictly forbidden in all areas.

An admission fee to enter a religious building is acceptable by law to aid the maintenance of it but the amount to be paid has to be the same for every religious building in the country and should be a small fee. This admission fee can only be applied when people are to attend a service. These attendees can pay more than the nominal fee if they wish but are not required to pay above the standard price. Visitors would not be charged to enter any building at any time but they would be free to offer donations to aid the maintenance. However, it is to be made clear that no visitor would have any obligation to donate.

People have the moral right to follow a religion and to practise it. There is no state religion as this would undoubtedly cause conflicts with other religions. Every religion has the same rights as the others.

Marx and Engels in The Communist Manifesto were wrong, on a moral level, to propose that religion should be abolished. Taking away people's freedoms in this way cannot be done. If some people believe in a religion that is not going to cause harm to others or influence others to believe in it, then it would be acceptable. If however, there are hidden agendas like the objective of converting as many people as possible to it, this would not be a legal practice, either in the country or with people who wish to travel abroad for this very reason. If you would not like someone to try to make you change your religion, don't do it to anybody else.

No religion has the power of being able to influence any law. There cannot be any dominant religion, irrespective of how many people follow any specific one. All laws are based on morality with respect to contemporary times. As virtually every religion is steeped in history, the issues contained in each holy book are not always relevant to modern society, which has to be adaptable at all times to reflect the needs of the people.

No forms of promotion or advertising are allowed for religions. There can be no public displays to attempt to convert more people as this is effectively a form of propaganda. People must grow up in a society to be open-minded about religion and to be free to choose whether they wish to follow one or not.

Religious symbols, dress or jewellery would be permitted in society. If they are inappropriate for safety reasons, a compromise must be made where the clothes are changed in a mutually agreed way by both parties concerned. Religious jewellery is also not permitted if, in a particular scenario, it has the potential to cause injury to the wearer or other persons. In this case, the jewellery must be removed for the duration of the activity which could cause risk to personal safety. A symbolic knife (as used in Sikhism) is also permitted with the condition that it is blunt and is worn with no intention of being used. Any misuse would result in penalisation depending on the method of misuse.

People are not allowed to publicly criticise any religion, be it their own or one that they don't follow. Every established religion has its foundations and justifications for being in existence. To criticise a religion is against human rights and is therefore unacceptable in a moral society as is the attempt of any religious groups to attempt to convert any other member of the public to its religion.

All religions have this limitation. They are not allowed to promote their religion upon anyone else or proclaim that their religion is better or any more correct than another or more correct than non-belief. To attempt to convert another person and alter their beliefs, non-beliefs or ways of thinking is also against human rights.

This is not to say that there can't be debates about religious practices or past events. The important point to make is that the choice of words used is of paramount importance.

A meeting to slander a religion and treat it like it is disgusting and evil is only going to provoke argument and probably violence, as is a meeting to claim how unequivocally fantastic a religion is. There are innumerable cases in history of this happening and it is a stubborn and childish fight for superiority with no evidence to prove unequivocally that any view is right. But to have a democratic debate to seriously question specific points is acceptable. We need to iron out the creases that leave religions open to interpretation. We need to adapt our thoughts so that there can be as universal an agreement as possible. Even if John, in Revelations, warned against altering the words of the Bible, there have been many variations of the Bible in the last century to make it more accessible to children and other groups and fortunately, no plagues have been sent that can be confirmed as results of rewriting the holy book.

However, Paine argues that "The best imagined history that could have been made, at the distance of two or three hundred years after the time could not have passed for an original under the name of the real writer; the only chance of success lay in forgery; for the church wanted pretence for its new doctrine, and truth and talents were out of the question." (AOR, p.174)

The book, The Age of Reason, is an extraordinarily persuasive piece of writing and I would recommend it as one of the most important books a person could ever read. It is difficult to argue against it, seeing as the only reference he used was the Bible itself. He challenged people to argue against his words and in a letter in the appendix stated "As I have now given you my reasons for believing that the Bible is not the word of God, that it is a falsehood, I have a right to ask you your reasons for believing the contrary; but I know you can give me none, except that 'you were educated to believe the

Bible' ... You believe in the Bible from the accident of birth, and the Turks believe in the Koran from the same accident, and each calls the other 'infidel'." (p.199)

Even though Paine very convincingly shows the Bible to be a work of falsehood, he pointed out early in the book that he believed in God and in Jesus, just not in the words of the Bible.

Religious Education

Any person must be free to choose a religion of their own accord but in terms of education about religion, which must be standard in schools from primary age to increase awareness, they are encouraged to contemplate every other major or culturally relevant religion before they decide to choose one. This means that children shouldn't be classed as belonging to any religious denomination until they are old enough to choose for themselves. This, of course, would mean a huge change in religious practice so why should this happen?

As Richard Dawkins has stated, it would be an outrage to talk about a young child as being Communist, Conservative, Republican or following any political group. They simply cannot comprehend such ideologies. The same is true of religion. Children of up to around ten or twelve years are not mentally developed enough to understand what it all means. I have heard primary school children say that they are Catholic, Evangelist, etc. with absolutely no certainty or understanding of what it means.

Why should children learn about religion if there is no state religion or they are not allowed to be a member of one? The simple answer is awareness. This is a major failure of society today that people are more than willing to criticise religions when their knowledge of them is either very limited or practically non-existent.

We get most of our information about religious tensions and wars from the mass media. However, we have to remember that they do not provide us with the facts, or at least not with most of them. Currently, the non-Muslim part of the world has a general feeling that Islam is evil because of the actions of the Taliban and Al-Qaeda. But these two groups are certainly not representative of Islam in a general sense. This is, however, all we get to hear about on the news and the ignorance of the religion in its pure sense leads to the general public suddenly disliking Muslims who live in their community when they previously might not have even acknowledged them as they had no reason to stand opposed to them. Not that in the light of terrorist attacks do they have a right or a reason to dislike Muslims in general as they would be able to point out clearly that these terrorist groups do not represent what they believe and practise. Non-fundamentalist Muslims in Pakistan and Afghanistan, for example, despise the actions of the Taliban and Al-Qaeda. This is the lack of awareness that seriously needs to be improved on a massive scale.

So in the school there would be no practised religions. The child who is sent to a religious school at a young age is not of a developmental stage to be able to decide if they want to follow a school's religion or not, or the religion that their family follows.

Instead children should be taught about the major religions of the world, being; (forms of) Christianity, Judaism, Hinduism, Buddhism and Islam or also those which are prevalent in the society in which they live. They are to be educated to accept that all these religions are as valid as the others and teachers or any other member of staff cannot encourage students to follow a particular one. Children will, for instance, learn about such aspects as the origins and developments of these religions, the beliefs of the followers, religious ceremonies, festivals and their reasons for them. They will be encouraged to discuss the merits and the failings that they perceive but must at all times be taught that speaking badly about a religion or any person that follows it is not appropriate or socially acceptable. Children will be taught that they must be knowledgeable enough about the various religions before they decide to follow one, if they wish to. It is not recommended for anyone under the age of 10 to actively follow a religion. It could be considered that children still in primary school should not be classed as religious at all but they are able to make their own choices when they are in the secondary school (or type of schooling from the age of around 11 or 12). It is for the reasons of a large-scale societal awareness and moral acceptance of all religions that they are to be taught equally in every school to every child.

Religious families do not have the right to demand that their children follow the same religion as them. They must be aware that their own children have the same human rights as they do and they must be given the freedom to choose or not choose to take up any religious practices or beliefs. Those parents who were brought up from a young age as followers of the religion of their parents must realise that they didn't make their own choice but they think it is right only because it was imposed upon them at a very young age. Hence, their entire lives were shaped by beliefs that they weren't given the chance to consider for themselves. Any child from a religious family who is brought up in this way is having their rights of freedom of choice removed from them simply because of the beliefs of the people around them.

Should a child wish to follow a religion once they have learned about it, they have exactly the same human rights as any adult to do so. If they choose to follow a religion that one or both of their parents does not, the parents do not have the right to have a say in their choice and are legally not allowed to try to dissuade them or convert them so that they will follow the religion that the parents or family wish them to follow. The parents or other family members are obliged to accept their children's decisions and, if they wish to follow a different religion, live with their different beliefs in a moral way so as to keep any conflicts of opinion to a minimum. This can be monitored by allowing the children to talk confidentially to advisors who, with training in dealing with this issue, can peacefully meet with the parents to try to get them to accept their own children's rights.

This brings us to the question of how valid are religions? If we are brought up to know about them before we choose to follow one or not, our society would be very different. For example, a televised debate took place in Britain in October 2009. It showed how awareness and contemplation about various points are important to people when formulating their own conclusions. It was organised by Intelligence Squared and broadcast by the BBC. First of all, before the debate took place, the audience of 2164 people were asked to vote on the motion "The Catholic church is a force for good in the world." The initial votes were 31% for Yes, 51% for No and 18% were undecided.

Then, the debate took place and to summarise, I will use the words from the Intelligence Squared website:

Arguing in favour of the motion were Archbishop John Onaiyekan and the Rt Hon. Ann Widdecombe MP.

Archbishop Onaiyekan begins by insisting that if the Catholic Church were not a force for good, he would not have devoted his entire life to serving it. He says that the hierarchy of the Catholic Church exists because of its 1.6 billion members worldwide, rather than in spite of them. He points not only to the spiritual assistance that his Church provides, but also to the tangible aid that is given internationally through Catholic projects. Finally, he admits that Catholics are not infallible, but are by necessity sinners trying to improve themselves through their faith.

Ann Widdecombe suggests that in trawling all the way back to the Crusades to find something to blame the Catholic Church for, Christopher Hitchens merely demonstrates how flimsy his argument really is. Why would the Pope have hidden 3,000 Jews in his summer palace during the Second World War if the Catholic Church was an anti-Semitic organisation? Admittedly, the New Testament does blame a Jew for the death of Christ; but it also blames a Roman, Pontius Pilate. Are we to infer then that Catholicism is anti-Italian as well as anti-Semitic? Widdecombe insists that the actions of the Catholic Church in the past should be judged with a degree of historical relativism; they were not the only people to murder and torture those deemed guilty of wrongdoing. She entreats us to imagine a world without the benefits of the Catholic Church, which provides hope, education and medical relief all over the globe.

Arguing against the motion were Christopher Hitchens and Stephen Fry.

Christopher Hitchens asserts that any argument trying to identify the merits of the Catholic Church must begin with a long list of sincere apologies for its past crimes, including but not limited to: the Crusades; the Spanish inquisition; the persecution of Jews and the forced conversion of peoples to Catholicism, especially in South America. He illustrates the vacuity of recent Catholic apologies by drawing on the case of Cardinal Bernard Law – shamed out of office in the US for his part in covering up the institutionalised sexual abuse of children – whose punishment from the Vatican was to be appointed a supreme vicar in Rome, and who was among those assembled in the 2005 Papal Conclave to choose the next Pope. Hitchens concludes by reminding the Archbishop that his own Church has been responsible for the death of millions of his African brothers and sisters, citing the Church's disastrous stance on Aids prevention, as well as the ongoing trials in Rwanda in which Catholic priests stand accused of inciting massacre during the 1994 genocide.

Stephen Fry concedes that his opposition to the motion is a deeply personal and emotional one. He criticises the Catholic Church not only for the horrors it has perpetrated in the past, but also for its ideology, and for its sinister temerity to preach that there is no salvation outside of the Church. With two words he refutes Anne Widdecombe's suggestion that the Catholic Church does not have the powers of a nation state: "The Vatican". As a homosexual, Fry reflects how bizarre it is to be accused of being "immoral" and "a pervert" by an institution that has persistently hushed up the rape and abuse of children under its care, and whose leading members, abstentious nuns and priests, all share an attitude towards sex that is utterly unnatural and dysfunctional. He concludes by questioning whether Jesus, as a humble Jewish carpenter, would have approved of all the pomp and excess of the Catholic Church, and whether he would even have been accepted by such an arrogant organisation.[2]

An interesting debate with certainly a lot for the audience to consider. It can be seen online on the Intelligence Squared website, the current address of which is given in the reference section.

In the light of this debate, the audience were asked to vote again on the same motion. Before the debate, 18% or 384 people were undecided which is quite a high number but afterwards, the uncertain ones were reduced to 1.6% or 34 people. Those who voted Yes went from 31% to 12.4% or from 678 people to 268. Those who voted that the Catholic church was not a force for good in the world went from 51% to 86% or from 1102 people to 1862.

We can take this as a significant event where by raising awareness of both past and present actions of religions people's opinions can change dramatically. It also shows us the status of this particular religion in the modern world when considered democratically.

Christopher Hitchins, in his book God Is Not Great[7], demonstrates that he has a broad knowledge of the history of many religions and the depth of his understanding is impressive. He highlights important issues, such as the likelihood that religion is man-made. Given the fact that there are so many sects of religions (more than 34,000 variants of Christianity, for example, according to the World Christian Encyclopaedia), people interpret and tailor them according to their own opinions. This concept alone has caused so many deaths all over the world due to the fact that religious sects argue against each other to stubbornly prove that each of them are right and their opponents are wrong. Would God really want 34,000 variations of his teachings? Or is it really that people have adapted the already many times adapted words to suit their own needs and desires?

In the gospel according to Matthew, chapter 5: The Sermon on the Mount, the authenticity of the Bible comes into question. Jesus said "You have heard that it was said 'An eye for an eye, and a tooth for a tooth.' But now I tell you: do not take revenge on someone who wrongs you." (38-39) "You have heard that it was said, 'Love your friends, hate your enemies.' But now I tell you: love your enemies and pray for those who persecute you..." (43-44) The words " You have heard that it was said" can only refer to the apparent words of God in the Old Testament, and therefore Jesus is refuting those words as though, considering Jesus is believed to be God incarnate, he is saying that he has changed his mind and he was wrong to say otherwise previously. This leads to contradictory books in the same Bible, apparently delivered by the same divine being.

Hitchins brings up the question that we don't need to follow a religion to behave morally. Christians have argued the opposite to be the case, claiming that if we don't believe we are acting so as to achieve salvation after death, then we would resort to anarchic, immoral hedonism. I have known many people who are atheists but in no way stand out as being less civilised than religious believers. To be moral, one does not need to have a religious background. We do need to have a background where we can make moral decisions that guide us to live our lives peacefully and productively but this can be found through philosophy without the need to look for a god to decide if we are doing things right or not. Often, religions use the method of fear to attempt to enforce certain behaviours. Children can be brought up with the belief that Hell is real and is a place where they will go if they sin or reject God. It is very easy to get children to believe in many things that aren't necessarily real, like Santa Claus. Young minds are easily malleable but this definitely doesn't mean that they should be exploited because of this reason. In fact, the amount of fear that some religious parents instil into their children could be argued as being not just immoral but purely evil.

When questioning the validity of the concept of Hell, as well as Heaven, we need to know of the evidence that they exist. In the physical world, science is unable to prove that these places exist or not. Religious believers will affirm that they exist on a spiritual level and cannot be located with scientific equipment. In that case, how do 'they' know that Heaven and Hell exist? Just because it says so in the holy books doesn't mean it's true. We have already looked at the controversy that surrounds the claim that Moses wrote the first five books, including the account of his own death. Religious texts need to be examined closely to decide if they really are as authentic as the claims suggest. It is very risky to take words at face value and in the modern world, where more notions are questioned and more facts are established through scientific study, we sometimes have no option but to change our beliefs when we see proof of something that we otherwise thought to be false or just didn't know about.

There are religious believers who often retort that non-believers can't prove that God doesn't exist just as they can't prove that it does. However, this goes entirely against the reasoning process. If we said that we can't prove that something doesn't exist, it won't mean that it must, otherwise we would believe in dragons, fairies and Father

Christmas just because someone said they exist. It is not the way to resolve doubts and should never be the way to develop our knowledge of the world. To be sure that something is true, we must be able to prove it. If we can't, we have to reject it.

Both Richard Dawkins and Christopher Hitchins give in-depth analyses of the histories and the influence of religions and whereas they definitely have an agenda from the outset that God does not exist and that religions have been more harmful than good, their amount of research is of great importance to consider. Even if you are a believer, I feel that it is important to read their books The God Delusion and God Is Not Great, respectively. For those who are devout believers, approach these books with an open mind. Unfortunately, at times, both of these authors can be too aggressive in parts and their views are not always empathic enough to gently convince people that they ought to weigh up the pros and cons of their religions. But the amount of historical evidence they provide is overwhelming and they do not approach the subject with the aim to irritate believers. I do feel that, at times, their words should have have been chosen a little more carefully but their arguments are certainly thought provoking and cannot be rejected as unverifiable rubbish in any way.

However, to continue the analysis of how valid religions are, let us look at the case of Jesus Christ and the story of his life.

In The New Testament, Matthew tells the story of Jesus' birth, in a short section which takes up less than a page in the Good News Bible, telling that "some men who studied the stars came from the East to Jerusalem and asked "Where is the baby born to be the king of the Jews? We saw his star when it came up in the east, and we have come to worship him." (Matthew 2:1-2). King Herod hears of the birth and sends people to find Jesus by seeing "the same star they had seen in the east." (2:9-10) The kings go with their gifts but there is no mention of shepherds.

Mark makes no reference to his birth but begins his story from when Jesus was already a man, performing miracles and healing the sick.

Luke tells a similar story to Matthew, although no star is mentioned; instead an angel appears to the shepherds and tells them "This very day in David's town your saviour was born – Christ the Lord! And this is what will prove it to you: you will find a baby wrapped in strips of cloth and lying in a manger." (Luke 2:11-12) So in this instance, there is a different way that people find out about Jesus; this time those people being shepherds and not King Herod, who is not mentioned.

In John, there is no biographical mention of Jesus until the line "John was standing there again with two of his disciples, when he saw Jesus walking by. "There is the lamb of God!" he said." (1:35-36) Therefore, Jesus was already an adult at the beginning of John's account.

So varying accounts of the birth of Jesus by two of the gospel writers and the other don't make any mention of it at all. It leaves me thinking that if Jesus was the most important person to have ever lived, why is it that we don't even know when he was born? The Roman calendar was in place in 46 BC and the years of births of many people such as Egyptian Pharaohs, Greek philosophers and many other historical figures who were born prior to Jesus have been well estimated or recorded. For example, Plato is recorded as being born in either 428 or 427 BC: quite a long time before Jesus but only with a variation of 1 year in his estimated year of birth. Therefore, why is it still unknown when Jesus was born? Scholars have estimated that he was born between 7 and 2 BC – that is, up to 7 years before himself.

Going back to the story of the star that guided people to Jesus on different days, Peter Joseph of The Zeitgeist Movement examines stories of gods and creators through history Before the Common Era (BCE). He notes that Horus, the Sun God of Egypt was born on what is now classified as the 25th of December to a virgin, as was Attis of Phyrigia.

Krishna, of India, born of the virgin Devaki with a star in the east signalling his coming, performed miracles with his disciples, and upon his death was resurrected.

Dionysus of Greece, born of a virgin on December 25th, was a travelling teacher who performed miracles such as turning water into wine.

Mithra, of Persia, born of a virgin on December 25th, had 12 disciples and performed miracles, and upon his death was buried for 3 days and thus resurrected. He was also referred to as "The Truth," "The Light," and many other things.

Hitchins mentions other virgin births: Mercury, born of the virgin Maia, Romulus to Rhea Sylvia, although he refers to "the god Buddha", which is factually incorrect as Buddha was never thought of as a god but a mortal who was born into a royal family (even though the story is that it was a virgin birth).

So it appears that there was a trend of mythological stories of virgin births happening on December the 25th. Scholars have not been able to confirm that this is when Jesus was actually born, so why is this date so important?

Peter Joseph sums it up well:

The star in the east is Sirius, the brightest star in the night sky, which, on December 24th, aligns with the 3 brightest stars in Orion's Belt. These 3 bright stars are called today what they were called in ancient times: The Three Kings. The Three Kings and the brightest star, Sirius, all point to the place of the sunrise on December 25th. This is why the Three Kings "follow" the star in the east, in order to locate the sunrise -- the birth of the sun.

The Virgin Mary is the constellation Virgo, also known as Virgo the Virgin. Virgo in Latin means virgin. The ancient glyph for Virgo is the altered "m". This is why Mary along with other virgin mothers, such as Adonis's mother Myrrha, or Buddha's mother Maya begin with an M (and also have similar sounding names). Virgo is also referred to as the House of Bread and the representation of Virgo is a virgin holding a sheaf of wheat. This House of Bread and its symbol of wheat represents August and September, the time of harvest. In turn, Bethlehem, in fact, literally translates to "house of bread". Bethlehem is thus a reference to the constellation Virgo, a place in the sky, not on Earth."[3]

Paine also referred to the similarities of stories in the Bible with older fables, for example when Satan made war against God, which is similar to the ancient myth of Jupiter and the race of evil Giants. "The Almighty,(who) defeated him and confined him afterwards, not under a mountain, but in a pit. It is easy to see that the first fable suggested the idea of the second; for the fable of Jupiter and the Giants was told many hundred years before that of Satan." (AOR, p.28-9)

Additionally, the death and resurrection of Jesus is noted as Easter Sunday, which is the first Sunday after the first full moon on or after the March equinox. This period is symbolised as the advent of new life, which coincides with the Spring equinox and is dated as happening on the 21st of March. It also refers to the dawning of new life in the animal kingdom in the northern hemisphere. Thus, there appears to be a coming together of religious stories and natural cycles, which could be seen as quite a convenient way of illustrating the story of the rebirth of Jesus. This time was deliberately chosen to symbolise the resurrection of Jesus as the time when it was supposed to have happened is also unknown but it gives a feeling that the story was created to fit to events already in existence.

The amount of historical connections between these stories is curious and doesn't seem to be merely coincidental considering that there are so many that follow the same formula. As Matthew wrote "We saw his star when it came up in the east" which seems to indicate that it was indeed something connected with astrology as it was said that this star, Sirius, was seen again (i.e. the next night). The four gospels have been dated by scholars to have been written only, at the earliest, 3 decades after the death of Jesus (Matthew's c.65-70 AD), and the names of the writers didn't become established until 180 AD. At a time when the only way of recording events was by hand, there seems to have been no-one who wrote about Jesus during his lifetime, not even by the Romans whose empire had spread to the middle east decades before Jesus and were known to keep written records of people and events.

As I have already said, I don't intend to try to tell you what to believe but this is intriguing evidence (or a lack of) and it is recommended that you investigate it and make your own conclusions.

From this, we need to have doubts about religions when they claim to be the Truth, that is The Word of God, to investigate whether they really are worth their status. Religions and church leaders have had an enormous impact on people's lives, especially in the early centuries AD where they were the governors of nations and empires and formed laws based on the religious texts.

It is understandable that this kind of perspective would be treated with condemnation by religious followers. After believing in these texts for possibly all their lives, they don't want to be told that it is all wrong and they were believing in something that was created by humans for the purposes of power. But faith is a dangerous thing and if we believed everything that people in power told us without any evidence for it being true, we would be worse off than we are now, which is bad enough already.

In Biblical times, science was in a very embryonic state. There was little evidence to be able to explain various phenomena anyway. But now, we are at a stage where we can prove theories like that the Earth orbits the sun, the sun is just one of many billions of stars, why earthquakes, hurricanes and tsunamis happen without the need for bringing a sentient being into the explanation. Without science, we wouldn't have cures for so many diseases and we wouldn't be able to understand our bodies as much as we do.

But of course, science isn't everything. We need to have ideas about how we are going to live our lives; guides to enable us to interact more productively and morally. And again, the concept of God is not actually necessary for this. If someone helped you when you fell over and broke your leg, you would have respect for them and feel you owed them something. It is unlikely that you would instead go and find the person who helped you and, because you didn't believe in God, wouldn't think twice about robbing them and torturing them. We can see from the animal kingdom that we instinctively look after each other if there is no reason to think that one of the members of the group is dangerous to our well-being. If it wasn't like this, there would probably be no end to the fighting and killing of all species, irrespective of whether they were members of their own groups.

With the possibility that some people may examine their religion and decide that maybe they don't think that it is what it is said to be and instead reject it, what would we turn to instead?

Some people don't like the idea of not being able to turn to God and pray for salvation, an end to their troubles or strength to succeed in some aspect of their lives. There is a comfort in that and sometimes, even if someone is not a strong religious believer who regularly attends church, they may still think that, in their hour of need, it is reassuring to turn to God. This whole principle is understandable because we do feel that we need someone or something else to be there for us. Unfortunately, there is no evidence to say that when one asks for God's help, there is ever an answer. Even if it feels comforting to think we have spoken with God and it has given us inner strength, it would be better to go through life following principles that we can rely on because we have evidence for believing in them. If the truth be said, there has never been any incontrovertible evidence that God exists. There have been many claims of hearing his word or of holy symbols appearing in physical media but this is wish-fulfilment and superstition that cannot be proven in any way. For example, people claim to have seen the face of Jesus in various things but there is no reference to Jesus' appearance in the Bible, and the idea that he had long hair and a beard is a cultural creation, handed down and enforced by so many religious paintings over the millennia. Considering that none of the gospel writers knew or even saw Jesus, we have no undisputed record of how he looked. Therefore, the apparent face of Jesus is nothing more than wish-fulfilment. This phenomenon is known as pareidolia which, as Carl Sagan, the astronomer and astrophysicist hypothesized is an inbuilt survival technique where people are "hard-wired" to identify the human face. This is evident when we think we see faces in clouds, trees and other objects. Of course they aren't but we can't help to perceive them.

This difficulty with letting go of superstitions is something to address. There is nothing about the number 13 that brings bad luck but probably millions of people really think it does. Many people have the superstition that they must touch wood when they say that something bad has never happened to them. It doesn't mean that it is necessary to do it. Similarly, to think that some unexpected event that happens is a sign of God doesn't mean it is true. We try to use reasoning to explain such things but this is only our naïvety which gives us a comfort zone of thinking we understand things that happen by coincidence.

So where do we go from here? This is the big question. We need to offer an alternative path for life that doesn't just give us something that is all that we have if we decide to turn from religion. It needs to be something that is essentially a liberation and an enlightenment to take us to a higher level of being. There are two ways to look at this.

Firstly, those people who want to retain their religious beliefs still make up many diverse groups. These groups tread through life with the firm belief that there way is the right way and that other religions are wrong. This is where awareness and education come in. In all religions, there are common principles. These need to be identified so that there can be reconciliation between opposing groups. No progress can be made if we only look for differences between people. It is fundamental that we search for and celebrate the similarities and question the differences with the aim of rejecting those which lead to conflict. Religion has been the biggest cause of war and killing within our species. If God exists, would he really want us to live in this way? Or would he want people to achieve common ground and live harmoniously, following the same positive and productive principles? A huge amount of research and cross-referencing between the holy books would need to be undertaken so that a consensual text can be formed and that people can retain their religious beliefs but not be in disagreement with people who label themselves differently.

This notion has been addressed by the Bahá'í Faith, founded in the 19th century. This is a monotheistic religion which has around 5 or 6 million followers worldwide, mostly based in former Persia. In the Bahá'í Faith, religious history is seen to have evolved through a series of divine messengers, each of whom established a religion that was suited to the needs of the time and the capacity of the people. These messengers have included Abraham, Buddha, Jesus, Muhammad and others, and most recently Bahá'u'lláh.[4]

A fundamental principle to the followers (Bahá'ís) is the progression of the rules by which one should live their lives, which as societies changed, needed a new prophet to update the teachings.

It is a very forward thinking and moral religion that has sought to reconcile the differences between religious believers. For instance, one of its views is that God and the universe have always existed, without a beginning or an end. This is important in bridging the gap between religion and science, which is one of its aims.

Shoghi Effendi, the appointed head of the religion from 1921 to 1957, summarised the faith's ideals in this way:

The independent search after truth, unfettered by superstition or tradition; the oneness of the entire human race, the pivotal principle and fundamental doctrine of the Faith; the basic unity of all religions; the condemnation of all forms of prejudice, whether religious, racial, class or national; the harmony which must exist between religion and science; the equality of men and women, the two wings on which the bird of humankind is able to soar; the introduction of compulsory education; the adoption of a universal auxiliary language; the abolition of the extremes of wealth and poverty; the institution of a world tribunal for the adjudication of disputes between nations; the exaltation of work, performed in the spirit of service, to the rank of worship; the glorification of justice as the ruling principle in human society, and of religion as a bulwark for the protection of all peoples and nations; and the establishment of a permanent and universal peace as the supreme goal of all mankind—these stand out as the essential elements [which Bahá'u'lláh proclaimed].[5]

So you see, it would be nothing more than prejudiced if a moral government were to view religion negatively. The principles quoted above are so similar to the principles that should also be emphasised by non-believers that they show there is no good reason as to why one side should condemn the other side as, apart from the difference of believing in a divine being, the morals are and should be the same. It is not about our differences; they will not bring us together harmoniously. It is about our common goals. What one person decides to adopt as their truth is just that – their truth.

The Bahá'í faith is committed to world peace and it has never been involved in a holy war. Unfortunately, however, as the religion formed in Persia (what is now Iran), it has had fierce opposition from the Shi'a Muslims who have persecuted and executed members of the faith as they believe that Islam is the perfect and final religion which cannot be superseded in any way. Therefore, Bahá'í Faith is seen as a threat and a rejection of Islam and has been outlawed as a religion.

Considering that the Bahá'í Faith is purely peaceful, this persecution is a sad reflection of how well-established religions can be so aggressively protective of their own faith, even when the other religion has no intentions of causing any kind of conflict between the two. If we can't live in peace with varying religious groups, there will be no adequate evolution of humanity.

If we, or some of us, choose to look for a way of life that doesn't rely on the belief in a god or gods, it needs to be one that uses the same positive principles as the religions (of which there are many) but which can be used to live in harmony with those who still choose to believe in a deity.

The stories from the Bible and other religious texts can be viewed as a starting point for a new philosophical text. The teachings of Jesus, if their 'divinity' is removed can be adapted so that they are more like the Philosophies of Matthew, Mark, Luke, John and the Apostle Paul. Such stories as 'The Sermon On The Mount' (Matthew, 5) are an excellent example of how to view life and could be edited thus:

"Happy are those who know they are spiritually poor;
Happy are those who are humble;
Happy are those who are merciful to others;
Happy are the pure in heart;
Happy are those who work for peace."

Instead of concluding with "the Kingdom of heaven belongs to them!", it could be rephrased as "The satisfaction of a clear conscience belongs to them!"

Or the 'Love for Enemies' chapter (Matthew, 5:43-47) could be reworked as:

"You have heard that it was said 'Love your friends, hate your enemies.' But instead, love your enemies and give empathy to those who persecute you so that you may become respected and admired by others. The sun shines on bad and good people alike, and the rain falls on those who do good and evil. Why should you feel peace if you love only the people who love you?"

One which applies to current materialistic society also offers a great deal of insight. Based on 'God and Possessions', (Matthew 6:25-34):

"Don't be worried about the food and drink you need in order to stay alive, or about clothes for your body. After all, isn't life worth more than food? And isn't the body worth more than clothes? Look at the birds: they do not sow seeds, gather a harvest and put it in barns; yet the world takes care of them! Can any of you live a bit longer by worrying about it?

And why worry about clothes? Look how the wild flowers grow: they do not work or make clothes for themselves. But I tell you that not even King Solomon with all his wealth had clothes as beautiful as one of these flowers. It is the Earth that clothes the wild grass. Accept yourself for how you are, you are already beautiful!

Instead, be concerned above everything else with the pursuit of happiness and with what it requires of you, and all these other things will come with it. So do not worry about tomorrow; it will have enough worries of its own. There is no need to add to the troubles each day brings. Marvel at what is already here and how it is of benefit to all of us alike. Do not concern yourself with possessions. Concern yourself with what really matters, that being the oneness of us all."

There are countless other teachings that can be universally accepted without needing the crutch of them being seen as coming from God or Jesus. Many of them are beautiful philosophies by themselves.

The concept of a deity, whether we agree it is humanly-constructed or not, must be explored to find out the reason for its manifestation.

God is said to be invisible and omnipresent. That implies that He is everywhere - in every atom of our bodies, in every part of any other creature, plant, rock or substance on the planet (and beyond). In this case, God is everything and everything is God. This is the same as simply saying everything is everything, or just that Everything Is. It is also a metaphor for saying that everything is intertwined and interdependent. Everything on this planet all comes from the same life source, that is the Earth. It is unnecessary to think of it as coming from God but instead simply coming from itself. The Earth is one big self-reproducing organism which uses parts of itself to regenerate life. There is very little outside interference from matter outside of the limits of the atmosphere (apart from the sun's energy), meaning that the amount of base material to create life is effectively constant. This shows the oneness of life on this planet and the scientific basis of creation of life from what is already here. Everything doesn't have to be seen as happening because God wills it to. Everything happens because it has the potential and capacity to happen, and causes and effects (or karma) is what makes things happen in the ways that they do. We interact with the world, with people, and these interactions are the causes and effects of what results from the interactions. There is no need to think of it as a God, it is simply Life.

When Gandhi was asked if he thought of God as a spiritual personality or a force which rules over the world, he replied "God is not a person, God is an eternal principle." Although being a Hindu, this has a lot in common with the Buddhist view that there is no almighty personal God that is in one way separate from us in that it created us and is an entity that has complete power over us. An eternal principle is not a concept that needs to be thought of as an omnipotent deity. It can be thought of as being the force that drives us and that guides our actions and thoughts in a monotheistic, polytheistic and atheistic way. The concept of God can be substituted by the concept of conscience or life-source. Religious people can think of God as being their saviour and the one that they look to for advice for how to live their lives. Buddhism knows no saviour other than the person who is looking for salvation. One finds their own salvation and treads the way by their own efforts. The Buddhist way of understanding this principle is similar to there being no external God that looks over us but that 'God' is within us all and is part of what makes us active humans.

Wallace Stevens said "God is in me or else in not at all."[8] (p.166) Meister Eckhart said "The eye with which I see God is the same eye with which God sees me." (p.24)

How we act and how we think depends on our conscience. It guides us to how we should act and live our lives. Religious people think that God knows and sees everything that we do or think, atheists themselves know everything that they do or think. This can also be applied to anyone at all, irrespective of what they believe in or not. If we do something and nobody else is there to observe it, we can't get away from the fact that we know what we are doing. How we feel about our actions, be they morally good or bad, depends on our conscience. We might, for example, steal something while no-one's looking. Religious people would say that God saw them do it and frowns on such behaviour, non-believers may think that it doesn't matter because they don't believe in God but they can never escape the fact that they themselves know what they did and if it leads to consequences that the thief would subsequently feel guilty about, then their conscience is what makes them feel guilty. In essence God and Conscience are the same concepts but the way that they are explained differs only in the concepts associated with them; essentially the humanisation aspect. Some people may think that we need a God to judge our actions, others may think that we don't need anything more than our consciences to make the judgements.

However, to be able to have a set of principles by which we can judge ourselves and others, we need to understand the consequences that are likely to result from them.

Wallace Stevens and Meister Eckhart were referring to the idea that the concept of God is our inner being and without it, we are nothing.

The concept of the soul is a similar notion but is used with reference to the idea that when we die, our soul will go to Heaven or Hell. This comes from the difficulty we have had, throughout history, with understanding what it is that makes us think – the mind and body dichotomy. With the development of neuropsychology, that studies the structure and function of the brain related to specific psychological processes and overt behaviours, we have been able to understand that our thought processes stem directly from the physical matter that comprises our brains.

The idea of us having a soul that leaves our physical body when we die is another one that has become so deeply entrenched in history that it is difficult to let go of. However, there is no scientific evidence at all that the soul exists.

So these are some examples of how can move our perspectives of life forwards, by searching for the truth. To conclude, in the words of Christmas Humphreys, from Exploring Buddhism:

"It calls for no faith save that the Buddha did achieve Enlightenment and strove to offer some of its principles to mankind. The rest is experience, the personal rediscovery of the truth put forward. It needs no apparatus, of ritual or prayer, of incense, rosary or shrine... It is infinitely adaptable... It is essentially a Way, a way of coping with the day's adventures, crises and situations, a Way of reaching Enlightenment for those who truly yearn for it, or for the better helping of mankind for those whom that noble ideal is sufficient unto the day." (p.132)

"Yet if life 'is' one, and the least form of it holy with that life, why is a world that should be learning by the experience ever at war? Because each man is at war within, and not until the war is won for compassion against the powers of hatred, lust, and illusion of separation in each individual mind will the mass-mind of a nation, or of the few who direct it, truly want what only then they will achieve, peace." (p.167-8)

The Age of Reason, Thomas Paine. Dover Publications, Inc.
1. Exploring Buddhism, Christmas Humphreys. Unwin Paperbacks, 1980.
2. www.intelligencesquared.com/iq2-video/2009/catholic-church

3. Zeitgeist, a freely available series of documentaries by Peter Joseph. See www.thezeitgeistmovement.com/
4. http://en.wikipedia.org/wiki/Bahá'í_Faith
5. Effendi, Shoghi (1944). God Passes By. Wilmette, Illinois, US: Bahá'í Publishing Trust. p.281. ISBN 0877430209
6. The God Delusion, Richard Dawkins. Transworld Publishers, Random House.
7. God Is Not Great, Christopher Hitchens. Atlantic Books.
8. The Little Zen Companion. Workman Books.

Education

"Originally this set-up (was) to serve society,
Now the roles have been reversed
(For) society to serve the institutions"
Stereolab – "Tomorrow is Already Here"

The education system of a country is the foundation of the building and maintaining of a successful society. For this reason it is one of the most important departments to monitor, develop and enhance. There are many aspects of the education system to address to ensure that it is a success.

Education should be free and available to all children who are resident in the country and compulsory for all children from the ages of four years to sixteen years. The progression of the school system is set out thus:

Nursery – for one year beginning for the child in the calendar year that they are four years old.

Primary – for six years, beginning for the child in the calendar year that they are five years old until the calendar year when they will turn eleven.

Secondary – for six years, beginning for the child in the calendar year that they are eleven until the calendar year when they will turn seventeen.

Note that nursery education is compulsory. This is for the reason that some children won't be starting primary school with a disadvantage compared to those children who attended nursery. After secondary school, there will be an optional two years to undertake further studies to gain higher qualifications. This could be called Tertiary or Upper School.

Currently, in the western world (as in many developing countries) the education system generally works in a similar way. There is the primary school which is usually in place until the children are around 11 years old. The secondary school carries on until the ages of 16 or 18. In terms of what the children study, the principle subjects are usually the same: first language, Mathematics, Science, Humanities, etc. Before we look at how effective this system is, we need to find out if it is felt as worthwhile and relevant to those who are required to work through such a system.

The NEF did a study with Nottingham City Council to measure the level of well-being in the local area. Over a thousand youngsters completed a questionnaire which included looking at how satisfied they are with their schooling. The age range of the subjects was 9 to 15 years. The level of satisfaction with life and curiosity in life was quite respectable in primary school but it fell dramatically for those in secondary school. The percentage of those who 'strongly agreed' with the statement "I learn a lot at school" was 71% in primary but only 18% in secondary. For the statement "School is interesting" 65% of primary children strongly agreed, compared to 12% in secondary school. For "I enjoy school activities", primary scored 65% and secondary 18%.[1]

This is the first point where we have to stop and think why this is the case.

As a teacher myself, primary school provides more activities that are exciting and meaningful as the children at still at a stage where they are learning new skills and new knowledge. As long as schools also use lots of practical methods of learning, such as science experiments, art, physical education and so on, the children are more likely to engage in the subjects taught. Children like to get their hands on and get stuck in to things. They feel they are really getting involved and their actions can influence the outcomes of the topic being studied. With a developing curriculum, we have tried to make the studies cross-curricular so that a certain topic can be used as the basis for different lessons, e.g. learning about Ancient Greece can include history, physical education (the ancient Greek Olympics) PSHE to show how Greek philosophy developed and democracy began as well as looking at Greek art. One of the main reasons why this can be done is because often in primary schools, the children have one main teacher for each year who teaches almost all of the subjects. This changes in secondary school where the subjects are taught more in isolation, due to the fact that each teacher teaches their specialist subjects and the cross-curricular aspect diminishes.

Also, students then perceive school as being something where they have to work towards certain goals, that is the tests and exams they will continually take until their final years. The element of curiosity is not so strong and the feeling that they are there because they have to be is a commonly held notion.

The obvious aim of school should be to help children develop their skills and give them a good grounding to be able to move into the adult world equipped with knowledge and qualifications to succeed in whatever path they take in life.

This, however, is much more limiting and restrictive than it might appear. When they feel that they have to study certain things just to be able to achieve good exam results, the interest can get lost along with the inspiration that they could and should have gained. A lot of what they will study, especially in Maths, doesn't seem relevant to them. It's all very well learning lots of methods and formulae but what use are they going to be to for the general population? Of course people need to learn the basic skills in Maths as it is used in many aspects of real life but the necessity to study it to a high level is questionable.

School has to be an institution where the students are going to feel inspired and that what they study has meaning for them. Two educational organisations at least have looked into addressing these issues more recently with the aims of making school more multi-disciplinary. The International Primary Curriculum (IPC)[2] is based on such core values as providing a broad range of curriculum subjects, fostering a commitment to learning both in school and later careers, developing personal skills to be good citizens, and developing a sense of their nationality and culture whilst respecting others in the world.

The International Baccalaureate has three programmes in place: the Primary Years (PYP), Middle Years (MYP) and Diploma Programmes.[3] The latter one has already gained a lot of ground around the world as a more holistic programme of study where students follow six areas rather than three A-levels, as has been common in the UK. These six areas comprise subjects from the areas of languages (native and foreign), social studies, the experimental sciences, mathematics and arts. Given that it has a much broader range of subjects to study, it needs the previous two programmes to prepare students for it.

For the PYP, there are six core themes to be used: who we are, where we are in place and time, how we express ourselves, how the world works, how we organise ourselves, and sharing the planet. The idea is that that these six themes are transdisciplinary and are to be used as the basis of the six subject areas of language, social studies, maths, art, science, and personal, social and physical education.

The MYP follows a similar structure and is based on the three fundamental concepts of intercultural awareness, holistic learning and communication.

Both the IB and IPC programmes are more progressive and offer approaches that are based on real life, in that life is not segregated into individual subjects and this should be implemented at a school level.

However, there is still more to what is required in education that what has been outlined thus far.

It is likely that some students, who are not academically apt, will struggle to achieve the first qualifications at age 16. In this case, they will be required to complete the first of these two years to get a basic level certificate and simultaneously, they will be encouraged to study an external training course to gain a vocational qualification in a line of work of their choosing. Note that this training would be in an area where they show interest and aptitude but doesn't necessarily mean that they require typical academic qualifications.

While at school, these students will be given advice to help them decide in which line of work they would like to be employed. The attendance level and required results of this training year would mean that the attendees will still be called 'students' and they will be expected to pass their training to be able to subsequently find employment.

An important aspect to focus on is that there are so many areas where people can have interest and even if they are not so academic-based, they should be supported and nurtured to follow their interests. We shouldn't be looking at how to set students up to be ready to fit into the current system. We should be more progressive and allow people to make use of their skills and interests so that they can find life satisfaction from what they would like to do. An example of this would be someone who is not interested in subjects like Maths and Sciences but may have a natural flair for drama or sports. When we, as teachers, can see someone's potential in any area, it should be focused on to help guide them to a path where they can move into that area of employment.

Children are required to start school in the Nursery year to help to make a start on any potential skills they may have. For example, if a child has an aptitude for Mathematics, it would be unfair to leave them unable to use their skill until they are six years old (in the case of countries that do not make education compulsory until that age). This can be a hindrance to the child's development and therefore is not something which would be desired.

The skills that a teacher needs to work effectively in the education system are very important and their initial and ongoing training will need to work on the following principles:

1. Students must be taught in ways that are inspiring and motivating. To be able to engage the students' attention and give them the reason to learn, they need to want to learn.
2. Students must receive a level of discipline that they are able to accept and respect. Whereas the classroom environment and the content of the lessons should be enjoyable, they must be

aware that certain rules of behaviour must be followed. Physical punishment of any kind is illegal so to emphasise the rules for behaviour, the students will be given discussion periods for them to understand the reasons for loss of privileges, etc. for unacceptable behaviour. They should also actively examine how they can develop more positively to be able to achieve better relationships with everyone and why this is so important. Rewards are more effective than punishments.

3. All students must be treated equally as people, regardless of any perceptible factor, e.g. religion, gender, etc. They will all potentially have the same opportunities which is relative to their level of good behaviour or amount of effort put into their school work.

4. Students will always be encouraged to try with their work and be praised more so for the amount of effort they put in, rather than the actual results they achieve.

5. Students have opinions and suggestions that will be listened to and respected. Their input is valid and they play an active role in their own and their peers' development, which is to be encouraged.

6. Teachers are not permitted to promote their own personal or religious beliefs in an attempt to guide those of the students. The teacher's role is to be neutral in terms of possible alternative beliefs or opinions and to make students aware that different opinions are valid as long as no-one suffers as a result.

Additionally, teachers must be flexible in terms of their teaching methods which, as society evolves, will need to evolve respectively. Teaching styles will always vary but as long as the above principles are followed and the objectives are reached, variation in methods are welcomed as much as they are accepted. As mentioned, teachers will receive ongoing training to aid development and their range of skills.

The students' families are to be encouraged to participate in their children's learning and kept abreast of the school work. Communication between staff and parents (or carers) is fundamental to ensure an effective system of learning and the positive development of the child.

The curriculum

The school curriculum is very broad but here, we shall see the basic principles of the subjects to be taught. Before we can start creating a curriculum, we have to think about what kind of people we should be developing in the country and in the world.

The UK schools secretary as of 2010, Ed Balls, said that children should be learning Mandarin Chinese and Arabic in primary schools. Why? To help UK businesses, he said.

The Guardian reported that Balls added that UK plc increasingly needed children to learn the languages of countries where Britain had "very important business contacts." Furthermore, in the Confederation of British Industry's poll of 581 businesses conducted last year, 38% of bosses said they were looking for staff with Mandarin or Cantonese.[4]

This article, reported in January 2010, didn't seem to get much of a negative reaction. But should it? After all, in the business world, there are stronger ties with the Arabic and Chinese markets now so shouldn't we be developing children so that they can work in these areas?

That all depends on whether you think children are people who should be able to choose what they want to do in life or whether you think that they are just the new generation of robots who have an obligation to support the capitalist system as it is and strengthen business links for the corporation executives to earn more money from their input.

I found this article on the government's proposals sickening. So what if the UK's businesses wanted people who could speak these languages? It is only for their own purpose and not in the interests of the people whom they basically require to be their servants in their quest for market domination. Balls clearly did not have the development of children's interests and strengths in mind in this instance, only the development of industries that effectively run the world.

This is a dreadful way to look at how to raise children. We have to be looking at important human skills that everyone should have, irrespective of any bias, be it cultural, religious or political.

Children (as well as adults) need to be aware of the world in which they live. They need to understand how it is so that they feel an absolute connection to it, in terms of the effects of our actions on other people, other creatures and the environment in general. First and foremost, we need to educate the children so that they understand that everyone belongs in this world on a completely equal level and that we all depend on each other and that we need to work together to have any chance of being happy. Discriminations of any kind need to be shown to be worthless, and a sign that having a discrimination against someone is a fault of one's character.

Children also need to realise that people do not own the planet. This is a horrible consequence of so-called human development; we think we own the planet and it is there for us to do as we please. In the light of climate change and pollution, there is no debate that this is a completely incorrect perspective. If this planet belonged to us, we would have made it or bought it. Inversely, the planet made us and we are part of the whole ecosystem that is life on Earth. We seriously need to drop this delusion that we can treat it as we wish for our own selfish desires and gains.

Hence, children need to learn about our role in the world – our connections with every relevant aspect of the planet and how to develop these so that we don't run into problems where people become divided into groups that are human-created, as discussed in Shaping A Society.

Also, even though the Bible says that man has dominion over all other creatures (Genesis 1:26), the fact that so many species have been made extinct directly due to human actions renders this idea as one that cannot be accepted. People have been the most destructive creatures in the history of the world. No other species has been responsible for the damage that we have inflicted upon the environment. We operate largely outside of ecosystems whereas other animals live within them and keep the natural balance steady without needing to be able to consider their actions. We, on the other hand, decimate it even to the point of spreading disease, poverty and death to our own species as well as countless others.

Therefore, we need to overcome this problem of ours and identify the real issues that are going to lead to true development.

As a school teacher, every year I have felt the need to teach a lesson on morality concerning people's attitudes to other animals. Concerning insects and other small creatures, children tend to view them as objects of their own amusement or torture. It is very common for them to kill flies, ants, spiders and the like, and this fault, of course, stays with many people throughout their adult lives. This is due to the lack of awareness that people have about our part in the web of life. Everything that lives on this planet has the right to do so because it has developed in accordance with the environment. Even if a fly comes into your room, I can assure you that it has no intention of irritating you. The same goes for any other creature that usually lives outside. They come to be in a room through exploration, which is a part of their instinctual behaviour. Even if it is crawling on your table or on your arm, it has no interest in you because it doesn't have the capacity to comprehend what you are.

However, what is the general human reaction to this kind of creature in our room? Kill it. Simple. You don't want it there, it's small, it's easy to kill and you won't get arrested for it. Well, maybe but does that make it right?

As I said, every living thing has the right to life. Tiny creatures like common spiders, flies and ants will not do you any harm and as to the fear that some people have of spiders, for example,this is learned behaviour. We are not genetically predisposed to fear spiders. The chances are that you learned it from someone in your family or one of your friends. It is undoubtedly irrational as it is millions of times smaller than we are and can't possible do any damage to us (of course I am not including poisonous spiders in this).

All these creatures play a part in the system of life on this planet. We are generally ignorant of their role and their crucial part in the chain of life. Everything that is here relates to something else, whether it is bees that extract pollen from flowers or spiders that eat flies. The interdependency is not just enormous, it is absolute. Everything works together in one way or another and carelessly causing species to become extinct upsets the whole balance, even if we aren't aware of it.

But ignorance is not bliss, it is a serious fault. We can learn from the multitude of mistakes that humans have made historically, although this should not be the focus of attention in education. We should use it implicitly so as to form a new way of developing humanity where awareness is the key, along with the knowledge of interdependency of all life.

The next role of education is to encourage curiosity – how things work, why things happen and what has happened in the past. Children need to feel inspired and motivated to understand how everything fits together. However, simply breaking these concepts down into individual subjects has led many children to lose interest as subjects such as Mathematics is effectively disconnected from the real world. Learning the times tables is all well and good but without a context in which to use them, the motivation is going to be lacking. In Science, learning about materials and why some are better than others for certain purposes will not leave the children with a lingering curiosity once the topic has been finished with. But if they are studied within real projects whereby many subjects come together and are actually implemented, the children will be able to realise how important certain mathematical and scientific knowledge is when they actually get to explore things that have a meaning.

Such project-based education can also combine Science and Maths with History or Geography or other currently segregated subjects whereas the real world is a blend of many of these areas that need to be comprehended in their holistic sense rather than merely specialising in one aspect of it. Even though this is necessary in some cases, like advanced research of a problem, children need to be taught how aspects fit together and how much deeper topics go when you think about how certain things developed such as limitations put in place by institutions such as the church which has prohibited many things in history because it didn't agree with them (e.g. Leonardo da Vinci's pioneering study of anatomy which was frowned upon when the church didn't allow the dissection of human bodies – Where would we be now if it wasn't for anatomy?).

So education should not be structured in a way that introduces separate subjects and topics that are taught in isolation but instead should work the other way around. There could be 6 (or more) projects for each school year which would be inspirational and from this top-down approach the areas of work that need to be studied to be able to understand how the project could be pursued could be fitted in to it, depending on what is age-appropriate for the children.

By approaching education in this way, it would be far more meaningful to the children and it would help them to explore their own interests more effectively. The chances that they will latch onto a certain part of a given project and want to know more are far greater than not using a real context in which to learn about something.

This approach would be suited more to primary education where the teachers usually teach all of these subjects independently anyway. Secondary education would need to follow on from this as much as possible, by having teachers of different subjects working together to provide education in a similar context-based, top-down way.

Each school year's projects would need to encompass many areas of study, ranging from scientific ones to artistic ones to give the students the scope that the world consists of as different children will have different areas of interest. Some might not be so successful with Maths or Science but they might discover that they love Drama or Fine Art. I have seen this kind of thing many times in schools where students who are seen to be 'weaker' ones as they don't get good academic results appear in a school play and you can see that they have a natural ability to perform, yet this strength and passion of theirs gets forgotten by the school in favour of pushing them to achieve more in the subjects that will help them to study some subject that they really have no interest in. Instead, whenever someone's strengths and interests are discovered by the teachers, they should be nurtured and the children should be supported to follow them in a constructive way so that, for example, the said drama enthusiast could work towards a career in the theatre, which they are likely to find both enjoyable and fulfilling, even if it doesn't earn them so much money. This side of it is not what is important – as long as they have enough money to support themselves that doesn't matter. But if they can end up doing something that they feel is their calling in life, then this should be supported by the school because enjoying what one does is worth more than having a high-profile office job where one works late, doesn't enjoy it, goes home thinking that they are glad the day is over but at least they have more money in their bank account. Well, life is less likely to be enjoyable for the person who works like that. So they have lots of money. Great, but their experiences are probably not bringing fulfilment to their lives so how can they be really happy?

When we can agree that these are the main principles for life, searching for happiness and fulfilment and enjoying what one does, we can start to build an education system that keeps these things in mind. They are the starting blocks and from these we can look at how to decide if something is worth studying or not and if it's not, how we can adapt it so that it will become inspiring and the children will be excited about coming back to school the next day because they will be able to carry on from where they left off.

Nursery

During the child's first year in school, they will be encouraged to interact and develop their social skills with their peers. They will learn about school rules and to be respectful of others and notably of the staff. They will learn the basic principles of using numbers and begin to understand and enjoy books as well as possibly beginning to learn to read.

They will learn pencil control (as well as other fine motor skills) to begin to write their name and draw simple pictures to represent things. They will partake in class discussions to develop their sense of their and other people's identities.

Play is an important aspect of nursery education to help develop their thinking skills, their gross motor development, their social interactions and concept of sharing. Productive activities like construction toys and those which will engage the children and stretch their mental skills would be given priority.

They will also learn aspects of personal safety and becoming responsible for themselves and others. Importantly, the children will begin to learn about their connection with the natural world. They will be introduced to caring for their surrounding in all ways: the natural environment, animals and insects and other people. This is something that isn't not given precedence in schools in general but to be able to prepare children for the future, they have to know the consequences of respectful and irresponsible behaviour, for example regarding pollution and selfish acts that could damage others or the environment. This area will be the most important aspect of the children's first year of education and it will continue to be emphasised in the coming years. Responsibility, awareness of others and the world and the capacity to live harmoniously with everyone is something that needs to form the foundations of educating children from the earliest age possible.

There is the possibility that there will be children from various religious, racial and socio-economic backgrounds as well as children with disabilities. However, as young children are non-discriminatory, these perceived issues will not be made apparent as this can influence their perceptions of each other unnecessarily. The only exceptions would be if children need to remember another's difficulty or inability to perform a specific action for the reasons of safety or help needed.

Primary School

In primary school, such lessons as Literacy, Mathematics, Science, History, Geography, ICT, Physical Education, Music, Art and Drama would be in place in the holistic, cross-curricular sense as described earlier. In addition to this, Personal, Social and Health Education (PSHE) would be a core subject which would include Religious Studies. This particular subject covers a broad range of topics that are related to 'real life' rather than just academia. It must be stressed that school is more than just rote-learning of facts but a whole life-forming experience. It must be as interactive and mentally stimulating as possible. School is not only to develop children's basic skills and knowledge but to develop them as people that are actively involved in their own learning.

The most important assets to give to a child are inspiration and motivation. They need to be given the chance to explore what they are learning about, to investigate more deeply with the intention of giving them more ideas from what they discover. This idea can be implemented into every subject in many different ways. If children are just being taught to remember methods, stories and facts, they are likely to lose interest in school. First and foremost, we need to remember that children like to have fun, they want to play more than anything. If we can give them ideas that they can take on and become passionate about and that they want to get better at, we will be at a point of success in education. Being involved in their own learning can be on the same level as hedonistic play. But only if they are given the inspiration and the motivation.

Morals must be a central part of education as well. This is the reason for the importance of PSHE. The way the western world is moving (progressing or developing are not adequate terms in this sense), children need to be given the opportunity to explore moral issues to understand why people are how they are. With the number of different cultures and religions in the world, awareness of these issues is crucial if the western world is going to find its way again. Currently, it is stuck in a quest for endless material gain. The lifestyle of 'buy this', 'upgrade to this' is one that leaves people with no idea of where they are going or what they are aiming for. The ignorance of people towards those who are seen as belonging to a different group is tragic. I don't need to discuss the problems betweens followers of different religions, they are well known and well established. We need to educate children about religions so that they will become accepting either to those who follow a different religion to them or any religion at all. It needs to be made explicit that whether people follow a religion or not, we are all allowed to choose the path we wish to, even if other people choose other ways. If religious issues are avoided, the only thing that will develop is ignorance and ignorance will then develop into intolerance and ultimately, war.

The same kind of reason must also be given to other issues that can cause conflict in 'real life'. Racism, sexism, homophobia and other similar prejudices can never be justified. It is impossible to argue such points down to their fundamental meanings and find that any of them make any sense. The biggest problem that the western world has regarding these issues is that we tend to categorise everything to try to make sense of it. No person is black, no person is white and therefore no person can be classed as belonging to the opposite group. We are all different shades of the same colour. And what colour is that? None. It is like looking at a circular spectrum of colour and trying to find where it begins. There are countless shades of human skin which could be arranged in a circle where the shades flow from one to the next. Ask a racist to pick the one shade that they think is the 'right' one or the best one and then ask them to explain why the ones either side of them are not as good or why a shade three steps to the left is not good. It doesn't make sense.

Another way to justify that such prejudices have no valid reason is to watch how under-5s act with one another. They have no such prejudices because their minds could not see any sense in them. Children play with other children because they can. They do not judge by appearance or gender because they don't possess such conceptual thinking. As long as they can get on with one another, they will. It is only when adults' ignorant opinions become forced upon the children that things can start to go wrong in society. As adults, we can actually learn as much from small children as they can from us if we have such invalid prejudices.

Therefore, primary education has an important role in developing children to become moral, non-judgemental people. Academia is only half of its purpose.

Secondary School

Secondary education is based along the same lines as primary and moral and social awareness is equally fundamental to its basis. However, the academic side of it must be more adaptable than it is in most western countries. It has been traditional to emphasise the importance of the most academic subjects- Literacy and Mathematics and to enforce that they are mandatory subjects and that at least one of them must be studied at higher level education. This needs to be questioned in terms of their relevance. Whereas they are undoubtedly important subjects which are the foundations of others such as sciences, literature or history, they have been over-emphasised in the western world. Latin and Ancient Greek used to be studied until relatively recently despite the fact they were largely redundant languages in the twentieth century. But it took a long time before they were eventually thrown out. Literacy and Mathematics, of course, are not redundant subjects but they don't need to be mandatory subjects up until the final years of study. We need to be more practical in terms of the subjects and skills that are relevant to students.

For example, it is not going to be fruitful to force students to study subjects for which they don't have an interest. Mathematics is not a popular subject in general and advanced Mathematics is not applicable to everyday life. We need to make sure that before anything else, we can guide students to their interests and the potential application of the subjects. Not every student is academically strong but they are not guided towards learning other skills that may be more useful to them. This refers to those who are likely to leave school at the earliest opportunity because they dislike the whole institution. There will always be school leavers who go away with either very few or no academic qualifications. It is a realistic fact. However, the educational establishment will probably not have offered them opportunities to learn practical skills to prepare them for work which doesn't rely on typical academic qualifications.

We need to be able to instil the work ethic in students. Students from less stable families who would normally be seen as those likely to not find work need to be supported the most. If a government states that it is going to give every child a chance, the system needs to work so that it will have the resources to develop skills relevant to each child.

To encompass this aspect, those less academic students would be able to study differently. They would need to complete at least 3 academic years in secondary school, during which their interests and potential skills would be monitored (by both staff and those students together) to be able to provide practical training courses that they could do for a further two years. This could involve manual skills like mechanics, electrics and so on as well as other career paths that they could envisage themselves doing. The most important thing in secondary education is to identify the students' interests so that they don't just feel that they will be doing work for the sake of earning money. There needs to be job satisfaction if we are going to develop a society that has a degree of happiness. It is common that people don't explore their interests fully and discover a path which will lead them to job satisfaction and the fault lies within the system. It is not always easy for teenagers to know what they want to do as a job before they have the experience. They need practical guidance to be able to feed their potential.

For those students who choose to continue in academia, subjects need to be provided and adapted to suit the times and the culture. Information and Communications Technology (ICT) has come into being and risen to a high level of importance since the later years of the twentieth century and assessments need to be carried out regularly to ascertain the relevance of any school subject to the real world.

However, given this increased emphasis on ICT, what has come with it is the increased funding needed to provide schools with all the relevant equipment that they apparently need. The ICT budgets of schools now are often the largest of any department by a long way. Despite being someone who has used computers for a long time and uses them for all manner of applications, I fail to see why governments and schools have felt the need to acquire so many resources in this area. I grew up at a time when computers were not commonplace in schools or in everyday life and therefore, I didn't need interactive whiteboards to learn anything, but I still learnt. Nor did I need access to a computer in every classroom I was in. Even though everyday life has changed with the development of the computer industry and the application of computers, they are not essential to education any more than Science, Maths or physical education. Such things as interactive whiteboards and projectors may make things look nice with graphics and videos and new ways of delivering lessons, they are not essential. It has also been argued that they help to maintain students' concentration better than using more traditional methods but this means that the way of teaching has been inadequate or the teachers' training has not been good enough.

Another argument is that it sets the students up to be more prepared to get certain jobs, where computer knowledge is essential. Maybe, but this is an example of wanting society to serve the institutions already in place.

Many ICT items are a luxury to some extent and a massive drain on the school budget where the money should be used more effectively to help develop the range of skills and interests that the students will have.

Similarly to primary school, the subjects need to be delivered in a way that is going to inspire and motivate the students. Active involvement is a key strategy to nurturing interest.

Along with the importance of educating the students about cultures and religions as described in the Primary section, these studies would play a significant part for secondary students, too. They can never be swept aside if we are going to improve the levels of awareness, understanding and acceptance of the next generations. Due to many factors such as hormonal changes and the influence of the media and marketing, adolescents currently develop in ways which are not sufficiently interpersonal and communal. They need to be taught the values of their peers in ways that go beyond theory and discussion.

Military service is something that has been in place in many countries until recently. It has only very recently been completely abolished in Europe, with Poland being the last country to end compulsory armed service in December 2008. The Hypothetical Government will have no involvement in war except for defence of its own nation in the case of attack and so would not make use of military service but key elements of it can be taken as inspiration for a similar kind of programme which would be for the purpose of developing working relations between people.

From the age of around twelve, students would attend camps where they would explore their own and their peers' strengths (and weaknesses) to complete group activities. These would be varied to explore different situations such as survival-type exercises which combine with more intellectual exercises to bring together the strengths of different members of the groups so that they can find their 'roles' and work out who is more suited to different aspects of the tasks so that the group works well together. The whole intention of these types of courses is to promote interpersonal skills and show in real ways how people, who may not think they relate to certain others, actually find that they depend on the others' areas of strength, for example the combination of the intellectual and the physical. Therefore, putting the emphasis on working together and coordinating the best ways to use everyone's skills to the best effect.

From the younger ages, the students would attend this type of camp for three or four days as an introduction and as they get older, the length of time will increase to two or three weeks for sixteen year olds. Students would be expected to attend these camps every year with different groups each time for a variety of people to work with which will give them a challenge when they don't already know their peers' skills in depth from the beginning.

The inclusion of this aspect of 'real life' education would also lead to more jobs becoming available for people to work at these camps, where the employees would need to exercise responsibility and motivation for the students, thereby increasing the overall level of solidarity between people.

To further aid the students' development as well-rounded and compassionate people, it should be standard for them to become involved in charity work. This would be so that they can actually experience difficulties and suffering (to a degree) first-hand. I have seen for myself how much of a difference it makes for the students to meet the people or be in the presence of the animals that need help, rather than just hearing abut them in a school assembly or even seeing videos and photos. This is an incredibly meaningful way of having the new generation become more empathic and feeling that they want to help as much as they can. It also goes along with the plan for the development of the community: we need to understand others if we are going to lose our prejudices and build a self-supporting society. The other benefit is of course that charities will be able to achieve more if students from every school contribute to their activities.

Conditions for Teaching Staff

Another important area to address is working conditions for staff members in a school. Considering that teachers are more responsible than parents for developing the knowledge and skills of children and that they spend more time with them with their development as the objective, teachers often get relatively little appreciation in return. Teaching is undoubtedly one of the most important jobs in society as without it, as in many countries in Africa and Asia, people would be in a state where they were unable to do many basic things like read, perform calculations, or provide clean water for a community.

A lot of the time, people who don't work in education often complain that teachers get so many holidays that they don't deserve anything else but if you put those people in a class of 30 children for six hours a day, five days a week, thirty-eight weeks a year and they have to teach them all manner of subjects, be aware of how to address their needs, maintain discipline, plan lessons, write reports, mark all of their work, etc., etc., they would then appreciate that it is not by any means an easy job.

We need to reflect this amount of responsibility in the conditions that teaching staff work under. It is not just that work finishes when the children go home at half past three. Sometimes, teachers can still be working in the school for another few hours a day and maybe finishing things off at home. Here, we see the first problem that needs to be addressed: in order to support teachers so that their workload is not excessive and they have a sense of well-being and calm with the potential to use and enjoy their free time, we need to look at how we can reduce the workload so that such important members of the community are not overlooked and they still feel that they are happy to continue their careers in education.

Even though education is generally a non-profit institution and there are limited funds to address all the issues that need addressing, we should find a way to bring more staff into the equation to support the teachers and share the workload. The main problem with this idea is how to pay for extra staff. It would be hoped that with the advent of the development of the local community, economically, there would be more funds available to gradually employ more staff who would work closely with the teachers so that they could help with marking work, marking tests, preparing resources for lessons and so on. A stressed out teacher is unlikely to be an effective one and of course this translates into a bad environment for learning. This cannot be ignored as the development of the students partly depends on their connections with their teachers. If the students feel they can't relate to their teacher because he or she is always in a bad mood (brought on by an excessive workload), they can lose their enthusiasm for school and therefore achieve less than their potential would suggest over time.

Other ways to look at how to improve conditions for teachers is how we can reduce the paperwork that they are currently expected to produce, in many western countries at least. If it is administrative work, it should be passed on to the administrative staff. Filing test results and other assessment grades can be done by other assistants without any real difficulty.

Teachers are some of the most valuable contributors in a country and we need to define their conditions accordingly.

Faith Schools

In the United Kingdom, there are currently almost 7000 faith schools which are allowed to design their own educational curricula. This effectively means that they can legally teach the attending pupils that scientific fact is only theory and that creationism is factual. They can also teach that homosexuality is wrong as well as other controversial issues to the modern world.

In the Hypothetical Government, faith schools would not be permitted under any circumstances. The whole notion that unproven ideas and opinions (that are detrimental to certain members of the public) can be taught as though they are proven facts is unquestionably immoral. To illustrate this, we need to address the arguments for and against faith schools.

An ICM poll in 2005 showed that 64% of the British public believe that "the government should not be funding faith schools of any kind".[5] Additionally, a large proportion of the public believe that faith schools should not even be legal institutions. Faith schools are typically very selective and mostly offer places only to those families who are practising followers of the schools' faiths. Arguments have been proposed to offer a compromise by saying that one quarter of places should be allowed to non-believers (though quite why non-believers would want to send their children to faith schools is mysterious) but this was actually defeated in the Houses of Parliament in as recently as 2002.

The main problem with faith schools is the idea that religious segregation should not be encouraged in any way whatsoever. Schools are obliged to make the pupils aware of all major religions without the freedom to effectively promote one religion over any other as this goes completely against human rights, as mentioned previously.

Therefore, faith schools, if present in any country, would not only be forbidden to receive any state money for funding but would be obliged to practise the education system of the country, focusing on equality of all people, awareness of all relevant cultures and religions and the bringing together of people from 'apparently' different groups of society to build a truer sense of community for all. The intention of doing so would be to eventually fade out the existence of faith schools.

The Selection Process

There is still a divide between schools depending on selection procedures for students to be able to attend. Private schools are also able to use this system depending on how much money people are able to spend on their children's education. In essence, this is discrimination and it simply exacerbates the divides between people, and the class system. In the UK, grammar schools use a selection process to choose which students will be allowed to attend depending on their academic results as well as other factors if there are too many applicants that could be accepted.

Whereas in one way this is understandable for those parents who would wish their children to be able to go to a 'better' school with higher achievers in general, comprehensive schools which allow anyone to attend regardless of results would always be seen as inferior. To address this issue, we need to be able to reduce the difference between students with respect to their dedication to their school work and their general attitude to school life and their peers. This, of course, would not be an easy or quick remedy but one which will need to be worked hard at for many years until society in general improves its level of solidarity, openness, work ethic and those characteristics which were discussed in the section about Virtues.

As has been outlined already, the plan would be not just to make all schools the same as this would imply that all children should be taught the same things, in the same way, without any aspect of flexibility. We need to provide opportunities for everyone so that they can constructively follow their interests and move to another institution that would be better suited for them.

There are already examples of music schools, drama schools and so on where the students may follow the standard curriculum in the mornings and then study music in the afternoons. These tend to be private schools, which would straight away mean that only a select few, the richest, would have the opportunity to go there. In principle, these kinds of schools have their advantages in that they allow students to follow their areas of interest more profoundly and these types of institutions can be used as a source of inspiration for general schooling. One suggestion could be that students aged 14 or older would attend regular school for most of the time and attend a specialist school to study drama, music, sports but also other vocational skills such as mechanics for, say, three afternoons a week. This would be one way of helping the new generation to feel that they have a purpose and an objective in life to aim for.

Depending on the specialism that they choose to follow, it wouldn't always mean that there would need to be new institutions built and managed, which would of course be a burden on the state funds. Drama or music could be specialised within the same school as there wouldn't need to be extra resources that couldn't realistically be included in the school. There would be a need for more specialist teachers as the workload for these subjects would go up but it wouldn't any unrealistic amount of extra work needed. One school in the constituency could be the drama specialist centre where other schools' students could travel to, another be specialise in art and so on. To become more progressive and flexible doesn't mean we need to start the whole system from scratch.

A society is never going to be successful until it is happy, has truly good relationships between its people, shows humility, charity and diligence. This is the main aim of the Hypothetical Government and through education, we have the means to be able to make this happen.

1. A Well-being Manifesto for a Flourishing Society, NEF: www.neweconomics.org/publications/well-being-manifesto-flourishing-society
2. The International Primary Curriculum www.internationalprimarycurriculum.com
3. The International Baccalaureate www.ibo.org/
4. www.guardian.co.uk/education/2010/jan/04/modernlanguages-languages
5. www.guardian.co.uk/uk/2005/aug/23/schools.faithschools

Animal Rights

Throughout history, humans have generally held the belief that they are superior to other animals and we can use them for our own benefit. In Genesis 1:28, God is said to have put humans "in charge of the fish, the birds and all the wild animals." Other religions, such as Hinduism and Islam have had respect for certain animals by prohibiting the killing of them but still there has remained the divide between human rights and animal rights.

Buddhism, on the other hand, has advocated the awareness of all life in the world and stressed the need to take care of and respect all living creatures. Unfortunately, this notion has not become widespread and people, in their quest for selfish development, have generally seen animals as being inferior and having no or very few rights.

This blind selfishness has led to a number of unacceptable situations concerning animals. The rates of extinction of some species has been disastrous and these have practically all being caused by humans, therefore rendering us as the most destructive species ever to have lived on Earth. The most important aspect of this selfishness is that humans have generally lost the idea that nature needs an equilibrium for the world to be able to function successfully. The eradication of (due to ignorance) or the depletion of (in great numbers) many species means that the ecosystems necessary for the planet to continue to survive, thrive and evolve are taking a battering because of the species that is said to be the most intelligent.

In terms of using animals for food, as was described in the section on Farming and Agriculture, it would be unreasonable and impractical to demand that people don't eat meat any more. The truth is that humans are omnivores although most of us can survive as herbivores so it should be down to each person's own moral judgement as to whether they feel it is right to eat meat or not. Just to reiterate, it would be the law that animals raised for food must be killed humanely and punishments would be given out for immoral practices.

As cows are one of the main animals used for the purposes of food, to use their skin as leather is an acceptable by-product as they will have been killed for another reason so it has to be admitted that it is economical to continue this practice and no additional animals have to be killed to produce leather. The fact that cows can reproduce easily and their numbers do not tend to dwindle as a result of human practices leaves them in a state where the species is not in danger. The same can be said for most other farm animals.

Fish, however, pose a different problem. Fish that are caught from the sea have suffered a great deal in terms of the survival of their species. This commercial fishing has come under criticism recently for the severe depletion of the numbers of fish caught for food. Quotas have been put in place to try to stop this happening and as every species on this planet does have the right to survive (otherwise they wouldn't be here), such quotas would be enforced. Even if it means that at times, there is not enough fish available in restaurants or shops, then so be it. Humans need to stop putting themselves before other species as they are not in any way superior, nor do they have any more of a right to survive than any other species. This planet has the conditions for so many millions of types of creatures to live, and as they have evolved, they have as much of a right to be here as any other. If species become extinct due to other animals (not humans) hunting them out of existence then this has to be seen as a natural selection procedure as it is true that other animals don't have the insight to analyse the numbers of other species but we humans do.

Animals are not only used by humans for food. This is where the contemptuous greed of people becomes more evident. Animals which are in low numbers but are used for their fur, such as mink, suffer a great deal. In fact, any animal that is not farmed but is killed for its skin will be totally protected under The Hypothetical Government and it would be entirely forbidden to carry out such practices. This is due to it being an utterly shameful display of conceit by some humans who want to show off their wealth (monetary, not their actual value) at the expense of a species on the brink of extinction. As this practice is in no way essential, unlike the need to eat, it cannot be allowed to continue. This means that animals cannot be killed in the country that applies this law, nor can their products be imported from other countries. The highly successful fashion house DKNY (founded by Donna Karan) imports fur from animals killed, usually brutally, in China, where there are no animal rights so that DKNY's products can be labelled as containing rabbit fur. PETA (People for the Ethical Treatment of Animals) has highlighted this case in particular, stating that "Chinese fur is often deliberately mislabelled, so, if you wear any fur, there's no way of knowing whose skin you're in."[1] This kind of unethical business practice needs to be made available for the public so that they can make their choices about which products they buy, depending on their own moral principles.

Similarly, fox hunting and the hunting of other animals that are considered to be a hazard to livestock would be outlawed. The most obvious reason for this is that the 'bloodsport' aspect of it is also deplorable and utterly unethical and humans should never be given the rights to perform such selfish acts. In terms of the protest that certain animals hunt livestock and can cause a lot of damage for the farmer's assets: So be it. You have to accept that those animals are only acting on their instincts. Of course they are not doing it deliberately to cause you trouble, it is part of their natural behaviour for the reasons of survival. However, as farmers are humans and are potentially a lot more resourceful, they should ensure that their livestock are securely protected from predators. If the farmers choose not to install fences or walls that would keep foxes and other predatory animals out, they have to live with the consequences. It is unacceptable to punish other animals for acting on their instincts.

Moving on to other bloodsports, other barbaric acts that are still in existence in some countries, such as bullfighting, would unsurprisingly be outlawed. It won't take the reader long to work out why this would be so. Any activity that could be classed as a bloodsport is immoral, selfish and has no place in a developing society. If that means that the whole business of maintaining a bullring would mean the loss of work for some people, then think about it and try to understand that there is nothing ethical about torturing and killing animals for entertainment. It is disgusting and when you can accept that, look for another job.

Animals are used in scientific research for testing purposes. This throws up some questions about the validity of such practices. There are many cases where it can be unequivocally made clear that there is no moral justification for their use. The main one being for the testing of cosmetics. This is such an unnecessary area of research that a ban of the testing of animals can be enforced. For one thing, there has already been so much research that the scientists should already know what chemicals are safe to mammals. If they decide to try to develop some other exploitative products that have no actual benefit to people and they want to test newly manufactured ingredients, they have a problem. So be it, if it's not necessary then the project should be dropped. The chances are that there is no need for the new project other than making a huge profit so the matter is settled without much need for deliberation. Testing cosmetics on animals is still legal in the US, to date, whereas it is banned in the UK, Belgium and The Netherlands.

Other kinds of animal testing which can be judged as being unnecessary would not be allowed, either. For example, psychological tests where animals are put through all methods of torture to see their reactions and outcomes are simply barbaric and have no real justification so obviously this would be banned on the grounds of immorality. Researchers would claim that it is for the advancement of human knowledge and to understand the brain better but in most cases, it wouldn't matter if we understood something better or not. There have been numerous cases of animals being abused in laboratories through deliberate torture, both physically and psychologically, which is obviously never necessary but shows the weakness of the researchers' characters. It would be important to put forward strong deterrents to try to stop such practices with long prison sentences and a ban on the guilty parties from ever working in the field of scientific research in the future.

The more difficult dilemma is when research is being made into new medicine. There will always be arguments that to find cures or treatments to certain medical conditions, we must use some other animals to experiment on as it would be unethical to use humans for the said research. As I have said earlier, it is also unethical to claim that other animals are not as important as us and that they have fewer or no rights. The devil's advocate would then put forward the question of what if you or your mother was suffering from an illness that could be remedied through experimenting on animals? This is a valid question and again, it is where we have to reach an ethical compromise.

P Flecknell wrote about the "Three Rs" of alternatives to animal testing, being Replacement (where non-animal methods are used whenever possible), Reduction (using fewer numbers of animals to carry out experiments) and Refinement ("methods that alleviate or minimize potential pain, suffering or distress, and enhance animal welfare for the animals still used.")[2]

Essentially, animal testing should only be permitted when it is unlikely to cause the test subjects pain in any way, after giving an anaesthetic to prevent suffering and if the animals are going to be in pain after the experiment, they should be humanely euthanised. If the research is considered to be non-essential and only for the reasons of advancing human knowledge, this is no ground for conducting experiments and it would not be allowed.

To determine what would be allowed or not, there needs to be a code of ethics that has a legal status which researchers have to adhere to. With the formulation of set criteria that have to be met, stating what can or can't be carried out, this would mean that researchers could see what they would be allowed to do or not from this code of ethics before they even put forward a proposal. Again, a violation of this code would have to result in significant punishments so that hopefully, the researchers would not even consider secretly performing illegal and unethical experiments.

1. www.dkbunnybutcher.com/why-donna-karan.aspx   (linked from peta.org)
2. Replacement, reduction and refinement. P Flecknell, 2002. www.ncbi.nlm.nih.gov/pubmed/12098013

The Environment

Over the course of the evolution of this planet, there have been ice ages and warm periods and each have had their effect on the how the Earth has shaped itself. Europe has seen the glaciers pushed back from the north and natural forestation take over all of the continent, also providing homes for animals that have migrated as the climates and temperatures have changed.

Before the dawn of humans the land was covered with highly enriched ecosystems, many species of animals balancing their populations through their natural need to use other species for food and keeping the ecosystems thriving in general harmony.

Humans then came along and with their mental development leading to the learning of how to transform forests into fields and how to tame animals for their own use in agriculture, and with their exploitation of the natural resources such as wood and metal, managed to upset the natural order of life.

Even though many good developments have undoubtedly come out of this development of humanity, such as how to feed themselves better and how to make infertile land fertile, they also, due to the lack of knowledge that their actions could have massive consequences, cared not for what might eventually happen once they had cut all the trees down or had captured all of a certain species for food. This lack of insight led to such catastrophes as the black death in the 14th century where half of the human population of Europe was wiped out. This plague was caused when humans, thinking they had advanced amazingly, lured rats into their unclean towns and villages by leaving rubbish and harvested crops in places where they were not managed properly. The number of rats increased dramatically, as did the number of fleas that carried the infections that got passed onto humans on a massive scale in a very short time, resulting in the epidemic known as the bubonic plague.

Easter Island is a good example of how humans have had total disregard for their desires. Once a thriving culture, given that it is an island that was practically inaccessible due to its isolation in the Pacific Ocean, the only resources they have to survive on were what they had on the island.

The population started to increase rapidly but so did their desire to create many Moai statues to reflect their spiritual beliefs that they would embody the spirits of their ancestors. The islanders continually cut down trees to make into canoes, shelters and equipment to transport the newly carved statues. Of course, this meant that it got to a point where the people had destroyed their own means for survival. The ecosystem collapsed and so with it the human population.

There are also arguments that diseases brought in by the European explorers (who could more accurately be referred to as invaders) were the reason for the decline in numbers. The downfall of the indigenous people was a combination of the two. Their population went from 2-3000 in 1772, as estimated by Dutch explorer Jacob Roggeveen to 111 in 1887. This was also due to the invaders taking the islanders as slaves to other Pacific islands as many people have done in history to gain power and money.

This isolated example of Easter Island is a useful warning to the population of the world – we can't just follow our own desires with no consideration of the consequences, it will be the cause of our downfall as well as all the other animal and plant species that we share the world with. We do not have free reign to do as we wish and in terms of what we do, our first responsibility is to look after the life source that we all entirely depend on to survive.

Of course, the lesson we have now learned from the downfall of Easter Island was not something that was well known at the time. Around the same time that its people were almost entirely wiped out, the Industrial Revolution was gaining ground in Britain. Factory machinery was rapidly developing and these means of production had to be fuelled. The discovery of coal proved to be more effective than trees and it was mined and burned in vast quantities. The amount of air pollution that was created left a thick layer of smog over major cities in Britain and mainland Europe once the Revolution expanded.

Other aspects of this have been discussed elsewhere but to summarise, from an environmental perspective, it can be argued that the worst thing to evolve on this planet was humans. All other animals live within their ecosystems until the climate changes and they have to migrate if they are going to avoid natural extinction. Humans, on the other hand, cause extinction to occur due to their irresponsibility and ignorance of the necessity to live in harmony with the ecosystems.

Fortunately, some humans have seen the errors of our ways and learned from our cataclysmic mistakes throughout history. Some people have dedicated their lives to finding out how we can begin to rectify our destruction of our home and giver of life.

Sepp Holzer, in the 1960s, sought to work out how to mimic the relationships found in natural ecologies on his farm in Austria. This concept, known as permaculture[1], was further explored and developed by Australians Bill Mollison and David Holmgren from the 1970s to better understand ideas about stable agricultural systems. Essentially, this line of study is all about how to design human settlements that are more self-sufficient and reduce the reliance on industrial systems of production.

Rob Hopkins, author of The Transition Handbook, believes that permaculture is the necessary foundation of moving past the oil dependency age and, whereas it is complicated to explain briefly, is something that most people are not aware of but ought to be.

To attempt to give a concise overview of permaculture, David Holmgren has identified 12 areas to be attentive to. These include observation and interaction, where we should pay attention to our environment to be able to understand how it functions and how we can design settlements effectively. Catching and storing energy refers to how energy passes through natural systems and is stored in various natural components such as soil. Obtaining a yield is about making our interventions productive like edible roof gardens or fruit-bearing trees in public places. This is an excellent idea – imagine there being fruit trees all over the neighbourhood, where people are free to take a piece of fruit from them as they wish. When ideas such as this are introduced, the people take care of the means of production because the trees would be there for everyone who lives nearby. It is in their best interests even though there is no monetary profit to be made.

Holmgren's fourth principle is applying self-regulation and accepting feedback. This is about being able to design a system that takes care of itself naturally, reducing the need for maintenance, very similarly seen in Masanobu Fukuoka's natural farming book, The One Straw Revolution.[2] Nature thrives at its best when it is left to do its own thing. We humans like to think we are able to advance everything, including nature, when we can't unless we add some unnatural aspects to it like chemicals. The ecosystems were in place long before you and I were here and long before humans arrived on the scene. The only help it needs is when we need to rectify the mess we have made to it.

Use and value renewable resources and services is fifth on the list. Again, as in natural farming, this means to allow nature to aerate soil using worms instead of trying to replace them with fertiliser and other harmful chemicals. Artificial additives are not going to be at all productive to make soil more fertile but the weeds actually play an important part in balancing the ecosystem.

In nature, there is no waste. Every output from one system is an input to another. We need to work much more on making our actions work in this way. Even though progress is slowly being made regarding recycling, there is a lot further to go, though I will discuss this later on.

The seventh principle is about being able to see things on the larger scale instead of focusing on individual details. We must learn to see how it affects things on the whole as every aspect of natural interactions make up a bigger picture. It is no good designing one small aspect in a settlement if it is not going to be congruous to the whole system. Natural clashes will occur and the whole will break down into its separate parts. This also leads on to the next one of integrating rather than segregating. Solutions are to be found in integrated holistic solutions rather than increased specialisation and compartmentalisation.

Using small and slow solutions is explained by Holmgren as "systems should be designed to perform functions at the smallest scale that is practical and energy-efficient for that function." This is all about efficiency and getting the most out of the minimum input.

Using value and diversity is analogous to the desire to bring a variety of culture to cities instead of following the same monoculture that globalisation has brought about. Diverse ecosystems are more resilient to pests and disease than those which are structured to achieve specific results like the growing of a single crop.

The eleventh principle is about ecosystems that meet and overlap. This can, as seen from observation, maximise their potential and be more productive than the two systems on their own.

The final principle of Holmgren's permaculture is one that ties in with the Buddhist observation that everything is constantly changing. Natural systems constantly evolve and grow, that's how the planet has managed to thrive for billions of years. It has outlived ice ages, earthquakes, volcanoes and even meteoric collisions. However, we must respect that the Earth has to go about its business in its way and we are nowhere near understanding how it can do this so efficiently. We are just another of the products of the living world and we have only existed for a microscopic fraction of the time that it has been in existence. We have to be much more sensitive to its needs and not our own desires that have caused, in a little over 200 years of industry and selfish capitalism, untold destruction and extinction of species just to serve our own misguided interests.

The idea of permaculture is one that is fascinating and as it is only in its initial stages of study, is one that should be embraced by society in general to appreciate and understand the world as well as one that should be taught in detail in school to develop the coming generations into ones that would be shocked at the idea of any kind of pollution or deforestation.

In terms of pollution and waste from industries, it is quite simple where we need to start if we are going to evolve a new era that eliminates all traces of our mistakes as a species. We *are* mentally developed enough to be more efficient with waste management. It may be cheap and easy just to send the effluent into the rivers and seas, but it shouldn't be legal. It would just take a short amount of time to devise better methods of dealing with waste so that it can either be sent back into the land if it is of a type that would be productive or be processed to be both safe and useful again as an input to another system. If neither of these results can be achieved, then the means of production have to change. It may only be transferring the energy used from fossil fuels to renewable energy. If it gets to a point where nobody can see any solution to the waste produced, we have to decide whether the production of whatever it is is needed or can be phased out.

Recycle everything

Over the recent decades, people have started to become more aware of the need to recycle. Until then, and it still happens, rubbish was taken away to places where nobody would go and dumped in a landfill. This idea was extremely primitive and was undertaken without any insight at all. In the beginning it would have seemed like a good idea in the short term – there were big holes in the ground, often after the natural resources had been exploited through excavating and they would hold enormous amounts of rubbish. The problem is, of course, that not everything is biodegradable and whereas organic material such as food would break down and re-fertilise the earth, glass, metal and plastic would remain almost indefinitely.

So when this was realised, what did the local councillors and government ministers decide to do? Carry on as before. Who cares? The holes are really big and nobody goes there so it doesn't matter.

Well, it does, it really matters. Already it is common knowledge that animals that go there to scavenge for food get trapped in discarded packaging and suffocate or suffer injuries, and they can pick up and spread diseases in a way that is similar to the onset of the Black Death.

But in the light of climate change awareness, recycling has started to take off more (in some countries) but it is still in its early stages of development. In Portugal, it is standard to have many recycling containers to collect paper/ card, glass, and packaging such as plastic and metal containers. They can be found very easily and one is usually never more than 5 minutes walk from a set of these (the UK, considered to be a more developed and richer country lags very far behind Portugal's example). If people are given the facilities to recycle, they will. If they have to travel long distances to find a recycling centre or bin, they won't bother; they will just dump everything in the same rubbish bag.

Evoking responsibility in the general public to look after the environment is not easy; people get set in their ways and think "We've done it like this all our life, why should we change?" Because it is and always has been one of your duties as a citizen. Remember, this is not *our* world; it created us and we have to lose this selfish apathy for it.

Communities need to have easy access to be able to recycle everything that they don't want. It is more than just recycling plastic, glass and paper. Organic waste should not be thought of as waste but as seen from Holmgren's permaculture principles, every output should be seen as an input for something else. If the organic leftovers from food were collected separately, they could be used to fertilise the land substantially and not just on farms but on areas that are thought of as wasteland within towns and cities. If there is an area of scrub land where nothing grows apart from a few weeds, it should be transformed following the permaculture method of practical design. The land can be ploughed and the organic matter can be added, which will bring in the more natural contributors such as worms to help restore the land to a natural, productive state.

We have so much that we throw away that could actually be used for very good reasons. All that plastic which won't biodegrade for hundreds of years could even be used to create the recycling bins that you are going to collect the next lot in. Home insulation could be made to make people's houses and flats more heat-efficient and less reliant on external heating sources, therefore cutting people's heating bills and reducing our carbon footprint. Old bricks from dilapidated buildings could be used again to build more artistic structures and decorations for the host of new parks that are spread around the town.

There has been a resurgence of an ancient method in construction; that of building using straw. This is when bales of hay are taken from farms, instead of having them burnt as unneeded waste, drying and compressing it into large bricks that work better as building materials than manufactured bricks. This is because they provide natural insulation and sound-proofing and are actually more resistant to fire due to the lack of oxygen in the densely compressed straw (which is plastered over in the same way that bricks are). This is another excellent example of turning waste into something useful. For more information, visit Andrew Morrison's website at strawbale.com.[3]

Not only are the innovations for recycling endless, but the number of jobs that can be created that have a real meaning is also something to think about. Working in areas of innovation to bring about real development that follows the permaculture principles is an exciting challenge where the results would be very rewarding.

There is a great scope for building a more resilient community through recycling. Considering the vast amount of items that get thrown into rubbish tips, if this was organised better, people could create their own jobs relatively easily and simultaneously protect the environment.

The way it could work is that if there were collection centres for unwanted items such as old furniture, washing machines electronic appliances, etc. in various places in communities, these can work as the starting points for new business as these items would serve as resources that don't require any capital or extraction from the ground to acquire, don't cause environmental damage (in fact totally the opposite as it means these items wouldn't be ending up in dumps any more) and would be available to the local people to collect, recycle and create new items with.

For example, if metals were needed for some project, they could be extracted from the unwanted items and re-fabricated so that they could be put to use again. Old furniture could be restored or just taken apart and used to make something different.

The plan would be to inspire the community to become involved in this as the only real capital they would need would be human capital, i.e. their own work. It would engender creativity in the community so that they could create things that they could sell, therefore creating their income. It could bring like-minded people together to be their own bosses (and workers with equal rights) who can develop their ideas and skills together, with an emphasis on supporting the members of the community who are otherwise unemployed to give them the chance to find a role in their lives. Being community-based, it would really develop the local economy (rather than create economic growth if say one business took control of this whole project and made all the money that was not equally shared out with the employees).

This is something that is entirely realistic, productive, creative and social, with, of course, the benefit of greatly reducing the amount of waste deposited in the environment.

Using an example from The Transition Handbook[4], we can make the transition from clone towns to more individual towns with character by taking disused land and returning it to its natural state. Where a building has been demolished and the area is abandoned, communities should get together to remove the artificial traces and help restore it to a more attractive natural area. Becoming involved in renewable energy projects as outlined in the Energy section will give the ownership of energy back to the people and motivate them to maintain it. Growing the community's own fruit and vegetables will encourage people to spend their money on local produce so that they support each other.

Easier said than done? Rob Hopkins addresses the problems that people might face when wanting to start a transition.

1. 1. We have no funding – Funding is not necessary and is an easy way of disguising a lack of enthusiasm and dedication to achieve results. Don't sit back and complain that the council are not sorting out something that you have an issue with. Do it yourself. Get like-minded people together and even if it's only a few of you, everyone else in the vicinity will see what you have done and will respect you for your work and some of them will be inspired by you to undertake a similar project.

2. They won't let us – Thinking that the local council will reject your idea has been found by Hopkins to be untrue. If you approach them positively, those in power are likely to be supportive of your plans, especially if they can see that you have nothing to gain from it other than a more pleasant environment for everyone concerned.

3. There are already 'green' groups and we don't want to step on their toes – You very probably won't. Groups need to join forces and share ideas and initiatives. People with the same goal will be willing to hear more ideas and it will only make the overall enthusiasm stronger.

4. No-one here cares about the environment anyway – Hopkins also states that we might perceive an apathetic consumer culture surrounding us. But if you start a program, you are likely to find that other people will come out of the woodwork and want to join you, they just didn't know how to begin.

5. Surely it's too late to do anything – We are not yet at a point where the world is collapsing around us and we can see impending doom marching on. If we sit back and don't do anything, it will get to be too late. If we start immediately, we can be the change we want to see in the world (adapted from a quote by Gandhi).

6. I don't have the right qualifications – You don't need any. All you need is the willingness to learn, work together, develop ideas and get your hands dirty.

7. I don't have the energy to do that – It may seem like an enormous project to undertake but as long as everyone is rational and makes sure that everything is organised effectively, it will move from being a daunting task to one that you really don't want to stop doing!

I strongly believe that the environment that people live in affects their mood. People are less likely to be content with their surroundings if they are full of plain, grey concrete buildings and dilapidated structures. It does not give a feeling of enjoying living there when it looks so ugly but people who live in well-managed and maintained areas that have a significant amount of natural elements such as trees and flowers, the ambience helps people to feel more content with their neighbourhood. This is an example of how we are instinctively connected to the natural world. People love to be by the coast and see the expanse of the sea, or a vast area of land as seen from a mountain top. But why? There is no more to it than our natural connection with the world. This is something that we have lost sight of in the west, with city-living and getting used to countless buildings that have been primarily designed for their function rather than their aesthetics. People like to go to parks and escape from the concrete jungles because they are more peaceful and beautiful. They bring a sense of well-being and we should make a great effort to increase the amount of areas like this; even integrating them into the built-up areas.

For many of the well-established business practices such as extracting non-renewable resources for fuels and leaving behind untold amounts of pollution, regulation is again the key. Whereas we can't simply prohibit companies from mining altogether, we can offer them support so that, on hand, we can help them find solutions to disposing their waste efficiently, we also support them to look for alternative business practices so that they move from exploiting non-renewable resources to green energy. It is not a case of treating them with an iron fist, but trying to bring everyone together in a well-planned and well-managed system of transition.

In the case of the BP oil spill in the Gulf of Mexico (beginning in spring 2010), this has to be seen as a wake-up call to the world that has similarities with the Easter Island case: if we keep trying to push things too far for our own irresponsible interests, we are going to have to pay for the consequences, often in a massive way. We are still in a primitive state of how we provide for ourselves. There is an exciting challenge to harness renewable resources so that we don't need to worry about the problems of such disasters or pollution. It may still seem like a long way off before we get to this stage, but the more people work together, the more quickly we can get there.

1. Various books by David Holmgren and Bill Morrison. Example: "Permaculture: Principles and Pathways Beyond Sustainability". Hepburn, Victoria: Holmgren Design Services.
2. The One Straw Revolution, Masanobu Fukuoka. Other India Press.
3. Strawbale.com, Andrew Morrison
4. The Transition Handbook, Rob Hopkins. Green Books.

Agriculture

The agricultural sector would need a large-scale redevelopment. In the modern world, the vast majority of it is conducted as Chemical Agriculture, that being agriculture which is almost fully dependent on the use of chemicals such as insecticides and fertilizers. This is something that came about towards the end of the 20th century as the big chemical manufacturers devised a way to con farmers and governments into believing that they needed these products to produce better crops.

With the problems of plant diseases and harmful insects, these two groups welcomed the idea of the use of chemicals to address these problems.

Thus, chemical agriculture took over quite quickly and although there are, of course, a few farms in the world that use the traditional method, the chemical manufacturers have been the greatest beneficiaries of this revolution.

The research for proposing a large-scale redevelopment of agriculture comes from a book by Masanobu Fukuoka called "The One-Straw Revolution".[1] He was a 20th century Japanese farmer who had, over many decades, developed another method called Natural Farming. It is a method which, as you will read below, appears to be so basic as to be implausible but is the most effective type of farming for many reasons.

Natural Farming (or Do-Nothing Farming) follows four main principles. Firstly, there is no cultivation necessary. According to Fukuoka, the earth cultivates itself naturally with plants, creatures and micro-organisms.

Secondly, there are no chemical fertilizers or prepared compost. This is simply due to the fact that people try to alter nature to improve it but as we are merely another product of nature, we can't understand nature as a whole and cannot attempt to improve it when it works perfectly well on its own.

Thirdly, there is no weeding or use of herbicides. Fukuoka found that weeds actually play a part in providing nutrition to the soil and keeping the biological community balanced. Just because we perceive them to be unattractive or of no use to us, there are reasons why they grow otherwise they wouldn't. Nature knows what it is doing and we, in this sense, don't.

Fourthly, there is no dependence on chemicals. This is fundamental to the agricultural regression that is needed to improve farming and its resulting produce. The use of chemicals, whereas it provides a short-term solution to disease and insect population, actually leads to a long-term problem which cannot be easily undone. Plants become weaker with the use of chemicals and they become dependent. The soil is put off balance and it cannot provide adequate conditions to grow the plants unless more chemicals are used to artificially stimulate growth. This, therefore, leads to an eternal circle which greatly increases the costs for farmers, makes a huge amount of work to produce food that will sell and most notably, consistently provides the chemical manufacturers with huge profits for something that is actually completely unnecessary in the agricultural sector.

Marketing of food has also helped to maintain the use of chemicals. Advertising food that looks good (the 'right' size, the 'right' colour) has become a standard method recently, which has been enough to dupe the customers into buying what 'appears' nice. The whole 'judging by appearance' has become standard all across Western society recently and we can use the problems with marketing of food as an analogy for marketing in general.

To be able to produce food that naïve customers will obediently buy, the farmers have to go through a tough process. Only those products which are the right size, shape and colour will be able to be sold to the markets, even if the other products are as good nutritionally but don't look as appetizing. Once enough chemicals have been used to attain the desired look, they are sold and the farmers barely make enough to cover their own costs of production.

There has been a trend recently of buying organic foods or those grown without any unnatural additives. But, as this is a trend or a fashion, organic food is sold at a higher price due to the status of it. However, properly organic or naturally produced food will not have used any chemicals or will not be 'dressed up' in any way or rejected if it doesn't meet the above-mentioned criteria. The cost of production for the farmer is minimal so the higher costs cannot be justified in any way. That's to say, not in any moral way. The retailers can justify the higher prices in their own greedy way.

Another problem with chemical farming is that the nutritional value of the food drops dramatically. The fight that nature has with the interference of chemicals reduces the level of vitamins and flavour in the food, especially in those that have been grown out of season in greenhouses and other artificial environments. The reason why such foods are grown out of season are to meet customers' apparent demands of having them available all year round. However, these demands do not come from the customers, the idea of demand has been forced upon the customers by the marketing companies.

Organic farming has been developing recently although the first noted practices of it were in the 1930s. It differs from natural farming in that it uses cultivation (which upsets the natural balance of the soil and leads to deterioration), and still uses pesticides, although in a limited sense. The very fact that pesticides are still used proves that, again, the ecosystems are being challenged and thrown out of balance, which does not equate with the very notion of organic farming.

This is some argument about the yields of organic farming compared to chemical farming but in general, to balance out the arguments, they are more or less as productive as each other, though organic farming can survive better in severe weather such as droughts. This is probably due to the crops being stronger because of their lower dependency on chemicals and their ability to grow under unfavourable conditions. However, organic farming still requires machinery and some chemicals to function, whereas natural farming requires no chemicals, no machinery and very limited labour as most of the work can be left to nature and the yields are also at least as good as by chemical methods or even better in severe weather conditions.

Applying the natural method to livestock

Whereas I am vegetarian, in the Hypothetical Government I cannot simply demand that no meat production should be allowed. The majority of the population eats meat and we could not force such dietary changes. However, humane treatment of animals is the fundamental condition to be put in place before any questions of productivity are raised. As humans are merely another animal species on Earth, they are equal to all other living creatures in terms of rights. Any animals have the right to be treated as humans would expect to be treated and in livestock terms, this means that stressful and painful forms of killing livestock must be illegal. Humane methods would have to be used in every agricultural institution to ensure that immediate and painless death is achieved. No animals will be allowed to be kept in restricted surroundings, such as chickens. Battery farming will be illegal, even though this may result in lower food production initially. It will only be a case of farmers providing enough space for the animals in a 'number of square metres per animal' ratio which will be enforced by law and subject to random checks. Government subsidies will be available to help with this transition to adequate living conditions for these animals. This would also mean that kosher and halal methods of killing (slitting the animal's throat until it bleeds to death) would be illegal and punishable for reasons of inhumanity. In

2003, the Farm Animal Welfare Council concluded that the way halal and kosher meat is produced causes severe suffering to animals and should be banned immediately.[2]

Another important factor in keeping livestock is the animals' diet. No artificial substances will be allowed to feed any animals and their diet must be kept as natural as possible, for example, chickens would be able to eat seeds and smaller creatures such as worms and insects, thereby maintaining the balance of the ecosystem as naturally as possible. Failure to comply with any of these conditions will lead to advice as to how to improve the farm and subsidies if the farmers cannot meet the costs of transition. If this advice is not followed up, the farmer can be forbidden to keep livestock. The imposing of conditions to maintain a lawful farm must be as agreeable as possible to avoid conflicts between farmers and authorities.

Certain foods would be banned due to their inhumane production methods. For example, foie gras, which is made from the liver of ducks and geese which have been force-fed to fatten them is unquestionably immoral. If you think it isn't, imagine doing that to your dog or having it done to yourself. Some EU countries, along with Turkey and Israel have already banned the production of this so-called delicacy.

Making the transition to natural farming

To change from chemical farming to natural farming would, of course, be a major transition and couldn't be achieved with immediate effect. First of all, the natural farming method as expounded by Fukuoka describes how he developed it in Japan. The climate, crops, soil and ecosystems are variable for each country and therefore a natural farming method would have to be researched and developed depending on the country and different regions of a country if there are wetter and drier/ hotter and colder regions. To reach the point where the methods have been adjusted for all these criteria, researchers would have to experiment on where and when particular crops can grow effectively based on the knowledge already used by farmers in their regions.

Then, a gradual transition would be made over a number of years to gradually convert fields or sections of fields to the natural method until the entire farms have reached a self-sustainable level. This transition would be estimated to be in effect within about five years of an agreed method.

The effects of this transition would also influence chemical manufacturers and marketing in a large way. The chemical manufacturers would lose a lot of revenue and their businesses could either face collapse or a turn to manufacturing chemicals for alternative markets. Morally, the potential collapse of such an industry is of no concern as chemical dependence in any way is to be condemned as it has no benefit for the natural balance of either the human immune system, general level of health or the environment and would always be discouraged.

Food imports and exports

It will always be the case, due to varying climates and soil types, that not all foods can be grown in every part of the world and rely on imports and exports to make them available worldwide. There are a number of controversies with this, however, and regulation would need to come into place.

First of all, countries which export great quantities of food that is more specific to their region are often poor and unable to supply their own people with enough variety of food to maintain health. It would need to be firmly regulated with an international agreement that these poorer countries are not exploited so much for the greedy desires of richer countries that they are unable to feed themselves adequately. It would need to be enforced to make sure that food can only be exported if it exceeds the national quota for the required diet of the native people.

The prices that exported foods can be sold for would also need regulation so that, again, poorer countries are not being exploited simply because the western world can pay them a minimal amount which translates into a still acceptable amount for the farmers and producers of food. The Fair Trade movement is one which seeks to help producers in developing countries obtain better trading conditions and sustainability. Currently, certain products bear the Fair Trade label to give customers the opportunity to decide if they wish to support this movement. But this is not enough. Whereas I would recommend giving people alternatives to which they can turn rather than outlawing some companies' practices, there needs to be a far greater push for fair trade so that all food exported reaches the objectives that this organisation has laid out.

The key principles of the Fair Trade movement are:
- Connecting producers to customers and allowing access with fewer middlemen.
- Provide higher wages than typically paid to producers as well as

helping producers develop knowledge, skills and resources to improve their lives.

- Raise awareness of the movement's philosophies among consumers in developed nations.[3]

It doesn't need much examination to see that this is a far more moral way of conducting the export and import of food and one that needs to be standard all across the world.

To enforce fair trading globally, we would be actively playing a part in helping the developing world to become more resilient economically, as well as helping the people to become more educated and skilled so that progress towards equality between nations can become a realistic goal.

Furthermore, we need to try to reduce the amount of exports overall to reduce the amount of transport costs, fuel costs and environmental damage that such transportation accrues. We need to accept the idea that we have no real need for foods to be available all year round and that we can live quite comfortably without having some foods available in the country if it is not viable for them to be imported over enormous distances where the environmental impact does not justify their transportation.

This is all part of the education procedure that needs to take place to get people to accept that some things do need to be scaled down and we can't always have everything that we want just because our country is an economic powerhouse or so influential and controlling that we get things cheaply without any regard for the consequences.

1. The One-Straw Revolution, Masanobu Fukuoka. Other India Press.
2. The Farm Animal Welfare Council is a UK-based organisation and its reports can be found at www.fawc.org.uk
3. www.fairtrade.net

Energy

"Oh, human life, we would like to value it.
But if there is no profit in it, what's the point?"
McCarthy – "I'm On the Side of Mankind as Much as the Next
Man"

At the current time of late 2009, there has been a lot of discussion and debate about energy crises, the effects of greenhouse gases on the environment and especially the oil crisis. As there have been many conflicting viewpoints that have been put forward by various people or institutions, it's hard to know who to trust or who to believe. To be able to address this issue, we need to analyse the various viewpoints with the same criteria to be democratic and to arrive at the truth. Conspiracies are useless as they will be argued to the end of time without any proper resolution.

It is generally agreed that climate change is happening, although there have been a number of cases where data has been falsified from both sides (those who argue that it is happening and those who argue that it is not). We are still at a point where we need to be more honest to establish the extent that climate change is happening so we must look at the facts of what we know (or strongly suspect) are the reasons for it. First of all, there is the possibility that some of it is due to a natural change in the cycle of the planet. There has previously been an ice age and there have been times where the average global temperature has been higher than it is now. The difficulty with ascertaining whether it is purely due to natural changes is that such fluctuations in the climate take a long time (the last glacial period, or Ice Age, lasted for around 100,000 years) so even though the average temperature of the world has been rising noticeably over the last few decades, we can't really know where the plateau would be in terms of when and how hot it will get before it naturally falls again. However, as the temperature rise appears to be increasing a lot faster than would naturally occur, from studies of the history of the Earth's climate[1], it looks very likely that it is largely due to what began as human naïvety and ignorance (when we didn't realise that pumping tons of CO_2 out of factories during the industrial revolution was actually harmful in any way) then continued as human knowledge and ignorance (knowing full well that too much CO_2 in the atmosphere is harmful to everything on the planet but not really caring because there is profit to be made from it).

It has not been difficult to analyse the effects of pollution from smoke and effluent from factories to the levels of smog in densely populated cities such as Los Angeles and Lima, Peru because of the amount of vehicle exhaust and factory emissions. The use of fossil fuels such as coal in the earlier part of the 20th century and oil in the latter part and in the 21st century has caused most of the pollution that we are now aware of and wondering what to do about it.

To give a quick explanation as to why fossil fuels have been used so much, it all comes down to the development of industry during the 19th century and the use of heavy machinery that needed some way of powering it cheaply so that production levels could increase. To create this power, human force was simply not going to work so the burning of coal was found to be viable as it was found in abundance and it could be mined cheaply. As the development of industry continued into the 20th century, oil was found to be just as cheap and abundant to produce for the purposes of heavy industry and with the development of motor vehicles, and it all looked like a wonderful way of developing the world. Through this blissful ignorance of the effects of burning fossil fuels, the developed world began to race ahead of itself and businesses started to flourish as car production rocketed, aeroplanes became a normal way of travelling long distances and trade and export was able to expand globally, sending products made cheaply in poor countries to the rich countries so that the consumers could have anything they wanted and the effects of attaining such products were conveniently hidden away so that the average citizen wouldn't know how much pollution had been caused in the developing countries, how poor the workers were who made the products and how many tonnes of CO_2 were spewed out by the ships that transported the products tens of thousands of kilometres across the oceans.

Of course, it's not just due to industry that we use a lot of energy as the vast majority of the world's electricity is generated by burning fossil fuels. As, in the western world, most people have televisions, computers, stereos, washing machines, microwaves and the countless other electrical appliances, the amount of electricity that has to be generated so that the demand is met is phenomenal. On top of this is the amount of work-related appliances that are electrically powered to provide the essential resources such as in schools and hospitals. It has become so much a part of our way of life that we are used to it, it's normal and we don't see the effects of what we do.

Oil is not just used for generating electricity and powering vehicles. In fact, many of our regular items are made from oil. From the following list compiled by Rob Hopkins, try to work out which of these things are made directly from oil and which are not.

Aspirin, sticky tape, trainer shoes, lycra socks, glue, paint, varnish, foam mattresses, carpets, nylon, polyester, CDs, DVDs, plastic bottles, contact lenses, hair gel, brushes, toothbrushes, rubber gloves, washing-up bowls, electric sockets, plugs, shoe polish, furniture wax, computers, printers, candles, bags, coats, bubble wrap, fruit juice containers, rawl plugs, credit cards, loft insulation, PVC windows, lipstick.

That's a lot to choose from but try to sort them into two groups of oil-based and non oil-based products.
When you have sorted them, you can see the answers at the end of this chapter.
So what this means is that we have become an oil dependent civilisation. With our current lifestyles, we cannot live without it. Apart from the threat of global warming, at least we won't have to change our lifestyles dramatically. Well, that would be the case if fossil fuels such as oil lasted forever. Unfortunately, fossil fuels of any kind are non-renewable. They will eventually run out. There have been debates about this issue already, most notably in the first decade of the 21st century but still, the vast majority of the public is not sure what the situation is.

Effectively, there are two sides to the argument concerning oil – it's not going to run out any time soon vs. it's going to run out very quickly at the rate we are currently using it. Let's have a look at who are arguing the above cases.

Case 1: Oil is not going to run out any time soon

This is argued by energy companies, whose businesses rely on the continuing production of oil.

It is also argued by a lot of western governments who want to keep the current pattern of lifestyle as it is because people seem comfortable with it; they have access to thousands of products made from oil, thereby stimulating the economy and it's easier to keep things as they are rather than uproot everything which could cause problems for the general population.

The media also do not support the theory of oil running out soon because they think that people are not going to want to hear that their lifestyles will have to change and that the very fuel of economic growth is going to run out (literally). Such a declaration would cause national and international panic, would cause people to hoard oil for themselves and they don't want that responsibility.[2]

The International Energy Agency (IEA), which is an intergovernmental organisation, acts as a policy advisor to its 28 member countries as well as other major countries like China, Russia and India. As reported in The Guardian in November 2009, a 'whistleblower' has revealed that the world is much closer to running out of oil than official estimates admit and claims the IEA has been deliberately underplaying a looming shortage for fear of triggering panic buying. The IEA source said:

"The IEA in 2005 was predicting oil supplies could rise as high as 120m barrels a day by 2030 although it was forced to reduce this gradually to 116m and then 105m last year. The 120m figure always was nonsense but even today's number is much higher than can be justified and the IEA knows this."[3]

This has left the IEA in a position where people should not have any faith in their predictions or claims. They have been deliberately deceiving us (probably under the member states orders) and should be referred to as the International Energy Conspiracy Agency.

The average carefree consumer is also going to be unwilling to believe it because they want to keep their cars, all their electronic gadgets and their lifestyles that depend on the production of oil. It's cheap enough and they can't see the problems that lie behind the industry.

<u>Case 2: Oil is going to run out very quickly at the rate we are currently using it</u>

The other side of the debate is argued by independent scientists who have researched and objectively analysed research about when oil production is going to peak and the supply can no longer meet the demand. Such people are concerned, not because their careers depend on it, but because the world depends on it and if there is no longer enough of it to maintain our lifestyles, things are going to get very difficult for everyone.

There are varied conclusions from independent scientists about peak oil but only in the case of when it is going to happen. The Association for the Study of Peak Oil has one some of the best research of the possible future of oil and gas production. It is easy to see that the peak for all types of oil and gas look to peak around 2010 and that by 2020 regular oil will be produced at the rate that it was in 1970, i.e. significantly less.[4]

Other researchers are only torn between whether oil has already peaked as of 2008 or will peak around 2020. Whichever year proves to be right, there is not a great deal of difference between them; it is going to happen not just in most of our lifetimes but it may have happened by the time you have read this.

Environmentalists accept the predictions because we need to start looking at how we are going to adapt our lifestyles so that we are not going to decimate the planet any more than we are currently doing.

Basically anybody who is aware of this problem of peak oil is concerned that a very big change is going to have to come about very soon and that we need to prepare ourselves so that it is not going to be the apocalypse that the media would like to declare for the sake of sensationalism but doesn't dare to do for the sake of their own jobs.

So from the perspectives of the two sides, the "denial" team in Case 1 have an agenda – their money and power could potentially dry up and the "awareness raising" team in Case 2 only have the agenda that they want to make everyone aware of the problem and, most importantly, the alternatives that we could choose to adopt to avoid descending into panic. That and wanting to actively help the planet maintain its self-sufficiency that is obviously vital to all life on Earth.

From this, we can very clearly work out which side is telling the truth and it's not difficult to work out that it is the side that has nothing to lose personally.

This leaves us with the knowledge that we are either already at the point of peak oil or we are going to reach it very soon, meaning before 2020. What implications does this have? When oil becomes more scarce, the price of it will increase as the oil companies will want to protect their own assets above anything else, such as the stability of the planet. This is the capitalist model for business – put profit before everything else. So if we persist in maintaining our carefree lifestyles and intend to use oil and oil based products, it is going to become more scarce more quickly. This would lead to a shock to humanity as it stands, with panic buying exacerbating the scarcity and violent behaviour between people and towards governments for not letting its people know about the huge problem. Civilisation in the western world would effectively collapse as we know it in all forms imaginable unless we act now.

To put people's minds at rest, at this point, it needs to be said that there are alternatives and the potential results of these are actually far more beneficial for humanity than the throwaway illusion of reality that we have been led into.

Alternatives to oil as a major energy source

If we look at the pros and cons of oil, the pros show that it has been in abundance and relatively cheap to extract and refine. With its abundance, it has been able to be sold relatively cheaply so that many people can afford it without it affecting their finances too much. It has been a major factor in the development of industry and technology throughout the twentieth century. The cons are that it is a finite resource and through research of searching for new oil fields, it has been found that it is ever more difficult to find new oil fields that can produce substantial amounts of oil. Oil production peaked in the USA in 1970 and the discovery of it peaked in 1930. Since then, obtaining a monopoly on the oil industry has been of paramount importance to the American government and those that govern it (corporate executives of large companies such as car manufacturers and energy providers). It has been effectively proven that the American invasion of Iraq was conducted for the sole purpose of gaining access to and control of its vast oil fields by inventing a reason to invade the country (weapons of mass destruction that didn't exist).

Another other major con is that the use of oil causes catastrophic damage to the environment; to the atmosphere in terms of its CO_2 emissions, as well as causing vast amounts of pollution to rivers and water in general as oil tankers spew out waste into the oceans. This, in turn, has the result of damaging lives – the sea life that ingests the waste via their breathing, human and other animal life when having no access to purified water, especially in the developing world. The CO_2 emissions that cause greenhouse gases also significantly reduce the quality of the air that we breathe. This aspect is not touched upon so much in climate change debates, but those people who live in large and densely populated cities with millions of vehicles and hundreds of factories have to breathe this dirty air which can provoke cancer and other medical problems such as bronchitis and asthma. It has a direct effect on our health but we have become so used to it that we don't even notice that we are taking in so many pollutants that, obviously being unnatural to our immune systems, can cause permanent damage.

Yet another factor is the growth in world population. Between 1990 and 2000, it increased by almost 1 billion people. This is a frighteningly large number and there are predictions that it increase from 6.5 billion as it is now to 9 billion by 2050. The effect this would have on energy demand is that world's energy needs could increase by 50 percent or more by 2030.[5] With governments unwilling to change their policies to seriously tackle the oil crisis and merely offering weak proposals of reducing CO_2 emissions by say 10% over 20 years is worthless. As population increase spirals upwards, energy demands do likewise and as the amount of oil available drops dramatically with the prices of it undoubtedly due to sky-rocket as a result, it is time to move on and take the next step in world development.

To conclude, cheap oil, for all its worth in enabling us to manufacture products beyond our wildest dreams (and far beyond our needs to live happy lives), the damage that it causes leaves it with the status that it really isn't worth it when it comes down to its profound effects.

Then what should we be looking at to provide us with energy on a worldwide scale?

1. Other fossil fuels, such as coal, petroleum and natural gas have the same pros and cons as oil. They are all non-renewable, in terms of how much of demand there is for them compared to how long they take to form. To form the amount of oil that we have used in the twentieth century, it would have taken millions of years and for this reason (and the others stated above) they are not a viable or sensible option.

2. Tar sands have been put forward as an alternative to the dwindling oil fields. This is oil that is a mixture of sand and clay that is very viscous. The province of Alberta, Canada contains huge amounts of tar sands but to extract them, from the surface and shallow areas not only causes massive environmental destruction but the amount of energy that is needed to extract and wash it makes it a ridiculous proposition. Greenpeace estimate that by 2011, annual CO_2 emissions from tar sands production (that is, before it is actually used) will exceed 80 million tonnes, or more than that which is currently emitted by all of Canada's cars.[6] In this time of climate crisis, tar sands are seriously not worth considering.

3. Nuclear Energy. This form of energy is one that, despite ongoing arguments against it, governments are now readily turning to. The reason being that the amount of net energy that can be gained from nuclear power is very high (47 to 59:1, depending on the studies, for centrifuge enrichment, or 10.5 to 21:1 for diffusion enrichment).[7] Again, as with the case of cheap oil, uranium is a non-renewable resource and the planet has about 60 years' worth of it left. As more nuclear reactors are planned to be built, this would become less with the increase in production of nuclear power. That's not to mention that the cost of building a new nuclear plant, which, in 2009 in the USA, is between $6 billion and $10 billion. Furthermore, the dangers linked with nuclear energy are shocking; nuclear waste is a problem that has

no known answer. It is currently buried deep underground, for example under mountains as well as taken to developing countries where the residents will not directly know about it and it can be hidden far from so-called 'developed citizens.' Due to the fact that nuclear waste has a half-life of 100,000 years – that is, it will have depleted by half in that time and that it is seriously toxic, causing damage to internal organs, if the production of nuclear power were to increase in the wake of the reduction in oil production, its effects would be far more severe than CO_2.

Proponents of nuclear power claim that it is a carbon-free way of generating electricity. However, the mining, processing, enrichment, treatment and disposal sides of it are certainly not carbon-free; they cause about one-third of the emissions of a conventional gas-fired generating plant. (Transition Handbook, p.49) It may be lower but it not the answer, we can do better.

As countries are turning to nuclear power more at the moment, a doubling in the number of nuclear power plants also means a doubling in the possibility that a nuclear disaster could occur. Commercial power plants use nuclear fission reactions, although nuclear fusion reactions are thought to be safer but technically more difficult to achieve. If we moved from being an oil-dependent world to a nuclear-dependent world, the amount of disasters akin to Chernobyl, Ukraine in 1986 would undoubtedly increase with the change. Whereas there are now much tighter safety regulations for nuclear power plants, in the USA, the Nuclear Regulatory Commission does not enforce them consistently.[8] In developing countries, the likelihood of nuclear disaster will be higher still and this makes it a very contentious issue.

In short, nuclear energy is probably the worst possible option currently known to humans when looking for the transition from oil dependency.

4. Hydrogen. The recent exciting buzz to an alternative to oil has been the use of hydrogen to power cars and other machines. The business community has been advocating its use with the intention of making people believe that their lifestyles can remain as they are but just with this minor difference.

These claims are false. Hydrogen is not an energy source, it is a carrier of energy. It is something that needs to be created in its pure form by running electricity through water. Immediately we run into a problem because, of course, we need an energy source to produce electricity to then produce hydrogen. David Strahan estimates that to reach the demand of the power needed for the cars in the UK, we would need "67 Sizewell B nuclear power stations, a solar array covering every inch of Norfolk and Derbyshire combined, or a wind farm bigger than the entire southwest region of England." (Transition Handbook, p.72)

As all of these options to create pure hydrogen via renewable energy or potentially very dangerous nuclear power stations would be practically impossible to use, the other alternative would be oil, which as you can hopefully see by now is no longer an option.

To be able to evaluate the best options for energy sources, looking at them from a business perspective is totally unacceptable as the only factor that would be considered in this way is profit. If something could be extracted, processed and delivered in a way that brings in a high return, then nothing else is considered important. Certainly not environmental factors, destruction of habitats and ecosystems, certainly not humanitarian factors such as effects of pollution from waste produced from the procurement of a source of energy.

5. Biodiesel is another much lauded option as using oil grown from crops can generate power with almost no CO_2 emissions. It sounds like a good option on the surface, but again, talking about the scale on which we would need to use it to replace conventional oil, the amount of land that would be needed to grow enough crops would be impractical and the amount of energy needed to harvest the crops and convert it to liquid oil such as ethanol from sugar leaves it with a very low net energy ratio of 2:1, meaning that the amount of energy that we get from it is only double the amount of energy that we have to put into it. It is an option that can be used to a degree, i.e. on a relatively small scale as the CO_2 emissions and environmental effects are low enough to be worthy of more research.

6. Natural gas is another hyped alternative fuel, undoubtedly focusing on the word 'natural' to sound more appealing and acceptable. However, considering that it consists primarily of methane, it is a greenhouse gas. It needs to be extensively processed to remove all other elements apart from the methane, which means that a large amount of energy needs to go into the processing so the net 'clean energy' that results from it is minimal. It contributes substantially to global carbon emissions and if its production increases as an alternative to oil, of course the emissions will grow. An IPCC report showed that in 2004, CO_2 emissions from natural gas was about half of that of oil but it is projected that by 2030 the level would be higher than that of oil in 2004[9]. It goes without saying that it is also a finite resource and requires substantial environmental disruption to produce it. So, whereas it might sound good on the superficial level, practically speaking, it is not a viable alternative, either.

From a true development perspective, we need to consider the options available that are not going to cause destruction in any way (if at all possible) or on a very limited scale whereby the damage can be repaired quickly and effectively. This means that we can't start invading other countries to obtain access to their natural resources while displacing people from their areas of residence just because we have the power, the money and the say on what goes. This is another example of pure immorality and it cannot be allowed to happen if we want to bring stability and happiness to the world, both on an environmental and humanistic level.

What can be proposed are energy sources that are already in use and if they are not too economical in terms of their energy return:energy invested ratio yet, it doesn't mean that they are not useful, practical options but ones that have room for technological development.

Renewable energy sources such as solar photovoltaic (solar panels), wind turbines, geothermal and tidal energy, have been talked down by energy industry officials although the truth of it is that they can give more net energy than they misinform us about. Hopkins shows that the net energy ratio of oil in the US has fallen from 30:1 in 1970 to around 15:1 today with a global average of 20:1. This refers to how much energy can be obtained versus the amount of energy that needs to be used for the extraction. Wind energy currently has a ratio of 11:1, which is quite good and could make up for a large part of the oil currently used to generate electricity. The problem with wind is that geographically, some areas would have more access to it than others depending on the weather systems and how windy places are in general. The other is that wind is a naturally occurring phenomenon and it doesn't blow at a constant level – some days might be windy, others might not. It would always need a backup system in place for when there are shortages. However, to generate the total electricity used in the UK annually, 6% of the land area would be utilised, an area of about 70 miles by 70 miles, and this would not preclude that land from being used for other purposes.[10]

The same can be said for solar power. Photovoltaics don't currently have the capacity for a great net energy ratio (between 2.5:1 and 4.3:1 as of 2008) but as they have only been used on a large scale recently, there is much room for improvement and efficiency. For example, the potential energy from solar radiation exceeds human energy needs by 1800 times.[11] It produces no CO_2 emissions, as is true for wind power, so could be used as part of the jigsaw that we need to assemble to answer the crisis that we are facing. Considering that the potential energy is far more than we would actually ever need to use, this is definitely an option for future development and research.

Hydro power or hydroelectricity is the production of power through use of the gravitational force of falling or flowing water, such as through dams. It is the most used form of renewable energy with a good net ratio of 23:1. It produces no direct waste and relatively low CO_2 emissions, compared with fossil fuels. In 2006, approximately 20% of the world's electricity was generated through hydroelectricity and 88% of the electricity from renewable sources.[12]

The disadvantages of this form of energy are that many of the planet's potential hydroelectric sites are already developed, some existing schemes have problems due to silting and drier summers in the changing climate lead to reduced output. (Transition Handbook, p.51)

But whereas such renewable energy sources have their problems, combined, they can currently account for a lot of the energy demand with the potential to improve dramatically in the near future when we think about how quickly technology has developed over the last century. As we need to move into a transition stage right now, we should be looking at ways to reduce the demand for oil so that the supply can keep up but as the demand goes down, so do the emissions, which would need to be a continuing trend.

There is no question that we should be looking towards renewable energy sources as our future in providing power. But what is likely to change is that as oil has been so readily and cheaply available up to now, the transition required would be a seriously big movement – oil that is not used for generating electricity, like in motor vehicles, cannot be replaced by wind power or as yet, solar power. New innovations are necessary to address these issues and although it does require a change on a massive scale, we should embrace this challenge as our path towards to a new era in human development. It should also go hand in hand with creating new jobs. Renewable energy production accounted for 2.4 million jobs worldwide in 2006.[13]

The IEA, which was formed in 1974 has become established as the authority on energy issues for the developed countries. It has 28 members, including the USA, UK, Germany, Japan, Canada, South Korea and France. With these members, the IEA can be seen to be the ultimate power for energy advice on a global scale. Unfortunately, as seen above and in other instances, it has been criticised, especially by renewable energy groups who have accused it of consistently underestimating the the potential for renewable energy alternatives.[14] It is currently losing its ground on such issues and is an organisation that needs to be replaced.

Easier said than done?

The International Renewable Energy Agency (IRENA) was founded in January 2009. It is another intergovernmental organisation for the promotion of the adoption of renewable energy worldwide. It was formed by 75 countries who signed the IRENA charter[15] and now has 137 member states. The USA joined it under President Obama, reflecting the effort to support renewable energy technologies. Founded by the German government, other member states include the UK, France, Japan, South Korea and India. This is a very positive step towards our development as a united civilisation with the advancement of future technology.

IRENA's aims are to become the main driving force in promoting a rapid transition towards the widespread and sustainable use of renewable energy on a global scale:

"Acting as the global voice for renewable energies, IRENA will provide practical advice and support for both industrialised and developing countries, help them improve their regulatory frameworks and build capacity. The agency will facilitate access to all relevant information including reliable data on the potential of renewable energy, best practices, effective financial mechanisms and state-of-the-art technological expertise."[16]

IRENA is committed to giving assistance to developing countries as much as developed ones by offering assistance with gaining access to renewable technologies with regard to buying, maintaining and repairing the equipment with the future goal of achieving the capacity to produce such technologies autonomously. Visit the website at irena.org for more information.

Following on from the information given above, what we would expect to happen as a result of this awareness of the need for change is that the oil, gas, electricity and other power companies would respond to the issues at hand and change their practices accordingly. In fact, that is exactly what they would like to be seen to do. There have been adverts on TV for energy companies who claim they are embracing the global warming issue by researching into other fossil fuels such as natural gas, which they falsely claim is a clean fossil fuel. Other adverts have informed us of the need to diversify the sources of energy to include nuclear, gas and oil, as well as a token gesture to mention wind and solar power. As long as these companies maintain their interest in non-renewable energy sources, they are not to be trusted. We mustn't forget that these are big monopolies who, working in the capitalist model, have profit as their main goal.

But what can we do if that's the only way of us getting energy – by buying what these energy companies provide us with? Aren't we just at their mercy? After all, they have the means to provide energy and we, as average citizens, do not.

This is where we need to bring about change. There is no way that, if we leave all the decisions and power with the energy companies, anything significant will change. At the most, there would be reported figures of decreases in CO_2 emissions of around 2% per year (i.e. insignificant) but everything will function in the same way, with no attempts to reduce the amount of energy we consume or any attempt to make us aware that maybe our lifestyles need to change. And then, when the big oil crash happens, as mentioned earlier, no-one will be able to cope with the disruption to their lives.

So, whereas a favourite phrase of Margaret Thatcher was TINA, There Is No Alternative, I would like to inform you that there certainly are alternatives and they have been extensively written about and researched already.

Globalisation of the economy is a major factor with which corporations keep hold of their power and control. This leaves us with the feeling of powerlessness and a dependency on what the governments tell us and what their powerful friends (CEOs) tell us is going to be the way of life. It seems like an unchangeable system. We can't extract our own oil or generate gas pipelines to power our neighbourhoods – that has to be done for us and then we pay the bills that ensure that the energy companies gain more power and more profit and the public get further away from being able to have any effect or control over their own lives. Obviously, from a moralist perspective, this is not anywhere near good enough. If people feel helpless to influence their own lives and gain their own mastery, then it does not make for a happy society. People need to have a purpose to their lives and they need to have ownership of the things that have a direct effect on their lives.

How this can apply in the field of energy production can only really be achieved by using renewable energy sources. A movement has begun in the west where solar panels are being fitted to houses more, usually for heating water. This is the first step to ownership of the means of power. This happens on a personal level so that each home caters for itself to a small degree. An even better step to take next would be to give the power (both metaphorically and literally) to communities. Solar panels are non-intrusive and can be fitted to roofs or on stands requiring either no or little movement (other than rotating to follow the sun's path). Wind power can provide energy on a larger scale at the moment and communities should be encouraged to come together to be able to buy and install (or even manufacture) their own turbines which provides their own power. In this way, the ownership of the the means of power will mean that the people will be far more concerned with its maintenance and development of its potential for energy because as a community, they will own it. Some people can receive training to be the ones who can make any repairs or adjustments, who again come from the community itself. This has the capacity to really bring people together, give the ownership to them and enhance their lives as interdependent human beings.

Along with this, the community can select people whose responsibility it is to research developments in renewable energy, to work with the installation of it and report directly to the community the progress that they are making together and how much money they need from the community to maintain the energy systems effectively. As has been seen from the cooperative method of factory reclamation, when you give the impetus to the people whom it directly affects, they are going to be far more responsible, enthusiastic and practical to ensure that the work is done as efficiently as possible.

To embark upon such a strategy, the big energy companies would undoubtedly feel like they were being fought against in an attempt to either eliminate or substantially reduce their level of power. It needs to be stressed that this shouldn't be the case and that an important reason for aiming to transfer the production of energy back to the people is to provide an incentive for the energy companies to collaborate with the people and support the development of renewable energy. Whereas they would probably be unwilling to relinquish their power, the companies would be encouraged to change from the globalisation of energy to the its localisation. If they want to remain a part of the energy industry, they must be prepared to downgrade and remove the barrier between the corporation and general public. For example, an energy company could switch from being a producer of fossil fuels to the manufacturer of wind turbines and solar panels but there would also be the possibility that the people could run their own factories to produce the same items, thereby preventing prices that the energy companies would try to set with the aim of making the products affordable for everyone instead of being the monopoly that makes extensive profits at the public's expense. Any attempts to get around this ethical principle by an energy company whereby they offer greater production at a cheaper price (for example by outsourcing production to the developing world) would not be legal and seeing from the factory reclamation movement in Argentina, the public would be more likely to support their own communities than the global corporations. Restrictions and regulations would be firmly in place to ensure a balance between the corporation and the people so that the people are not becoming worse off in terms of money and control over their own destinies.

The next question is how can this work on a practical level? How can we empower people to be able to undertake such a project? Rob Hopkins, the author of The Transition Handbook, has been researching how we can make the change from oil dependency to local resilience. He has worked on how to provide a strategy that will make people aware of the problems of climate change and peak oil without leaving them with a feeling of despair and that our lives are going to collapse. Instead, he focuses strongly on the idea of collective evolution and a change of mindset to inspire people to regain their destinies by being in control of their communities as much as possible on a local scale. It is very important to make sure that people are aware of the truth regarding the impending energy crisis but also that they see that the necessity to adapt to less is an exciting new adventure which can be achieved as long as everyone works together. The difference here is that people, knowing that what they do will directly affect and improve their lives, will be far more motivated to succeed than if they were just doing uninspiring work for a multinational company. Hopkins approach fits wonderfully with the whole idea of a moral government and a society that feels connected and empowered.

First of all, it is important to realise that, at least to begin with, the idea of self-sufficiency of a town or region is unlikely. Not every resource, be it food or steel, etc., is available in every part of the world. We do rely, to some degree, on imports to be able to provide us with certain things that can't be grown or extracted from the region in which we live. However, the main aim of the Transition Handbook is that a community needs to strive to be resilient, that is, in the event of disturbance to the system, like not being able to have a material transported to the community for various reasons, political or economic, the community can still function without suffering a shock. It is a case of being able to adapt and continue adequately with what the community already has.

Hopkins draws on the fact that during the World Wars, when transportation of goods was extremely limited, people were able to pull together and manage with what they could produce for themselves. Of course, these days, the idea of needing provide for ourselves is largely forgotten as we can import cheap goods from China and the developing world without worrying about the prospect of their unavailability. It is certainly true that in the western world, people in general are at their lowest skill levels for everyday life than they have ever been in history. If fruit and vegetables became unavailable in the supermarkets because the price of oil spiralling upwards meant that it was too expensive to import them, most people would be unable to fend for themselves. The weakness in the level of community in the 21st century would provoke riots and people battling against each other to try to obtain food. This lack of resilience would lead to a collapse in society that could be avoided if communities were educated to be more resilient.

The Transition Towns project has been developing since its conception in Kinsale, Ireland in 2004. It began by showing its students a documentary called "The End of Suburbia" (which is highly recommended viewing) to raise awareness of the problems of what is due to happen in the next decade if we are not prepared. Over the months, meetings and workshops were held to enable the people to come up with their own ideas of how to make the transition to their own local resilience. The main perspectives that were worked on to create the most effective project were avoiding the idea of 'Them and us' so that the local council and the people involved in the project were to be seen as part of the same vision. It is important to create cohesion between all units so that the aims are the same for everyone. Creating a sense that something is happening is important so that people don't just watch videos and presentations, have meeting and attend workshops while not really feeling that they are actually going to act on their knowledge. People need to know that they are going to be able to make progress with the ideas that they themselves develop. Creating a vision of an abundant future is fundamental so that people are not left feeling that life is going to get a lot worse but instead is going to be even better and created by themselves. Design in flexibility is also very important because as this was a new project that had to be developed from scratch, people needed to accept the fact that some ideas that seem great in principle might not work as planned and they need to be willing to admit to their mistakes and listen to anyone who might have ideas of how the plans could be adapted.

Even though Hopkins led the project initially, he wanted to be able to give over the reins of control to the people so that when he left, they would have the feeling that they could continue it on their own. The kind of things that were involved in the project were how to produce their own food to a resilient level, how they could return much 'developed' land back to its natural state, hence creating a permaculture: a human settlement and agricultural system that mimics the relationships found in natural ecologies. Also important was how they could develop their town's own identity instead of it being a 'clone town' which features mostly the same shops and chains of pubs, restaurants and cafés that almost every town or city in a developed nation is made up of. This idea of bringing the ownership back to the people is one that fits with the previously mentioned idea that people would be much happier and settled with their lives if they feel they are working for themselves, not for a global corporation.

Hopkins then moved on to a small town in Devon, England called Totnes and launched the UK's first Transition initiative in September 2006. Built along the same principles as the one in Kinsale, the organisers hoped that it would go viral and spread throughout the country. Eighteen months later there were 30 Transition Towns there as well as the first few in Australia and New Zealand.

Reading The Transition Handbook leaves you with a great feeling of inspiration, hope and that such initiatives can and do work. The New Economics Foundation showed that 62% of people in the UK have jobs that they find uninteresting or stressful and that 87% of Britons agree that 'Society has become too materialistic, with too much emphasis on money and not enough on the things that really matter'.[17] This shows clearly that people wish their lives were different but without this kind of awareness they find it very difficult to imagine how things could change and improve.

The reaction to the Transition Initiative has drawn very moving responses: "When I think of what Transition Town Totnes is doing, I feel so full of hope I could cry." (Transition Handbook p.131)

Whereas Hopkins has stressed in his book that it has not all been plain sailing and that plans had to be altered or rejected at times, if people put in enough work with motivation and the desire to achieve, which seems to naturally happen, then changing from an oil dependent society to a local, resilient one has left people feeling unquestionably happier, knowing that their futures lie in their own hands and that when the time comes, the oil crisis is not going to cause any major disruptions to their lives and their communities.

Therefore, to conclude, there are solutions to an energy crisis and climate change can be addressed in much more effective ways than most western governments proudly claim that they are going to implement. In the end, it is not going to be enough if we wait for the governments to change things minimally while trying to maintain our materialistic and ignorant lifestyles. The impetus can be given to the people so that they can make it happen when they have no faith that the government will do anything significant.

A hypothetical government will see that such things can happen and certainly encourage the people to take the reins and build their own futures where they decide how their lives are going to be. Changing to local resilience is an exciting prospect that can have an enormous effect on how the planet can be guided back towards a stable state, where humans don't need to plunder its finite resources to feed lives that are not even benefiting from the practice on any real level. By downscaling the frivolity of life, we can actually enrich life by bringing people together, finding our purpose and managing things by ourselves.

Answer to the sorting activity: All of them are made directly from oil and oil is also used indirectly to manufacture them. (The Transition Handbook, p.19)

The Transition Handbook, From Oil Dependency to Local Resilience- Rob Hopkins, Green Books
1. http://ipcc-wg1.ucar.edu/wg1/wg1-report.html
2. The End of Suburbia – Richard Heinberg (www.endofsuburbia.com)
3. http://www.guardian.co.uk/environment/2009/nov/09/peak-oil-international-energy-agency
4. peakoil.net
5. http://irena.org/downloads/IRENA_brochure_EN.pdf (p.8)
6. Greenpeace Canada (2007) Questions and Answers about the Alberta Tar Sands
7. www.world-nuclear.org/info/inf11.html
8. UCUSA - Nuclear Power in a Warming World (2007): www.ucsusa.org/nuclear_power/nuclear_power_and_global_warming/nuclearandclimate.html
9. www.ipcc.ch/ipccreports/ar4-wg3.htm
10. www.claverton-energy.com/what-areas-of-wind-turbines-would-be-needed-in-reasonable-sites-in-the-uk-to-in-one-year-generate-all-uks-power-demand.html
11. Founding an International Renewable Energy Agency (IRENA)
12. Renewables Global Status Report 2006 Update (2010)

See www.ren21.net

13.   IRENA brochure, p.11

14.   Guy Pearse (2009). "Quarry Vision", Quarterly Essay, Issue 33, p. 93

15.   http://irena.org/downloads/Founconf/ Signatory_States_20090126.pdf

16.   http://irena.org/ (See "Our Mission page")

17.   www.neweconomics.org/sites/neweconomics.org/ files/Are_You_Happy_1.pdf

Transport

This is an important area to include, in the light of air pollution and the crises that happen within this industry, particularly in the global recession of 2008-9.

As of 2010, the state that we are in in the western world is that there are numerous car manufacturers on a global scale who are committed to constantly producing more and more cars. It is their business and they don't want it to collapse. Understandable, but the negative implications of this industry far outweigh the positives.

Firstly, there are already far too many cars and other motor vehicles in operation in the world. In 2008 alone, 80 million motor vehicles were produced.[1] Of course they are necessary for a lot of reasons but one of the main problems is the cost to the environment, which is staggering. To keep the motor industry going, they need to persuade and convince (deceive) people into believing that they need a new car every two years or so or that it would be in their best interests to buy another one. With new models being continually produced, it is easy to see that there would be the temptation to sell your old model and get a new one with lovely new gadgets and a more streamlined body. This is extremely superfluous and a massive strain, not only on the atmosphere in terms of CO_2 emissions, which, even if we can't be completely clear about whether this has a profound effect on climate change and global warming, we can be certain that it is making the quality of the air that we all have to breathe less than desirable and indeed less than healthy.

The continued production of new cars is also a huge strain on natural resources. So much metal, oil and materials that are used to form the plastics are being being exploited massively for no justifiable reason. Of course, from time to time, we need to get a new car if the old one breaks down but it's not likely to break down two years after buying it. Even in the light of global warming and the issues with CO_2 emissions, the car manufacturers continue to pay most attention to sustaining their industry.

If we regulated the industry and put a limit on the number of new cars that could be produced, there is the problem of the loss of jobs of the assembly line workers. As this is an area that provides jobs for so many people, we have to take this into consideration when thinking about the reforms that are needed.

Already there are plans to produce more environmentally friendly motor vehicles, which don't use carbon-emitting fuels or which emit less CO_2. The latter is not a particularly effective way of changing the industry as the emissions they produce are not significantly less to make a real difference to the air quality. With more than 800 million motor vehicles on the roads in 2007, even a 50% decrease in emissions is still going to leave us with enough air pollution to affect our health and the stability of the planet.

The new era of no-emission vehicles is one to be supported but again, it needs to be regulated in such a way as to demand that the manufacturers produce vehicles which are, under normal situations, going to last a long time, i.e. with good quality materials.

But of course, it would be a long, gradual transition to change the 800 million vehicles to ones that do not emit CO_2. This would simply be like any other adaptation in the manufacture of any products that develop over time. As the amount of green vehicles increases, the amount of new environmentally-damaging ones decreases.

In the meantime, what are the big manufacturers to do if their businesses and indeed their industry is not going to collapse when they can't produce so many new models? Well, instead of producing new cars all the time, the assembly line workers can use their skills in other ways. There should be developments in the industry so that instead of having to buy a new car every time they become more efficient, we should be able to take our current cars back to the manufacturer to have the engines upgraded or replaced if this is not possible. Even though it would still use a lot of natural resources, it would be less than having to replace all the body work as well when one buys a brand new car. This would be a more effective use of workers' skills, keeping them in their jobs and using resources more efficiently.

With air travel, a scaling down would need to take place. Too many people think it is a right of luxury to be able to travel wherever they want, whenever they want. As aeroplanes produce vast quantities of CO_2, restrictions need to be brought in to reduce the number of flights available. This may mean that people can't travel to far away places as often as they might wish, but this is how it was before the 1980s anyway and people then didn't complain about it. It was just how it was and we had to accept it. We have to get things into perspective and be able to weigh up the pros and cons of taking frequent holidays. It is selfish to complain that one can't go somewhere at the time they want just because there aren't enough flights available. It is for a good reason. We are only able to exist because the environment is in such a state that it provides all that we need to survive. We absolutely cannot live in ignorance to what we need to be careful of to make sure that the planet is not being disrupted by our faulty behaviour.

To start addressing this issue, we could actually halve the number of flights that we currently have at our disposal and the world would still be able to function effectively. In terms of business travel, we have advanced methods of communicating through video conferences using the internet so there are always ways around such insignificant problems.

Otherwise, there need to be moves to improve public transport to encourage people to use it more. The cost of using public transport needs to be regulated to give the public an incentive to switch to using the bus instead of their car but along with this, routes may need to be improved and restrictions placed on cars so that they can't be used on certain roads that suffer from congestion. It is not really very wise to say that people have to pay more road tax or tolls to use certain roads in the hope that they will use their cars less as this is going to upset a lot of people and simply having to pay more to use roads is going to do absolutely nothing to improve the quality of the air.

People need to be able to think that something is a good strategy for them if they are going to consider changing their actions.

To finish this section, the bicycle is a wonderful invention. It produces no emissions, uses no fuel, is easy to navigate through traffic congestion, is effective to use for short journeys and it is an excellent way of keeping fit.

1. "World Motor Vehicle Production by Country: 2007-2008" . OICA. http://oica.net/category/production-statistics/

The Economy

Before we look at what would be the most ethical way to structure an economy, as it is an area that is very complicated and full of specific terminology, I will attempt to give a clear outline of what the economy means, how it is made up and how it operates.

Firstly, it is made up of certain components, like a living body that needs to be nurtured to enable it to remain healthy and grow effectively. Those base components are things like the money to be used (the capital), the workforce (the people that basically 'sell' their skills to employers in return for payment), the resources to be used in the various industries and the economic agents, which generally refers to the people who make the decisions in an attempt to optimise their area in the economy, like managers and chief executive officers (CEOs).

All of the aspects of organising the manufacture, marketing and sales, evolution of products, impact on the environment are what give the result that is the economy of a country. So basically, the function of all the above-mentioned parts and interactions give an overall model of what is happening concerning work and finance.

Historically speaking, economy was effectively another word for trade where goods were exchanged for unregulated sums of money and the pricing of various items depended on their scarcity and the demand for them. Merchants were only able to sell things at prices people could afford but if there was a great demand for something that was scarce, like imported products that were not otherwise found in the given country, they could charge more because they knew that the richer people liked to show off their wealth and status by owning rarer items.

The first economist was said to be Adam Smith, a Scotsman who lived in the 18th century. He defined the elements of a national economy – that being that a natural price comes from products due to their supply and demand. He stated that the basic motive for free trade is human self-interest. This refers to people selling whatever they can to make as much money as they can. If they are aware that there is a demand for some product, they could set up a business like a factory and offer employment to be able to supply the product. This happened especially when the industrial revolution began to emerge in the 18th and 19th centuries. It was also the birth of capitalism, whereby people with enough wealth to own a factory could employ the poor people at a low rate because for them it was better than having no money.

It is argued in the 2007 book "The Improving State of the World", that capitalism has improved life by increasing wealth for all, higher life expectancy, reduced working hours and the abolishment of child labour. This book argues many points for how capitalism has effectively been the saviour of mankind.[1]

For example, people on average are better fed today than they were 50 years ago. They use a statistic that chronic undernourishment in developing nations has declined from 37 to 17 percent of their population between 1969-71 and 2000-02. However, 17% is still a huge number of people and that is only the 'chronically undernourished'. It could just as easily be argued that the reasons for this are the provision of humanitarian aid and enough people actually having morals to help develop communities internationally rather than the desire to become as rich as possible.

It argues other issues in similar ways, such as that child labour has decreased worldwide from 24.9 percent in 1960 to 10.5 percent in 2003. Isn't this mainly due to pressure from human rights groups like Amnesty International and the United Nations? In most of the developed world nowadays, it is illegal to use child labour as society has generally decided that it is an abuse of children's rights. It is not because some countries have become richer.

Karl Marx quite rightly pointed out that with the influence of the industrial revolution, society became polarised into the Bourgeoisie and the Proletariats, or the rich bosses and the poor workers, respectively. The Bourgeoisie are the people who own the means of production, i.e. the businesses, and the Proletariats who perform the labour necessary for the making of money for the Bourgeoisie, hence increasing the rich-poor divide, which is still happening today.

Marx wanted this system to change by removing the power from the Bourgeoisie and allowing the Proletariats to take control of their production. Unfortunately, as this developed into Communism, it became severely distorted and abused so that the rich did indeed lose their wealth by force but the workers did not gain control of their destinies. Instead the totalitarian leaders such as Stalin, Mao-Tse Tung and Kim Il-Sung decided they would have all the power for themselves and practically everyone else could suffer in poverty. Well, not quite everyone – they needed protection from counter-revolutionaries so the leaders made sure they took good care of their armies so that the general population would not dare to oppose the 'Great Leaders', as they generally became known.

So whereas Communism has only been a total failure, mainly due to the abuse of the dictatorial leaders, Karl Marx's principles, in this case, were theoretically moral. He believed that the wealth should not be controlled by a few but should be shared equally, which from a moral perspective is far more desirable. Marx set his Communist Manifesto up for failure due to his wording -

"The proletariat will use its political supremacy to wrest , by all degrees, the capital from the bourgeoisie, to centralise all instruments of production in the hands of the State, i.e., of the proletariat organised as the ruling class; and to increase the total of productive forces as rapidly as possible." The Communist Manifesto, p.34.[2]

The aggression implied by his words did indeed cause revolutions to occur in Russia, China and a few other states, inspired by the ferocity of Marx's words. If he had been more careful to word his manifesto more compassionately, things may have turned out quite differently but he spurred on megalomaniac individuals to crush the Bourgeoisie and the Proletariats at the same time.

This still leaves us with the problem of "If Communism doesn't work, then Capitalism must be the answer." Unfortunately, it is not as simple as that. Under Capitalism, the Bourgeoisie has continued to flourish and gain more money and power than it can possibly need, and as a result, 80% of the world live on less than $10 a day. (ref: The World Bank).

There are plenty of other statistics that would amaze and shock you that are the real result of living under a capitalist model, which you can find at the Global Issues website[3], but I'll give you one more for now:

In 2005, the wealthiest 20% of the world accounted for 76.6% of total private consumption. The poorest fifth just 1.5%. (ref: The World Bank)

In the western world, the economy is based on preserving and expanding businesses. The misguided presumption and propaganda is that an economy can flourish if the biggest companies can thrive and offer jobs to the 'regular' people. It is true that the most successful and profitable corporations provide work for millions of people but what those jobs actually mean is more than just financial security and life stability. What we don't tend to hear about is that working for these corporations is the way that the divide between the rich and the poor, the powerful and the unheard is not only maintained but enhanced. For example, McDonald's employs a huge amount of people in all the countries where it has fast food restaurants and these people are able to find work, albeit low paid and horribly uninspiring, and look after themselves in terms of paying rent and buying what they need to live.

Being such a big company, McDonald's makes an enormous profit because it pays low wages and uses low quality raw materials (beef, bread, etc.) and every time it opens a new restaurant, unskilled workers have the possibility to find employment.

The problem with this is that its employees are kept very much in a state where their financial options are very limited. Earning around the minimum wage will not leave them with the opportunity to develop their skills or their lives based on what they can do with their money. It's very much a hand-to-mouth scenario, which is an example of oppression. What I mean by this is that McDonald's workers are kept on the bottom rung of the ladder, earning a pittance, while the company executives are continually climbing the ladder of financial gain. The company becomes more successful while it keeps its foot firmly on the heads of those who work for it and therefore make it successful. Such big companies simply cannot survive without such workers (and of course its consumers) yet they give practically no reward or thanks to those who are fundamental to its success (along with the managerial staff).

This is the same for all multinational companies that are the most profitable and powerful. They exploit their workers so that those at the top of the pyramid earn more and those at the bottom stagnate. As most people are aware, this gives us a highly unfair system that keeps the majority of the world struggling to survive and gives the minority who work at the top far more than they need to live comfortably. This is called the Capitalist Model.

So, it is easy to see that whereas it is effective in providing jobs for people on a large scale, such people will probably spend their lives on the poverty line while a handful of people control the world with their extreme wealth which provides them with extreme power and influence; not only over the general public but the governments as some use their wealth and power to bribe governments so that they will be able to maintain their business practices without being questioned over their oppression and corruption. It has also left the majority of workers in the western world feeling unfulfilled and dissatisfied with their jobs and this is an issue that demands a lot of attention to attempt to rectify.

What this leads to is, due to the division between the rich and the poor, the poorer people resent the richer people or they have the desire to climb the same ladder so that they can be on a comparable level with them; i.e. having a lot of money. Humans are terribly susceptible to greed but firstly, it must be noted that this is not in our nature as some people think. It is due to the concept of thinking that in order to be happy, we need to be rich. This whole concept has been established by the Capitalist Model as was outlined earlier in this book. People have it rammed down their throats that they should aim to own countless products that will do nothing to enhance their feeling of deep-down happiness. But because this mind-state has been so entrenched in western society and is currently being thrust upon developing countries, who now yearn to have lives like those in the west, the public thinks that this is what life is about. Celebrities and other excessively rich people are paraded on television and in the media in general in a way that they have the status of being our role models. "This is what you should be aiming for and by buying our products, you can have a life like this." That's all very well, but if the majority of the population doesn't have anything like the money that would be necessary to possess such meaningless products, they will be jealous of those that do have them, wish that they could have them as well and become greedier and resentful as a result. In some cases this leads to crime, such as theft to achieve the goals that have been forced upon them.

In order to address the problem of the big companies controlling the poor by exploiting them, regulation needs to be put in place and on a large scale. The net income of a company (the amount of profit after all deductions) is and should be public knowledge. Taking this net income, which would be shared out among the people at the top of the pyramid, regulation should be in place so that the net income at the end of each financial year would be paid out in bonuses to the workers who not only helped the net income to be made but are responsible for it and should be paid accordingly. The consequences of this would be multi-faceted: firstly, the executives would not be in receipt of the amounts they get under the present system but a far more modest amount, the workers would be better off as a result of their own work, the workers would be more respectful to their employers, they would also have the incentive of wanting to do their jobs well so that they would receive more of a share of the net income at the end of each year, the workers would have more purchasing power in the country to be able to support the economy and the gap between the rich and the poor would decrease.

Whereas it would be difficult to argue against most of these points, the executives would be less welcoming of such regulations but they would not exactly be left in the gutter, struggling to survive. They would still be receiving a good income, just not so excessive. This would require them to look into their consciences and understand that their company could not survive without their workers and therefore, the income should be spread accordingly. This system of regulation would actually serve them better in the end if the employees are happier and feel themselves to be a real part of the whole team. The company would thrive more and even if it didn't make so much profit that the executives can legally receive, the business would potentially be more stable.

But, of course, we need to take into account the fact that corporate executives are more likely than general workers to be guilty of corruption. The rich love their power and wealth and often would do any possible underhand tactics to be able to hide the figures so that it appears that they are not making as much net income as they really are. This is simple to resolve. Such figures would be public knowledge and completely transparent and would be investigated by independent committees to ensure that the books were not being cooked. If it was found that they were guilty of such offences, those guilty parties could have their assets frozen, would be subject to imprisonment and would not be allowed to work in similar positions in the future. If that sounds harsh, bear in mind that the Capitalist Model works on the principles of incentives and deterrents. If they know that these consequences would happen to them if they were guilty of such crimes, the deterrent is clear beforehand; it's better to avoid such temptations if you know that you are going to lose everything as a result. If you don't want that to happen, don't do it.

Outsourcing is another issue that needs to be firmly regulated. This is when production is sent abroad to poorer countries so that the products can be created for a lower price, hence resulting in higher profits for the company. In terms of the business model, it makes more sense and there is the argument that otherwise unemployed people in developing countries would have the chance to make more money than finding employment with a local company. There are many moral issues with this idea. Firstly, it means that jobs are being lost in the country where production originally occurred, weakening the purchasing power of the local population as they could be left unemployed when their jobs have gone to Asia, for example. This means that the country's economy is weakened as people can't afford to buy products in general as readily as they could when they were working in production for a company. It is an extremely naïve business practice in this sense; making products available more cheaply is going to be of no real value if the public can't buy them. Additionally, even though it means that people in developing countries can earn money, on a global scale, it is relatively little and this means that the country is being kept at rock bottom by highly profitable companies from western countries, therefore enforcing an enormous divide between the rich countries and the poor countries. On a humanitarian level, this is very bad news for the development of all countries; the poorer, developing countries are being kept as slaves to the wealthy developed ones.

As a result, regulation would be put in place so that companies who use outsourcing as a business practice would be required to pay significantly higher wages to the workers as a way of helping to develop the economies of the developing world. Due to the high levels of corruption that tend to occur in such countries, an independent, international regulatory board would need to be established to attempt to see that the workers' incomes were not being unfairly taken from them (for example by unfairly high tax rates) by their own governments.

Companies who use outsourcing would also be subject to higher taxes on their revenues to deter them from using this practice. This regulation of outsourcing would also have the potential of companies deciding to keep production in their own country as outsourcing would not have any significant benefit to their income. The ultimate aim of this would be to try to narrow the divide between people's incomes on an international level.

In the section on prisons you can see the proposals for how to begin to bring production back to the countries where it originated or where it used to happen before outsourcing became the trend. As is mentioned there, this would also benefit the population in general in that convicted people would be given the opportunities to develop their own skills, not just in manual labour but in the management of the production. For an economy to be successful, the public needs to be employed so that they are the ones who make things available to buy and they also have the money to be able to buy other things. This might sound like naïve idea which it is as long as the economy is maintained in the way that we currently live. It is one of the causes of the failure of a nation and indeed the failure of the world from the perspective of humanity.

Thomas Paine, in "Rights of Man" stated that "the prosperity of any commercial nation is regulated by the prosperity of the rest. If they are poor, she cannot be rich, and her condition, be what it may, is an index of the height of the commercial tide in other nations."[4] (p.148) This refers to the imbalance between exports and imports. A country that trades more in exports than imports will be better off but only for a limited period. The countries that import more than they export will only be able to do so until they have no more money to import. It is a very simple fact to understand and points to the need for resilience in every country as much as can be achieved. For if the rich country that prospers due to its exports finds that no other country can afford to buy them any more, the rich country in going to end up in dire straits. They might try to remedy this by loaning money to the poorer countries (as generally happens) but as we have seen repeatedly, this is never going to work in the long run because if a poor country borrows money at interest and they have not the resources to prosper in a resilient fashion, they are going to be in constant debt and the country that loaned the money is unlikely to get it back. It is a ridiculous system but one that has been irresponsibly used all over the world for decades, always resulting in financial collapses.

Economic Growth versus Economic Development

For a nation to be stable and sure that there will always be jobs for people, a lot of things would need to change. Firstly, the persistent misconception that a country needs to have economic growth needs to be examined. Economic growth refers to an increase in the quantitative output, which is measured by the Gross Domestic Product (GDP) of a nation. Therefore, the more that a country can produce, the more money it can make. This is usually the favoured comment that politicians make.

That's all very well but money alone is not going to make a country develop in terms of its standard of living in a meaningful sense. Economic development, on the other hand, is more concerned with these aspects, such as literacy rates, poverty levels, leisure time, environmental quality, freedom, or social justice. This is an enormous difference between the amount of money that the state has versus the quality of life of the people. In the book "Three Cups of Tea" it is noted that the king of Bhutan said that the true measure of nation's success is not gross national product but "gross national happiness."

It goes without saying that a moral government would be more concerned with economic development. It is not essential for GDP to increase from one year to the next but it is also important to note that a country needs to have enough resources to make sure that all its areas are being properly managed and looked after with no possibility for corruption to take place, for example, in the case of funds being illegally diverted to individuals' bank accounts. Very stiff penalties would be in place for such acts.

In order to build an effective economy in terms of its development, that is its technological and social development, we need to gain a consensus on what would be meaningful to everyone in terms of what work we should be expected to do. Infrastructure refers to many structures that support a society, such as roads, water supply, sewage, power grids, etc. It is the backbone upon which a country can function well.

Such things need to be given a priority, not just in terms of whether they are all well maintained and managed but how well developed they really are. For example, the sewage system is not effective if it is simply pumped out into the sea in an 'out of sight, out of mind' way. Third world countries dispose of sewage in this way, mainly because it is too expensive for them to treat it effectively. Sewage tanks are used more in developed countries, although it can also be converted into fertiliser through sludge processing plants to make fertiliser pellets, which is a much more efficient process. Where it is disposed of in rivers and the sea, it is extremely primitive and irresponsible and it needs to be addressed, as with other aspects such as energy, so that the environmental effects are the first criterion to be met. If it is going to cause destruction in some way, it has to be changed. I don't need to go through the details for all of these issues but the basic principles need to be highlighted to form a basis of how the infrastructure needs to be reformed.

This means that it would be necessary for employment to occur in infrastructure. Unfortunately, some of the jobs that would be required might not be personally fulfilling but an awareness from the general public about the importance of such jobs, good working conditions: pay, holidays, healthcare and working hours would need to be put in place to make the workers feel that they are being valued and respected and that we recognise the importance of what they do for the rest of us.

Other areas where it is necessary to have enough jobs and enough qualified people are education, health, agriculture and the emergency services. These are the most fundamental aspects of human development to ensure that people have enough food, can receive health care easily and quickly, develop in terms of their skills and knowledge and will be taken care of efficiently when necessary. Again, those who work in these areas, given their level of responsibility, need to have very good working conditions. It is common at this time for doctors and teachers to be working long hours and having very little leisure time. This is not good enough and a possibility is that these professionals should work more on a job-share basis so that more people can be employed but working fewer hours. The disadvantage of such a system would be that the workers would receive less income but it could be agreed on by the professionals themselves, via a union, as to whether they want to do a job-share or not. The main point is that these professionals, upon whom we depend for a well functioning and well developing society, must be given working conditions that reflect their roles in society.

There are secondary levels of jobs regarding their importance as, of course, there are other things that we need. The construction industry is one that needs to be stable as buildings need to be repaired or replaced. This is not something that a government needs to be concerned with as it is generally a private industry and it can be self-managed via a union. It does, however, need to be regulated so that all construction businesses offer standardised prices. It could also be something that is subject to localised restrictions – certain businesses are only allowed to construct in their designated areas. The reason for this would be to eradicate competition between companies and to ensure that all existing companies get an equal share of the work. This is the cooperative system where the emphasis is on people working alongside each other, not stepping on each others' toes and working under pre-defined agreements. If, however, in the case whereby there is no work in the prescribed area but there is an abundance of work in a neighbouring area where the demand is more than the supply, arrangements can be made so that workers who currently don't have any contracts could take on work elsewhere because of the demand. Again, the details of such a practice could be defined and agreed on by a union.

Manufacture of clothes and typical non-food products found in most supermarkets need to exist and would be considered as secondary level work. Due to the extravagance, selfishness and greed of the fashion industry which is currently enslaving a huge number of people into a world of delusions and false promises, before we can adapt the clothes manufacturing industry, we need to work on helping people to realise how they are being deceived and try to free them from their dependency on clothes shopping. If we can reduce the amount of clothes that people buy, we can form a manageable industry that can be maintained in the same country in which the items are sold and implicitly break down the global monopoly of the fashion houses that emphasise their logos and the utterly false claims that theirs are the best. By raising people's awareness that buying such things not only fails to bring them happiness in a true sense and that the industry is maintained by keeping the buying public oppressed by the dogma of the industry, we can start to find our path towards real human development.

Moving down to a tertiary level of work, we reach the area whereby people need something to fill their leisure time. At the current time there are countless distractions that have the aim of keeping people entertained while giving them an escape from reality – TV shows, commercial pop music, computer games as well as the fashion, beauty and cosmetics industries. In one sense these distractions have developed at an incredible rate because people are willing to buy them and forget about their unfulfilling lives, at least for a short time. The main problem with this way of life is that the majority of people need to escape from reality. And this happens in what is known as the developed world.

Why is it even called the developed world? Certainly there has been a lot of development in terms of what we are able to produce but a significant amount of what we produce is worthless. The current Dalai Lama said "We have become long on quantity but short on quality." It is not development just to be able to produce countless rubbish just to keep us from having to think about the real world and all its problems. Development is about bringing a real sense of purpose to what we do and bringing comfort to our lives in a way that doesn't cause divisions between people or cause destruction to the environment. We are already very able to keep ourselves entertained with simple activities that don't require a designer label or meet the approval (or jealousy) of other people. Playing sports, playing board games, having dinner with our families and friends, watching performances of all kinds at the theatre and enjoying music are all things that have been popular to do over the centuries and even millennia. To be able to fill our leisure time in a way that leaves us feeling with a sense of true happiness, we need to contemplate what is worth doing and what is not.

If it is going to bring people together in a positive way, then it's worthwhile. If it is going to leave us feeling like we have personally developed in some way (becoming better at a sport, better at cooking, better at writing music, etc.) then it should be emphasised even more so. We need to focus on creativity and personal growth when deciding what activities we are going to partake in. Just playing on some hand-held computer game where you have to shoot the aliens is never going to achieve the same goal. It is only a way of filling time without having to think too hard or to get up out of the chair.

We should be developing our entertainments so that these things are going to happen and that they are going to encourage people to do them more often. We need to realise the pointlessness of having a new hairstyle done, applying enough make-up so that we no longer look like our true selves but instead give a false appearance. We need to support each other to explore our real characters, our interests that we know we love to take part in because they sincerely make us feel happy.

To achieve these goals we don't need to rely on a global economy or big companies to provide us with products, in fact quite the opposite. We can obtain the items we might need to partake in an activity that we enjoy through the simplest means – buy a guitar, buy some football boots, buy a ticket to the theatre, buy some ingredients. All these things are well within our means and we don't need to go far to get them.

Additionally, with this intention of inspiring people to develop their interests productively, we can work together on a local level as the demand for these simple items increases. We can create our own objectives, our own purposes and be the ones who make them happen. Resilience is not only a concept that can be applied to energy and food but also to the economy.

By following these principles we can take the control of our own lives and not be dependent on what multinational corporations implicitly demand that we do, for we must remember that they have their own interests at heart and nothing else. They care not for the development of humans, in fact quite the opposite – they want people to be unable to realise their own potential for being independent thinkers and doers. We don't need to tax the corporations to reduce their level of control. All we need to do is abstain from buying their products. It is like Gandhi's 'passive resistance' - show that you are not going to comply by simply not contributing to the demand that they want to maintain. Importantly, we should also offer encouragement and support to convince these types of companies to change their practices so that they produce more worthwhile products and share the profits and management with the workers so that we can achieve a smooth and peaceful transition from global monopolies to locally managed businesses. The NEF has a proposal in place to support companies with this type of transition. Called Ethical Business, the project is to support businesses to "achieve positive impacts on the world around them." What they refer to as the three Ps, Purpose is to "deliver a social or environmental objective and ... not operate solely to achieve financial bottom lines." Production is to "to alter the way goods and services are traditionally produced, and find innovative ways to tackle a problem, for example, by providing environmentally friendly products or employing groups that are socially excluded." Power is to "see their stakeholders as integral to the success of their business and (to) adopt governance and new ownership that empower(s) their stakeholders."[5]

The public is more likely to support ethical businesses if they see that they have the choice to buy the products or use the services of those that operate ethically rather than of those that have a more unethical reputation.

To reach these objectives would take time as the awareness and agreement of people would not come overnight. While this transition is taking place, what we currently have as a way of life can be altered to help the shift from globalisation to localisation. As an example, the cyclical consumption issue will be used.

As previously mentioned, this is when products are regularly updated so that the buying public 'need' to keep buying the latest model so they won't be left behind by their peers or by the planned rate of technological development. This is unacceptable and a totally avoidable problem in the Capitalist Model. It is an utter waste of finite resources and causes massive environmental damage when the outdated version of the products are thrown away.

In terms of electronic devices such as DVD players and mobile phones, it is common knowledge that they are constructed with components that are designed to last for a short time (usually until just after the warranty has expired). This means that even if some people are quite happy to keep their existing model without getting the new version after a year, they will be unable to as it will either break or malfunction within say 4 years. To get around this problem, it would be simple enough to enforce companies to print on the packaging how long the product has been designed to last for. If this was a legal requirement, there would be a new side to competition in the market. If you saw a DVD player that had a warranty for 3 years and another of equal functionality that had a warranty for 10 years, which one would you buy? Even if it cost twice as much it would still be worth it. This simple requirement would mean that the manufacturers of such products would be unable to keep releasing new models with unnecessary extra features as long as the currently owned one did the job. If the DVD player could play and record, there is little else that is necessary. They could be developed so that, like computers, if they needed updating with the advent of, say, a new video format (e.g. Xvid, flv) then you could update the software on the player via a USB flash drive and it would still work fine.

A way of limiting products could be conceived so that the manufacturers are not allowed to produce as many products as they currently do. This would have the effect that simply not so many products are available to buy and therefore the amount that are thrown away is less. Of course, it goes without saying that it would be required that people should have access to electronic product recycling centres where they can be disposed of so that they wouldn't end up in landfills – poisoning wildlife and polluting the ground that plants grow from. These drop-off points are already in place but their numbers would need to be increased so that there is no excuse not to use them.

But what would this mean for the economy if the amount of sales dropped drastically as a result of this regulation? For the average person, very little. Fewer products would be available in the shops as they would be designed to last longer. This would mean that shops would be frequented less often and therefore jobs would be lost. This is very likely to be true but as the policy for creating employment would be radically changed, this would actually be a good thing.

There would be fewer jobs that are unsatisfying and uninspiring, such as working in a large department store for some multinational company. As most people in Britain are unfulfilled by their work (62% according to the NEF), this would lead to the the opportunity of training people to do more constructive and meaningful work, such as reducing the work hours of teachers and doctors or becoming involved with the research into the development of renewable energy for their community. Otherwise, they could move into the arts if they had an interest in music, acting, dancing, etc.. Remember the idea of voluntary untaxed teaching of skills in the Shaping A Society section?

There is always a way that people can find work in this system and it is far more likely that people would find work that they actually *want* to do as it has a real purpose. The NEF have written a document precisely about this issue, proposing that the working week should switch from 40 hours to 21 hours. They argue that "A much shorter working week would change the tempo of our lives, reshape habits and conventions, and profoundly alter the dominant cultures of western society."[6]

Mikhail Gorbachev, the former president of the Soviet Union who ended the political supremacy of the Communist Party which led to the dissolution of the Soviet Union has called on political changes since leaving office. He wants a restructuring of societies around the world (perestroika) as he believes that the economic crisis of 2007-present shows that the Washington consensus economic model is a failure that will sooner or later have to be replaced. The term Washington Consensus was initially coined in 1989 by John Williamson to describe a set of ten specific economic policy prescriptions that he considered should constitute the "standard" reform package promoted for crisis-racked developing countries by

Washington, D.C.-based institutions such as the International Monetary Fund (IMF), World Bank, and the US Treasury Department.[7]

This model, which touted the dogma of free markets, deregulation and balanced budgets at any cost, entails super-profits and hyper-consumption for an elite few, unrestrained exploitation of natural resources, social dislocation, environmental irresponsibility, and public spending cutbacks that hurt the most vulnerable members of society. According to Gorbachev, countries such as Brazil, Malaysia and China which rejected the Washington consensus and the International Monetary Fund approach to economic development, have done far better economically on the whole and achieved far more fair results for the average citizen, than countries that accepted it.[1] In the light of the global recession starting in 2008, it turns out he was right.

So, we need to turn now to the market system to find out which would be the most ethical, fair and functional model.

According to Wikipedia, "a free market is a market without economic intervention and regulation by government except to regulate against force or fraud. This is the contemporary use of the terminology used by economists and in popular culture; the term has had other uses historically. A free market requires protection of property rights, but no regulation, no subsidization, no single monetary system, and no governmental monopolies. It is the opposite of a controlled market, where the government regulates how the means of production, goods, and services are used, priced, or distributed."[8]

A regulated market or controlled market is the provision of goods or services that is regulated by a government appointed body. The regulation may cover the terms and conditions of supplying the goods and services and in particular the price allowed to be charged. It is common for a regulated market to control natural monopolies such as aspects of telecommunications, water, gas and electricity supply. Often regulated markets are established during the privatisation of government controlled utility assets.

Basically, the concept of the free market is a bad idea for people in general as companies are effectively free to trade as they wish, focusing on high exploitation of the masses and without any regard for any damage it causes, either financially or environmentally.

In principle, a controlled market has the potential to be fairer but every government to date that has used this version has exploited it for their own interests, such as in the communist system where the people have no choice as to what is on sale and companies have to sell at fixed prices.

Therefore, what we need is a market economy that falls somewhere between these but where no company, group of companies or individuals have more influence and power than any other.

Regulation is the key. Mixed economies include a variety of public and government control, or a mixture of capitalism and socialism. There is no one definition of a mixed economy as this term has been used to describe the systems in place in the Untied States and Cuba. Obviously these two work in extremely different ways so it is too ambiguous a model to be satisfactory for a moral government.

There has to be regulation in place to ensure that current multinational companies' grip on the market is significantly reduced, which is very detrimental to small businesses, many of which have closed down with the advent of huge superstores that stock much more variety at a lower cost to the public. Whereas this appeals to the public, hence their willingness to shop there instead of at the more expensive shop with limited product range, the public is unaware in general that the profits made by the big superstores disappear from the community and probably from the country into private bank accounts so that the community suffers on the whole.

The question is how to convince the people that they should go back to the local shops, even though they are more expensive. This is where regulation comes into place.

Multinational companies are able to sell their products more cheaply because they can buy in bulk and have the goods made in developing countries, due to the freedom of the free market. It spells nothing but stagnation for a local community as they can't afford to compete with such large businesses, smaller businesses close and the public has no realistic alternative to shopping with the big companies, i.e. they are trapped in grip of the multinationals, clone towns are formed and people merely become the consumer puppets of this system – buying what the controlling elite provide with the mistaken belief that the increasingly worthless products are our salvation from the melancholy of everyday life.

Well, everyday life wouldn't be melancholy and something to feel the need to escape from if the general public's lives weren't so controlled.

To be able to regulate the free market of the multinationals, limits would need to be imposed so that they wouldn't have the potential to build new stores wherever they liked. There would need to be a limit on their scope to restrict them from taking all the wealth from the people.

To illustrate this, let's use an easy-to-visualise example to show

how the globalised economy works, in terms of the multinational companies that are listed on the stock exchanges due to their size.

The FTSE 100 is a share index of 100 of the most capitalised companies in the UK. They sell stocks and shares of their companies and other people buy them with the intention of making money when the value of the shares go up and the shareholders can then choose to sell them for a profit. The companies sell shares so that they can raise more capital to expand their businesses. The people buy them because they believe they are well-established and usually relatively secure enough so that there is less of a risk that the shares will plummet in value and the shareholders will lose their money. In reality, it is not always the case as shares have been seen to be very risky assets.

The consequence of this activity is that the people who are shareholders want to make some easy money by effectively gambling on the companies that they buy shares from and the bigger companies get more capital to pursue their interests of market domination, or in other words, control of the general public's lives by defining what they will have available to buy.

Now, when companies grow and their market share increases, they will be able to move from being a small local business in their outset to a nationwide company and then, if all goes well for them, a multinational company. Let's say for the sake of argument that the owner of the company remains the same throughout the company's expansion and that he (as they are usually men) stays based in the country where he was born. As the company is now global in scale, the amount of sales are dramatically higher as they are occurring in countries like Malaysia, Argentina and Ukraine. As the sales are made, the money that is not deducted in tax by the state and by the distributors, etc. becomes net profit and will likely end up in the bank account of the boss who does not then distribute it. This means that money is being sucked from all over the planet into one big bank account; a lot of people are therefore transferring their hard-earned money to one central place. 1% of the world's population owns 95% of the world's wealth. The poorest 40% of the world own 5% of the wealth. The difference between the richest and poorest countries in the world in 1820 was 3 to 1, in 1992 it was 72 to 1.[9]

So this is the consequence of having free markets operating under the capitalist model. It is grossly unfair as wealth is not distributed even slightly evenly and is becoming more uneven as each year goes by.

So, what's the alternative?

Localisation of the economy

Imagine this alternative scenario: People in general become more aware of how economics work and decide that they don't want to be a part of the system of consumerism as it means that they are effectively causing the rich-poor divide to happen by themselves. Instead, they decide to support their own community by buying locally made produce wherever possible. They support the local shopkeepers, thereby helping them to stay in business, securing employment in the area for their neighbours and their reluctance to go to the chain stores means that the multinational companies' revenues fall and because people are spending their money locally, the employment shifts from SuperMegaCheapShop to a whole variety of small businesses that sell more products that come from the area.

The NEF also states that "Real local shops have been replaced by swathes of identikit chain stores that seem to spread like economic weeds, making high streets up and down the country virtually indistinguishable from one another. Retail spaces once filled with a thriving mix of independent butchers, newsagents, tobacconists, pubs, bookshops, greengrocers and family-owned general stores are becoming filled with faceless supermarket retailers, fast-food chains, and global fashion outlets." (In a recession, chain stores are the most likely to abandon the high street and close branches.)

But how can the public afford to buy products from the local shops when they are so much cheaper in the big stores? Because the money that is being spent in the local area is staying in the local area. It is going to the local workers who will in turn spend it in the same way. The money is not slowly and invisibly drifting away from the community into the bank account of someone who regularly appears in the Forbes list of the richest 100 people in the world. The people are holding onto it and keeping their local economy stable just by changing their spending behaviour.

And because they are actively choosing to buy local produce instead of those imported from third world countries, they are giving themselves the scope to create their own jobs to supply the local community. They have the money to do so now and as a moral government would support this scheme and promote it fervently to help the local citizens gain control of their own destinies and financial stability and in turn their well-being and stronger, interdependent community, the wealth is being spread much more equally, there is more employment, on a meaningful level because more people own their own businesses and they reciprocate each other, there is less crime because there is no reason to commit crime when people's well-being is so much better and people have more of a purpose to their lives.

"Imagine the local economy as a bucket. If someone has £5 and spends it in the local grocers, the £5 stays in the bucket. But other activities, such as paying utility bills, or spending money in out-of-town stores, causes money to leak out of the bucket, away from the community. By plugging the leaks in the bucket, we can keep money flowing within community and create strong local economies." (NEF)

But what about if people stop buying products made in China and Bangladesh? Won't those poor people lose their livelihoods because, even though they are being paid an absolute pittance by western standards, they actually earn a good amount by their local standards?

This is where the next part of the scheme comes in – the globalisation of financial equality. The people who work in the factories and sweatshops in the third world need to receive support from the developed world so that they can make the transition from supplying the west while remaining their slaves to supplying *their* local communities with the products that they manufacture.

The multinational companies that use the sweatshops to produce their products make very few of the sales in the countries where they are based. The general public in the third world cannot afford these products, so the vast majority of them are shipped abroad to the rich countries that pay no attention to where they are made and how appalling the conditions are. More so, the multinationals conveniently neither own nor have written contracts with the sweatshops so that they couldn't get caught out on a legal level by using inhumane working conditions such as 16-hour working days and child labour because they only have a verbal agreement with the factory owners, who reciprocate the agreement by maintaining the bad conditions in a dictatorial manner so that if the workers complain, they're out and they'll be replaced by someone else within an hour.

So, if sales of clothes and plastic rubbish with some cartoon cat's face stamped on them drop, the industries would be in trouble if they couldn't refocus their market. They would still have the machines and other equipment to make products but instead they would need to receive training from moral volunteers from the west who have more understanding about how the whole market process operates so that they could instead start manufacturing products that could be sold in their own countries and actually have a use as, at least in the beginning of this transition, the local people in a country such as Bangladesh wouldn't have neither the money nor the interest in buying pointless plastic brand name objects. The reason for making them would diminish and hopefully, over time, the demand for such tacky junk would disappear as the world becomes more productive, democratic, educated and developed together.

Value Added Tax

VAT is the amount of tax that is deducted from every item that is sold to the buying public. It generally goes through three stages – the manufacturer pays tax on the purchase of raw materials, the retailer pays tax after purchasing the item from the manufacturer (at a higher cost), and the retailer sells it to the consumer, again at a higher cost and a percentage of what the consumer pays is the tax that also goes to the state. It is not necessary to explain all the details of how this works, but instead, I would like to look at how VAT can be reformed depending on the 'real' value of items for sale.

Products that are considered to be superfluous to our needs (i.e. sold by deceiving the public as to their use) and that use the weaknesses of people to make profit will be taxed accordingly. The actual price of the product should go up in an attempt to deter people from buying it and the amount of VAT would go up at a higher rate so that the profit made on it would be less but the amount of tax earned from it by the state would be higher.

The effect of this is that instead of such high profits going eventually to the owner's private offshore bank account, more of the money would stay in the country to be used for the benefit of the citizens.

For example, if a high-sugar/ low nutritional content breakfast cereal was being sold at £2, where 17.5% of it was VAT (i.e. 35p), it would change in this way - the price of the cereal would have to increase to, say, £3 where the amount of tax being earned from it would be 50% or £1.50. The company would, instead of receiving £1.65 from it (minus the sale price to the retailer), they would earn £1.50. Not significantly less to put the company out of business but it would be with the aim of encouraging them to produce better quality products.

The consumer might feel they are the ones being cheated, but they have the choice to buy something else that is healthier and cheaper as the VAT on it would be much lower, say, 10%.

If the public then changed their buying and therefore eating habits, the companies that make low-quality, unhealthy foods would have an incentive to change what they make or risk going out of business due to rapidly falling sales.

The intention is to give people a reason to want to buy healthier foods, which are often more expensive at the moment because of the marketing opportunity that is being used to extort money from people who wish to eat better quality foods. This is unacceptable and needs to be changed around the other way.

This system would require a lot of VAT bands but would be proposed for the reasons of the well-being of the public as well as the ethical business practices of companies. Weaknesses are far less likely to be exploited (if chocolate is considerably more expensive, people would eat less of it) and the incentive to produce more ethically better products would be likely to increase significantly.

The minimum VAT rate would still have to be one where, if all products were altered for this reason, the amount of tax going to the state would still be in the same range as it is under the current system of a single VAT rate where the products do not already qualify for reduced VAT rates (as in the case of newspapers and certain magazines being subject to less VAT in Belgium or certain goods and services in Iceland: books, hot water, electricity, radio station licences, etc.).

Corporate Tax

Corporate tax, which refers to the amount that a company has to pay in tax to the state depending on their profits, varies from country to country. As with income tax, it often works at different rates according to how much profit is made. For example, in the USA, the lowest rate is 15% on taxable income less than $50,000, increasing and, strangely enough, decreasing in stages to 35% for incomes greater than $18.333 million. Though, if one's company makes profits between $100,000 and $335,000, the tax rate is 39%. In the UK, there are only tax bands currently, starting at 21% for incomes of less than £300,000 to 28% for incomes over £1.5 million.

There are many complications along the way, such as relief for expenses, but in order to look at how corporation tax should be set according to morals, we can establish many criteria that would have interesting effects on companies.

In the free market system, very few morals are used, especially when the companies are larger and more profitable. And having a maximum tax rate depending on the annual income, of around 35% in the USA can be criticised for not providing a deterrent for unethical business practice.

The moral criteria that can be used to set a company's tax rate can consist of the following:

Outsourcing – If a certain percentage of a company's products are produced by cheap labour in developing countries, this can be considered a factor in increasing the tax rate due to the unethical nature of exploiting people in poorer countries to be the slaves for the ever-expanding western businesses and also due to the loss of jobs in the country where the business is based.

Environmental impact – If a company is guilty of pollution, deforestation, destruction of other natural areas and habitats, harmful waste deposited or buried underground, an unnecessary exploitation of natural resources due to planned obsolescence in the business plans and so on, this too can increase the company's tax rate. In fact, in a United Nations study, as reported in The Guardian, it was found that if the biggest 3,000 companies had to pay for the environmental damage they cause, it would cost them £2.2 trillion.[10] In other words, this would wipe out one-third of their profits. But they would still be left with two-thirds of their profits, so it wouldn't be a catastrophe.

Exploitation of workers – If the workers are not considered as outsourced, but work in developed countries but are exploited through such things as low salaries compared to company profits, long work hours, lack of democracy in the workplace (such as non-Union agreed principles), and bad working conditions in general, this would also be another factor. However, all of these issues would be outlawed anyway under a moral government, as discussed in the Employment and Welfare section but while the transition from immoral to moral business practice is happening, it would be a significant deterrent for a company operating in such a manner.

Exploitation of consumers – It is not only the workers that can be exploited but those who buy the products. This was raised when discussing such industries as fashion, beauty, cosmetics, pharmacology, food and drink and children in general. Regarding the first three in that list, the public are constantly exploited to believe they are not as beautiful as they should be in order to be happy with themselves and that they ought to look at the 'solutions' that the companies 'offer'. As has been mentioned, this is unacceptable and certainly immoral with the aim of making people suffer from low self-esteem and depression where the only apparent answer is buying some product that has no real use or even does damage to the body.

Regarding pharmacology, people are often deceived into thinking they have some imaginary illnesses or that something that is quite insignificant is actually a serious matter for concern, even though it could probably be treated with a simple aspirin tablet. Such attempts at exploitation would be punished via this moral corporate tax system.

With food and drink products, people's weaknesses are exploited as much as is possible within the law. They are told things like chocolate is good for you because it contains milk or products are made to be addictive by adding specific chemicals that lead to addictions. The results of people continuing to buy such products as pre-packaged foods, soft drinks, confectionery, alcohol, cigarettes and other similar products are that people become unhealthier, fatter and are more likely to suffer from illnesses from their consumption of such products. If we were to make these kinds of foods and drinks more expensive, because of their exploitation of weaknesses, and liable to a higher corporate tax, the combined deterrents would lead to far lower prevalence of such bad food and drink.

Exploitation of children – This is one that is quite easy to determine. There so many thousands of products made for children that have no use in building their skills or giving them constructive ways to use their time. Certain toys such as games which can develop their motor control or their mental abilities in some way would be encouraged and not liable to a higher corporate tax rate. However, such junk as any merchandising products that use celebrities or fictional characters to promote them or that are seen as having no real use for the children would be subject to a higher tax rate.

The other benefit of such a corporate tax rate system is that the general public, or consumers, would not be the ones who are really affected. Even though some products would be more expensive because of the moral VAT already discussed, they wouldn't be totally out of the public's reach – they would be simply less inclined to buy them as they might not justify their higher costs. But most of the onus would be on the companies. With a graded tax rate system that affects all companies in place and the moral tax criteria, a company would really be more likely to think about what they intend to make their money from.

Let's look at a basic example. Imagine the standard corporate tax rate were as follows:

Income less than €50,000 – tax rate of 10%
€50,000 to €100,000 – 15%
€100,000 to €350,000 - 20%
€350,000 to €1 million – 30%
€1 million to €3 million – 40%
€3 million to €10 million - 50%
Over €10 million – 60%

These are just figures to illustrate how the higher the corporate income, the more tax they should have to pay to the state and not an actual proposal. But if a company made €10 million annually and paid 60% tax, they would still make a profit of €4 million in just one year. That is a lot of money and cannot be justified if it is only going to the bank accounts of a few people.

But if the same company used outsourcing and produced goods that were of no practical use, like expensive trainers that were considered to be a status symbol, the company could incur an extra 5% tax for both of these criteria. So, the €6 million paid to the state in tax would increase by another million that the company could have saved if their business model was more moral. Now there's an incentive for good practice. If they disposed of their waste more responsibly, they could again save half a million. And when big companies are so addicted to money, this has the potential to make them sit up and listen.

The UN study of the 3,000 biggest companies led to an initiative called the UN Principles for Responsible Investment (www.unpri.org) where it aims to encourage investors to follow their proposals, receiving support along the way so that they can adapt their practices more easily. There are four key support activities: Providing guidance to implement strategies, building networks so that signatories can form groups to brainstorm ideas, enhancing collaboration between signatories and evaluating progress to report and assess the ongoing activities. The UN emphasises that it should be voluntary for businesses to sign up to this agreement, although it may be necessary to enforce deterrents such as the additional taxes described above. To date there has been an increase from 50 signatories to 500 in the first three years, which is promising but it is likely that some companies refuse to sign up to this agreement and need a little more coercion.

Supporting companies to sign to this agreement is a good example of moral practice and allowing them to voluntarily sign is a good way of showing that the UN's intentions are supportive.

The Nordic Model is an economic model that has been highly regarded for its ethical practice and welfare provisions. It is an adaptation of the mixed market economy. Even though the income tax rates are very high compared with most other countries, the social provisions that they are used for reflect their need and the Model's aims are that the people will trust it and understand the benefits of high taxes. Other aims of it are enhancing individual autonomy, ensuring the universal provision of basic human rights and stabilizing the economy.

However, the downside of this model is that it is still focused on globalisation and the free market and little market regulation. The Nordic countries of Finland, Sweden, Denmark, Norway and Iceland also rely heavily on imports and international developments. This meant that when the global recession kicked in in 2008, the Nordic countries were hit very severely, despite not being directly responsible for the failures of such banks as the Lehman Brothers.

When addressing why the Nordic Model was hit so hard by this crisis, the authors of Nordics in Global Crisis[11] concluded that "Regulation was not up-to-date, supervision was inefficient, rating agencies made serious mistakes, and the incentive schemes faced by managers of financial institutions encouraged excessive risk taking." (p14)

Therefore, "What the world needs now is more effective regulation and supervision to reduce the likelihood of financial instability and/or better access to macroeconomic stabilization tools in times of crisis. However, this is not a call for going back to the policies and regulatory structures adopted after the Great Depression. New circumstances require new approaches and solutions." (p19)

They admit that "The Nordic countries have been hit harder by the crisis than the OECD countries on average, with the exception of Norway. This is no coincidence but a consequence of the economic strategy of these countries, which is oriented toward exploiting globalization as a means of raising productivity and income." (p28)

Unfortunately, the authors of this report are unable to think outside the Capitalist Box, stating that "Globalization and sophisticated financial markets are here to stay, and more or less serious shocks will continue to impact the world economy." (p29) This is absurd. If we know that this is the case and following the capitalist model is always going to lead to such crises, then we have to change the system. It means that the current one is ineffective and guaranteed to fail repeatedly.

On the next two pages, they feel that "For the economy to recover and grow, to be resilient, it is crucial for relative prices and costs to adjust in a way that enhances competitiveness and the reallocation of labour and capital from less to more profitable uses."

This notion of 'competition is essential' is a dreadfully flawed idea that guarantees that at certain times, every business will succeed and fail, depending on what is happening to their 'competitors'. On a large scale, as Finland suffered worse than Sweden in the global recession, "one might argue that Sweden is benefiting at the expense of its neighbours by capturing market shares from its closest competitors, notably Finland." (p24) This shows that even entire countries that work under an effectively unified system still view each other as competitors.

The way forward would be for such countries that operate economically as part of a union to support each other in times of crisis and to help them to avoid dramatic losses of market shares, not capitalise from them. It is like seeing your friend's business collapse then using this as a strategy to get the customers to come to you because you still have a better range of products.

Despite the good points of the Nordic Model, it is no surprise that it was hit so badly. Whereas the structure of it may be built from solid, high quality materials, building it on sand and rebuilding it in the same place when it collapses is woefully ignorant and irresponsible.

The idea that capitalism is here to stay has been revoked by the NEF in their New Economic Model: "There is nothing 'natural' about our current economic arrangements. They have been consciously designed to achieve a simple objective: growth. But growth is not making us happier, it is creating dysfunctional and unequal societies, and if it continues will make large parts of the planet unfit for human habitation. This means starting from first principles and building a new model for how the economy functions. Right now every one of us is dependent on growth. The way our economy is structured means that unless there is growth people lose their jobs, the tax base shrinks and politicians struggle to fund the public services we all rely on every day. At NEF, we want to break that vicious cycle by building a new macro-economic model that is geared not towards growth, but towards achieving the outcomes that are important to society and that can be sustained by the planet's finite carrying capacity. This will not be easy. But we believe that if we can create an economy to achieve the goal of growth then we can also create an economy that delivers for people and the planet."[12]

The UK government's figures for receipts, expenditure and borrowing tell an interesting story. The total income for 2009/2010 was £541bn, the total expenditure was £704bn, while the amount of money that the government borrowed was £163bn. Practically every country borrows money from the World Bank (a private business that literally makes money out of nothing then lends it with interest to governments). This shows, apart from other things, that the government is unable to function in a self-sufficient way, very far from it, and it is also unable to function in any kind of a resilient way. To be so deeply in debt and have debt interest of £43bn for a single tax year points out that the country is economically very unstable. And considering that the way that this problem is planned to be rectified is by cutting public spending means the economic model is of no use to the general public. Countries that have such high debts often aim to rectify the situation by cutting public spending. This is an unacceptable solution as the taxpayers effectively have no say as to how their taxes are going to be used. They should have their money spent on public services because they are what the public needs and deserves. Such governments should instead be looking into how they can reduce the need for state benefits by increasing the amount of work available as described above and in the chapter on Prison. They should also be aiming to reduce the reliance on imports and make the economy more resilient so that more of the money remains in the country. Another important way to avoid cutting public spending is to reduce military expenditure which is money that is simply lost once it is spent. More information as to why and how this could be done can be found in the Foreign Policy chapter.

The most moral and realistic answer to the problem of governments being so obsessed with economic growth rather economic development is to look to the New Economic Foundation.

Their New Economic Model is "to establish what broad structural conditions are needed so that an economic system that has positive social and environmental outcomes, rather than growth, as its primary goal is able to exist."

When comparing it to how it would fit with a moral government that would plan to make everything work for the well-being of everyone and everything, it is difficult to find any contradictions. Therefore, it would be recommended to use the NEF's principles as a basis for managing any economy.

To show some more examples of how their policies fit with an ideal government, the other two branches of their 'business, finance and economics model' would be:

Sustainable business – to establish ways of aligning the interests of society with those of business, for example through pricing that approaches 'real value'.

Financial reform – to identify what a finance sector that serves the real economy and society looks like, and how it can be regulated.

To illustrate how well the NEF's policies would fit with the system of Moralism and the proposals for an alternative economic structure, here are some more examples of their statements.

"From 2009, we will be working with other economists on a radical new approach to economic modelling. Standard models take no account of resource use and environmental constraints, and are blind to social outcomes in terms of equity and, of course, human well being. They are open-ended by nature, with growth being the primary output of interest. Inputs feed in, interact with each other, achieve balance (or equilibrium) and outcomes result.

Our approach turns this on its head. We will start with the hard outcomes we need - environmental sustainability; equitable economic justice; and high levels of human well-being - link these to relevant economic determinants within the model (aggregate output, income distribution and working hours, respectively, for example) and to 'reverse engineer' what this would imply for the levels and types of differing inputs."

"We believe that local businesses should be at the heart of all regeneration projects, and produce research, policies, programmes and training which help communities protect the diversity of their high streets and the growth of independent enterprise. We also help communities to reinvent their local economy in response to climate change, seeking a new low carbon, high well-being model of local economic development. Whatever your role is in a community - whether a business leader, a government official, or a concerned resident - you have a vital role in shaping the local economy."

"High Street UK programmes are driven by the creativity and passion of local people and supported by NEF's national coordinating centre. NEF will develop the programme with a group of representatives from the local business community, resident organisations, statutory agencies, voluntary sector, youth and faith groups. The programme will focus on four main areas: local co-ordination, design, promotion and economic development. All representatives are volunteers and the only criterion for membership is a passion for the place they live and work in. Initially the group will be supported by NEF but the programme is designed to lead to the employment of local people in the long term."

The only way that I would disagree with some of their proposals is that they are looking at how to adapt practices within the current system so that it would be more effective and fairer. I believe that the current system is never going to lead us to a point where practices are universally agreed and where we have fairness. The current systems of government are always going to fall short because they don't have the interests of everybody in mind. They are more concerned with pleasing those who support them through their 'donations' and who would stop 'donating' if their free market model was restricted.

However, the NEF's range of studies, reports, ideas and policies are vast and have the aim of developing the well-being of everyone. It is recommended that you find out more from their website at www.neweconomics.org.

Banking and Finance

The global recession that began in 2007is generally thought to have been caused by a subprime mortgage crisis. In simple terms, this is when banks decided to offer mortgages to customers who were considered to be unable to pay back their loans (default on them). As house prices were rising up to 2006, defaulting on mortgages increased and a lot of the money lent by the banks was lost. This is a classic example of greed running blindly through fields of flowers straight to a lake of fire. Bankers wanted to exploit the poor, with the intention of making them pay extra on the interest rates of their mortgages but being ignorant of the probability that these customers would not be able to pay them at all. The value of houses then started to drop so that they were worth less than the mortgage loan, so the borrowers had an incentive to enter foreclosure, where the lender was able to take possession of their properties. Thus the wealth of the consumers decreased and the financial strength of the banks did likewise.

But how could this be allowed to have happened in the first place? The free market. A lack of regulation of banking practices allowed them to risk whatever they wanted, including the livelihoods of its subprime customers, in a vain attempt to steal their money through interest rates of their choosing, and not only did it fall apart for the people involved but on a global scale, 200 million jobs were lost in this recession, partly because international investors had invested in the booming US housing market. These financial institutions made losses when the housing bubble burst and it sent a shock through the financial markets across the planet.

Quite clearly, this is a practice to not only be learned from, but regulated very tightly. Such predatory lending should not be allowed to happen and there should be national or even international credit criteria that makes it a lot harder for subprime and prime customers to borrow, for the reasons of loaning such money is utterly immoral and is only intended to be for the benefit of the bankers concerned.

Also, such phenomena as house prices increasing does not do anything to help a society develop economically. House prices can't keep rising indefinitely, otherwise hardly anyone would be able to buy a house in, say, 20 years, let alone sell their houses should they wish to make a return on their investments. The housing market is one that needs to be stabilised so that prices will only be able to fluctuate very slightly. This is to ensure personal financial stability and the knowledge that people aren't likely to suffer from having their houses repossessed or their investments making a loss for them. The downside to this is that the housing market would become one that is not really a tool for investment as the amount of profit that can be made from it would be minimal. However, we need to find compromises that actually work better for the people and don't leave them at risk. It is worth being more secure knowing that your mortgage payments would be fixed and that the value of your house will be relatively stable, and also that you are unlikely to have to default on your payments or enter foreclosure. Forget about trying to make easy money, remember that you deserve what you work for, not what you gamble on.

Banks would not have the freedom to lend money to whoever they want. The customers would need to pass strict criteria that is standardised nationally and enforced by law. However, with the implementation of a localised economy that gives more of the power to the people to determine their own successes and that would improve the financial stability of people more, the need for borrowing would decrease and such exploitative banking practices would eventually become a thing of the past, which the majority of the population would certainly welcome.

Other causes that have been suggested as factors for the global recession are things like the government deregulation of financial institutions, notably by George Bush Sr in 1992 so that Fannie Mae and Freddie Mac would have more money to issue as loans, widespread miscalculation by banks and investors of the level of risk inherent in certain unregulated markets and the creation of credit which made it easier for people to get into debt that they couldn't repay.

All of these possible causes, which together formed a dangerous combination, show that capitalism and the free market economy are disasters that will keep causing recessions regularly, causing untold misery to millions of people worldwide. It has to be replaced.

The NEF "works on economic policies and financial models which support inclusive, fair and sustainable economic activity. We believe that banks often work better when they're embedded in communities, in the middle of local economic life, and we support policies, such as the USA's Community Reinvestment Act, which bring banks closer to the needs and lives of everyday people."

To provide alternatives to the large banking institutions that operate on a global scale and to provide people with services that they can trust, in a similar way to making the transition from the global economy to the local economy, local banks would be a far more sensible option.

Banks all over the world generally work in the same ways. They obtain most of their funds from regular people and businesses becoming their customers and opening accounts so that they can store their money safely and access it easily enough. With this money that is collated from thousands of people, the banks will use it to lend to other people or businesses with the intention of making a profit from the interest that they charge for lending it. This is the main purpose of a bank, which is a profit-making institution. The very fact that they charge interest by lending other people's money is immoral to begin with.

They use many other tactics to achieve the same goal, such as offering bonds/ term deposits. This is where you fix a certain amount of your money into the bank for a period of time. During this period, the customer is unable to withdraw their money but they will earn more interest on it than their interest rate on their current account. The bank, meanwhile, knows it has secured this money and can use it to lend or invest as it wishes because it knows the customers can't access this money. The incentive is that the customer can earn a few extra pounds, which is unlikely to make much of a difference to their lives but when they know their money is secure, why not?

So, in effect, the banks use our money for their own gain, although they offer a tiny bit of back in interest (in some countries – in Germany, for example, the customer is charged to have a bank account). They never ask us if we allow them to use our money for whatever projects they implement or if we agree for them to lend our money to other people. The little incentives that they offer keeps them looking caring and giving but none of the money they use is theirs, only the money that they make in profit.

But when the profit comes mostly from encouraging people to get into debt (credit schemes, mortgages, etc.) it doesn't appear to be such an acceptable practice. What we have to remember is that all money is owned by people because it is a human construct. All money changes hands in ways that leaves some people richer and others poorer and banks' intentions are to make those at the top of this profession rich by effectively forcing many people to hand over their money (loan interests) which is what ends up as a bank's reported profits. It is all a case of a few people's profit is many other people's debt.

As I noted earlier, religions such as Islam and Judaism prohibit the idea of making profit from other people's misfortune or need. This is an excellent principle because it is also another way where the money that could be seen as collectively owned by people in a given community gets reduced bit by bit over time and cannot be reclaimed. Imagine that 10,000 people who add up all the money they have in their bank accounts at any one time and it comes to 1 million units. If 4,000 of those people were in debt and paying off loans, including mortgages, with 10% interest all that money will be transferring to the people who run the bank while the other 6,000 are earning minimal interest that doesn't add up to the difference. If it continued for a year mechanically like this, this collective amount will get less but the bank's profit will increase because they are illegitimately stealing money by encouraging people to use credit cards and take loans. How can this be seen as moral or just? We need an alternative.

In Islamic banking, there are many principles that could be incorporated to a new western system of banking due to their morality. Apart from the total lack of interest charged on money loaned, they use a novel way of lending money to businesses. The 'floating rate interest loans' work by lending money to a business and charging them for the service depending on their profits. Therefore, the money that the bank makes is a percentage of the company's profit and not an accumulating rate of interest. This is very moral as it means that the figures are adaptable according to what the business makes. The only loss from the business is the fixed cost, which, as it depends on their profits, is not going to lead to bankruptcy.

An Islamic mortgage transaction works in a similar way. Sometimes, the bank will buy the property from the seller and then re-sell it to the agreed buyer for a profit. This means that, again, there is no accumulation of interest from an APR and the customer simply pays until the fixed amount is cleared. As western banks make huge profits through mortgages, with their vast amounts of interest that builds up over the decades of repayment, it can be shown that there is an alternative and it works. The bank still makes a profit, albeit a far smaller one than in the so-called developed west.

There has been controversy and criticism of Islamic banking but only in isolated cases of malpractice rather than of the general principles. Therefore, it can be used to assimilate principles into Moral banking.

Money is used as a generally finite resource. For it to have any value, it needs to have the scarcity element attached to it. If a state just kept churning out money non-stop, it would be as worthless as using grains of sand for currency. It keeps its value by being something that is more difficult to obtain. The World Bank, which represents 186 countries effectively is the machine that makes money. Its intentions (which have adapted after repeated criticism and protests) have been to achieve humanitarian goals, such as eradicating extreme poverty and hunger, achieving universal primary education and ensuring environmental stability. However, it is run by a small number of the most powerful of the 186 member countries, who have been seen to tailor the actions of the World Bank to their own interests.[13] For example, the president of it is always American and is always nominated by the president of the USA. Therefore, it is easy to see how it operates in a subjective way and that even if it does help many humanitarian causes, it could also be managed more objectively with the interests of all the member countries at heart. We need an alternative here, too.

The Bank of the South was set up by seven South American countries to reduce the amount of US influence in their economies. After reducing their International Monetary Fund (IMF) debts significantly, Argentina and Brazil have since refused to borrow from the IMF again. The various countries had to pledge money to provide the start-up capital so that this money can be used for the development of the member countries with the deregulation of conditions such as loans. This is an example of providing an alternative that doesn't aim to destroy what previously existed. They just said they didn't want to be a part of it and set about creating their own version on a smaller, more contained scale.[14]

This principle can also be used on an even smaller level in terms of local banks. The idea is that each designated region of a country, be it a town or a county (depending on the number of total inhabitants) has its own bank. The people would be free to close their current accounts and switch them to the local bank. In some cases, particularly in areas where the income levels are low, there would be a need to attract rich contributors to help with the start-up capital. This would work in a way that some rich but very moral individual or company would provide, say, €5 million to the bank which the inhabitants could borrow to help develop their area in the way of employment and resilience.

The start-up capital would be loaned out at the rate of interest for the country, which hopefully would be minimal but with no added interest rates from the banks. This money could then be used to create opportunities so that the money that people spent wouldn't be going out of the area to the multinational companies that supply a significant amount of the goods on sale. Instead, because the people in the area would ideally be producing and manufacturing more of their own produce, the local economy would be a lot more stable and prosperous, and due to this non-leaking of the money to foreign sources, the loans would eventually be able to be paid back to the contributors.

This proposal fits in very closely with the whole moralist, cooperative ideal. It is also one that is very possible. It doesn't require a government to close down any existing institutions. It is just a case of making the transition from the national and international level of control to local control. The rules and regulations would be the same for all of these banks across a country to ensure that no-one was losing out by paying loan interests and as it contributes significantly to the development of the community, along with all of the other proposals in this book, there would be less of a chance that anyone would even need a loan, other than for starting a new small business.

To ensure that the money was being used for real development, it would not be easy to secure a loan from this local banking system. There would need to be written contracts that show what the money would be used for. The emphasis has to be on the development of the community, not money for personal gain. If someone just wanted a loan to refurbish their house, they would need to find other ways to fund the project. But if it was to to open a new shop that sells items that are not available from a local origin, it would be investigated by the local council to see if it would fit the needs of the community and not be too large that is not really practical in terms of the likelihood that it will prosper. Proper management of a community is fundamental to its success and avoidance of business failure. Stability is possible, it just needs to be managed effectively and doing such things on a small scale, following a set of well-reasoned principles, is much more manageable and likely to create a real sense of purpose for everyone concerned.

"There is nothing 'natural' about our current economic arrangements. They have been consciously designed to achieve a simple objective: growth. But growth is not making us happier, it is creating dysfunctional and unequal societies, and if it continues will make large parts of the planet unfit for human habitation." (NEF)

The concept of local banking would also have the intention of removing the dependency of the national economy on the large banking groups and other financial institutions. It is simply not fair that so many people suffered from the malpractices of these groups. The majority play no active part in the current system where the economy depends on the banks and the largest companies and therefore the people should not be ones who have to bail them out via their taxes being used to try to restabilise this eternally problematic set-up. The very fact that there are cycles of booms and busts shows that it is ineffective and that the failures happen on such a large scale that the average person has to suffer. We need a system where smaller communities (e.g. states as in the USA or counties in the UK) are more economically autonomous and they have a real incentive to ensure that their resilience and therefore their own hard work will keep them economically stable.

Regarding bankers' bonuses, which have understandably come under fire in the wake of the global recession, in the case of such people receiving millions even when the taxpayers have had to save their institutions, it would simply be illegal to implement a bonus system. The money that would be used for this purpose would have to be paid back as a fine to the state to recuperate the losses from the state funds. When the system is more stable and there is money to deliver as bonuses, it should be either equally distributed between the banks' employees or, as the NEF propose, it would be subject to a "95 per cent tax... that would take a year's remuneration for an individual employee beyond £1 million."

However, under a moral government, it would be expected that the capacity of the current banks would diminish as the people would choose to take their business elsewhere, i.e. local banks that they can trust their money with and that won't be used to try to immorally make profits from.

To summarise, the days where people are aiming to make as much money as they can needs to end. The system whereby the general public become poorer due to a deliberate intention by banks to maximise their profits at all costs needs to be regulated so much that most of their possibilities to exploit the people would be outlawed. People need to be more in control of their own destinies, also in an economic sense, so that they understand that because the money they make mostly stays within their community and will be used to increase the community's funds, there is more of an incentive to contribute to it through their work. The stabilisation of the local economy has to have a real purpose for the people so they can help themselves to develop their economy, not just make it grow, and so that the measure of their success will be their level of happiness, not the level of their own bank accounts.

New Economics Foundation www.neweconomics.org
1. Improving State of the World: Why We're Living Longer, Healthier, More Comfortable Lives On a Cleaner Planet, 2007: Indur M. Goklany, published by the Cato Institute.
2. The Communist Manifesto. Karl Marx and Friedrich Engels. 1996, Orion Books Ltd.
3. Global Issues. www.globalissues.org
4. Rights of Man. Thomas Paine, Dover Publications, Inc.
5. Ethical Business. New Economics Foundation. www.neweconomics.org/publications/ethical-business
6. Towards 21 Hours. New Economics Foundation. www.neweconomics.org/projects/towards-21-hours
7. Washington Post, June 7, 2009, "We Had Our Perestroika. It's High Time for Yours" Op-ed piece by Mikhail Gorbachev

8. http://en.wikipedia.org/wiki/Free_market
9. www.globalissues.org/article/26/poverty-facts-and-stats (point 3)
10.   www.guardian.co.uk/environment/2010/feb/18/worlds-top-firms-environmental-damage
11.   Nordics in Global Crisis. Gylfason, Thorvaldur - Holmström, Bengt - Korkman, Sixten - Söderström, Hans Tson - Vihriälä, Vesa
www.etla.fi/files/2427_nordics_in_global_crisis_(kannet).pdf
12.   A New Economic Model. New Economics Foundation. www.neweconomics.org/projects/new-economic-model
13.   Woods, Ngaire. The Globalizers: The IMF, the World Bank, and Their Borrowers. Ithica and London: Cornell University Press, 2006, pp.190
14.   Williamson, John: What Washington Means by Policy Reform, in: Williamson, John (ed.): Latin American Readjustment: How Much has Happened, Washington: Institute for International Economics 1989.

Employment and Welfare

In the western world and many other parts of the world, employment has been an issue that is difficult to stabilise. The general public are kept dependent on opportunities that are made available mostly by the multinational companies, which depend on the stability of the free-market capitalist system. As we have seen in recent years and throughout history, these dependencies do not offer a model of stability with the booms and busts of the free markets and the big corporations.

The problem of the multinational companies is that as long as they have the monopoly on their markets, they will have factories and shops all over the world. This means there are lots of jobs available for people, which in one sense can be seen as positive. But the jobs are there as long as the workers are going to be the servants that keep the monopolies thriving, expanding and keeping control of the workers' lives. And this is where the problem lies. People can get jobs as long as they work for the big corporations and as long as they work for them, the corporations keep hold of the power over the market and the public in general.

Ordinary people are not able to start up their own businesses so easily if they know they are going to be competing against something like a supermarket or fast-food chain. They won't have the resources to be able to sell at such low prices because they won't have access to imports from somewhere on the other side of the world or to be able to buy in bulk which can give them discounts, so they are practically either doomed from the start or they have to live with the fact that they are never going to achieve much and maybe just stay in business for 2 or 3 years.

But some businesses can start small and grow; it depends on what it is, what competition it will have and how well received it is by the general public. This requires either very wise entrepreneurs or people with a lot of capital to begin with. In the first case, such people are few and far between. It can work for some who have amazingly clever ideas and business plans but not everyone is geared for that kind of success. In the second case, it's not very different from the multinationals if the owner of the business already has a great deal of money to use. He or she will be able to eventually get a chain of shops or cafés going, become rich but at the same time exploit people by using them as servants to create his or her wealth for them, i.e. through the capitalist system.

So with this system of the rich multinationals, the problem of being trapped by them (because they provide the jobs and it's hard to find a job elsewhere because the smaller businesses are collapsing) will not only remain but become worse over time.

The other problem is that with the boom and bust scenario of the capitalist market, where recessions are part of the the whole process, if a huge company fails, it can save itself by closing some factories or branches somewhere where it can do without them. This leads to thousands of people losing their jobs in certain areas without having a say in the matter. The workers' voices are not heard. If they are told they don't have jobs any more just because the company has crashed, they have to walk away and accept it. The control over one's own destiny simply isn't there. These people have not been sacked because they are not working well or are guilty of any other sackable offence, they are just thrown out like bags of rubbish.

Therefore, what we need to develop is a system whereby the ordinary people have control over their own destinies. They need to be able to have jobs that they themselves have created and would only lose as a result of their own bad management or bad workmanship. The fate of people's jobs need to be in their own hands.

That's easier said than done, you might be thinking. Well, of course it's not going to happen overnight but it can happen over a period of a few years, possibly even less than ten. It's not a case of being immoral and putting legislation into place whereby the big companies have to close down, sell their places of work to the public or impose higher taxes on their revenues. In the Hypothetical Government, that would not be acceptable as it is actually being unfair to the businesses that already form the monopolies just as it is unfair that they lay off thousands of people in a week. We can't fight fire with fire, it is never going to bring about stability and peace.

The big companies only succeed because the ordinary people buy their products. Take that away and the companies are in serious trouble. If people aren't buying their low quality burgers and their trainers that were made by poor, undernourished, illiterate children in Bangladesh, then they cannot survive. People need to be awakened and realise that they are unknowingly maintaining the big businesses' profits and their own relative poverty (or lack of opportunity to make it on their own) because they are being tricked into buying what the big businesses produce through their adverts full of happy, slim, beautiful, cool actors and models (i.e. fantasy people) that also act as the role models that the general public should be aspiring to. People need to be given an alternative to these multinationals and their products. They should, instead, support their local small shop owners.

Their prices may be a little higher, but if they are bringing in more revenue, they will be able to lower their prices as their own opportunities increase. People need to move away from the convenience of being able to buy a burger quickly that they know they like the taste of and that it will always be the same. If the local café around the corner is getting more customers, it will raise their spirits and they will ensure that their service gets better and with a little advice (and regulation if necessary), will improve the quality of their food so that it is much healthier than the manufactured junk that is sold in the big chain restaurants. This will also have a positive effect on the environment if we can cut down on the factory farming and deforestation of land that is vital to ecosystems.

But what about the jobs that the big corporations so kindly provide for people? These 'servants' will then be even worse off. Not exactly. If people regularly eat out for their lunch every day and the business goes from café A (big) to a range of smaller cafés, then these cafés will have more demand and will need more staff and the revenues stay in the local area instead of being siphoned off into some offshore bank account where it will not be used again in that area or even in that country (apart from when they invest in creating another branch for their company). The jobs will simply go from one place to another.

Again, we have to be careful not to think that this kind of change is going to happen from one day to the next. It is a gradual process that would be started, supported and finally established by the people themselves. For it to happen on a large scale, it has to be made aware of to everyone possible. This is where the government can, of course, come into effect. Even though the government would not be there to make things happen against the will of the people or the big company executives through force and legislation, as the Hypothetical Government is in effect the institution that represents the people (both rich and poor), it has a duty to guide the people in terms of how they can make change happen. Change is not something that a government should be responsible for in terms of restricting what can be done or not (wherever possible) but something that it has to present to the people in terms of a plan that the people, if they genuinely want it to happen, will be the coordinators for. In a country of millions, an institution of one or two hundred people cannot make things happen. They can provide the opportunities and develop the programmes but everyone has to be a part of it.

Ideas of how all the different individual plans for the bringing back of industries, services, etc. to the people can be organised and put into effect by the people. It is not only a case of bringing the ownership back to the people just because the government arranges and allows these things for the public; it is a joint effort that cannot be achieved without the input from everyone concerned.

Concerning the funding, the local bank idea would be how it could be realised. The money that is saved in the local bank would be used only for the development of local projects. A new business could lend money to start at a low interest rate (of, for example, the national interest rate plus 1% APR) and providing the business plan is deemed to have the potential to succeed, the loan can be repaid depending on their monthly revenue (to prevent the possibility of closure due to financial problems). If the general public is aware that this is how their community and local economy can develop, they are likely to want to be a part of it and switch their savings to the local bank.

The typical argument against this proposal is that it is just idealism; just a pipe-dream or a theory; it would never work in reality.

Fortunately, there is evidence to show that it is possible and it can work extremely well. A documentary was made in 2004 by the journalists and political activists Naomi Klein and Avi Lewis called The Take (www.thetake.org) which tells the story of factory workers who reclaimed control of the former workplaces.

In Argentina, after their economic collapse of 2001, many factories were closed and workers lost their jobs, many not being able to find other work. This is an example of what is typical of a capitalist system – for every boom, there is a bust. In the light of this, an organisation was formed, called The National Movement of Recuperated Factories (NMRF). This was conceived for the reason of allowing the laid off workers to return to the factories where they had worked and simply take control of it themselves. The NMRF's slogan is "Occupy, Resist and Produce", which was in opposition to the government who did not want the workers to control their own destinies, but to make sure that the businesses remained in the hands of the rich and corrupt owners even though they had failed with their fraudulent plans.

So the workers occupied factories across the country and they managed them by themselves. They did the same work to produce the goods that they used to and increased the productivity and revenue without any bosses or higher management of any kind.

This 'cooperative' system is in opposition to the rulebook of capitalism, which runs along the principle that there has to be higher management to run a company, while the workers do as they're told, earn a meagre wage and feel grateful that they have the privilege to do so.

The workers had to learn by their own trial and error to make the factories function but they have in many cases made the businesses more profitable than when they had the administration to do it for them. One factory, Ghelco, has no owner but the workers have equal say and receive equal pay. In 2007, they were earning more than double their previous salaries and the staff had weekly meetings to make joint decisions.

The reason that this can work is that there is a lack of corruption because there is no higher management. The workers control their own destinies, have no-one to answer to, work as they choose to and because they are in full control, are much happier with their work and their lives. They use their money carefully and everyone knows how it is used.

In this example in Argentina, it has not been an idyllic progression by any means. They have had to battle with the courts and the threat of the re-election of President Carlos Menem, who having created economic growth through his widespread privatisations was also the reason for the economic collapse of the entire country. He was almost re-elected in 2003 but withdrew after winning the first round when he knew that he was going to be defeated by his main opposition rival, Néstor Kirchner.

Thus, the NMRF gained ground and by 2007, it represented around 10,000 people in 80 factories. The reason for this growth of the cooperatives was that the workers of these factories support other cooperative factories by helping them to understand how to manage the businesses by themselves and because the general public is in complete support for their local communities.

This recent, real-life example shows that people can control their own destinies, maintain stable jobs and live comfortably due to their own hard work which lies entirely in their own hands.

Therefore, there is proof that the cooperative system can work, not just well enough to survive on, but even better than the capitalist system, and that it is not idealism in any way. It is important to point out that the workers reclaimed the factories in a moral way. Even though they had to stand up to the police, who at times had to prevent them from entering the factories due to the bureaucratic obstacles, they did not force the owners out but simply took the workplaces back when they had been closed.

Due to the political corruption that has been rife in Argentina, to achieve their goals, the workers had to use force which generally wouldn't be advocated. If it is possible, workers should exercise passive resistance, as advocated by Gandhi to peacefully take control. Under a moral government, this would be possible. The closure of factories and other workplaces due to economic collapse would provide the opportunity for workers to legally occupy and take control of the places where they had worked so that they can take the first steps into reforming the work conditions of the country, and morally and peacefully reclaim their destinies from the multinational companies. They are their own bosses and corruption is effectively eliminated.

From this system, we would end up with production by the people, for the people. It is also important to try to reduce the amount of globalisation of the economy, which can be achieved as a side effect of the cooperative system. We would aim to produce as many of the things that are needed (not just wanted) for the country to support itself without relying on imports wherever it is practical. This would mean an end to cheap goods because they are made in sweatshops for the westerners' convenience and ignorance. In a country like the United Kingdom where there were 2.47 million people unemployed in August 2009[1], that means that there is enormous scope for the workers to bring back manufacture from abroad, from providing the resources to producing the final products. Industry has declined dramatically with the outsourcing of production in the last few decades. By aiming for this situation, we would also need to discuss what products would actually be worth manufacturing. This is where the question of "what do we really need to be happy?" comes into play. Without going into it again, it would require awareness, education and analysis from the people themselves to determine what it actually necessary to be produced. The importance of this is because of the need to eliminate the concept of cyclical consumption which is a huge waste of finite resources. This practice can be reformed when we start to shape our culture so that we are not delusionally depending on things that are, in essence, useless.

But what will happen to those poor people in countries like Bangladesh who, by working in sweatshops are actually earning money for themselves with which they can support their families? Simple – instead of manufacturing the products for sale overseas, they can occupy the factories that the western companies stop using due to their decreasing market and they can use them to manufacture products for their own country. It would be exactly the same concept of the NMRF, except that they wouldn't need to manufacture fancy rubbish plastered in logos but downgrade them to functional items that would actually serve the Bangladeshis who can't even afford to have shoes or new t-shirts currently.

This would be a project whereby people of developed countries who are well educated in the cooperative system would be required to go to the developing countries to train them how to take their own control. Step by step, we would be able to reform the world, reduce poverty and remove globalisation with its culturally polluting elements. Your average Bangladeshi has no interest in big name brands, nor should they have these things imposed on them. But if we give them back the means to support their own population, things will start to improve dramatically.

Talking about the Third World is, of course, another issue due to the extreme levels of poverty and underdevelopment. One could think again that this idea really is unworkable. How could you go about changing a country already at the point of collapse? Well, again, there is evidence to show that it is possible.

Another recent documentary, "The Road to Fondwa" (fondwa.org), depicts how the people of Haiti, the poorest country in the western hemisphere have got to the point where they know they can't rely on anyone, let alone their own government, to provide them with food and basic infrastructure. In the face of disillusion they took their own control. There are projects where the people are working together to provide for one another, are learning methods to be able to farm, fish, build schools so that the children can be a part of the future of the country and they are making progress. This also shows that it is inadequate to expect any government to fulfil your needs. The people have to take the initiative and do things for themselves. In underdeveloped countries, they will need help from outside to even be aware of how to create a sanitary water system or how to have electricity in their village. There are already countless volunteer organisations that are dedicated to such causes so it is unnecessary to have to try to justify that it can work.

Unfortunately, since these projects started up, Haiti suffered a massive earthquake and the newly-found hope of the people was crushed with it. Credit has to be given to the World Bank, who cancelled Haiti's debt of $40 billion.

So, in the place of a capitalist system which certainly doesn't satisfy everyone or anywhere near the majority of the people of the world, evidence shows that a cooperative system is the way forward. It brings people together, it gives them control of their own lives, it makes them supportive of one another and it removes the power of those who already control the world and that are aiming to control it even more tightly.

The way that employment works is such an important issue, which directly affects the lifestyles of practically everyone. It has been discussed in Shaping A Society but it is worth going over the main points again.

Firstly, work has to be meaningful to the workers wherever possible. To achieve this, we should aim to give people as much control and influence of their own destinies as possible. Removing the concept of middle and upper management is one of the key points – It has been shown that the workers, when given enough training and having enough time to work out the best strategies to run their own businesses, can do it in such a way that their lives are far more satisfactory. They earn more, they have an equal say in how the business develops and the have the power in their own hands, collectively.

It is also important to organise work regulations on a large scale so that competition is not going to get in the way and cause some businesses to collapse because others have a greater market share. To ensure this, things need to be scaled down so that they mostly work on a local level but with national agreement. A business that manufactures tyres should have its limits and not be allowed to encroach in other businesses' territories, so to speak. If business A sells its products to the people in region A and it works at a good level so that the workers are neither overrun nor under-worked but they keep the production levels steady and sufficient for their own well-being and that of their community, there is no good reason why they should be allowed to expand and try to be the leading manufacturer in the country. This competitive business practice would damage other so-called 'rival' businesses and probably cause unemployment in other areas or, if they buy out the smaller company, make the other workers lose control of their own destinies.

Workers' conditions are equally important to make sure that they are not just happy that they earn enough money to live comfortably on but that they feel secure and happy and that they actually like to be in their workplaces. Each worker should have insurance and the health and safety regulations must be strictly adhered to. They should be allowed to have regular breaks and work in an environment that is inspiring. There is a great psychological advantage to working in an environment that one finds pleasant – with enough light, good air quality, attractive décor, comfortable furniture and pleasant rest areas.

Another important condition is making sure that people don't have to work too many hours. People need to be able to enjoy their free time and not feel stressed by having to work late every day. To reduce unemployment levels, work-hours can be divided and jobs shared between more people so that the workload is reduced and employment is increased. If they are working under a cooperative system, there is more chance that three people can reduce their work hours from 40 to 30 but still earn a good salary and provide another job for someone else to make up the 30 hours that have been cut.

Unions

Unions are very practical institutions so that fairness can be attained on a smaller level, locally as well as nationally, and so that issues can be better managed such as the working conditions. This is as long as the unions are not being unrealistic. The concept of unions have been criticised in the past for demanding too much and causing more trouble than they are worth so, as with everything, a compromise has to be reached.

Trade unions would need to be standard practice in any country and every worker would automatically be a member of their union to ensure that their needs and interests are not marginalised and that they will be unable to be exploited by company executives. This means that money would need to be deducted from workers' salaries in order to fund them and pay for the work of those who represent the union so it would need to be agreed that it would not cost too much for the average worker. Of course, they would have the option to abstain from joining the union but the plan would be that it would definitely be in their best interests to do so.

The New Unionism Network (NUN) has been established to try to bring democracy to the workplace. It is morally wrong to say that workers shouldn't have any say in what conditions they have to work under. Their jobs directly affect them as well as what can measured in the output of their work. The difference is that the workers are people and they have rights which are far more important than work quotas and profits. If the majority of workers in any employment sector are dissatisfied with their jobs, they absolutely have the rights to speak up and demand that their conditions are improved, for they are the majority in the sector as opposed to the upper and middle management. They also have absolutely equal rights to everyone else as does everyone on the planet and this fact has precedence over every decision that is taken in any aspect of human life.[2]

A problem that unions have historically had is that there has always been competition between the agendas of the management and the agendas of the workers. Countless arguments and strikes have occurred as the result of these conflicts. This is something that needs to set straight right from the beginning so that it has no scope to occur. Compromise is the key so that when the need arises to debate issues that one side doesn't agree with, it is simply law to reach a democratic decision through voting where anyone's vote, be they managers or workers, all have the same weight. This would mean that those in higher positions of power wouldn't have the last say. It would simply come down to the result of the democratic principles.

This would also have the effect of the management's influence becoming less influential. As the NUN states, decisions don't have to be made. They would come about by themselves when all the factors relevant to an issue have been considered and the resolution is put to the vote.

This is the only ethical solution to organising workers' rights and the development (not meaning competitive expansion) of the business or institution.

One particular issue tends to arise with the idea of giving more power to the people – If you give people their own power, they will demand more and become some megalomaniacs. This is a quite bizarre notion – why would people, whose own work and rights define their own outcomes, working under agreed regulations, become megalomanic? They would be working on a smaller scale, with practically no opportunities to suffer from megalomania, their working conditions and pay would be far more agreeable, they would be happier with what they do as they are in control of what happens to themselves, therefore have much more job satisfaction and job security. Happiness, comfort and fulfilment don't seem like reasons for people to demand more from their jobs. On the other hand, working for someone who they'll never meet, who also walks away with most of the money made from their work, being paid relatively little, having no say in how their careers progress or how the business operates, having no insurance as well as no respect and compassion from the middle management do seem like reasons for people to demand more from their jobs.

The kind of people who make such a claim are those who know they would lose their power and disproportionate salaries, i.e. it would damage their own greedy, selfish aspirations to continue exploiting the masses for their own benefit. If we are looking at implementing morality at every level, some people's lives would have to change – negatively for the exploiters, positively for the exploited who are the ones that really count considering that they may comprise of more than 90% of the people involved.

But could this concept work in practice on a large scale? In the UK, there is a department store chain called John Lewis. As of March 2010, reported in The Guardian, it had 69,000 employees. It also has the Waitrose supermarket and together there are 251 premises nationwide. Its operating profit was up 20% during the global recession and the company's constitution states its purpose as "the happiness of all its members, through their worthwhile and satisfying employment in a successful business".

So far it sounds like any other chain store that can *say* that is its purpose but it doesn't mean it will follow through on it. It just sounds nice. But each year, one of its employees opens an envelope and reads out a percentage. It is usually between 9% and 22%. Every worker waits to hear this number because it means that is how much of a bonus they will receive for the year, where 8% is an extra month's pay. But who are 'they'? The store managers? The owners? Yes, as well as every checkout assistant, every shop floor assistant and everyone who works there. Because these 69,000 people are not really employees, they are partners in the business. John Lewis doesn't exist to make the few at the top of the pyramid rich, for there is no pyramid here. Everyone is on the same level in a democratic sense. They can all share their thoughts on how to improve their business model, which are passed onto the board, which is elected by an 82 member partnership and who can sack the chairman if they feel necessary. Not that the partners are usually in that kind of position – they want to keep their jobs at all costs for they feel valued and looked after with all the benefits. The partners decided they didn't want to work on Boxing Day, so that's how it was.

Not only do all the partners receive the bonus each year as that would be a nice extra little package but it really sticks to its purpose, that of the happiness of all of its members. They collectively own holiday centres for the partners to stay at, along with a 16th century castle with a private beach, a 24-room outdoor and water sports club on Lake Bala in north Wales, and a country house hotel in 4,000 rolling acres of Hampshire as well as many others facilities. All for the employees, sorry, partners, to enjoy.

They also get 25% off most products in John Lewis and 15% off in Waitrose and are rewarded with a non-contributory final salary pension scheme. The partners stay with this company for twice as long as the industry average.

But surely this model cannot work in the long term, can it? Well, John Lewis Partnership Limited began life in 1928 and is still as strong as ever because practically everyone who works there feels a part of it. What they gain from their time at work depends on how much they contribute to it. If they work hard and organise and manage departments well, the business will succeed, they will all be able to take the holidays at the places that the company provides and they will receive the bonus depending on how much money they were able to help the company earn.

But how does it compare with the companies listed on the FTSE 100? They outperform it by about 10% each year – that is, they outperform the 100 biggest firms in the UK by that much.

Jon Henley also reported that research by the Cass Business School indicates that employee-owned businesses also create jobs faster; are significantly more resilient in an economic downturn; deliver far better customer satisfaction; boast substantially higher value added per employee; and, depending on the sector and size of the business, can deliver markedly higher profits (co-owned businesses seem to work best when they've got fewer than 75 staff and operate in knowledge- or skill-intensive sectors).[3] This means that for John Lewis, it has been a long period of learning how to work with this model on a large scale but it does and very effectively but to achieve this kind of success on a smaller scale is much easier because there are fewer factors and problems to deal with.

This John Lewis model is one that should be used for all private sector businesses. After its implementation and evolution over currently 9 decades, it can be evaluated as being very effective and most importantly worker-friendly. This model is also in effect a combination of a job sector and a union where those two parts work as one and do not exist independently.

For these reasons, a moral government would make it a legal requirement that every business works along the same principles: democracy, partnership, workers' bonuses, workers' benefits including leisure time facilities.

In fact, such a model would also work very well with the Creativity in the Community proposal. Take an example of small scale textile manufacture. A small group of designers living in a designated council/ neighbourhood would love to use their creativity to design and sell their own clothes but it's difficult because of the large retailers and well-known brands. They decide to get together and they find some people to be involved in the manufacture of their designs. They produce a small number of garments and rent a shop to sell their own work. The profits made go equally to the group of workers, who then, because of the knowledge of their potential, continue working because they know that if they put the work in they will gain from it. No management, no factory supervisor, no commands from high office in the capital city that they have no choice but to comply with. It's all theirs – they own it, they make it happen and the people in the same community support them because they know them and buy their clothes from the shop. Consequently, the money made stays in the community and can be used to buy other products and services which also are community based. The taxes from the businesses go to their local council, which then funds their own public services. The money is not drained out into overseas bank accounts and the community becomes much more resilient, meaning more economically developed and the people are the creators of their own well-being.

Other ideas could include a similar takeover scheme to the one of the reclamation of factories that have been closed down by large businesses. In the event of companies who run a chain of shops closing some of their branches, as in a recession, the building should then become under the control of the local government. It wouldn't mean that they own it but have the rights to it. With this newly acquired building, a local consortium can be formed whereby local people would be able to use the existing building and its equipment to joint manage a department each. Say, for example, a medium sized department store closes down; a group of 20 people take control of the electronics department, another 20 take the food section, etc. Effectively, the shop would continue to function but it would all be managed by local people. The emphasis should be on the sale of locally made produce wherever possible, thereby encouraging the manufacture of local clothes, local food and so on. A scheme like this would have the potential to create hundreds of jobs in a short space of time, but not just jobs where the employees work for an outside corporation; they collectively own it themselves.

While this new scheme is developing and earning money, the originating business can be gradually paid a percentage of the cost of the real estate. An agreement would need to be standardised for the country in this event but a potential figure would be that the former company would receive 50% of the market value of the property that would not be subject to an interest rate outside of inflation. The amount that is paid by the new cooperative owners would depend on their monthly net profits so that they would not be at risk of falling behind on payments, nor would they be having to pay more than they can afford considering their own costs.

This is a way of showing that there is no intention of trying to crush existing businesses that work on a national or international scale, but when the real estate becomes available, there is a way that it would benefit the local community, give them ownership of their work, inspire more local manufacturing and also contribute to the previous company's financial difficulties.

In 1998, when in Bratislava, the capital of Slovakia, I came across a type of fast-food market. This was an inspirational idea that would also fit in with these kinds of proposals. It was like an indoor market that comprised of individual fast-food stalls that provided all kinds of foods: Slovak, Chinese, Italian, etc. There might have been around fifty of these that appeared to be owned and run by a small number of people for each one. Customers would simply go and choose whatever food they felt like and with the variety available, it made an excellent business idea. This would be an alternative to the kinds of fast-food sections in shopping centres that are clones of each other in shopping centres around the country.

It could work in a cooperative manner, too, so that the raw foods that they need can be ordered and stored centrally, i.e. so that the bulk buying can lead to reduced overhead costs. The cooperative group could agree on fair prices so that no stall becomes more favoured because they charge less relatively. If one or a few stalls were having difficulty in making sales, they could be allowed to temporarily lower their prices or receive support from the other partners to develop their stalls to become more effective.

Under the current capitalist system, this type of cooperation and support is quite alien as the emphasis in the business world is on competition and being more successful than one's rivals. But what is the point of that? Why would anyone want to become so successful that their competitors risk losing their businesses? It makes no sense, especially on a moral level.

Given the amount of local support that has been seen in the reclamation of factories scheme in Argentina, and how well that scheme has worked in terms of salaries, democracy and working conditions, there is definitely the probability that it could work in the above ways, too.

Income Tax

Nobody likes paying income tax. This is the first problem that a government has to address. Why don't people like paying it? It is most likely that people think of all that money automatically going out of their monthly wage and it seems to disappear into obscurity and we never know how it is really being used. We are told that it is used for public services like schools, the police, the infrastructure such as building or fixing roads but the anonymity of it leaves people thinking that for all they know, their money might just be going into the bank accounts of corrupt politicians. In some countries, this is true but people don't have any reason to trust the system because all the decisions about how the money is spent are made behind closed doors without consulting the workers who have no choice but to hand it over.

In the UK, the areas of public expenditure, in order of amount spent, as of March 2010 were social protection (the welfare system at £196bn), health (£122bn), education (£89bn), other areas such as sport, culture and international development (£74bn), debt interest on the government's borrowing (£43bn), defence (£40bn), public order and safety (£36bn), personal social services (like social work and home help at £33bn), housing and environment (£27bn), transport (£22bn), industry, agriculture, employment and training (£20bn).[5]

Knowing that the most of the tax money is spent on those who are out of work would make many people uncomfortable because immediately they would think of the free-loaders, although since the recession kicked in the unemployment rate has increased dramatically through no fault of those workers, but through the fault of the multinational companies who used a faulty business model that was based on fraud and exploitation.

Of course the state's income is a lot more than just income tax. According to The Guardian's piece, income tax amounted to £146bn for the 2009/2010 tax year. This is because the other deductions imposed on the public are just given different names. National Insurance, which covers the medical care that is otherwise freely available brought in £97bn. Other taxes include stamp duty and vehicle excise duty plus others (£81bn), council tax (£26bn) and VAT (£78bn). These taxes, which directly affect the general public, apart from corporate tax, excise duties and business tax, more than double the amount gained in income tax.

But again, the money deducted personal taxes just goes to the state and the people get no say in how it is spent. If, however, cities and regions were given more economical autonomy, it would change the way people see both their work and the value of paying tax.

For example, imagine that a constituency of 10,000 inhabitants were responsible for some of their own public services: all those listed above except for defence and debt interest. This would mean that the employed would be contributing to the schools that their children attend, the hospitals that they may need to go to and the police who they want to instil public order for them. Obviously the amounts would be far less than the national figures (one six-thousandth when comparing ten thousand people to sixty million in the UK in total). Of course it wouldn't be as easy as just dividing the figures by 6,000 as not every constituency would have the same number of schools or even have its own hospital but if the inhabitants were told how much needs to be spent on various sectors that are directly related to themselves, they would probably be more willing to contribute via their taxes.

It would also be an incentive to help the unemployed citizens to find their way back into work. Instead of criticising them as being free-loaders, they should be more positive and constructive, identifying areas where the community is lacking and falling short of being resilient, and work together to set up projects so that the unemployed could become a functioning part of the community, e.g. helping to improve the roads or the general environment, joining a local business group to manufacture goods that are sold in the local community.

If the unemployed are supported and seen as people who could fill the gaps where the community doesn't have a certain service that it needs, the strength of solidarity would increase substantially.

In the case of people who live in one constituency but work in another, their income tax can simply be split 50-50 between the two constituencies. If they are working in one area, they are contributing to that particular society but as they live in another, they would also be contributing to that one in terms of their personal expenditure.

In terms of tax rates, a graded system would be most fair, with the lower earners paying minimal tax of, say, 2%. The reason for this, as opposed to saying low earners should be exempt from tax, is to give them a feeling that they are still contributing to their local economy in some way. The rates would go up to around 50% for seriously high earners, which would be justified as again, no-one *needs* to be taking home millions each year. The more they earn, the more their duty is to contribute to their community.

As there are some sectors which should be managed nationally and some which would need an extra covering of funds to share between areas which have less than others, a part of every workers' income tax should go to the state to be divided appropriately. This would need to be negotiated but could, for example, be 30% of the total income tax paid (so 70% would go to the local community and 30% to the state for more general costs that have to function on a national scale).

Where a town has only one hospital but 4 constituencies, the money earned in income tax would simply be aggregated and used for that purpose.

This type of tax system is designed to, again, give the ownership and destiny to the people and show them that they have the responsibility to look after themselves as a community and don't feel that they are being used as puppets by a government that never asks the people how they would like the public money spent.

In the Nordic Model, welfare is seen as being fundamentally important to make sure it is available to everyone who needs it. To be able to achieve this, the income tax rates are high (averaging 50% in Sweden) but the justification for this is so that public services won't need to suffer. With the vast amounts of cuts in public spending that is going on in what used to be thought of as the richest countries shows that the system has again failed and the finances have been extremely badly managed.

A government needs to gain a high level of trust from the people and good management is obviously essential to make sure that public spending should never need to be reduced. The public need to be kept informed of how the public funds are being spent (transparency) and therefore why it is important that people pay income tax. It is something that again comes to the notion that the measure of people's success is how much they contribute to society.

Welfare

The concept of a welfare state is when the state assumes primary responsibility for the welfare of its citizens. To be effective, it needs to take certain factors into account to make it fair on everyone. Firstly, if there is little work available, the unemployed need to have a kind of safety net so that they can support themselves. In the UK, this is set out so that the unemployed can claim state benefits indefinitely if they are unable to secure a job. This has a serious disadvantage to the state and to the concept of a work ethic because it means that there will always be some people who depend on it indefinitely and it can lead to some people being unwilling to look for work. For this reason it is ineffective as there is no impetus to actively seek work if the people in question are content to live in this way. It becomes a burden on the state and therefore, a different system need to be devised.

In Spain and Portugal at least, the availability of unemployment benefits depend on how long as person has worked and how much they earned at their last job. For example, if a person has worked for at least 12 months, they would be entitled to the benefits at a rate of 80% of their last earnings for a four month period. After that, there would be no more benefits available. The length of time that people can claim for increases depending on how long they have held a job in the country. This is more effective as the claimants can still receive a substantial proportion of their previous earnings but as the period of time to claim is relatively short, there is the incentive and still a relatively long time frame to find new employment. It also has the ethical benefit of being relative to the amount of work the person has put into society, which makes sense if people deserve to get anything back if they are out of work.

By contrast, the Nordic Model of economics stipulates that anyone should be entitled to receive benefits that are not significantly lower than the employed. This is due to the ideology that everyone should be at a comfortable standard of living. The other side of this is that tax rates are very high. In one sense this is acceptable because it means that there are more public funds available to be used to benefit everyone but if someone is earning relatively little and they still have to pay a high tax rate, it will affect them adversely.

The Nordic Model, which is very highly regarded regarding economic efficiency and growth with a peaceful labour market, a fair distribution of income and social cohesion, is a complete system whereby the state is able to reciprocally help the citizens to a high level. It would be difficult to summarise the Nordic Model here as it is, of course, very detailed but it can be read online in full.[3] However, one of the precursors for it to work effectively is high employment rates. The Nordic countries are Finland, Denmark and Sweden (and to some extent Norway and Iceland, though the conditions are different for them as they are not currently EU countries). These countries have relatively small populations, which makes it easier to provide enough employment for its citizens. In larger countries, which may have ten or fifty times the population of Finland's 5.3 million, it would be more difficult to apply the Nordic Model due to the difficulty of managing such vast populations effectively with one model, especially where unemployment rates are higher, partly due to faster population growth as in many Asian countries.

However, there are many elements that would be practical to consider and adapt for countries with, say, 100 million inhabitants. For example, the concept of scaling down things to more regional levels rather than national levels would, in theory, make the task of government more achievable. Dividing a large country into its regions, provinces or states would reduce the workload of the overall government but each one could follow the same principles and be managed separately.

Of course, the main aim of the employment sector would be to keep unemployment as low as possible. To do this, it needs to either create jobs or make it 'straightforward' for people to create their own jobs. There would still be no guarantee that there would be permanent jobs available for everyone so temporary work agencies, which are already established, would be useful for helping people to support themselves in the short term while they are trying to find long-term employment.

In the case of people who claim that it is difficult for them to find the kind of work for the qualifications that they have, it needs to be asserted that people should be willing to take on a job that they might see as being beneath them and lose the idea that they are too proud to take on work that they see as menial.

For those who actively seek work but honestly do find it difficult to find it, there could be condition in place that states that if someone is unemployed for more than 12 months, they must take on voluntary work to entitle them to continue receiving state benefits. This is not meant to be seen as making sure that people are being used against their will but rather that they have a sense of purpose and that they can still be a contributing member of society even if it is in a not-officially-employed fashion. If people are doing voluntary work, it is likely that they are also developing their skills and improving their prospects of finding proper employment. Therefore, the intention is that they are seen as people that are being supported rather than criticised for living off the state, which can also lead to depression if they feel they are not achieving anything.

It is critically important that people are always supported if we are going to raise the level of well-being for everyone.

1. www.statistics.gov.uk/cci/nugget.asp?ID=12

2. www.newunionism.net/

3. www.etla.fi/files/1892_the_nordic_model_complete.pdf

4. www.guardian.co.uk/business/2010/mar/16/john-lewis

5. www.guardian.co.uk/uk/interactive/2010/mar/24/budget-2010-state-britain-finances

Personal Finance

In a report by the NEF, (Community Banking Partnership: A joined-up solution for financial inclusion), a quarter of British households do not have access to mainstream financial services. (1) This is because they are considered too poor to be able to pay back loans. The demand is there from people who need to borrow money but the supply was not there from high-street banks. This means there was a gap to be filled. Unfortunately, living in a free market capitalist system, 'doorstep lenders' were able to freely walk in and offer loans easily to these households with the freedom to charge as much interest as they wanted. These rates range from 160% to 1,500% APR. There is no limit imposed on interest rates and the NEF calls for alternative and affordable sources of credit.

However, this is only half of the solution. There needs to be a law that prevents these loan sharks from being able to set their own interest rates as their only objective to is make huge amounts of money from people who are desperate enough to lend at such exorbitant rates. They don't care in any way about pushing struggling families and individuals into a cycle of debt from which they will probably be unable to leave. They just want lots of money at any expense because the expense will not come from them.

As it is unquestionably immoral to make profit from the poor, serious restrictions need to be put into place as well as providing new sources of credit that aren't going to lead to misery and suicide. The credit union industry has tried to gain a market share of this business of lending by offering interest rates of 12.68% APR, which are restricted by law. This means that the credit unions are unable to compete in the higher risk area of the market as they can't change the margins needed. Some of the new community development finance institutions (CDFIs) have begun to provide personal credit at rates of about 25 per cent APR and are proving that low-cost alternatives can be developed.[1]

So the problem is still that the more ethical alternatives are struggling to succeed for the low income earners because the predatory lenders can give credit with no questions asked. The solution? Change the law.

If private financial institutions are restricted to offer credit with a fixed interest rate that is only 1 or 2% above inflation, they can still function as a business, but they will not have the freedom to exploit the poor and they are more likely to abandon their business practice.

In the NEF's words, a flexible model sensitive to local needs is what is required. The Community Banking Partnership (CBP) approach is to select the best team players able to respond to long-term demand within their specific local market, while simultaneously delivering the maximum social benefit in each different urban or rural sub-region.

The CBP aim is to provide financially excluded households with a seamless service offering savings facilities, affordable loans, access to basic banking services, bill and debt repayment systems, money advice and support.

The aim of a moral government should be to spread the wealth much more evenly in society so that there is almost no need for loans to pay bills, etc. By localising the economy and giving people the management of their own destinies through moving from working for multinational companies to local businesses that they collectively own, the wealth should be spread more effectively and the well-being of people will be a lot higher and more stable.

The only discrepancy I would have with the NEF is that it forms its principles around the existing model that we live under in the 'developed' world. It aims to provide alternatives to existing practices, without calling for an overhaul of the unethical, exploitative practice that is allowed to go on. To be able to achieve total success, we need a new system of government and a new way of life so that the alternatives become the norm and they are not alternative to anything else as no other practice would be permitted to exist.

The NEF still want credit to be available to less well-off people but the Hypothetical Government would be committed to giving the less well-off more opportunities to look after themselves, discourage the idea of lending and wanting more money and material possessions and eventually change the mindset of people so that they wouldn't feel tempted to have everything that is currently paraded in front of us, despite most of it having no real value to our well-being.

This is how the general public's mindset has been shaped by the capitalist system: want, buy, and if you can't buy - lend.

I see the concept of the Community Banking Partnership as part of the transition period but not the end product. The intentions are good, to support poorer people, to offer them affordable loans but this should only be a step towards the ultimate goal which is to not need a personal loan because people have the savings to cover their needs adequately.

There are far too many high earners in every country, even though they make up the minority. Take, for example, high-profile football players, commercial pop singers, Hollywood actors, CEOs of all the big multinational companies. There may not be many of these kinds of people but they have more than their fair share of the wealth that could be used to help deprived communities to develop and become more resilient. If we were able to persuade some of these people who have millions of even billions of dollars/ pounds, etc. to place some of their money in local banks that would be able to use it to lend at a rate of the national interest rate plus 2%, communities would have the capital to be able to build their own base to support themselves and through the practice of the local economy, be able to retain the money that they spend, make their communities more affluent and pay back the original deposit made by the high earners who were moral enough to put forward their money to help communities develop.

As mentioned in Shaping A Society, the Institute for Philanthropy is an example of how this end is trying to be achieved.[2]

A more resilient community that is not scraping by to survive will be happier, more crime-free, safer and those who lent their money to help all of this to happen should feel like they have really achieved something meaningful with their lives instead of just wasting their seemingly never ending fortune on another mansion, a big yacht or a new state of the art car.

1. www.neweconomics.org/sites/neweconomics.org/files/ Community_Banking_Partnership_Financial_Exclusion.pdf

2. Institute for Philanthropy www.instituteforphilanthropy.org

Immigration

This is a policy area that has provoked much debate and disagreement for governments, due to the fact that increasing the number of inhabitants of a country puts a strain on the welfare system and the jobs market where there are already unemployed native residents.

The reasons for immigration are varied: sometimes people want to leave their country because of a poor standard of living and the hope that their situations will improve in another country, people often want to study in another country because of the better opportunities or because it is cheaper to do so elsewhere, persecution, oppression or ethnic-cleansing leads to humanitarian reasons for wanting to find a more stable life, natural disasters that cause the loss of homes and/or livelihood such as earthquakes. Other employment opportunities may crop up in another country or retired citizens might simply want a change of surroundings.

With these reasons, immigration needs to be looked at both practically and morally. Those people who are against immigrants entering their country when there are not enough jobs for the natives usually fail to see the humanitarian reasons and refuse to tolerate the immigrants without using any reasoning or considering what it would be like if they were in the immigrants' position.

To form an effective policy, the practical elements need to be addressed in collaboration with the moral aspects. The society also needs to be kept informed as to why decisions are made to allow or disallow certain people to settle in the country.

From a practical perspective, if the country has a high unemployment rate, allowing tens or even hundreds of thousands of immigrants in per year is not going to be effective. It is likely that whatever their circumstances, the immigrants may attain more stability but they would cause disruptions in the functioning of a country as they would need monetary support in terms of welfare and housing that would need to be provided by the government which would in turn make the economy less effective.

For this reason and in this situation, it would be important to restrict the amount of immigrants that would be allowed to settle in the country, more so in the cases of those who would simply like the chance to live elsewhere but don't really need to.

In the case of the destination country needing more qualified workers in certain areas such as medicine that couldn't otherwise be obtained from the native population, it would be more effective to allow enough immigrants in to fill those positions. In this situation, there should not be any real problem as they would be entering the country with a job waiting for them, and they would then be able to support themselves and support the economy through their expenditure and tax deductions.

When the reasons are humanitarian, such as fleeing a war-torn country where their lives are in danger, countries should pull together to attempt to share the burden of the influx of immigrants and make efforts to provide them with employment. With high rates of unemployment at the time of writing, this idea sounds impractical but this can be used to counteract the amount of outsourced work as mentioned previously. If companies set up factories in the country to manufacture goods that would otherwise be imported, unskilled immigrants can be given work, therefore reducing the cost of welfare, adding to the national funding through (minimal tax) and raising the well-being of the immigrants so that they can care for themselves and even learn skills that they could take back to their native country when it is safe to return. To encourage companies to be a part of this scheme, there should be tax breaks offered if they create and maintain jobs in the country rather than outsource them.

This could be seen as simply moving sweatshops back into so-called developed countries but obviously, it would have to be law that the workers have good conditions such as a limit of working hours and they can live in clean accommodation that the company should provide. The other difference is that it is not using immigrants as slave labour but giving them opportunities to fend for themselves instead of having them in marginalised communities where they are not integrated.

The integration of immigrants is extremely important to ensure the well-being of everyone. We really need to educate the people to understand that the reasons for immigration are varied and important in many different ways. If the people in question are going to fill a job that couldn't otherwise be filled, there shouldn't be any difficulty with accepting them. If it is the case that they don't speak the language of the destination country, it would be mandatory that they receive lessons; either paid for by themselves if they have work or voluntarily provided if they do not have the finances. The same thing goes for integrating them into the culture and community: it would be required of them to integrate as much as possible and reciprocally, it would be necessary that the native inhabitants welcome them and aid their integration. It is always important to put yourself in the shoes of the other people to get an unbiased opinion to their situation.

This requirement of the existing population would also have a major impact on the levels of crime in their area. If the immigrants were not accepted by most people and they were not supported to find employment, what are their options going to be? They have to support themselves in some way and whereas they may receive some kind of benefit from the state, the lack of acceptance from the residents will instil in them a sense of anger, resentment and conflict, which could obviously result in crime. This has been shown to be the case in many countries, where the crime statistics show that immigrants are more likely to cause crime than the natives. If we supported them and helped them to integrate, there wouldn't have been any reason for them to turn to crime. Every cause has an effect.

Another issue is the right to remain in the country permanently. Again, this is a complicated one to make generalisations about as it depends on many circumstances. If a person in question was seen to be essential to the society, for example by being a local doctor, there shouldn't be any need to try to ask them to return to their country of origin. If a large number of refugees were allowed in, found enough work to support themselves but the circumstances in their home country changed and became stable enough for them to return, it may be more practical for them to return, to relieve the burden on the country that they emigrated to. In this case, it would not be moral enough to simply say that because the conflict has now ended there they have to leave because, as members of the same species, we have the obligation to support each other and help them to return so that they would be able to support themselves in their home country.

If they were to be sent back but they would be unlikely to find any work or suitable housing, projects should be formulated so that they would receive support from more developed countries to help them to learn skills that they could implement in their home country so that they wouldn't simply be going back to the same kind of suffering that they had previously experienced, but instead so that their country can develop more effectively. While living in a more developed country, the immigrants should be taught skills that they could take back with them, with the objective of making less-developed countries more desirable to live in.

The ultimate aim would be to make it less likely for countries to fall into disarray, politically and economically, and to help the world develop together so that immigration for reasons of necessity (war, oppression, genocide, etc.) would, by itself, decline by itself.

As a world and as a species, we must strive to achieve overall development and stability and this requires the support of the more developed countries if they are going to be a part of preventing problems that they claim to suffer from with respect to immigration.

Social Regeneration

To illustrate how it would be possible to transform a very deprived area into a successful one in terms of the residents' well-being, I shall take the example of a housing estate in Scotland, called Easterhouse, which The Guardian did a report on in March 2010.[1]

Easterhouse is a suburb of Glasgow, made up of grey concrete blocks of flats and houses that have been boarded up after they had been set fire to. The local reverend regularly cremates people between the ages of 45 and 55, due to lung cancer, alcohol abuse, heart failure and drug-related deaths. Syringes and rubbish litters the estate and the children have nothing to do to fill their time.

So, in a neighbourhood where there are almost no jobs, a feeling of fatalism (some residents even refer to themselves as scum), high levels of alcoholism and a low life-expectancy (it is said to be common for people die before they are 50 although the average is 66), where does one start?

The Conservative politician Iain Duncan Smith has been working on a project to fix the problems of the so-called 'Broken Britain', a term conjured up by the Conservative Party to illustrate the level of poverty and social decline. Duncan Smith had visited Easterhouse and was inspired to set up a thinktank to analyse the ways in which Britain is broken and to propose solutions (which these days seems an absurd idea - to get this particular person to undertake such a task). His work has won praise from charities and campaign groups as well as from some Labour MPs, which shows that it is futile to divide people into certain groups, such as political persuasion, but we all need to work together to find solutions.

Duncan Smith identified five areas which are the cause of poverty: educational failures, worklessness, debt, drug and alcohol abuse, and family breakdown. These aspects are correct but they are not exhaustive; bad planning from the local government and a lack of real support to help nurture the community is the main cause of poverty and social breakdown. This, of course, stems from the national government to begin with.

The article states interviews with local residents and people like a secondary school principal to attempt to understand the problems. The principal, Gordon Shaw, wants to ensure that children have ambition; "telling them not to see their future as working in a commercial outlet, but aspiring to manage that commercial outlet."

With no disrespect to Mr. Shaw, this is not the right way of thinking. In the first instance, it can be agreed that to be realistic, helping school-leavers to find a job in a shop would be a good start. Even though I am opposed to Capitalism in general, this is the system we currently live in and we can use it initially to begin a transition. If there are commercial retailers that can offer basic employment, the people can at least earn money. It is a form of using the capital and opportunities that are already there to start bringing money to the people in a deprived area.

We have to remember that to move from capitalism to cooperativism is a slow transition and not one that can be achieved from one day to the next. But it is also not as easy as saying that we should try to find similar jobs for every one who is old enough, for there simply aren't enough jobs to go around, or there are personal problems, like alcoholism, that would make it difficult for people to secure a job.

We have to start gradually to be able to improve the social conditions for everyone. In Easterhouse, when the estate was originally built, the planners forgot to add shops, obviously a fundamental aspect of the community to provide the means for survival and also employment. As a result, people have to queue at the back of old ice-cream vans to buy food. This is not a failure of the residents at all as they were sent to live there; it is a failure of the bureaucrats who managed the project dreadfully and caused the problems for the people who live there with no effective way of correcting the issue.

Another factor that we need to take into account at the beginning, before we start formulating a plan for recovery, is that there are hardly any recreation facilities for the people. There are locally formed youth clubs like Wellhouse, which offers ways for girls to spend their time, like using the computers, playing snooker or making bead necklaces. This is a step in the right direction and one that needs to be expanded to ensure that everyone has somewhere to go to pass their time instead of relying solely on alcohol to forget about their actual situations.

The only way to approach this is to talk to the people and find out what they would like to have. It would not be good to assume that they want a certain facility without consulting them as they would just feel they are being told what to do. It is a subtle but very important difference when we need to earn the trust and respect of the people that something affects.

The next question is how to achieve such goals as creating a sports club or whatever they would like to have in their community. Again, we need to be realistic and only aim for what can be achieved. If they would like a snooker table, these are expensive when new, but we can ask around in other clubs or pubs to see if anyone has one that they don't need and are willing to donate. It is not difficult to find such items in this way, especially when it is made clear that it is for reason of helping to make people's lives better. As Gordon Shaw said, in response to the money that has been given to pay for better housing, better provision for health and better local employment, "there is a lot more work to do. It's not about throwing money at the area; it's about changing hearts and minds."

In terms of the building that is going to be used for such clubs, we only need to locate unused buildings and allocate them for their new purposes. In the event that the building needs to be repaired, the local residents should be brought in to help out. If they are unwilling to do the work necessary, explain that they don't have the money to hire professionals to do it so if they want a facility where they can pass their time, they can easily make it happen by themselves. The main reason being that if they have to hire an outside worker to do the job, the local economy loses some money by having to pay for the work.

If, say, there was a newly refurbished centre for playing such games as snooker, darts, table tennis and other easily and cheaply attainable activities, it is not enough to simply leave them open for people to pass a couple of hours. It would be better to use the facilities to encourage ambition – set up tournaments to give people the desire to achieve something. It may be small and not something that has a prize at the end of it, but the small satisfaction of winning a tournament is a starting point and it can help people to think and act more positively. If they want to win, they know they will need to practice and some people would be willing to dedicate their time more constructively to achieve their goals.

So this is a way to begin to bring happiness to people's lives and to make them feel like they have something to work for. But it doesn't solve the problem of unemployment. This is the other side of providing a good well-being; the job and the leisure time both need to be addressed.

In an area where there are few shops and few jobs, the simple answer would be to allow the people to create their own shops, again, using otherwise unused buildings that can be converted simply. We need to look at improving the basic problems like providing food and other household supplies. Normally, it would be impractical to expect a community with very little money to be able to start up such a business, but there are ways around it.

For one, those people who are employed by a company that is not based in the area need to be persuaded to try to spend their money locally; that is, to spend it on produce that is grown or made in the area in question. What this means is the money that is coming from outside (the wages paid by the outside employer) should be kept inside the community. If people spend their wages on imported items, their money just leaves the area again. Money attained from outside goes back outside.

Similarly, for those on benefits, the money, that is coming from the state (i.e. outside) should end up staying in the community as much as possible.

For another way to build the economy of the community, it would be good to try to set up an agreement with food distributors so that food can be lent to the new shops and when sold, the balance can then be repaid. To be able to do this well, there can be no loans with interest as this is a way of making profit from the poor (which is forbidden by the Abrahamic group of religions: Christianity, Judaism and Islam). We need to set up a system of trust: If the goods are sold (at a small profit relative to the distributors cost), those items can be paid for. If the good are not sold within a certain time and they still have enough shelf-life, they can be sent back and sold elsewhere. The profit made on the sale of the goods becomes the income of the new shop workers, on which they would not have to pay tax so that the money stays in the community.

The plan would then be to work towards a resilient community that grows its own food, or as much of it as possible and provides its own services. Meetings should be held to pool the resources of the people from the area. It can be worked out how many plumbers, mechanics, electricians and so on would suit the population, allocate people to those jobs who have the skills and again, the money would then stay in the area. In the beginning, it would probably be unreasonable to charge income tax while the local system is taking shape. It would take time for a financial base to grow and it would require the awareness and action of most, if not all, of the people in that community. Starting from this kind of basic level engenders a work ethic and enables profit to be made from little monetary input. The Creativity in the Community project should also be implemented and training given to help people create products from basic materials, such as clothes, food and drinks that could be sold in cafés, as well as starting to teach each other how to play the guitar or how to cook good meals from the local produce. Ideally, this last one could also give rise to something like a monthly community festival where people bring the food they have grown, other people cook it and make drinks from it and the people celebrate their achievements together.

There are many ways that profit can be made easily from basic goods and services originating from a given area.

The results of this would be an increase in employment and an increase in the local economy so that people would eventually be able to manage their own locality, though locally retained tax.

Another option would be ask individuals or companies with a lot of capital to provide money that can be used to set up similar shops, where again, they would not earn interest on the money they provide and lend out. A local bank can be set up for this purpose so that newly establishing businesses can borrow money that they need to start and once the sales are being made, the money is paid back to the bank in reasonable sums that don't damage the well-being of the workers who borrow the money.

There is no room for debt to occur. The shop workers pay what they can, when they can. A level of trust should be emphasised to remind the workers that they have this capital at their disposal because some people willingly lent them money to begin their business and build their community and they require no interest to paid on it.

While this is taking place, the other way to rebuild a community is to bring in resilience. This has been described in detail elsewhere in this book but for example, support the residents so that they can grow their own fruit and vegetables.

If it is argued that none of this could be achieved without Capitalism, I would agree. But this is because Capitalism is what we have in place right now. The idea is to take aspects of Capitalism and transform it to Cooperativism and resilience. People can look after themselves; in previous centuries they had to. There weren't big corporations that employed thousands of people; they grew their own food, they made their own clothes. They developed skills because they had to. When one gets to the point where they can't rely on their own skills but depend on the big companies to give them opportunities, people are in a dire situation. We need to have skills to be able to look after ourselves. In the light of a financial crisis that has been brought about by bad management of finances by a small group of extreme capitalists, it is not fair that everyone has to suffer. But this is how it is because we depend on them to keep our lives stable. This way of life is unreasonable and with good organisation, no corruption, interdependency and solidarity in the community, it can happen.

1. www.guardian.co.uk/society/2010/mar/31/is-britain-broken

Housing

Housing is a key area that any government needs to address. It is much more complicated than just saying that everyone should have access to some form of housing, whether it is through private property or government led housing schemes such as council houses that were built in the UK over much of the 20th century.

Council houses or social/ public houses, were built to cater for the people who were struggling financially and were not in a position to buy their own homes in the private sector. The emphasis was on building good quality homes that were affordable because of below market rents that would eventually pay for the cost of building them after some years. The concept of this is good in principle but there have been many criticisms that showed the gaps in the planning and implementation of the projects.

For one, it became a stigma for the people who lived in council estates. They were seen as the lowest class of people, who were put together in a kind of ghetto. They had few incentives to be able to move from these areas into newer, better houses as being on the waiting list for council houses automatically placed them further down the list to move to another place because they were no longer seen as being in desperate need. They now had a secure home and were effectively left to fend for themselves.

Another criticism was that those families who occupied, say, a three-bedroomed house with two children were able to remain in the house once their offspring had left home. They didn't need to downgrade their home to a smaller one which left many houses or flats with extra unused bedrooms. When we think about waiting lists for council houses and how many people are kept on this register this is an issue that is difficult to address. You can't force people to move home just because their children have grown up and left. If they have been living there for twenty or more years and they want to stay, then it is their home and it is a basic human right to allow them to stay there as long as they are not causing any major problems such as anti-social behaviour or damage to the property.

Because of this issue, the only realistic answer is to ensure that there are enough homes for everyone in the country. Of course, this is a massive problem to address but there are other issues that need to be discussed before looking at how to achieve that goal.

Just building a housing estate is not enough to secure a stable and fruitful society. There needs to be scope for resilience for the people living in any given estate of this kind. This means that things like shops, other places of work, centres for activities and entertainment and social well-being need to be included in the plans. This goes along very closely with the idea of localising the economy. If the inhabitants of an estate have opportunities to work, both within it and nearby, and they have the responsibility to manage it effectively for their own interests, it is going to be far more successful. Also, if the money that these people earn is taxed so that most of their deductions goes back into the area to help it to develop, this is going to help their local economy develop. There is no need for economic growth to be maintained as long as the community is at a state of being comfortable, stable and affluent enough to ensure a general level of happiness.

It is a simple case of planning and organising an estate where the people are brought together to see who can fill the roles, in terms of work, that that community would benefit from.

This means that basic amenities need to be taken care of: food shops, other shops for items that the community will require, maintenance and service workers who can be called on to fix the plumbing and the cars, etc. in that area, taking care of the immediate environment so that it doesn't fall into disarray, places where the children can spend their free time safely and positively.

The kinds of provisions in this sense should be ones that are not only somewhere to go to pass the time but ones where children can develop their skills and become productive members of the community by combining vocational projects with fun and interesting activities.

It is not such a difficult project to formulate so that the people can take care of themselves and provide for themselves. It just requires looking at all the areas that need to be taken into account, with the partnership of the residents being an extremely important factor so that they feel that they are defining the area for themselves and not being told what they can do just because a handful of bureaucrats are following a set plan that is to happen identically across the country.

Of course there need to be certain guidelines and principles to work from that would be the underpinning of these projects nationwide but the details would be more individual and conducive to the needs and interests of the people living within the community.

When it comes to how all of this can be funded, the government would need to set aside some funding which should not be seen as their one-way payment to society but rather the foundations of developing a resilient estate that will be able to pay back the money when it becomes affluent enough through employment and taxes.

To reduce the burden on the government for funding, it would not be practical to borrow money from an independent monetary fund like the World Bank as this would mean that there would always be a debt to pay back but it would be more practical to encourage voluntary work from the people to develop their own area by asking them to contribute their skills when requiring nothing in return except for the development of their community, after which income can later be earned.

In terms of housing in a non-governmental way, that is, the private housing sector, serious reforms need to be made. There is a huge emphasis on the monetary value of land and property that makes it very unequal as to who can benefit from it. First and foremost, the land in which we live doesn't belong to anyone. It was there before us and we don't have the right to lay claim to it. The whole issue of landowning is one that developed as a way for some people to get rich and influential by then being able to sell it or rent it to poorer people and thus make profit from it.

This has escalated over time to become the real estate market that recently collapsed (the global housing bubble) which caused the value of real estate to plummet, making it difficult to sell property, making investors lose great sums of money which then had a knock-on effect for the general public.

It will be no surprise to know that the lack of regulation was to blame for this collapse. If house prices are allowed to rise dramatically, they will exceed the income levels of the general population who will either forget about trying to buy a new house or will default on their mortgage payments and leave themselves at risk of having their houses repossessed. This is an awful state of affairs which seriously undermines the well-being of very many people while investors are trying to make profits from the many.

Mortgages are currently dreadfully exploitative packages which serve no real benefit for the average buyer. They work by selling a mortgage loan to a person or family who then has to repay it with high interest rates so that the banks make vast sums of money and the buyers spend most of their lives trying to pay it off.

As mentioned in the Economics section, the Islamic Banking principles are far more favourable to implement so that housing bubbles are less likely to occur as very little profit is likely to be made from mortgages anyway. To reiterate, the bank or financial institution that has the money to lend would buy the house and then sell it to the buyer with no interest to be added except for the interest rates set by the national bank. The then home owners would have less to pay back and in the event of personal financial difficulties would be able to reduce their payments temporarily so that they don't become at risk of losing their homes.

If it got to a point where the home owner was unable to continue paying the mortgage, the bank would buy the house back off the person who would then receive the money they have paid so far (minus the interest rate mentioned above) and they could use this money to either buy a cheaper property or move into rented accommodation. The bank would then own the house again and be able to sell it to another buyer, with regulation in place so that they can't inflate the price of the property as they choose. There would need to be a legal restriction in place so that the price of the house can only be raised by the the increase in inflation from the time when the house was last sold and when it goes back on the market.

There is the possibility that some banks are unlikely to want to even sell mortgages in their first place if they are not going to be making their usual profits from them. That is their choice. To counteract this, there are ways that other systems can be set up so that people can still buy houses in this way.

One way would be to set up a government-managed institution that functions in the way just described. It is not actually essential that the institution has a vast amount of capital to buy properties when people all over the country make mortgage applications. Banks don't actually need all the capital already there to sell a mortgage as they don't give out the €150,000 to the buyer in hard cash or through a bank transfer. All they do is pay the money to the seller each month and take the extra that is their mortgage interest rate for themselves. It is much the same as renting a property except that the tenant will not get any closer to owning the property in this situation.

Therefore, if mortgages worked like renting, there would only need to be a legally binding agreement between the seller and the buyer so that the buyer pays €500 a month, the seller receives it and pays a percentage in tax to the state as part of their income tax. This would be simply worked out by seeing how much money the seller (who might also have a job) receives annually and they pay the percentage according to the tax bracket that they are in.

This would be a radical upheaval of the real estate market but what would the consequences actually be?

There would not be any real profit made from selling property, either by the individual sellers or financial institutions so would they suffer from this? They are not losing money, either, by selling in this way, so no. They just won't be able to rely on earning their money from real estate. It is hard to see how a housing bubble (which will always burst) could even have the scope to develop under this system. Property would just become a matter of fact issue where the buyers are at very little risk as they wouldn't usually fall behind on their payments. They would just have to take longer to pay them off or move out and find alternative living arrangements.

In the case where there is a contract simply between buyer and seller and the buyer has to move out, it would be more difficult for the individual seller to repay the mortgage paid so far. If this happened, there could either be a clause that states that should the buyer have to cancel the mortgage and vacate the premises, the money paid would be treated in the same way as renting (i.e. they wouldn't get any of it back) or they would get a percentage of it back as the seller would be able to start selling it again from scratch to the next buyer and be obliged to refund say 25% of the money paid by the previous buyer for a 3 year period. The reason for this would be to make sure that the buyer who is in financial difficulties can recover their finances to a degree so that they would not fall into desperate measures and a low state of well-being. It is almost like a private source of welfare

But what if the seller had already spent all of the money that was paid to them so far by the previous buyer? How could they then refund the 25% if they no longer have it? Obviously, this could be a serious problem which would potentially ruin the seller so again, we need regulation in place to make sure that this can't happen. The seller would be obliged at the beginning of the contract to place the 25% in a kind of bond with their financial institution that they wouldn't have access to until the mortgage has been fully paid. As this would only need to be secured for the first 3 years, it wouldn't be a great sum of money that they own but can't touch. In the example of the mortgage repayments being €500 a month, this would amount to €4500. Note that this would only need to be paid back if the buyer had to cancel their mortgage. If, after some years, they decided they wanted to move somewhere else, they would then be able to sell their share of the property. Note that this is not a specific proposal but some ideas to get people thinking about setting up a new system for mortgages that do not exploit buyers and make outrageous profits for banks that then have ultimate power over the home buyer who falls into financial difficulties.

In conclusion, the property market would not be profitable but this would mean that from this, people would not be getting richer or poorer than each other and it would help to address the issue of inequality in personal finances. House prices would not be able to rise significantly due to the regulations in place (unless the property was improved or extended that made it worth more), people would be at less risk of financial problems and there would be no scope for repossession or destitution of individuals.

Crime

The reasons why crimes are committed were explained in Shaping A Society. It was made clear that it is not how to punish the offenders that should be the primary goal, but how we can attempt to stop crime from happening on a notable scale. Of course, it would be too ideological to expect crime to disappear entirely as there will always be some isolated cases for many reasons; mental illness resulting in diminished responsibility being one of them.

Therefore, the aim of a moral government should be how to develop society so that there aren't individuals who feel that they are lacking so much or that their needs are ignored but instead, how to improve the well-being of everyone.

As a lot of the book so far has been examining how we can achieve this, this section on crime doesn't need much more to be said that hasn't already been. However, to recap the most important points: we need to put a lot of effort into expanding and supporting the opportunities of those who are judged to be most at need for development, in terms of employment, education, their feeling of inclusion into society on the whole, and compassion and understanding from people who are considered to be more developed in the above ways.

The cost of crime on a country is vast for a number of reasons: the damage or loss of possessions leaves the cost of replacing or rebuilding for both individuals or groups such as institutions or businesses, the likelihood that those who commit crimes will also be claiming welfare is high and the need for imprisoning some of those people is of a tremendous cost to the taxpayers and the government. So a policy which focuses on the need to increase penalties or to make it easier to arrest and prosecute people by making the criteria softer to do so is not going to improve a society at all. There may be some people who don't like the idea of such consequences as increased fines or a criminal record but these people would be in the minority. If other people think they have nothing to lose or they really don't care if they get caught, the problem is not going to go away.

Some of the ways that a country can create its own opportunities have been suggested earlier, such as in Creativity in the Community. The sections on employment and welfare and the economy also address how we can begin to overcome the problem of crime.

The following section on prison gives more details as to how we can effectively rehabilitate people in a way that is meaningful to them rather than how we can make them conform to a government's expectations.

As it has been mentioned, we should always keep in mind the teachings of the Buddha that the most important thing to remember is understanding people who commit crimes and look at how we can support them rather than judge and punish them.

Prison

Prison has long been a contentious issue all around the world. In many countries, it is seen to be the last step for criminals in terms of a judicial answer for their crimes. There are of course many different crimes that can result in a person going to jail but in general, the crime has to have reached a threshold on the continuum of moral indecency.

In the modern world, the prison populations of the average country have increased and this causes serious problems in terms of government spending (where a percentage of taxpayers money goes), prison overcrowding, efficiency of the penal system and re-offending which in turn affects the general level of safety for the population as a whole.

Before attempting to find a solution for prison reform, we need to look at the evidence of the mark that prison leaves on a society.

The success of a government and a society can be reflected in the statistics of the number of prisoners per 100,000 people. Currently, the United States, which purports to be a highly successful nation (economically) has the worst statistics in the world, where in 2008, 739 people per hundred thousand were in prison.[1] This compares to Germany, a similarly well-developed modern country whose number stands at 95 or even Canada, the USA's neighbour in more ways than just geographically, whose number is 107.

This means that levels of crime can be high in countries that are among the richest in the world, therefore a high GDP per capita has no relation to how well the society is managed. Other less developed countries such as Russia (611) or China (no data available) can have high prison populations which can easily be blamed on their systems of government.

So what can cause a so-called developed country to have the world's worst prisoner: free citizen ratio? There are of course many reasons and many arguments that people would argue over but the large economic divide in a population is undoubtedly going to be a factor. So is the lack of opportunities for the marginalised groups of people depending on what fictionally attributed group they are labelled with. If people think that they receive no support or are even oppressed due to their skin colour, lack of educational qualifications, etc., they will rebel. They will bite that hand that refuses to feed them.

Is that justified? Certainly not, but it is understandable. Living with the feeling that you will never get the chance to make anything of yourself is likely to eventually lead to serious rebellion against the system where one will break the law because they just don't care any more. Why should they care when they are not cared about? It makes a lot of sense that some people will react in this way. But whose fault is it? That of the perpetrators or that of the government? The Labour Party in the United Kingdom came up with a slogan in the 2000s: "Tough on crime, tough on the causes of crime."

That's an interesting one. Of course we can understand that a government needs to be tough on crime because they want to stop people committing crimes. But being tough on the causes of crime is a curious idea. The cause of crime is rebelling against the system because of the failure to address the issues that people have before they finally cross the barrier and break the law. So this means that the cause of crime is the government. It is the government's lack of an effective system to rehabilitate the poor and help the under-privileged to find a way out of their predicaments which, to them, feel like they are permanent. The British government has talked about how they will install CCTV cameras in areas where gangs are known to meet frequently to try to cut crime levels. This idea is absolutely absurd. By persecuting the people whom the government wants to stop committing crime will only make those people feel even more anti-government and likely to rebel. They will just do it elsewhere. If people felt that they were being treated fairly, given opportunities and looked at equally by the government and by society in general, they are less likely to even think about committing crimes. So the slogan of "Tough on crime, tough on the causes of crime", when it comes down to it is another way of saying "Tough on crime, tough on the government, i.e. ourselves for pushing people into situations where they commit crime, to show us how much they don't care about us because we don't care about them." But in the government's eyes, this is not the cause of crime and anyway, it's not such a catchy slogan/ piece of propaganda.

So now that we have found the fundamental cause of crime, let's take a look at what happens in a general prison and what happens to prisoners who get released to see how effective the whole process is that costs the governments millions each year.

Prisoners, being with like-minded individuals don't have a particularly comfortable time with life. So what's wrong with that you might ask. If they are in prison, they don't deserve to have a comfortable life. Well, possibly but but what happens to prisoners when they are inside? Primarily of course, they have very limited freedom of movement, i.e. they are not allowed to go into the regular world. They reside in cells which can be looked into at any time by the prison guards and sometimes, if they have seriously unacceptable behaviour while in prison they may be sent to solitary confinement for anywhere between 24 hours to several months. This period of isolation can have extremely detrimental effects on the prisoner due to lack of human contact of any kind or stimuli. This has been known to lead to forms of insanity, which isn't really going to be of any benefit to the prisoner or anyone else they might come into contact with, whether being released back into the general prison wards or into society.

Being among similarly criminal-minded individuals can of course also lead to more unacceptable behaviour, including mental, sexual or physical abuse from other prisoners as well as either becoming drug users or continuing as drug users. In the USA, approximately 35% of prisoners are already drug users.[2] This means that their acquaintances will expertly smuggle in all kinds of drugs, such as heroin or crystal meths, which causes a huge problem for the authorities. Due to the number of letters and packages that could arrive each day at a prison, they simply don't have the man power to search for and find every drug that gets smuggled in. Often, in the end, the authorities allow the prisoners to carry on using drugs because at least it keeps them quiet and out of some kinds of trouble for a period of time.

What about any privileges that they are allowed? Understandably, as the prisoners are supposed to be living under very limited freedom as their punishment for their crimes they have little else to occupy their time. They usually have recreation rooms where they can play pool or cards and watch some television. They will usually have access to a gymnasium or an exercise yard to help keep their bodies in reasonable condition and they will be able to see visitors under supervision or in a cubicle divided by bullet-proof glass.

So far, these kinds of entertainments will do very little to help the prisoners to develop as people and to be prepared as citizens who can operate positively in society upon their release. They are just ways to keep them from getting bored, i.e. treating the symptoms but not the problems. But rehabilitation is also an issue that has been taken on by some penal systems, at least in the western world. Sometimes it is possible for prisoners to read and study subjects which can lead to them earning a diploma which could be of use to them upon release. Some prisons will have connections with industrial or agricultural plants where the prisoners can work and gain some job-related skills which they can also take with them to help build a new life on the outside.

So why is it then that two-thirds of American prisoners[2] and almost 60% of British prisoners end up re-offending and returning to prison? The system can't be very effective if most prisoners will re-offend. Or maybe it's because employers will be reluctant to employ former prisoners. It is a combination of both of these issues, the second of which will guide ex-convicts back to their previous life of crime as they will usually find their old accomplices when they return to their roots and if they are getting no chances from society, it would be easy enough to slip back into the old routine.

However, if prisoners were rehabilitated more effectively while inside, surely they would be less likely to re-offend. This is where the main problem lies. After a prisoner has done his of her time, they are more likely to be back at the stage they were when they went in.

Therefore, the penal system needs a huge amount of reform to reduce the number of re-offenders and help to rebuild society. Considering that on average, in 2004, it cost British taxpayers £38,000 for each prisoner[3], this would require a lot of changes in how prisons operate.

Prison Reform

All in all, prison systems do not work. The only benefit of using prisons is to incarcerate those criminals who are caught and convicted, often for a relatively short period of time (6 months to 5 years). Unless they have received effective rehabilitation, there is a greater chance that the released prisoner will re-offend than not and the price of maintaining prisoners it at a great expense to the taxpayers and more directly to the government of any country.

So what could be the answer to these problems? There are many possible adjustments to the system that could bring about a significant change, not just for the sake of the prisoners themselves, the staff employed at prisons and the safety of the general public but also for the economy.

Starting from the bottom, we need to address the moral issues. It is commonplace for people who are aware of the severity of some offences to have the opinion that the criminal should be locked up for as long as possible without any privileges and that they should suffer for what they have done. However, this situation would not only be to the detriment of the convicted person, but to the public as taxpayers and the country as a whole in the economic sense. For example, using the current cost of maintaining a prisoner in the UK, a ten year sentence would cost £380,000 but to keep the person inside for life could mean around 40 years in prison or £1,520,000 (increasing with adjustments for inflation).

Thinking of it this way, do the taxpayers really want their money spent this way rather than have it allocated for public spending that might be of benefit to them? In times of recession and fiscal deficits, political parties talk of reducing the deficit by cutting public spending. They don't talk about reforming society to ensure that the prison population decreases. Looking at the short term solutions is not the most effective way of tackling this issue. If we are to reach a stage of economic stability, there is far more to consider than just looking at how the money is spent or not. It is about how we can make the fiscal budget increase while at the same time improve conditions for people on a national scale.

Obviously, to merely release the prisoner earlier would not be a sensible alternative if they were judged to be a high risk to the public. We have already looked at some of the reasons why someone might become a criminal. There are, of course, many possible reasons but in essence, the person will have been experiencing some kind of trouble (e.g. family, money, relationship, psychological problems). This is the root of the problem that should be addressed if there is going to be any chance for the person in question to recover their life and achieve some degree of personal success that will not be at the expense of someone else. To begin to resolve such problems would essentially require professional counsellors or psychologists, depending on the severity of the prisoner's problems. Ideally prisons would be staffed with a large number of such professionals to be able to adequately deal with such issues- in the case of the USA that currently has around two and a half million prisoners, we might need around half a million counsellors- but this is not practical when their salaries would be paid by the state.

To even begin to approach the issue of employing more people to help the prisoners to reform we would need some way of raising the capital to pay the salaries. Two and a half million prisoners at a maintenance cost of around \$60 billion[4] is an issue needs to be tackled in a large way.

But two and a half million people is an awful lot of human capital, which could be put to use to help maintain their own costs as well as indirectly contributing to the federal reserve bank of the country. A large proportion of prisoners will never have had much of a work ethic, especially considering that more than a third are drug addicts. Lacking a work ethic leads to ambivalence, both to themselves and the wider community. But if the prisoners' time was put to more productive use, they would start to develop more as people. Through many economic studies it has been established that people need some kind of incentive if they are going to be productive. While the thought of promotion or a wage rise can inspire workers to produce more, the notion of being able to eat well and earn small privileges can provide an incentive for a prisoner to work for their rewards. This could be seen as being ideological considering that the average prisoner might not care less about what food they get to eat or whether they can have a couple of hours off work to play pool or read in the sun, but any system has to begin with small steps until people cotton onto thinking that "Hey, maybe this is worth doing... at least for today... maybe tomorrow as well..."

Such incentives have to be meaningful to the prisoners so that they are going to pay any attention to them. This does not mean that they will be allowed to take drugs or whatever they would ideally choose as of course, prison is meant to be a punishment of a kind but more importantly, it should be seen as a method of rehabilitation.

To be able to make any kind of start along these lines, it is important for the prisoners not to feel oppressed by the staff. One can not earn respect if one is not willing to give respect. And gaining respect in a prison setting is part of the foundations to making a system work. The prisoners have probably passed through life getting little positive attention. However, as human behaviour goes, most people like attention in some way, so if they don't get positive attention, they will opt for negative attention as at least they are being noticed. It is a human behavioural trait that people like to be recognised for what they do and if they are failing to be noticed, they might take a stand and perform some anti-social action that gets them noticed even if it is in a hateful way.

So this is what must be avoided from the very day that a prisoner enters the compound. Anybody who is of a sound mind (and those of an unsound mind should not be there but in an institution that can adequately deal with their case) will react to being respected, even if they are known to have aggressive or vindictive behaviour. People react to other people in certain ways: if someone looks down on the prisoner and treats them like a low-life, the prisoner in turn will react negatively to the instigator. But if the prisoner is spoken to respectfully and equally, with small steps their behaviour will change, they will act more favourably to those individuals who show them respect.

All prison staff would need to receive training so that they would know how to speak to and act with prisoners so that negative interactions will be more unlikely. Already, most staff members will be experienced enough with dealing with trouble - fights, arguments and so on but it's not so easy dealing with situations verbally so that they are less likely to arise. Nobody, whether staff or inmates, would want to go through a day where all the experiences were bad, it doesn't make for a satisfactory day for anyone. And continuing with this way of interacting would only exacerbate the situation, hence the prisoners will not develop their attitudes and they will be more likely to re-offend when released.

Prisoners would, of course, continue to have duties to maintain themselves and their living quarters. They would be required to clean their cells and themselves but it must be made clear that it is for their benefit, e.g. to reduce the possibility of infections due to squalid conditions. If a prisoner refused to clean themselves or their cell, they would have privileges removed, whilst in the knowledge that other compliant prisoners can keep their privileges. No heavy-handed punishment is necessary, no negative attention of any kind. Simply being told that they can't go to the recreation room that evening would be enough to get them thinking that it was a waste of time acting like they did - they weren't able to antagonise the guards or start up a fight but were simply left quietly in their cell while the other prisoners were allowed to move around relatively freely. The non-compliant prisoners would just feel like they have achieved nothing, not even a scene where they caused a conflict with the guards.

The prisoners would also be responsible for making their own food, that is, preparing food for the masses, on a rota basis, where they would be taught how to prepare and cook food. Likewise, they would be required to clean up the dining halls and wash the dishes.

Of course, this does not sound like anything particularly revolutionary about prison life. It simply needs to be made clear what would happen in such reformed prison systems. Food is a great expense when prisons have to feed hundreds or even thousands of people every day. Therefore, to reduce costs, prisoners would be taught how to farm and grow their own vegetables and fruit as well as how to make produce such as cheese and bread. Prisoners are constantly there and should be used to their full potential to help to pay for their own maintenance as well as how to keep them occupied in a meaningful sense. It is not the same as forced labour camps where the prisoners are worked to the bone doing work that is meaningless to them, it should be about giving them a sense of purpose and developing the mentality that each of them depend on their peers to ensure that all their needs are being met.

Prisoners can be assigned roles in various ways like this as well as given other jobs that they can do for certain periods of time, e.g. working in the kitchen for two months then transferring to another point of responsibility to keep them from becoming bored and therefore unproductive if they have been in a position for too long.

The next point is something that has the intention of being of benefit to the country as a whole in an economic sense. Prisoners can effectively be used to work for low wages. Again, this is not meant to be slave labour, but as they have no overheads like mortgage or travel costs, they have no real need to earn much money. As large corporations often turn to manufacturers in cheaper countries, like in East Asia, Africa and Central America to produce cheap goods, some of this labour can be set up in the home countries with incentives for the businesses such as tax breaks if they use this system. This has many reasons to be implemented:

1. It again gives the prisoners a sense of value when they have the responsibility to work,

2. It trains them to be a worker, especially if they have never been employed previously, giving them skills and the chance to move to positions of higher responsibility both in prison and after their release,

3. From the relatively low wages that they earn, they can have a savings fund set up which they can either make accessible to their families or keep for their own access when they are released. This is a valuable incentive for a prisoner if they know they will have some money when they are free instead of having to start again from the bottom with no job skills, which is likely to lead to re-offending within a very short period of time.

4. The money they earn can be taxable, albeit at a very low level due to their low levels of income, but nevertheless it is tax which is revenue for the federal bank that will increase the countries' Gross Domestic Product. Such extra revenue could also be used by the government to set up further programmes to help people get back to work.

5. It will simply develop them as 'real people', that is: people that are accepted by society as a whole, as equals, as those who are able and willing to work to support themselves through ways that don't cause harm to others or at least on a lesser scale.

At this point there will be questions to be considered. Wouldn't this proposal mean that prisoners would be more likely to be eligible for parole earlier? Quite possibly. But would we really want ex-prisoners back out on the streets sooner than they were sentenced to be? Not if they hadn't been educated and aided with their personal development, but that is what this whole plan is about. If the ex-prisoners have been judged to be ready for parole, then it would mean that theoretically, we would have more desirable people in public and the cost of running prisons would be lower if the inmates didn't stay in for as long as they would under present systems. Therefore, this proposal for a prison system would be, in effect, a re-education and training facility which has the ultimate goal of making society both safer and more productive. And how about the question that many people might ask: Why should we give opportunities to those rapists and armed robbers and all the rest when there are unemployed people in the 'normal' world who don't get the same opportunities? Well, think of it like this: would you rather have rapists and armed robbers, who could, under the present system(s), be out again in around 10 years and be likely to go back to their old ways or be at a point where they are no longer like they were but have been armed instead with skills, values, education and morals?

But what about the jobs that would be taken away from the countries where labour is cheap? Wouldn't this then affect the lives of those workers that do actually rely on the relatively low-paid work from western companies that for them is more than the average wage and helps them to support their families? Possibly, if it isn't managed effectively. It would need to be organised carefully so that as little damage as possible could be done to the people who it could affect. There would be additional factories or industrial plants for example that could be set up in the host country which would also cut down on transport costs, not to mention the environmental impact of shipping goods all over the world. The prisoners in the host country would be used as cheap labour which actually benefits themselves while they are still being rehabilitated. They are part of a programme, a system of improving their own conditions to give them a basis on which to more easily shape their lives after release. The people who work in the 'sweatshops' of Asia are effectively used as slaves. They would continue to be used as long as their wages are low. If their wages needed to be increased, the firms would pack up the machines and look elsewhere. Such corporations are not based on morals and ethics, they are based on profit. They would prefer the sweatshop workers to remain in bad conditions where the standard of life is poor because they can use the people for their own gains. To be honest, this principle is one that should not be encouraged but if we could encourage the firms to set up their manufacturing plants in their own countries and contribute to the development of its own people, then morally speaking, this is more justifiable.

And what about the staff who would be employed to aid rehabilitation? As mentioned earlier, they would be various types of counsellors and psychologists, who are already employed in low numbers in prisons. Obviously, to start with, only a few of these staff members would be able to be financed but to increase the numbers, this would depend on developing other ways of raising money if the number of prisoners and the revenue they could create didn't match the necessary funds, but as was mentioned, it's a step by step process.

Other professionals could be used as they already are in some prisons to help to educate the prisoners from the basic levels of being illiterate to studying for recognised certificates and diplomas of various kinds that would set them up well to support themselves after release. In the case of low staff numbers, more educated prisoners could also be used to teach those who are at a low level of education, but this would require training for those who could be chosen to teach. However, this could provide a way of removing some of the problems of being short-staffed.

So, what if this prison reform system was implemented and the prison population declined? What would be the effects of this? Firstly, as mentioned, there would be more people in society that were less likely to commit crimes and more likely to have personal responsibility and a sense of personal worth. But let's say that there were 100,000 of these former prisoners operating productively in society. That would mean that there would be less of need for the prison staff described above and surely jobs would be lost. This is an important issue to consider but for the prison psychologists, they would need to be supported so that they could transfer their position and skills to other areas in society. Psychology is a university subject that is very popular and in the numerous branches of it, such as clinical, educational, occupational and criminal, there simply aren't enough positions for the number of psychology students unless they take employment where they can at least use their skills to some degree. With the above proposal in place, there would be more jobs available in the criminal psychology sector but they could decrease over time if the reform is effective. There could be a programme whereby psychologists are used more to act as advisers to groups, businesses and so on to help them improve their conditions and success levels in many ways. After all, the principal role of any kind of psychologist is to improve situations – to understand the workings of the human mind better and formulate solutions to alleviate the problems that can be identified. As the central principle of this book is to achieve such things on so many levels, psychologists would be an excellent human resource to participate in this process.

Regarding the economic effect of implementing this kind of reform, would it be effective? In the case of of it working as outlined, the government expenditure on prisons would decrease as prisoners are partly responsible for their own survival and maintenance through their work expectations and the number of prisoners would be expected to decrease. The number of jobs available would be increase if outsourcing of work to developing countries was able to be turned around, which even if the prisoners, upon release, might choose to leave would mean more work available for other citizens and therefore economic growth and stability as the country would become more resilient and produce a larger quantity of its own goods. This would lead to more tax generated as the employment level would rise, resulting in the means to maintain public spending and in the case of government loans from the International Monetary Fund and the World Bank, the deficits would be able to be paid off at the same time.

Of course, the economic effects would be more complicated than this but this would be a matter for experts to address and balance so that the economy is working more smoothly than it does in most countries in the world.

If we can start to remove the reasons for why crimes are committed, through a supportive system, and address how we can rehabilitate those who are currently in a position where they they haven't been supported in life, we can make a country more stable, peaceful and successful.

1. www.kcl.ac.uk

2. Lockdown, National Geographic television series. http://channel.nationalgeographic.com/series/lockdown/all/Overview

3. John Kampfner meets the man in charge of prisons, New Statesman. www.newstatesman.com/200405310003

4. Slevin, Peter (June 2006). "U.S. Prison Study Faults System and the Public", The Washington Post.

Health and Healthcare

The topic of health has been covered briefly before, regarding the value of natural foods versus pre-packaged foods. To add to this, there is also the problem with the saturation of fast food that is giving a quick and tasty solution to those people who don't like the idea of cooking for themselves, or at least not too often. Again, to make the junk food cheap, artificial ingredients have to be added to make them taste better and to make them addictive. Such multinational companies care not about how their foods are going to affect your bodies, they only have profit in their minds, so they use the cheapest raw materials that are imported from poor countries, thereby leaving those workers at the mercy of what the companies want, i.e. if their land is being destroyed by the demand for cheap beef but the people can make a living from it, they will do it. We, in the west, won't get to hear about this unless independent researchers want to make us more aware but such awareness raising only happens on a small scale when people actually want to find out more information on such issues.

Currently, scientists are 'researching' obesity levels and funnily enough are now proclaiming that there is an obesity gene. This means that some people are pre-destined to become obese and that's just how it is. If this is true, it's curious as to how this gene has only recently developed, going along with the recent development of the fast-food industry. People in the first half of the 20th century weren't suffering from this problem. You could also argue that the range of food was also more limited then but if there was an obesity gene then wouldn't they have become fat anyway? The massive production level of hamburgers, pizzas, chocolates, fizzy drinks, sweets and cakes might actually have a significant factor in the rise in obesity levels.

So why would these scientists be claiming that they have found this new gene? Well, expect a massive influx of products such as tablets and supposed health foods that will help you to lose weight. I don't like to repeat myself but... profit. There is a massive marketing possibility here and with enough advertising there will be billions to be made. Just tell people that their obesity is irrelevant to their lifestyle and their diet so they will keep eating junk food and keep selling them placebo products that may not damage them any more than they have done themselves, but they certainly won't help either. However, while there is time before people become so sceptical (they have to try these products over time before there can be any effect) that they just give up on them, there is still a huge window to make lots and lots of money.

With the recent press coverage on increasing cases of obesity, the advertising companies have had a field day, by selling their products almost entirely deceptively. People who are heavier than is healthy are not going to lose weight simply by eating more products full of artificial flavourings and chemicals. They will alter their immune systems to become more dependent on these products (which is what the manufacturers want, of course) but by eating certain products a person is not going to lose weight. They may simply not put on more weight but without doing some exercise, nothing significant will happen. It is interesting to note that in many popular magazines, the constant stream of articles about how to lose weight usually only refer to going on certain diets yet do not point out that exercise is actually the way that weight is lost.

We don't tend to see too many adverts about keeping fit, though. And why not? Because, apart from fitness centres, there's not much money to be made from recommending that people exercise so it tends to be ignored. The main reasons for rises in obesity levels are due to the food companies providing more and more products with artificial additives, electronics companies providing more reasons to stay at home and watch huge plasma TVs, DVDs, to play on games consoles, etc. and the mass media conning people into thinking that wearing certain types of clothes, listening to manufactured music and worrying about the effects of ageing instead of reminding people that first of all, they should be taking care of their own bodies and minds before diverting their thoughts to anything else.

Whereas a number of people are active by playing sports or by keeping fit on their own by jogging or swimming, for example, in the western world at least, it certainly isn't the case that people in general look after their fitness to an adequate degree. With the increasingly faster pace of the modern world, many people may think they don't have time to go to the gym or play a game of tennis. Other people may not even think about keeping fit anyway as it is something that has never really been a part of everyday life and there are too many distractions now to have a chance to consider it.

However, keeping fit should be a standard part of everyone's lives as much as going to work or going out with friends. It is not necessary to have money to keep fit. To maintain a decent level of fitness, one could simply jog two or three times a week or play football with friends in the park. The Hypothetical Government would make this kind of awareness its duty to help to develop a satisfied society. It is important to make exercise part of the weekly routine so that people don't forget to do it. It can be difficult at first to continue an exercise routine if one is not used to it, but after a few months it becomes established as part of what one does in life.

It is not only for the reason of keeping a person's weight down that fitness should be emphasised. Regular exercise provides a rush of adrenalin that cannot be adequately described in words but the feeling of completing one's routine more easily is something that has to be experienced to be understood. We feel better about ourselves when we know that we are really developing in a real way. This is not something that can be taken away from us by an identity-removing marketing strategy.

Being fit also makes us stronger inside so that we don't tire so easily and we have more stamina to cope with what may be a hard working day. Perhaps most importantly, it also strengthens the immune system so that we are less likely to become ill because we are working our muscles and organs to a point where they can combat minor viruses or infections more effectively or even prevent them from becoming manifest in our bodies. Again, the feeling of knowing that we are stronger people inside is a feeling of satisfaction that can only be understood from experiencing it and not something that can be obtained through chemicals that are alien to our bodies.

Once people get a fitness routine in place, they will become more in touch with themselves. This is not meant in a 'new age' kind of way that many people will immediately dismiss but insomuch as they gain more of an understanding about themselves and what they are capable of. The act of exercising subconsciously makes them more aware of how fit and healthy they are and it can lead to people being more comfortable with themselves- something that beauty product manufacturers claim they can provide for people but deep down, even the most gullible of people will know that such products always fall short of the mark, no matter how willing they are to keep buying and trying new products (where the active ingredients are effectively the same but the packaging is different...). Being told that a certain product can 'combat the signs of ageing' may work in a way that customers won't even stop to analyse what this actually means but it can never overrule the fact that every single one of us is constantly ageing and no matter how much cream you put on your face, the evidence will still be there when you remove it. This is an example of Bad Science[1], for which it is highly recommended that you read Ben Goldacre's book of the same name to gain more insight into how people are legally conned by companies that make false claims with no real scientific evidence to back it up (e.g. Gillian McKeith, who is not the doctor she claims to be). Making such claims in this way should, of course, also be illegal and subject to prosecution. Any deceitful or downright false information has no place in a moral society and the repercussions for companies who try to get away with this kind of business practice ought to be severely punished and there need to be deterrents in place that would make it not worth their while to even contemplate such marketing strategies.

There also need to be limits on what kinds of products can be allowed on sale to prevent companies from pressurizing people into having lower self-esteem and a lower level of confidence because they think (and wrongly believe) that they don't fit the norm of a 'beautiful-therefore-successful' person. We must be encouraged to accept who we are and how we look without feeling the propaganda constantly being forced on the western world by these companies that sell superficial and deceitful products. This is how we can begin to find our identities, both as individuals and as a society.

This may remind people of market socialism whereby the government owns the economic institutions and decides on what can be sold and at what price, however, there is an important difference here. It is all about protecting people from the exploitation of companies. There need to be such restrictions on products that are sold with the solitary aim of making profit from something that is worthless. The people may argue that this still removes the freedom to buy what they want but this is not the case. Imagine the difference between a shampoo that cleans your hair well and leaves it looking in good condition and a shampoo that is sold with the claims that it makes your hair stronger, shinier and gives you self-confidence without having any scientific evidence to prove that they are true yet still costs more. To help people to understand these issues more, independent research and scientific testing needs to be done so that the results are freely available for anyone to read and discussions should be conducted to reach a decision on what the majority think should be allowed to either be sold or subject to increased value added tax. If, for example, the public still wanted to be able to buy a product that had no evidence to support its claims, the penalty of a price increase could instead be implemented so that the additional VAT charge would go to the state funds.

The healthcare system

A national or state health service would be in place in a moral government. This is the kind of system, also known as Universal Health Care, that is in place in such countries as the UK, France,

Norway, Canada, Australia and in fact all industrial countries (plus some developing countries) except for the USA. It is funded by standard deductions from private incomes (national health insurance) so that healthcare is available to everyone for free, with the exception of paying a small cost for medicines.

The obvious reason for why this is the best system is that it is indiscriminate and nobody can be rejected healthcare for reasons such as being unable to afford it. This needs to be pointed out as the push for healthcare reform in the USA has had a difficult time because the Republicans are spreading lies and propaganda to the public by basically claiming that it is socialist (or in their terms, Communist and therefore evil). The truth of the matter is that Republicans have many friends who make unjustified amounts of money from private health insurance companies that only allow people to be accepted if they have absolutely no health problems prior to application.

There is also the problem that everything has to be pre-approved by the insurance companies in order to have the costs of treatment covered. This includes things like the cost of being taken to hospital in an ambulance. One would need to have this pre-approved before it could take place. How this would be possible if, for example, one was unconscious or in a state of trauma or injury that it would be a ridiculous idea to even think about doing is one way that the insurance companies hold on to their money.

As Michael Moore investigated in his 2003 documentary, "Sicko", there are around 50 million Americans who have no health insurance.[2] That's 1 in every 6 people or almost the the amount of the entire population of England. Why so many? They either can't afford it or have been rejected by the insurance companies for the reason of having something as insignificant as a yeast infection previously in their lives.

The truth of it is that it is utterly immoral and evil to deny the public free healthcare when such systems have been in place in other countries quite successfully since 1948 in the UK and the 1880s in Germany. It is even more shocking when the USA is said to be the land of the free and the most developed country in the world. Considering that volunteers that helped out in the aftermath of the Twin Towers catastrophe who then became seriously ill with respiratory problems could not get medical treatment in the USA but could travel to Cuba and easily receive treatment and medication is seriously disgraceful.

The two-tier system of healthcare would be allowed to continue whereby people could choose to pay for their own private health insurance. This is practical as the NHS in the UK sometimes has long waiting lists and if people earn enough money to bypass this, they should, of course, be allowed that right. To overcome the problem of long waiting lists, there would need to be a review of the system to try to provide more funding. Obviously this is a complicated matter that would be too long to discuss here but essentially, a universal healthcare system would need to have enough staff, enough funds and enough hospitals if it is going to be more efficient and effective. Reducing military expenditure would be the first option as this would need to be at a minimum in a moral society. It cannot be justified in any way that millions or billions of dollars, Euros or pounds should go into funding the killing of people instead of caring for people, especially the citizens of the country that one governs. Any government that disagrees with this is not to be trusted at all.

The other important way to try to reduce waiting lists is to encourage people to be healthier in general. As noted above, being healthy and fit reduces the amount of illness that we are likely to suffer from. A moral government would firmly support the promotion of a healthy lifestyle so as to reduce the need for using the NHS. There may not be any profit in promoting this but this is exactly the point. Profit is the least important thing when aiming for a healthy society.

The pharmaceutical industry

Even this is something that needs tighter regulation. It is a very profitable industry so under the free market system, the main aim is to make profit. Companies even invent illnesses or conditions to make people believe that they suffer from them so that, coincidentally, 'their' products can resolve these problems. Whereas, of course, we need to keep developing treatments for real illnesses and advancing our medical knowledge, we also need to ensure that new products are not geared for profit rather than for cure. This means that prices of products cannot be any more expensive than they have to be; taking into account that costs of production need to be covered, as well as scientists wages. It also means that there have to be investigations of new products so that the market is not inundated with pills and creams that are totally unnecessary because they don't actually do anything.

An example of this would be things like cellulite creams. Cellulite is something that occurs naturally, mostly in women, and is a part of life. With the massive influence of the beauty industry, it has been manifested as something that is ugly or even shameful to have and that women should try to get rid of it. There is at least one pharmaceutical (sic) company that advertises its creams with the slogan "Offensive cellulite". This is a disgraceful way of trying to sell their product by making women have a lower self-esteem if they have cellulite. It is not offensive, it is a normal condition that millions of people will develop. If anyone is offended by seeing it, they should just keep their worthless prejudices to themselves.

Regarding the treatment of it, creams will do nothing. A number of medics have reviewed existing treatments and concluded that there is no effective treatment available. Dr. Michael F. McGuire, a clinical associate professor at the David Geffen School of Medicine at the University of California, Los Angeles, confirmed that "realistically there is no cure for cellulite." Dr. Molly Wanner, an instructor in dermatology at Harvard Medical School and an author of a 2008 evidence-based review of existing treatments, asserted, "At this point, there is no outstanding treatment for cellulite."[3]

From this lack of supporting scientific evidence, the only thing to do regarding cellulite is accept it. You may not be happy with how it looks but it is just a condition that one can have, rather than suffer from. Presently, the causes of cellulite are unclear so there can be no real advice given as to how to avoid it or reduce it. It may not become manifest in everyone but a lot of men lose their hair, too, and there is also nothing that can be done about that, save having hair transplants.

The pharmaceutical industry discourages us from accepting ourselves and forces us into looking for ways of achieving physical perfection. Such products that claim to treat conditions when they have no supporting evidence cannot be allowed to go on sale. It is as simple as that – if you can't back it up, you can't sell it.

This takes us swiftly into the world of homeopathy. This is seen as an alternative to traditional manufactured medicine that has gained a lot of ground in terms of being known and selling its related books and products. The only problem is it is a complete lie from start to finish. It goes on the premise that medicines are more effective the more they are diluted. Dilution processes can go on until the active ingredient is 1 part in a trillion where the rest of the solution is water, sugar or alcohol. Common sense and an absolute ignorance to anything medical will be more than enough to know that this is a ridiculous idea. Again, Ben Goldacre goes into this subject in great detail in Bad Science and many doctors and medical institutions have concluded that homeopathic medicines are nothing more than placebos. The movement is likely to become banned in some countries with the serious doubts that have been raised. In the UK, in February 2010, the House of Commons Science and Technology Committee concluded that "the NHS should cease funding homeopathy" and "The funding of homeopathic hospitals — hospitals that specialise in the administration of placebos — should not continue, and NHS doctors should not refer patients to homeopaths."[4,5]

Furthermore, as reported in The Guardian, Tom Dolphin, a member of the British Medical Association's junior doctors' committee stated that "Homeopathy is not witchcraft, it is nonsense on stilts." He has compared homeopathy to witchcraft but later apologised as he thought this was unfair to witches.[6]

The reason why the pharmaceutical industry has been able to legally produce medicines that don't work is that the unregulated free market has the potential to be very influential. Doctors are more likely to prescribe quick and easy drug treatments to patients because, for one, it's a quick way of sending them on their way, and two, because the money spent on marketing some drugs has put them more in the spotlight for the patients as well as the doctors. In the USA in 2002, $21 billion was spent on drug marketing.[7] This has been seen clearly in the recent Prozac craze.

Depression is a difficult condition to treat: it takes a long time to work through the psychotherapy that is needed to uncover the causes. However, in most cases (even though it is very diverse) it is a reaction to one's circumstances and is therefore behavioural. This means that the only effective way to treat (most) depression is through a course of psychotherapy which could take months or even years. In this day and age, people want a quick fix because we are seen to be at a stage where we can rectify problems with the flick of a switch or the popping of a pill. However, drugs such as Prozac do not and cannot get to the cause of the depression, they can only hide the symptoms. It may feel better in the short-term but luckily for the manufacturers, the patients need to keep taking them as once the effects have worn off, the real problem is still there.

The 'New Scientist' in 2008 reported that the US Food and Drug Administration conducted a meta-analysis of these drugs and found that for most patients, they do not work. Their conclusion was "compared with placebo, the new-generation antidepressants do not produce clinically significant improvements in depression in patients who initially have moderate or even very severe depression."[8]

There needs to be a crackdown on lobbying in the pharmaceutical industry. Sales representatives visit doctors to influence them to prescribe their drugs. And this happens on a massive scale due to the competitive nature of capitalist business. In the USA as of 2003, there were said to be around 120,000 pharmaceutical prescribers and 100,000 pharmaceutical sales reps.[9] The number of sales reps doubled between 1999 and 2003. This competitive nature of the business world needs to be seriously addressed to try to reduce the competition and increase the cooperation, and scale down their greed to focus more on making sure there are enough medicines to go round, each company has their own share of the market by, for example, only producing certain drugs which other companies don't (through an agreement) and forget worrying about making so much profit.

Another way that drugs companies seek to keep selling their products is by putting a use-by date on them that is far sooner than it should be. This date is to show until when the drug is still fully potent and safe. The U.S. Food and Drug Administration carried out a study on over 100 prescription and over the counter drugs and found that about 90% of them were still safe and effective 15 years after the expiration date. But, of course, people looking through their pills when they feel an illness coming on would rather buy new ones instead of using ones that had an expiration date that was one or two years ago.[10] And so the pharmaceutical industry keeps reeling in the money. In fact, the combined total revenues of the top five pharmaceutical companies in 2008 was US$225 billion.

We need to make a concerted push to regulate the pharmaceutical industry so that drugs are independently investigated to make sure they work and the public is not being deceived or ripped off. We also need to try to encourage people to have healthier lifestyles so that they are less likely to need medical treatments and our goal should be the well-being of the patients, not the profits made by the companies. A possible option would be to persuade the highest earning companies to set aside a certain percentage of the profits to use as charitable funds to send medicines to developing countries as aid. If it didn't really make a dent in their revenues but the public knew about their contribution to curing the poor, they might just become more respected and valued.

1. Bad Science, Ben Goldacre. Harper Collins Publishers, 2009.
2. Sicko. A Michael Moore film. The Weinstein Company, 2003.
3. www.nytimes.com/2009/06/25/fashion/25skinintro.html? ref=fashion
4. UK Parliamentary Committee Science and Technology Committee - "Evidence Check 2: Homeopathy www.parliament.uk/parliamentary_committees/science_techno

logy/s_t_homeopathy_inquiry.cfm
5. Evidence Check 2: Homeopathy, Fourth Report of Session 2009–10, House of Commons Science and Technology Committee, 20 October 2009, parliament.uk www.publications.parliament.uk/pa/cm200910/cmselect/cmsctech/45/45.pdf
6. Ban homeopathy from NHS, say doctors www.guardian.co.uk/society/2010/jun/29/ban-homeopathy-from-nhs-doctors
7. Sufrin CB, Ross JS (September 2008). "Pharmaceutical industry marketing: understanding its impact on women's health". Obstet Gynecol Surv 63 (9): 585–96 http://dx.doi.org/10.1097%2FOGX.0b013e31817f1585
8. Prozac does not work in majority of depressed patients: www.newscientist.com/article/dn13375-prozac-does-not-work-in-most-depressed-patients.html
9. Robinson, James T. (November 2003). "Changing the Face of Detailing by Motivating Physicians to See Pharmaceutical Sales Reps". Health Banks. www.healthbanks.com/PatientPortal/Public/support_documents/PMT_Robinson.pdf
10. Cohen, Laurie P. (2000-03-28). "Many Medicines Prove Potent for Years Past Their Expiration Dates". The Wall Street Journal 235 (62): pp. A1.

Pensions and the Elderly

Another policy which has been difficult to balance effectively by many governments is the pension system. This is due to the amount of money that is in the state funds as well as the decreasing birth rate in the west, which results in fewer workers having to pay contributions from their income for an increasing older population. In this latter case, it is not very practical or dependable to try to convince people to reproduce more as there is no way of monitoring this. It may turn out that too many people decide to try to overcome this problem and the population increases too quickly, leaving other problems with provision!

The idea of state pensions is an excellent concept as it means that the people have the obligation to prepare for their own retirement. A fixed percentage is deducted from their salary throughout their working life, leading to the financial resources to pay for their needs after they have retired. The best thing about this is that people have to contribute to society to help look after each other. Every worker is part of the same grand scheme that they will then all benefit from as long as the accounts are managed properly. The money that gets paid for this purpose has to be kept in a separate state pension fund that cannot be used to pay for anything else.

In the case where there are not enough funds available to provide for the retired population, money would need to come from elsewhere to subsidise it. One way of addressing this is to raise the percentage rate of social security for those people who earn over an agreed amount and to whom it would not cause a significant financial problem. In the case where the pension funds become balanced again, this rate can return to the ideal rate. Another would be to charge the largest profit-making businesses with the intention of showing them that, because of their high net income, they are expected to contribute to society. They have the means and it is their responsibility to help out the public who have made it possible for them to make such profits, from their sales and other payments. All the time we should be looking at strengthening morals in everybody, particularly if they have far more than they need. Everyone has a moral obligation to contribute to society as we are all a part of it. That can't be argued against.

People should also be allowed to have private pensions if they wish but again, as such institutions are in existence for the aim of making a profit, there would need to be regulations in place to ensure that the profits made are minimal after their own costs have been covered. A way of ensuring this would be to create government-monitored pension schemes whereby people can pay as much as they like to their own savings account and this money is secure and will be available to them when they retire. This would be like the state pension system described above but individuals who choose to save more would be able to and have more at their disposal after they finish working.

The next thing to address is the retirement age. Modern politics has been dogged with immoral decision-making where the retirement age generally keeps increasing. The reason for this is bad economic management from the banking sector as well as the government who end up with not enough funds to pay pensions. One big problem with this is that politicians make the decisions with consulting the public. For a minister to announce that the retirement age will go up by one or two years is unacceptable. For one thing, it is to cover the debts that the government is probably responsible for, not the people, which should not be the responsibility of the people. It is unquestionably unfair to tell people that they have to work for more years. For another, the lack of discussion and agreements made with the general public means that the government has no concern for what the people think. The people are the ones who have to have the burden of working longer, not the politicians! This is an example of where democracy fails entirely.

It is also an example of how the capitalist, free market system is completely ineffective. We can't have these kinds of issues regularly coming up just because a few greedy, immoral people took risks that were even bigger than their bank accounts.

The retirement age should be equal for both males and females. A typical age that has been used across the world is 65 and is acceptable. However, people should be allowed to work longer if they choose to. This would be welcomed, although not obligatory, as it would mean that pension funds would continue to be paid for longer by some people.

In the case that ill health means that someone cannot continue working, disability benefits would be received if it has been proven by medical officials that the person cannot be expected to work any more. Of course, these checks would need to be stringent to ensure that people aren't cheating the system. However, along with the morality that should be evident in most people by implementation of this whole moral system, the likelihood of wanting to cheat the system should be less. As long as the people have a good level of trust in the government and they believe that their needs and well-being are seriously being addressed, the level of trust from the government to the people should also improve.

In terms of care for the elderly, this is also an issue that has been difficult to manage. As elderly people are more likely to suffer from illnesses, medical care needs to be provided sufficiently. The national health service is where the guarantee needs to come from, as private medical care is currently not affordable by everyone. It is difficult to say whether the amount of care necessary is going to be possible to provide until this moral system is in place. The main idea concerning general health is that we are at a stage where we should be looking at preventing illnesses from occurring whenever possible. The World Health Organisation is looking to promote complete health with "a state of complete physical, mental and social well-being and not merely the absence of disease or infirmity."[1] As mentioned elsewhere in this book, we should be aiming to convince everyone to be fit, to take care of what they eat and to not feel the need to engage in unhealthy activities such as heavy drinking or taking drugs.

Another point worth mentioning is the western attitude to death. Many people find it difficult to come to terms with the fact that we are all going to die. There have been so many medical advances into helping people live longer. The only aspect we should be concerned about is trying to alleviate suffering from medical complaints. If it is the case that an ailment is prevalent because of old age but it is not causing too much discomfort, this may sound shocking but it should be seen as the time to accept the onset of the inevitable.

Buddhism sees death as part of the change that is always apparent in life. For Buddhists, it is seen as the time when the being transcends to the next lifetime (reincarnation) and it is nothing to be feared. This is a difficult concept to accept, particularly as we have no proof or evidence that such a thing occurs. However, what we do know is that death will always occur and that it is part of the natural cycle of all beings. We mustn't be so concerned with trying to prolong life as much as possible, for it will only end in failure. We must accept that we have a limited time and that we should try to make the most of it from the perspective of society. If we have led a fulfilling life where we feel that we have achieved something, be it great or small, how can we fear something that is unavoidable? To have a fear of death is to have an unhealthy and deluded state of mind. Of course, sometimes death happens prematurely, as in the case of a fatal accident, and it can be a time to mourn but we should also keep in mind that we should be able to adapt to our loss after some time and that there is nothing we can do to change what has already happened.

The most important thing is to make one's life as constructive and positive as possible so that we won't mind coming to terms with the end. If we can work on alleviating suffering and lead fruitful lives, our friends and relatives should also try to remember us positively, as people who enjoyed life and achieved something.

1. Preamble to the Constitution of the World Health Organization as adopted by the International Health Conference, New York, 19-22 June, 1946; signed on 22 July 1946 by the representatives of 61 States (Official Records of the World Health Organization, no. 2, p. 100) and entered into force on 7 April 1948. The Definition has not been amended since 1948.

Foreign Policy

Foreign policy, or how the country will interact with other countries, can be broken down into various areas: economically, politically, socially and militarily.

First of all, the main aim to interact with any country has to be with the intention of maintaining peace, good relations and reciprocal actions that lead to strengthening of the bonds with other countries. Policies that set out to exploit another country in any way are not acceptable. We shall now examine the four main areas individually.

Economically

Each country needs to become as resilient as it can; that is, to be able to look after itself in terms of food, manufacturing and the general well-being of the citizens. In the cases where a country needs to form partnerships with others when certain resources are not available, it is important to make sure that fair trading is in place. For example, if a rich country cannot grow certain foods but a poorer country can, it can only form a business deal whereby the poorer country will not be selling too many of its resources so that it cannot feed its own people. Those resources which are then exported must be sold in a way that is going to be fair, and likely to be beneficial to the people, i.e. by bringing more money into the poorer country. Of course, this would also mean that there would need to be strict regulations in place that are monitored so that the money going into the poorer country is being distributed fairly and not being taken by either the company owners or the ruling party.

This is likely to mean that the prices of the imported products in the richer country would be higher and that fewer people could afford them but as long as they are not essential items and they could be replaced by indigenous crops in terms of their nutritional content, there is no practical issue with this situation. It is simply not good enough to say that if the poor country would still be happy to export its resources for a lower price, then it should go ahead as this would make the poorer country remain in a state of bad economic development and a low standard of living. We must remember that we cannot only look after our own country but we must make sure that we are trying to eradicate the corruption and exploitation that keeps some countries rich and others poor. This is another problem with capitalism – taking care of ourselves while having no regard for other people is only going to prevent humanity from progressing. We must be aware of our impact on others and allow the freedom to have such unfair trade reported in all cases to the general public.

Politically

Exactly the same principles apply in the area of politics. Whereas one government should not try to tell another how it must behave and act, it should be willing to offer its advice to a country that uses bad practice on its citizens in a peaceful way to attempt to persuade the other government to change its actions and policies so that it can be honest with itself and accept that their actions should change. This type of diplomacy is extremely important to try to prevent any international conflicts from beginning. It is all about having democratic meetings with other countries' leaders to almost 'guide' them towards more peaceful and fairer treatment of its citizens. Resolution of such problems should only be attempted in a helpful and non-judgemental way, otherwise, as in the current case of Iran and its nuclear enrichment programme, the Iranian government is constantly receiving aggressive demands from the west to abandon its practice with sanctions and threats being made. Keep in mind that those countries that are making such demands are also guilty of having nuclear enrichment programmes. You really cannot use the old adage of 'do as I say, not as I do' if you are going to make any progress with international relations.

Instead, strategies must be used to peacefully request Iran not to produce nuclear weapons with offers of international aid, both monetarily and with human resources to help improve relations with the west, if they agree to not threaten countries that are considered their enemies. Both sides involved need to be able to reach a compromise so that they will not be in a state of aggression with each other. The west needs to be willing to drop any plans they have, such as wanting to invest in and ultimately take control of Iran's natural resources.

One of Iran's two strategic principles for its foreign policy is to eliminate outside influences in the region. This quite clearly means that they don't want the west to meddle in its culture and affairs, particularly in its oil fields. Interestingly enough, Iran ranks second in the world in natural gas reserves and in oil reserves.[1] It is quite understandable for Iran to not want western oil companies barging in and taking control of their oil and gas, making ridiculous profits that the Iranians are not going to benefit from in any way. And when they feel threatened by the west and that they are being told what to do and not to do, they don't exactly feel very content with this, which is understandable.

However, if they were instead offered a peace deal where they were assured that there was not going to be any plan to exploit the Iranian natural resources or anything else about their country and that if they improved their human rights then they could receive training and support to improve their infrastructure and improved trade with other countries, all in a non-intrusive way, there is a far greater chance that relations with the west would improve and that peace would prevail.

There would be far less of a chance that arms manufacturers would be making so much money if they can't maintain tension between the countries involved and when the likelihood of war is practically non-existent, but that is exactly what we should be working towards.

The book "Three Cups of Tea" was published in 2006 which tells the true story of a former mountaineer, Greg Mortensen. After failing to reach the summit of K2, Mortensen found himself in a small village in northern Pakistan. After being treated courteously and compassionately by the inhabitants and learning that there were no schools in the region, he made a promise to return and build them a school. Mortensen was a man who had practically no money to support himself but, after travelling back to America, sleeping in his car and finding part-time work in a hospital, he set about trying to form a plan to raise money so that he could fulfil his promise.

He faced an almost impossible battle to do so, receiving no donations from the 580 rich and influential people and groups he had contacted in America, except for one, a physicist called Dr. Jean Hoerni, also a former mountaineer who had scaled peaks on five continents. Hoerni provided all the money needed himself and Mortensen was able to return and build the school, which was intended to be for girls as well as boys. The story tells of the reluctance of the native people to provide education to girls, but through Mortensen's undeniably good intentions to help develop the northern regions of Pakistan and through their admiration and respect for him, he succeeded in building the first school they had ever had.

He continued to work unscrupulously hard to raise money to build more schools but while he was in the process, the 9/11 bombing of New York's Twin Towers took place and started the war between the west and the Taliban. At this point, most western readers would expect that Mortensen, being American, would flee from the area for his own sake, but as he had become so well-known to the people there over the years, the Pakistani people spoke of how much they would risk to save his life.

The Taliban recruited its soldiers by offering something that they would otherwise have never had – money, to study in their 'madrassas' – extremist schools which would make them ruthless martyrs, whereby they would be so brainwashed that they would follow the orders to attack whoever they were instructed to. Mortensen's mission was to stop this recruitment by offering people something else that they had never had and were likely to never have in life – education. His work continued and despite facing opposition through fatwas and threats to destroy his schools, the organisation that he had later set up – the CAI or Central Asia Institute, had built fifty-five schools by the time the book was published.

What this one man had dedicated his life to, from a starting point of nothing, is testimony to how much can be achieved worldwide. As his pilot, Brigadier General Bashir Baz said, in the light of the offensive from the President Bush-led hunt for Osama Bin Laden, "Osama is not a product of Pakistan or Afghanistan. He is a creation of America. Thanks to America, Osama is in every home... You can never fight and win against someone who can shoot at you once and then run off and hide... In America's case, that's not Osama or Saddam... The enemy is ignorance. Your President Bush has done a wonderful job of uniting one billion Muslims against America for the next two hundred years."

Mortensen had previously been receiving hate-mail and death threats from Americans after it was known that he continued his work post-9/11. Some time later, he collected five sacks of letters from his PO Box from Americans and from other countries following a story in the "Parade" magazine which detailed the story of his work and said "...after I finished reading every message, there was only one negative letter in the whole bunch."

Needless to say, Three Cups of Tea is essential reading.[2]

Socially

Regarding social relations between countries, one thing that would need to be worked on is the elimination of rivalry and hence, xenophobia. There are so many cases of neighbouring countries that have bad relations simply because they live next to each other and they want to assert their own superiority over the other in a competitive way. There is no logic in this, as was explained in the section on national identity. People can relate to each other not depending on where they were born but on how compatible they are with each other. It is childish to say that someone is worse than you in some way because they hold a different passport to you or live within different political borders that they had no influence in deciding where they would be placed.

We need to focus on bringing falsely divided groups of people together to show that they can relate well with each other. They may speak a different language or dialect but we are all people and the potential is already there for us to become friends, simply because we come from the same species. We must stop clinging to prejudices just because other people have, over time, established them. It doesn't mean that they are right, nor does it mean that everyone from a certain country has the same character as the badly constructed stereotypes that we have all heard about regarding certain nationalities respective to our own.

Strengthening international relations on a social level is something that everyone can get involved with. Bordering countries should be encouraged to join together in festivals and other events that emphasise the welcoming feeling that really is going to make people feel more comfortable with each other. It is not enough just to tell people that they shouldn't be xenophobic or racist, we have to help them to experience the friendships that can happen. How can anyone feel truly happy if they portray other people as the enemy or rivals? Arguments, fights, bitterness and even killings occur in this situation and no true satisfaction can come from this. If one has a grudge against an entire nation, it is extremely unlikely that their prejudices are of their own making, but instead come from the press and the government that wishes its citizens to hate them, so that the people will support the government's desires to destroy the nation that they themselves have a personal grudge against.

We need to lose the emphasis that is put on national borders as they keep people apart on a social level. We need to build compassion and encourage and educate people to be willing to mingle with others or be willing to give everyone a chance, however they may communicate with them. This is something that has to come through school education to increase the children's awareness of other peoples in the world so that their compassionate understanding will replace the selfish and ignorant prejudices that are so prevalent today.

Friendly competition, such as in sports competitions, would still be fine as long as it remains friendly. If another team beats your country's team, then don't get into conflicts with the opposing fans but congratulate them and accept that it was only a game, even if a trophy was won. So what? It's only a trophy, it doesn't actually mean anything substantial. We need to work on our priorities and not let things get out of scale.

Bringing about peace is fundamentally important. Raising people's awareness of others and being educated about the cultural differences between them is crucial to increase good relations, not just between separate countries but also between people of the same country. Don't categorise yourselves and others. Break down the barriers. They don't exist anyway.

Militarily

As you will have worked out from the above sections in this chapter, war with other countries is something that we should be aiming to avoid at all costs. Declaring war on a country is completely immoral and could never be allowed to take place. It is, however, a more difficult subject to address when military intervention is used to help citizens of another country who are being persecuted and killed by either their military or rebel groups. For the sake of the citizens, it has to be reluctantly accepted that this type of involvement is often necessary. But essentially, wars are often declared because of what is in it for the perpetrators. They want resources (that they may declare are in their national interests, so as to attempt to convince the public), power, control and money. Well, what are they going to do with it when they die? And how many of their own citizens' lives are they going to waste in order to get what they want? There is never any moral justification to invade a country simply because you have provoked them to attack you.

Defending one's own territory is another issue and of course, it would be necessary if another country decided to invade. In a truly moral government, neutrality would be the position to take so that if the country was never going to threaten another or support a country to attack another, then should be no reason for another country to threaten or attack the neutral one.

This may be seen as idealistic but it has been in practice for some countries for almost 200 years at the time of writing. Sweden has not fought in a war since the Napoleonic Wars in 1814. Switzerland established its neutrality in 1815 and both of these countries were left untouched in both world wars. There are only a few other neutral countries as of 2010, the larger ones being Japan, Austria, Finland, Ireland, Costa Rica and Turkmenistan. Since establishing their neutrality, these countries have not been threatened or attacked so clearly, it is not just idealism but a fact that it works.

There is rarely any justification for war. However, in the case of the

Second World War, the revolting aggression of Adolf Hitler needed to be stopped. Even though his regime was eventually stopped, it came at a cost of millions of human lives to those who fought in the war (and the civilians who died as a result of invasions), as well as those who were murdered in the concentration camps.

This is one of the most extreme cases in recent history of undesirable governments. In other cases invasion of a country is not done for reasons of liberating the people but of what can be gained by the invading allies' countries. There have been recent genocides in countries such as Sudan, Burma and Rwanda but there was no NATO intervention. Why not? Because they have no significant stocks of natural resources that could be exploited. They simply weren't profitable so NATO was not interested.

War is never going to be an effective solution to international problems because there will always be people who die or suffer great losses, such as their homes in a bombing, and most importantly because acts of aggression will not be seen by the other side as acceptable. If country A attacked country B, B wouldn't like it and they would want revenge. If they carried out their revenge on A, A would respond by attacking B again, and so on, ad infinitum. It will never result in a peaceful resolution between two sides.

To conclude, all countries need to work in harmony with each other to establish real human development, true peace and to eliminate exploitation.

1. www.eia.doe.gov/emeu/cabs/Iran/Background.html

2. Three Cups of Tea, Greg Mortenson and David Oliver Relin. Penguin Books, Ltd.

Section 3: Laws

For a large part, laws don't need to be explained here as it can be taken that certain laws will be in place as they already are in democratic countries. This means that certain laws are obvious to have in place, like murder, fraud, physical violence, etc. However, there are certain laws which are still currently open for debate and opposing sides claim that their views are right and the opposition's are wrong. Such controversial laws will need to examined in the following chapters to be able to understand the true morality of them so as to arrive at a point whereby they cannot be up for debate.

The only way that such a decision can be reached is to analyse them starting from the moral perspective. This means that particular influences such as personal opinion, religious beliefs and tradition may not play a part in the process of establishing the laws in question. It can never be justifiable that something should be illegal because only the minority might do something that the majority don't like. It may be the majority but if their views are only opinions, they are not facts and never will be.

Laws can never made in a way that the ruling classes decide what they think is right as there is often a hidden agenda that they are going to benefit from or a loophole that leaves them free to be able to stay clear of the law. The first rule in making a law is to decide what is going to be best for everyone concerned or in the case of the environment, what is not going to cause it any upset wherever possible. A law cannot be made which is going to be an inconvenience to people just because they belong to a particular minority group if there is no justifiable reason for it (i.e. if the action in question is not going to be detrimental to anyone outside of the group).

At times, laws have to be made which are going to cause inconveniences to some people but if it has a reason that is morally above the people, then it will be explained clearly and without any ulterior motives that remain hidden from the public. For example, if something was causing environmental damage, say pollution, and whatever was making it was not necessary to maintain, then the people would be asked to understand the reason for changing the law and helped, if need be, to make alternative arrangements that wouldn't inconvenience them too much when the law has to be changed.

If there is no justifiable reason for making a law (on a moral level), then it would be reconsidered and changed accordingly.

Human Rights

Human rights are in place around the world to varying degrees. The United Nations set out the Universal Declaration of Human Rights (UDHR) in 1948 with the intention that it should be

"a common standard of achievement for all peoples and all nations, to the end that every individual and every organ of society, keeping this Declaration constantly in mind, shall strive by teaching and education to promote respect for these rights and freedoms and by progressive measures, national and international, to secure their universal and effective recognition and observance, both among the peoples of Member States themselves and among the peoples of territories under their jurisdiction."[1]

Unfortunately, we are still at a time where far too many countries have not adopted this declaration and some have atrocious human rights records. Obviously, there should be a continued effort to try to persuade those countries to declare allegiance to at least some of the rights, step by step, to bring about greater internal peace in the countries. This is pointed out because many western countries that have adopted the declaration in full still continue to trade with those who largely ignore most of the rights in the list. By acting in this way, there is no real incentive for other countries to sign up to the declaration as they feel they will not lose any business connections or suffer from imposed sanctions if they continue to operate in inhumane ways to their own populations.

Therefore, an important policy should be that a country should not trade with another country that falls short of implementing human rights. It is not intended to be aggressive, in fact quite the opposite. It is a way of saying "If you don't respect your people's rights, it is in our constitution that we can't trade with you." It is not a way of outwardly criticising the country in question but a way of letting it known that the country has to establish trade links elsewhere.

There are number of issues regarding human rights that have raised controversy that fall outside the articles in the UDHR.

Lesbian, Gay, Bisexual and Transgender rights (LGBT) are certainly one of them, even in supposed developed countries. There is no specific article in the UDHR relating to the rights of sexual orientation but there are certainly limits around the world, ranging from the prohibition of marriage of two persons of the same sex to execution of homosexuals by law.

The recommended attitude to sexuality was addressed in Shaping A Society but we should also look at the issue of gay marriage.

As it is something that has recently come under discussion about whether it should be allowed by law, we need to think why shouldn't it be allowed by law? If two people of the same sex are already in a relationship and already live together, why shouldn't they be allowed to get married? To be married means you get a legal document that shows that you are registered as married and you wear wedding rings. Where's the controversy? Some homophobic organisations claim that it will affect family values and the sanctity of 'regular' marriage. I can tell you that it won't. It will not affect anybody else at all because nobody else is involved in the marriage. If they already live together, it is effectively the same thing, the only difference is that their relationship has been made 'official' (for what that is really worth).

Gay marriage will not have any effect on straight marriage, families or anything. However, having an open mind and the willingness to say "There's no problem because it's none of my business" will have an effect – a positive one that shows strength of character.

The only reason that anyone opposes such rights is due to their ignorance, their stubborn refusal to accept others who are different to them in certain ways and their arrogance in believing that they have the right to dictate to others how they should act.

Other human rights than can be raised here are to do with legal ages for various activities. In some cases, they need to be no more than recommendations, in others, due to reasons of protection, they need to be strictly enforced.

A lot of this has to do with with when a person is deemed mature enough enough to engage in something. Regarding all forms of drugs, please refer to that chapter in this section. But continuing the sexuality theme, we should consider the age of consent.

Biologically, a person is mature enough to have sexual relations when they reach puberty and in some cultures this is how it is expected to be. However, it ought to be recommended through sex education that teenagers don't have the maturity or levels of responsibility to look after themselves emotionally or financially. In Spain, the age of consent was *raised* in 1999 to 13. This, for a developed country, ought to be considered as far too young for the above reasons.

It can be debated as to whether the ages of 16 or 18 are the best ones to establish an age of consent. I would favour 18 to try to help teenagers develop a sense of self control and responsibility. But if the two people involved are both younger than 18 (which is when one 'officially' becomes an adult in many countries) they would not and need not be prosecutable by law. Sex education should be in place to help them understand why it would be better to wait until they are older. Of course, we all know that this is difficult to do as many teenagers like to pretend they are already adults or they are keen to experiment with things that they are not yet legally old enough to do but the key to improving this situation is being able to earn respect and give support to teenagers so that they feel there is no good reason to rebel.

However, with sexual acts, when one of the people involved is older than 18, we move into different territory. This is when we are talking about laws for the protection of minors. It should be illegal for anyone over the age of 18 to have sexual relations with anyone younger than 18 (or 16 if the general public feel that this is a satisfactory age to set as the limit). The reason for this is of course to protect the younger people from being taken advantage of.

Both of these sides of the law for the age of consent would apply to people of any sexual orientation. It would simply be unfair and discriminatory to set different ages for 'different' people.

Taking into account other legal ages, such as the voting age, marriage age, driving age, etc., it would be better to agree on a standard age for all of the relevant activities, perhaps of 18 so that they tie in with when a person is deemed to be an adult and has individual responsibility for themselves. This again comes down the aspect of the level of maturity in general.

Amnesty International and War Resister International has called for another article to be added to the UDHR – that of "The Right to Refuse to Kill". These groups feel that it is not explicit enough in article 18 ("Everyone has the right to freedom of thought, conscience and religion; this right includes freedom to change his religion or belief, and freedom, either alone or in community with others and in public or private, to manifest his religion or belief in teaching, practice, worship and observance"). This is a valuable proposal to make it clear that nobody should be able to be forced to take up military service and that it should be entirely up to the individuals to choose whether they want to respond to the requests of their country's ministry of defence.

In a government that wants to promote peace in every way, this resolution should be completely adopted with the additional intention of showing other countries that it does not want to go to war unless it is unavoidable (i.e. if another country attacks it – which is unlikely for neutral countries as mentioned in Foreign Policy).

Some Islamic countries have criticised the UDHR for not taking into account the cultural and religious contexts in place in those countries. They believe that it trespasses Islamic Law (Sharia), especially concerning article 18 as quoted above. The 'freedom to change his religion or belief' would be a massive violation of Islamic Law. Instead the Cairo Declaration on Human Rights (CDHRI) in Islam is an alternative to the UDHR which states that people have the "freedom and right to a dignified life in accordance with the Islamic Shari'ah".[2] This entails a lack of freedom of religion or gender equality, however, and with respect to the Islamic faith, it has to be treated with some scepticism.

Some specific issues relating to Islamic Law and how it differs from what is stated in the UDHR include the lack of agreement between it and democracy. There is effectively no allowed alternative to Islamic Law and the dogma is to be strictly implemented. There is no freedom of speech allowed concerning criticism of Muhammed. Although I feel that this is acceptable, the belief that such an act should be punishable by death is definitely not.

Homosexuality is illegal under Sharia. The penalties for homosexual acts vary from region to region but as I have already explained, one's sexuality appears not to be a choice of any kind and therefore, it is wrong to say that it should be punishable.

In the CDHRI, women are given equal dignity but not equal rights, stating that "All men are equal in terms of basic human dignity and basic obligations and responsibilities, without any discrimination on the basis of race, colour, language, belief, sex, religion, political affiliation, social status or other considerations.", therefore not explicitly stating basic rights.

The Organisation of the Islamic Conference should be encouraged to try to redress these controversies as, from a moral perspective, it does fall short of promoting total equality and adequate freedoms in some instances.

1. The Universal Declaration of Human Rights. www.un.org/en/documents/udhr/
2. Cairo Declaration on Human Rights in Islam www.religlaw.org/interdocs/docs/cairohrislam1990.htm

Drugs

This chapter is to consider the legality of certain drugs, depending on their effects (medicinally, harmfully, physically and psychoactively), their naturally available or manufactured status and the governmental control.

Those drugs which are generally legal and readily available in most countries comprise caffeine, tobacco and alcohol. Some countries have a tolerance of cannabis and in some cases legalise or decriminalise it and other drugs, such as heroin, cocaine, amphetamines and LSD are classed as illegal drugs on the whole.

In terms of those widespread legal drugs, they would be legal under the hypothetical government but would also have a level of governmental control and guidance. For example, caffeine can be harmful to the body if taken in great quantities so it would be mandatory for adverts to show warnings that advise against drinking a certain number of drinks containing caffeine for health reasons. There would also be limits on how much caffeine manufacturers of high-caffeine drinks could put in their products per 100ml. This is because it is morally incorrect to sell such products with the intention of making money from people who, seeking a legal 'high', actually end up damaging their bodies due to excessive caffeine consumption.

Additionally, the VAT applicable to these manufactured drinks would be high to try to discourage people from buying them.

Tobacco

Tobacco would have a legal status as it would meet a large amount of protest if it was outlawed. As it has many damaging effects on the body, particularly on the lungs, there would be programmes to try to reduce the amount that people smoke as well as to help people give up smoking altogether. Cigarette manufacturers would have to provide three levels of each brand they produce with varying levels of tar, nicotine and carbon monoxide (CO) content. To attempt to encourage smokers to smoke weaker cigarettes, the VAT imposed could be a varying rates depending on how strong they are. For example, low content cigarettes would be at the standard price, for examples' sake at €4, the medium content would be €5 and the high content cigarettes at €6. This significant difference should influence smokers' choices so that they are more likely to at least reduce their intake in terms of the amount of the damaging content. It could also be law to limit the highest possible levels of tar, etc. that can be allowed. The varying levels could be:

High content cigarettes: Tar 8-10mg, nicotine 1mg, CO 8-10mg
Medium: tar 6-7mg, nicotine 0.6-0.7mg, CO 6-7mg
Low: tar up to 4mg, nicotine up to 0.4mg, CO up to 4mg

The reason that these levels don't include 7-8 or 4-5mg, etc. is to prevent manufacturers from beating the price increases by selling medium strength cigarettes at 7.9mg of tar, etc. There is a definite divide between the levels permitted to make the cigarettes notably different.

Whereas normally, the practice of genetic modification would not be encouraged in the hypothetical government, due to the damaging effects of cigarettes, especially the tar content, research could be encouraged to develop tobacco plants that produce less tar while retaining the nicotine levels. Although we would like to reduce and eliminate the practice of tobacco smoking in general, we would have to respect that it is addictive and difficult to stop, but there would be governmental adverts to encourage people to try alternative methods to reduce the amount they smoke by giving advice in a respectful way.

Nicotine still has detrimental effects on the body. It is not believed to increase the likelihood of cancer but has been shown to impede apoptosis, which is the body's ability to destroy unwanted cells (such as damaged cells that can become cancerous).[1]

The legal age to be able to smoke would be 18. The reason for this is because of the harmful effects. It is not expected that teenagers would fully respect this legal age but it would be hoped that a growing number of them respects and follows the legal age limit and that establishments that sell tobacco products would only sell to those who are of the legal age, where proof through identification would be required if the salesperson had any doubts. There would be punishments for salespeople who are found to ignore this law in the form of significant monetary fines and if the failure to comply continued, they could lose their business.

There are already products on sale that give alternatives to smoking, like 'alternative cigarettes' that supply the dose of nicotine that smokers are used to but that give no tar. As yet, there is no evidence to say that electronic cigarettes are a safe and effective nicotine replacement therapy.[2] These cannot be seen as ways of giving up smoking as they are merely there to simulate the effects of smoking and maintain a market for people who have an addiction to nicotine.

Simply giving smokers something else to be hooked on will not help them to overcome their habits.

Smoking in public places has, in the first decade of the 21st century seen major changes in the law in a number of countries that prohibits the practice. A lot of the time this law has been very strict and can be seen as being against the rights of people who smoke. Understandably, for health reasons, it is acceptable to limit smoking to reduce the amount of secondary smoke inhaled by non-smokers, although we have to respect that every person has the same rights, whether they are smokers or not. But, as passive smoking can also have damaging effects on people, to address these issues, a compromise has to be reached rather than simply favouring the rights of non-smokers. Public buildings such as cafés and bars would require a separate enclosed section where people could smoke in a room that has air-conditioning that meets specific standards. The same could be provided in workplaces but ensuring that secondary smoke does not escape from the provided room. This is not to encourage people to smoke but to respect their rights and allow them their freedom if they wish to continue smoking while not contributing to any potential health problems of non-smokers. What happens otherwise is that we get smokers gathered in doorways and on the streets as though they are social outcasts, so it would be better to provide them with their own area rather than ostracise them.

Governments often increase the prices of cigarettes in an attempt to convince people to quit (as well as raise the taxes payable on cigarettes), which considering that this practice fits in with the proposal of higher VAT for unhealthy products, should continue as long as it is made clear that tobacco manufacturers are not the ones who are making extra profit from these price increases.

The overall objective would be to help people to give up smoking altogether but we have to be respectful and understand that it is a step-by-step process that is likely to take time.

Alcohol

Alcohol, whereas it is legal in the majority of countries and, depending on the society, causes relatively few health problems in relation to the number of people who drink alcohol in moderation, but it is still a drug that requires special attention. It is known that alcohol can damage the body if consumed in large proportions and has easily noticeable effects on those who consume a large amount in a short period of time. These effects seriously affect the motor control of the individual as well as behaviour and level of aggression in some people. In some countries such as the United Kingdom, alcohol consumption is a big problem and can lead to hospitalisation as well as arrests for anti-social behaviour. In many other countries such as Spain and Portugal, alcohol consumption does not cause such a big problem in terms of its effects on other people as, due to the difference in the cultures in general, drinking alcohol does not generally lead to fights and aggressive behaviour in the public on the same scale.

If it was the case that alcohol was seen as being a large-scale problem for society, there should be strict laws on the limits of alcohol available. In establishments where alcohol is sold, it would be illegal to sell alcohol to people who are perceived as being drunk and it would be illegal for someone else to buy them an alcoholic drink on their behalf. This, of course, could lead to undesirable behaviour from the customer, in forms of protest, but hopefully, the customers would get used to the law over time (as generally happens) and they would accept it. But to address the issue of alcohol abuse, programmes and advertisements would be used to try to change the attitude of those who drink excessive amounts of alcohol due of the peer pressure/ group identity issue to encourage them to seriously question what the point of getting heavily drunk is.

In the United Kingdom, for example, alcohol abuse has become almost a tradition or a way of life for a large number of the population. It is seen as simply 'what you do' on at least a Friday and Saturday night because everyone else does it. However, it is difficult to see why people perceive getting to the point of being unable to stand up unaided or speak clearly, to get into a fight, vomit and suffer from a hangover is a definition of a good night out. When this happens on a large scale and regularly, it is time to get very strict regarding the laws on selling and consuming alcohol.

Other options could include the sale of low or no-alcohol content drinks at the standard price in the establishments to attempt to encourage people to change their drinking patterns and raise the prices of normal-level alcoholic drinks significantly in both public houses and off-licences. This price difference would again be due to the VAT imposed on the drinks.

As alcohol is an escapism in this case, it is more important to continue the support for people to improve their level of well-being so that they don't feel the need to escape from their unfulfilling circumstances by turning to alcohol. This depends a great deal on the reshaping of the society so it is difficult to say how long it would take to make a significant difference to this type of behaviour.

Illegal Drugs

There are many drugs which are generally classed as illegal in most countries. Drugs such as heroin, crack, amphetamines, LSD, ecstasy, cocaine, etc. would be illegal and possession and selling thereof would have similar implications as in the most of the western world (fines, criminal records and imprisonment). Cannabis, which is constantly under debate and is legal in a few countries deserves a separate discussion.

Cannabis is a drug which, if taken in moderate doses and using specific methods of consumption, is relatively safe, has some medicinal qualities and causes very few changes in behaviour that are potentially harmful to others. As it is also derived from a naturally growing plant, having an illegal status is hypocritical with respect to its effects. As Bill Hicks pointed out, how do you make something that grows naturally on the planet against the law? Furthermore, against the high numbers of deaths annually that are linked to tobacco and/ or alcohol use, there are no reported cases of death due to cannabis use.

The method of consumption is quite important to reduce its harmful properties. The most common form, smoking, is actually the most harmful, potentially leading to the development of bullous lung cancer far sooner than tobacco smokers. Cannabis smoke contains greater levels of toxins such as ammonia, hydrogen cyanide and nitrous oxide. Therefore, even though it would be classed as legal, cannabis cigarettes would not be allowed to be manufactured and the smoking of them would be discouraged. Using a vaporiser pipe would be a more recommended way of consuming it because fewer toxins are released when the hashish (resin) form is used and is heated to a gas which is then inhaled through the pipe.

Another method of consumption which would be preferred would be to mix it with cooking food, such as hash cakes (or space cakes), as again, toxins would not be released as much as with smoking and even though its psychoactive effects would take longer to become apparent, they would not be so strong and would give a more relaxing effect of being high.

Such information and advice would be freely available to encourage responsible methods of consumption and moderation of intake to ensure that it is being used sensibly.

Regulation concerning cannabis consumption would be that it is not permitted to be under the influence of cannabis when operating any vehicle or machine, or when at work of any kind of paid employment.

The medicinal qualities of cannabis include slowing of the growth of cancer cells, treatment for depression and reduction of muscle spasms for sufferers of multiple sclerosis. There are other medicinal uses which would deem it inappropriate to outlaw cannabis.[3]

As its effects are almost exclusively of a calming nature with a pleasant, peaceful feeling, it is relatively unknown that people under the influence of cannabis cause aggressive actions to others, which gives it a preferential effect over the consumption of alcohol.

Regarding the availability of places to consume it however, it would not be permitted inside any public buildings as it would require extra rooms separate from smoking rooms to avoid undesired inhalation by non-users, which would be generally impractical for proprietors. Therefore, consumption in outdoor areas or in private homes only would be permitted. Otherwise, it would be requested that no methods of smoking are practised while in the vicinity of other people in case of their objections to either secondary smoke or having children see the practice.

The legalisation of cannabis would also have some benefits to the country: illegal smuggling and sales of cannabis would be rendered virtually non-existent. It would be available either through private shops or medical prescriptions and in the case of sales for recreational use, it would be taxed. Cannabis would also be sold in specific quantities to try to discourage excessive consumption and the packaging would be required to contain information about the various methods of consumption and their comparative risks. The private growing of cannabis would also be legal as you cannot prohibit anyone from growing natural plants that do not cause a significant amount of damage to beings that use them.

Initially, the legalisation of cannabis may provoke opposition and overly-zealous usage but as it became more commonplace, the consumption thereof would reach a level of moderation as with tobacco and alcohol in general.

Regarding other drugs which are derived from naturally growing plants, there are many varieties but concerning their legal status, as they become more known, research would have to be conducted objectively to ascertain whether they would be safe enough and likely to produce behaviours that are of no risk to the user or to other people. From this, there could be more drugs that get legal status but would follow similar regulations and guidelines as described above.

In terms of what to do about drugs that should remain illegal due to their destructive properties, like heroin, crack cocaine, crystal meths, etc., trying to stop the smuggling of them will always be an issue and one that realistically is unlikely to ever be completely solved. However, education about the effects of such drugs such be mandatory in secondary schools as well as in the press and on the television and internet. To do this with any chance of success, the schemes would have to be presented in a way that is neither condescending or likely to meet with rebellion against the state because of an implicit degree of propaganda. People will not react favourably to something if they feel they are being told not to do something as though they were small children. The facts only can be given and the use of words by which the facts are given must be carefully chosen to approach people on their level.

Again, taking such illegal drugs is usually a form of escapism so improving the overall conditions for people and society are imperative to be able to make any progress with such issues.

1. "Toxicology" eBasedTreatment.
   www.ebasedtreatment.org/drugs/treatment/nicotine/toxicology
2. "Marketers of electronic cigarettes should halt unproved therapy claims". World Health Organization. 2008-09-19. www.who.int/mediacentre/news/releases/2008/pr34/en/index.h tml
3. Meyer, Robert J. "Testimony before the Subcommittee on Criminal Justice, Drug Policy, and Human Resources, Committee on Government Reform" U.S. Food and Drug Administration. www.fda.gov/ola/2004/marijuana0401.html

Abortion

Being a very controversial issue which has many divided opinions between groups, analysing abortion is one that is necessary to try to achieve a moral compromise for its legal status.

The main division is between pro-life and pro-choice groups where the former believes that every child, be they yet unborn, has the right to life. The latter believes that there are many important factors that have to be taken into consideration and that women have the right to choose whether to keep the baby or have it terminated.

Religious beliefs commonly influence those who believe that pro-life is the only acceptable stance on this issue. However, there are exceptions where abortion is permitted. For example, by the Roman Catholic church it is permitted if the mother's life is in danger from continued pregnancy and the National Association of Evangelicals allow abortion to take place if the foetus shows evidence of severe deformity or if the pregnancy is a result of rape.

In Islam, abortion is permitted before 4 months of pregnancy as, after this period, the foetus is thought to become a living soul, although it is still permitted after 4 months for reasons of rape or when the mother's life is in danger.

In Hinduism and Sikhism, particularly in India, pro-life is the most common stance although it is unclear as Hindu theologians believe that personhood begins at three months of pregnancy, implying that abortion would possibly be permitted before this time. Most abortions in India are carried out for reasons of sex selection, favouring the birth of boys as girls are not seen to be of as an equal status as boys. Clearly, this idea is morally very wrong as gender equality would be a fundamental right in a moral society.

In Judaism, there is a more liberal approach although there is some controversy from various Jewish leaders. Some Jewish pro-life activists agree with the same permitted cases as the Christian groups mentioned. An interesting concept is that of Efrat, a pro-life organisation in Israel, which aims to raise funds to relieve the financial and social pressures on pregnant women so that they would be less likely to seek abortion. Finding solutions to problems rather than simply making laws to forbid things is a more positive, constructive way to tackle such issues.

The religious perspectives, whereas they are certainly not to be ignored, have to be said not to have any evidence that they are the truth, especially considering that there are conflicting views within each religion.

Incidentally, as in the USA, protesters who use violent actions against abortion providers, such as arson and bombing of abortion clinics and even the murder or attempted murder of physicians leave themselves in the position of being pro-life yet anti-life at the same time. This hypocrisy implies a 'do as I say, not as I do' attitude which, in the case of murder has them effectively protesting against the very act that they are guilty of themselves.

The reasons for pro-choice are, of course, much more liberal, and follow the notion that it is a human right to decide on something that could have a very negative impact on the lives of both the parents and the children in question. Things to take into account are, again, the health of the mother and the possible danger to her life, the health of the foetus that may show signs of physical or mental deformity or illnesses and diseases and the idea that if abortion was illegal then those women who were desperate to seek one would have to resort to illegal and potentially life-threatening abortions in so-called back street clinics.

There are also issues such as the mothers being the victims of rape, having no financial security to raise the potential child adequately, the failure of methods of contraception leading to accidental pregnancy and pregnancy happening at a time in the mother's life that would make it detrimental to keep the child, such as in the cases of depression, the interruption of the career, relationship breakdown and others.

So far, we can see that there are commonalities between the two groups. Because of this, it would be possible to arrive at a compromise as the reasons for allowing abortion from religious perspectives have moral aspects, as do those of pro-choice groups.

The first criteria that could be agreed on for the legality of abortion are:

4. In the case of the mother being a victim of rape.
5. Where the mother or the infant's life is in danger from continued pregnancy.
6. Evidence of severe deformity of the child.
7. Evidence that the unborn child will suffer from an incurable disease (such as AIDS) or a condition that will be severely detrimental to their life because of constant pain or the inability to ever look after themselves independently.

There are other criteria that could be accepted by both groups mentioned that should not be too controversial. If the mother is considered to be too young to be pregnant (e.g. 14 years old), abortion should be allowed as she would probably be too immature to cope with the burden of raising a child. The actual age of 'consent for abortion' is one that should be discussed and agreed upon, although 16 years of age is a reasonable suggestion as to a criteria for warranting abortion.

In terms of other criteria which would cause arguments, such as simply not wanting to be pregnant or contraception failure, which could be argued against with the judgement that they should have been more careful and they should have to live with the consequences, the other side of it shows a very different story. If the female became pregnant 'by accident' and didn't want to have the child for whatever reason, there is the very real possibility that they wouldn't bring up the child in a satisfactory manner. The unwanted child may be unloved and not cared for and as a result is likely to live an unhappy life that could lead to undesirable consequences, such as violent behaviour, drug addiction, crime and other such behaviours that would not only be to their disadvantage, but to the disadvantage of the community that has to suffer with such badly-developed people. What is more morally correct, to terminate a very undeveloped foetus that has no experiences of life or to have hundreds of thousands of people that were unloved, unwanted, abused, rejected and therefore potentially dangerous to themselves and to society?

A report in the Guardian stated that in 2009, the Mary Stopes abortion helpline received 350,000 calls from females in the UK.[1] What if 200,000 of those didn't meet the criteria of pro-life groups to permit them to have an abortion? This is a very real issue that could have a significant effect on society, along with the fact that the population would also be rising more rapidly, making it more difficult to maintain economic development (that is, the overall development of human life).

The same article was about the introduction of television advertisements for abortion services late at night. This raised controversy with pro-life groups. Michaela Aston, a spokeswoman for the anti-abortion campaign group Life stated "I can only express utter disbelief that this is being allowed, given the opposition to abortion advertising expressed during the recent public consultation."

The important point to consider regarding this reaction is that that is only their opinion. Abortion is legal in the UK so just because she didn't agree with it doesn't mean that it breached any laws or rights currently in place. Raising awareness and giving support to those females who have worries about being pregnant is a positive step. It helps them to be able to find a calm, legal solution to their dilemmas. As long as the adverts were not controversial in any way, there is no problem with allowing their transmission.

In terms of the time period where abortion can be performed, most are carried out in the first 12 week period (the first trimester), although in some cases it is still safe to do so during the second trimester up to 20 weeks of pregnancy. In other (later) instances, it would be the doctors' decisions as to whether an abortion would be safe to carry out.

Abortion is something that, for many reasons, is something that should be legal if we are going to develop society more effectively. Compromises can be reached as long as we use morality for the basis of discussions.

1. www.guardian.co.uk/media/2010/may/19/abortion-advertising-television-uk

Euthanasia

Euthanasia is the practice of ending the life of something or some creature to relieve pain and suffering. It is different from suicide in that an authority has to make the decision on whether or not a person should be allowed to die. There are various forms of euthanasia which need to be reviewed before deciding on whether it should be legalised or not. Involuntary euthanasia on any person or group of people is illegal worldwide and is effectively the same as murder as it is the ending of someone's life against their will. This means that if the person in question cannot give consent and the parents or nearest of kin do not give consent, then it cannot be administered. Voluntary euthanasia should be legal but certain criteria have to be met before it can be performed. Before we get to the criteria, we must look at why it should be legal.

A person who is suffering from a terminal illness which causes pain psychologically and physically or who suffers from an irreversible medical condition and who is in a relatively stable state of mind to give consent for voluntary euthanasia should be the only person who can decide on their own life.

For example, a person suffering from a form of cancer that cannot be cured and will lead to increasing internal damage as the disease progresses and to whom it causes considerable distress has the right to decide on their own fate, be it life or death. No doctor or other figure of authority can lay claim to that patient's decisions concerning their life. Any individual in any perceived position of power has no relevance to the fate of the sufferer in this kind of case where recovery is currently impossible.

To attempt to overrule a patient's decision on their own life is to play God. Who can decide if someone else should be allowed to decide on another's fate in this way? One could argue that a position whereby the figure of authority is deemed to have more knowledge or expertise on the case should be the one to decide. But this again is playing God. Nobody can forcefully overrule the consent of the sufferer.

However, this does not mean that anyone suffering from a terminal illness can simply say that they want to die and they will then receive a lethal injection. This is where the criteria have to be met, which are as follows:

1. The person in question is of a stable mind to give consent for euthanasia. The minimum age to be able to give one's own

consent therefore could be thirteen years of age. If they are below this age, then the following conditions must all be met.

2. The person in question is suffering from a terminal illness for which there is currently no cure and is suffering from considerable physical pain. Alternatively, the person has a medical condition, such as paralysis which means they are largely dependent on other carers which causes considerable psychological pain and possible physical pain.

3. If the person in question is not in a state to give consent for euthanasia but they meet criterion number 2, then at least two of the next of kin (if as many as two are available) must give signed consent.

4. The person in question or the next of kin must receive regular counselling from a qualified professional over a period of at least two months (if possible, depending on the medical problem) after which the professional must give an unbiased judgement that the person in question gives justifiable consent.

5. If all of the criteria are met, then the person in question may be granted euthanasia in one of the following ways:

A consenting doctor will be allowed to give a lethal injection if the patient chooses this method. If a consenting doctor cannot be found, the patient may be given a strong potion that is known to cause death in a relatively painless fashion. Otherwise, if the patient is physically able to do so, they may administer an injection, either manually, or from a device which can be attached to a part of their body that is appropriate to receive a lethal injection and they can initiate the device to perform the injection.

In any of these ways, there must be at least two other professionals present to guarantee that the procedure was carried out correctly by signing their names on the relevant documentation.

Therefore, it is paramount that every person is the only person who can decide on their own life. It is a human right to be allowed to apply for euthanasia. But equally importantly, to be able to finalise one's own decision, the person will be helped and encouraged not to opt for euthanasia. It is certainly not a preferred end to one's own life unless it is entirely justified and unquestionably meets the above criteria.

It should also be stressed that other people should not pass judgement on the person who chooses euthanasia. Nobody else can know what the person in question is or was suffering. This is an individual and personal experience that can only be truly understood and felt by the person in question. Morally speaking, nobody else can make the decision about another person's right to die if the person is of sound mind to be able to choose to do so. Similarly, the next of kin must not be judged if they are the ones to make the decision about a relative who is unable to decide, as other people cannot experience what the next of kin are or were experiencing.

This point is also fundamental regarding any opposition to euthanasia on religious grounds. It must be respected that people have different beliefs which are as valid as each others' (as long as the beliefs do not involve the suffering of others). If a person who wishes to receive euthanasia follows or does not follow a religion, judgement cannot be passed by another person as all people are equal and cannot claim that they have more authority on such issues than another person. Any attempt to do so goes against human rights and is neither permitted nor will it receive any official attention. If a person wishes to receive euthanasia but family members who are religious try to stop the practice from taking place because they think it is against God's will would not have the power to change the decision of the sufferer as this is an example of not allowing this particular human right.

A person who chooses not to receive euthanasia because of their religious beliefs is permitted to live until they believe it is their time to die. This is, of course, acceptable as there is no question of requesting euthanasia. Again, no-one else can claim the right to make the decision for them.

The controversy that has surrounded euthanasia has included opponents feeling that it is the same as assisted suicide or involuntary murder. Regarding the former, the difference must be made clear that yes, it is a form of suicide, but for very specific reasons which have been explained. It cannot be legally administered for anybody wishing to die and it has a very strictly defined set of criteria that must be reached.

Regarding the latter, as already explained, this would equate to involuntary euthanasia, which would not be legal anyway.

With animal euthanasia, this is an area that has not received much controversy and the 'putting down' of animals is usually seen to be 'for the best'. The reason why there is such a difference between the cases of humans and animals is likely to be due to the fact that species instinctively want their members to survive wherever possible and due to our mental capacity and reasoning skills, we see it as a more difficult area to agree with.

However, this has to be seen as being due to the difficulty that people often have with the letting go of their relatives or friends, and the anguish that their death may cause to them personally. Human attachments can be strong but ultimately, the relatives or friends have a selfish desire to not want to suffer themselves, and if this is the case, they need to receive counselling to help them overcome this psychological difficulty.

Whereas we should be of the viewpoint that human (and other animal) life should be valued in all circumstances, sometimes the experience of one's life is not free from significant suffering and we should respect that it is sometimes more moral to allow someone to die if they have no chance of overcoming their predicament.

Prostitution

Prostitution has been recognised for millennia as an activity or a profession but is one that has been a controversial topic for many governments. Currently, a few countries give prostitution a fully legal status and some countries either decriminalise it or ignore it. Other countries view it as fully illegal so around the world it is an issue which has not reached widespread agreement.

Understandably it is seen as taboo. Being a very personal practice, humans have come to be largely secretive about discussing it, especially in detail. Not until recently has sex and the sex industry been viewed more liberally and traditionally in many countries; it has been a topic that is not seen as one for everyday discussion unless with close friends or partners. Religious groups generally view prostitution as wrong and punishable but the fact of the matter is that it will never disappear as an activity. For this reason, we need to investigate why the legality of it should be considered.

Humans are, in general, sexually active creatures and for different reasons to most other animals. It is not simply the instinct to reproduce that makes people want to have sexual activities. Of course, the level of desire differs greatly among people but on the whole it is a popular and sought after activity. Due to the behaviour patterns, social skills and social etiquette of many societies, it is not always easy to find a partner with whom to engage in what is seen as the most intimate interpersonal actions. Therefore, the desire to engage in sex is sometimes sought after by way of finding a prostitute to fulfil the desire. Similarly, some partners in a relationship may no longer desire the other partner but still want to have intercourse, thus do likewise.

As much as some individuals or groups may condemn the act of sex for non-reproductive reasons or may condemn prostitution as a concept or practice, the number of people who seek the services of prostitutes will always remain notable enough to maintain the numbers of prostitutes working legally or illegally.

In the current permissive society of the western world, sexual activity has become less of a taboo and the status of women as sexual objects has become more prevalent through vacuous TV series and films, not to mention the vast majority of pop music videos and pornography on the internet, which prey on the wantonness of those men who will happily look at it if it is there to be seen. As a study into why men use prostitutes was conducted to interview subjects to find out their opinions on why they paid for sex, 32% of 398 responses denoted that it was "to satisfy their immediate sexual urge, for entertainment or for pleasure." 20% said it was because they can't get what they want sexually and emotionally in their current relationship and 15% wanted convenience, no commitment and no emotional connection.[1]

There has undoubtedly been a decline in moral decency in recent decades; sexual symbolism has become more mainstream (and of course if you can get people's attention that way, there is always a way to make money from it). However, this is not to say that sexual activity is wrong. But just believing that one should be able to get it when it's wanted is a lack of self-control and weakness (exacerbated by the capitalist model, as previously discussed). If sexual activity is conducted responsibly, there is no problem with it. The difficulty is that it is a very exciting thought for very many people.

So when we accept that this is a fact of human life, reluctantly or otherwise, it makes sense to legalise prostitution in society. However, for many reasons which will be explained, there need to be many conditions met for it to function as an appropriate profession.

Firstly, with the prevalence of sexually-transmitted illnesses (STIs), especially incurable ones such as HIV and AIDS, prostitutes must have regular tests to determine that they are clean of contagious infections that can result through sexual intercourse. For this to be effective, they would require a test every calendar month.

But how could these be checked and enforced? Institutions such as brothels or sex clubs would need to be privately available for the act of prostitution. They would only be privately owned and managed so that it is not seen as a state profession, to help opponents of the practice accept that it is not directly linked with the government. This would then lead to the official status of prostitution as a form of work, for which they would receive income legally and have to pay tax on. The institutions additionally would need to pay corporate tax which is high enough to prevent superfluous profits but low enough for them to keep the business running comfortably.

Legally employed prostitutes would be required to show documentation of their blood tests and other relevant tests at a clinic every month. Failure to do so would first lead to a warning, but after three omissions they would lose their job. To ensure that prostitutes would not want this to happen and resort to working illegally, their work conditions would have to be beneficial to them.

These conditions would include the security of the staff employed by the institution, who would be able to monitor customers, discounts for receiving their medical tests and the comfort of working in a safe environment. To aid the security of the establishments, tax breaks would be provided for the owner(s) to install closed circuit television (CCTV) cameras at the building's entrance and in the reception area. Rules can be enforced to use contraception and to prohibit aggressive or violent behaviour towards the employees. And with the legal status of their profession, the workers would not feel anxious about being caught as they would if they worked illegally.

There would also be rules about how the institutions can function. They would not be able to use signs, writing or pictures of any kind on the façade of the building to advertise the business but would only be allowed to display a small symbol that would show the specific purpose of the building. This would have to be accompanied with a certificate to show that it is legally recognised. Thus, the general public would not be exposed to any writing or images that may offend some people. They would be allowed to advertise their business in newspapers, other publications or via the internet but only to show the symbol and the address, no other details would be permitted. Whereas other workers would have legal status in such institutions, pimps of any description would be illegal, either inside or outside a recognised establishment and would be heavily penalised.

The interior of the establishments would need to be kept clean and healthy and would be open to regular checks from the authorities which could lead to closure and loss of business if the levels of cleanliness are not maintained after three written warnings.

For the safety of the employees and to help keep undesirable or under-age people away from the premises, the front door would have to be locked and only unlocked after the person on duty in the reception has seen the potential customer via CCTV and is willing to allow them to enter.

For the customers, the following conditions are applicable:

The prices of services and times can be set by the owners but they must be displayed in the reception. Payment must be given before entering the room to engage in the chosen activities. The activities that are available can be seen in print for each prostitute as some employees would be willing to engage in different activities to others. If the customer desires, they may receive physical pain or degradation if the prostitute is willing to administer it. Physical pain or any type of degradation may not be given to the prostitute and any attempt to do so could lead to dismissal of the customer without refund or, if need be, the arrest of the offending customer. Customers would not be required to give any personal details or identification for the right of personal privacy.

What would be the implications for the problem of human-trafficking? As legally employed prostitutes would need to be registered, their identification cards and work permits would need to be provided, therefore keeping a check on any immigrants that come forward for this kind of employment. This doesn't mean that women couldn't be trafficked to be used as illegal prostitutes but as it would have a legal status, there would be far less of a demand for illegal prostitutes if clients knew they would not be in danger of breaking the law by visiting legal establishments. So the implications of legalising prostitution would potentially be beneficial to the aim of eliminating the trade of human-trafficking for this reason.

Using recent estimates for the number of prostitutes working in countries where it is legal, there could be as few as 1 prostitute per 1000 inhabitants (The Netherlands) to 1 per 300 (Czech Republic). Therefore, in a population of 50 million, there could be between 50,000 and 100,000 legally employed prostitutes working in institutions that all pay tax to the country.

This would mean that a significant amount of money could be additionally obtained to benefit the country (potentially hundreds of millions of Euros/ pounds/ dollars a year) rather than keeping prostitution illegal, unsafe and the money that is made from it separate from the Gross Domestic Product, instead of being used to aid public spending that may otherwise be lower than required.

We have to face facts and think of what would be the best solution for the prostitutes, victims of human-trafficking, people who feel they need to meet their sexual needs, no matter what (when their alternative could be rape if laws were brought in to punish clients of prostitutes), the amount of STIs prevalent, and the economy.

1. Men Who Buy Sex. Melissa Farley and Julie Bindel. www.eaves4women.co.uk/Documents/Recent_Reports/Men Who Buy Sex.pdf

Weapons

The use of weapons has always been a controversial issue throughout the world and the argument for the ownership and accessibility of weapons will be discussed in this chapter.

Firstly, knives and other similar objects such as swords or axes should be illegal to be carried in public. This law is applicable regardless of size or perceived level of danger. Similar objects which are to be used as tools may be transported in public as long as they are placed in a container which renders them inaccessible for use, such as a sealed plastic package or larger container in the case of distribution to shops.

Bladed objects can be used at home for various standard cutting activities but certain types of knives and swords may not be owned or kept by any individual. These are the types of implements that have been designed as weapons such as hunting knives, knives with serrated edges or any other knife that is not seen as a having typical design to be used for home cutting activities.

Whereas this law does not permit certain types of knives, the use of any knife to attack a human or any other animal is illegal and will leave the attacker susceptible to punishment by law. Similarly, attacking any human or other animal with any type of weapon is prohibited and will lead to punishment by law.

As the use of some bladed objects may be necessary to kill animals for food, the ownership and use thereof are subject to the ownership of a licence for doing so, which will state the limited ways in which the implements can be used.

Regarding the issue of gun and ammunition ownership, drawing on the gun laws of many countries, there are some countries where it is permitted to own and use a gun under certain conditions such as hunting or in licensed shooting clubs. Other countries allow the ownership of many other types of guns. This would not be so under a moral government.

It would be generally illegal for anyone outside of the military to own or to handle an active gun. Persons employed by the military can have access to state owned weapons for training and in the case of defending the country from a foreign attack. This is also the only way that anyone would be allowed to have access to and use live ammunition.

Hunting of any kind is illegal. The reason for this is that it is inhumane and morally unacceptable to kill any animals for personal entertainment. No other animal is capable of using weapons and few have the instinct to attack humans. Therefore, to make the situation equal for all living creatures, humans should be prohibited from the murder or attempted murder of another animal.

In the case of hunting to protect domesticated animals such as farm animals, it would still be illegal to own or use any type of gun or live ammunition. It is simply the humans' responsibility to ensure that the farmland cannot be entered by predatory animals such as foxes and if they choose not to ensure that their land is protected, they can do nothing but accept that they may suffer losses of livestock due to their own ineffective protection. As stated previously, other animals are driven by their instincts to hunt for food and that is their right due to the limited capacity of their brains. Humans can have no opinion or say on changing these instincts and we have to accept that is part of nature.

It was said that it would be generally illegal to own a gun or live ammunition. Certain guns would be permitted for use at shooting clubs which have been given a licence. All guns used at such clubs must always be kept at the clubs and it is not permitted that they can be taken away, except for the reason of repair. Absolutely no live ammunition would be permitted at any shooting club. Shooting clubs could only be used to shoot at inanimate objects such as standard targets that have no explosive potential.

The reason why no person may otherwise own a gun or live ammunition is simply because of the immoral nature of doing so. Guns were invented for the sole reason of killing. It is merely a by-product that shooting has become a sport. It is widely agreed that the worst crime is to kill another human being and guns are manufactured mostly with this in mind. Some people (especially in countries where it is legal to own guns) may argue that we need guns to protect ourselves but the question is "To protect ourselves from what?" The bottom line of this argument is 'other people that own a gun'. This is where the problem lies. It is circular. If one believes that many people carry guns in public then they feel that they must own a gun to protect themselves from this threat. There is no justifiable argument to say that there is anything positive about owning a gun. Having the potential to kill someone quickly is about as negative as one can get. In the initial stages, there would be a gun amnesty which is mandatory. Anyone found still owning a gun after the end date of the amnesty would be liable to be punished according to the law that comes into place.

However, if we remove guns and their availability, we can take a major step in the level of fear of ordinary citizens as well as reduce the number of gun-related crimes. To do this will inevitably create a larger black market of gun smuggling and sales. This is a problem that cannot be ignored. This would require police investigations to try to locate those people who are responsible for any continuation of a black market of this kind. It would also require that very tough penalties would be put in place to aim to deter individuals from becoming involved in the illegal sale and distribution of guns. If found guilty of mass distribution and/ or smuggling of guns, a penalty of life imprisonment with a minimum sentence of thirty years could be given. If an individual is involved on a smaller scale, such as the illegal sale of a single gun then a minimum sentence of ten years in prison would be given. Steps such as these long prison sentences would help to deter at least some of the people involved in this activity.

Another factor in the high level of gun crime is the amount of coverage in the media that it receives. Gun crimes and especially murder command high priority in the news. Mass murders such as school shootings get even more air-time. The reason that this is a problem is that it inspires others to do the same. Individuals who are at a stage in their life where they may be volatile to a point of committing a similar crime may take inspiration to copy the crime or try to do it on a larger scale. This is the sensationalist problem that the media in general is guilty of. Such coverage can make certain types of killings fashionable for certain people.

What this would mean in terms of aiming to lower the amount of gun crime is that the media would be very limited to how much of such incidents they could report. They should only be allowed to state when and where a murder took place, the number of people that were killed and information about the killer to aid their capture by the police. No other information would be permitted by any type of media. If so, the company responsible would be subject to a significant fine for each instance that they step over the limits of reporting. We must be very careful about potentially giving other people ideas of how to carry out such crimes as well as delivering such negative news stories with the frequency that they currently are.

On a related note, it would also be illegal to manufacture and sell toy weapons. This may seem like a harmless form of play for children but even the idea of play-shooting/ killing is immoral. We should not encourage the idea that harming other people is in any way entertainment. To allow this kind of activity through retail products gives the impression that it's all right to pretend to kill. Such an attitude should not be accepted. Children can become more open to the idea of obtaining weapons that actually do harm others, such as air pistols, and the more they see the use thereof as acceptable, there is the possibility that as they grow up, they will be tolerant to the idea that it's fine to have a real gun. This is something that we should try to avoid when aiming to create a more moral society.

Advertising

The problem with advertising is one that has been briefly mentioned earlier in this book. It is an issue that needs to be looked at carefully if we are going to improve the level of well-being of everyone.

The advertising industry works with the objective to make as much money as possible for their business clients. Working under the free market system, this leaves it with a lot of freedom to try to convince the public that they should buy their products. Lies, deceit and delusion are very much a part of many companies' strategies to achieve this goal. As we live in a very materialistic world, many of the products that we buy are ones that will not provide us with any real benefits, in terms of our overall development. We shall look at different sectors to try to arrive at laws that are required for advertising.

Fashion and accessories are a prime example of this materialism. Adverts appear on TV, the internet and in printed form with the aim of making people believe that these products will do them good. They often use celebrities or beautiful models (usually both of these groups will have had their photos 'enhanced' to achieve an image of perfection) so that the public will want to aspire to look like them. Already, we have a moral problem in that the public are fed propaganda as to how the ideal person should appear. It comes in such large quantities that some people will be left feeling that this is true; that to be successful, they have to look beautiful. From what we have forced upon us through celebrity magazines and programmes, it appears that the most successful women are beautiful and dressed in amazing clothes and jewels. The delusion here is that some people think that this is the measure of success. So they feel they should emulate them to try to achieve a similar state of well-being.

However, this is not true well-being. Well-being, as you will hopefully have picked up on by now is a state where one has enough financial security to not have to worry about covering costs, having good relationships with friends, family and the community, having a job and interests that bring satisfaction because one feels a real purpose with doing them and enjoying one's leisure time in a way that is not an example of escapism. How can buying and wearing an elegant dress or a diamond ring contribute to any of this? Obviously, it can't. It is not going to change any of the above factors in one's life in any way.

So, what does the buying of these types of products do for the customer's benefit? A common answer would be that it makes them feel good, or they feel more confident when having a more attractive appearance. But, confident to do what? To find a meaningful job? To improve one's relationships? Both of these things depend on how you are as a person, not what you look like. You can't get a better job because of wearing fashionable clothes, you need to have qualifications or relevant experience and be able to demonstrate that you could perform well with that kind of work. Your relationships with people are not going to improve unless your character is going to improve with it; and fashionable products are not going to be the crucial factor that makes that happen.

So, in short, the fashion industry does nothing meaningful for us. Yet, it is a massive industry that thrives because of its ability to deceive vast quantities of the general public (the celebrities that wear designer brands are actually paid to do so, not necessarily because they want to wear them). But the general public is not paid to do so, quite the opposite. As I mentioned before, the public actually becomes the advertising for the companies by displaying logos on their clothing to promote them. Such logos are seen as a status symbol. But a status symbol for what? What does one actually achieve by showing other people that they wear X brand jeans or trainers? They show that they wear X brand jeans or trainers. And that's it. There is nothing more that is gained by the person in question. But there is something lost and that is, of course, their money. And most of it goes to the fashion houses (via the retailers and manufacturers).

Therefore, this highly immoral industry needs to be regulated. They should not be free to advertise their products in ways that are judged to be delusional, as in offering a false ideal to people that they would benefit from their products. The adverts that they create would have to go through a advertising standards authority (as are already in place in some countries) before they could be used in any media. This would provide a deterrent to advertisers so that they would have to work through a set of regulatory rules, otherwise their adverts would be completely rejected. If companies decided to air them anyway, say on the internet, they would be liable to pay a substantial fine (something like $500,000) and subsequently have those adverts banned and removed.

The full list of criteria needed would have to be very detailed and precise and it is not necessary to try to list them here as the principles behind such a law give the reader the starting point to understand how and why these laws should be implemented.

The beauty and cosmetics industry would have to follow similar principles in its advertising as it, too, uses the power of deceit and lies even more so. I wrote about such things as anti-ageing products earlier, which are nothing but pure lies. Other products which also represent the 'cult of the body' ideal would be very tightly regulated so that any claims that they make have to be independently scientifically proven before any advertising can be considered. If the potential products cannot be shown to do what they are claimed to, they would not even be allowed to go on sale. This is another deterrent to convince companies that it would not be worth their time or money if it is unlikely that the products would pass the stringent tests necessary for them to be allowed to enter the marketplace.

Again, photo manipulation would be prohibited, as would slogans, such as 'beauty is confidence', that are completely unsubstantiated lies.

Regarding other fashionable items, such as electronic gadgets, the advertising companies would be restricted to delivering the facts about their products (e.g. the size, capacity, speed, etc.) and not how it would change people's lives in any way. There would also be stringent regulations for this sector so that the claims made are truthful and clear to understand. Simply stating that a product is the best or the fastest would not be allowed, nor would be the use of complicated terminology that the majority of the public would not understand.

The food and drinks industry would not be allowed to promote their products in such a way as to make them seem like there are the 'coolest' ones to buy. This would be an example of deceit that would lead to the adverts' rejections before they were due to be aired.

I have also mentioned that regulations should be in place to put pressure on companies to reduce the likelihood that they will make available products that prey on the weaknesses of people. If the product is judged to be of no real nutritional value, such as chocolates and carbonated drinks, they could even face not being allowed to advertise them at all, as well as having their corporate tax rate raised so that it is not in the company's interest to keep manufacturing them as they are. The idea would be that the companies would be encouraged to improve their products, for example by removing chemical additives that aren't necessary for the human body but instead possibly cause the products to be addictive, or by reducing the fat content so that they can be advertised (with mandatory information of the fat content).

Cigarette and other tobacco products would not be allowed to be advertised in any way, as is already in place in the UK, as, of course, they have not just no health benefits but they are harmful to health. More on this issue can be found in the chapter on Drugs.

Alcohol is one that is still currently allowed to be advertised but in a more regulated sense than in the past. Reasons for this include aiming to curb the amount of alcohol that people drink and also to protect children from seeing adverts for alcohol. According to CQ Researcher in 1992, by the time teenagers reach driving age they will have seen 75,000 ads for alcohol. Therefore, younger people will have been influenced by these adverts and are more likely to experiment with under-age drinking. Whereas one might argue that it is unfair for moderate drinkers to be prevented from seeing adverts for alcoholic drinks, there is the more pressing issue of heavy drinking and its affects on society and individuals. Television adverts that show, for example, a group of people having the time of their life while they are drinking beer would not be permitted as this is an unverifiable claim, even if it is not made explicitly. One way of restricting this type of advertising is by only allowing short, five-second adverts that show the product, show the alcohol content and have a simple slogan that does not have the power to convince people that they should drink it.

Advertising to children under 12 is something that has already been banned in Sweden and Norway. In the UK, Greece, Denmark and Belgium it is restricted. There are many good reasons as to why this should be so. The European Union has set out minimum provisions on advertising to children and its EU Audiovisual Media Services Directive[1] has the following rules:

Advertising shall not cause moral or physical detriment to minors, and shall therefore comply with the following criteria for their protection:

a. it shall not directly exhort minors to buy a product or a service by exploiting their inexperience or credulity;

b. it shall not directly encourage minors to persuade their parents or others to purchase the goods or services being advertised;

c. it shall not exploit the special trust minors place in parents, teachers or other persons;

d. it shall not unreasonably show minors in dangerous situations

In addition:

e. Children's programmes may only be interrupted if the scheduled duration is longer than 30 minutes

f. Product placement is not allowed in children's programmes.

g. The Member States and the Commission should encourage audiovisual media service providers to develop codes of conduct regarding the advertising of certain foods in children's programmes.

This is a comprehensive and strict set of rules that ought to be in place in every country, whereby any breach of them would result in a substantial fine and removal of the adverts.

There are other ways that companies can advertise their products or services, such as telemarketing or through door to door sale representatives. In this age of the internet where spam emails are considered illegal, the former two practices are no different. The public receives unsolicited calls to their phones or their door as spam is unsolicited emails to inboxes. Unless the public want to hear of such promotions, these practices should not be permitted. The likelihood is that if we want to find out about something, we will do it by ourselves. If we don't want to, we won't. Any unsolicited calls are an invasion of privacy and often, important contractual details would not be given by the people who are representing the companies, i.e. using deceit.

The reasons for needing such tight regulations in advertising are entirely for the well-being of the public. The public need to be protected from parting with their money for reasons that are not going to be of any benefit to them and along with this, it is planned that people's awareness of such delusions will encourage them to change their perspectives on life and pay more attention to improving their true well-being.

1. http://ec.europa.eu/avpolicy/reg/avms/index_en.htm

The Press

The press covers the responsibilities and regulations of the media in the following formats: newspapers, magazines, television, radio and official websites.

The press is, of course, bound to the law in that it has to provide truth in its coverage of events. To do this, a story deemed to be of interest to the general public must be reported in an objective manner. However, what the press sometimes states is in the public interest can actually be an exposé into someone's private life. This is the issue where regulation and restrictions need to be considered.

There can also be articles of commentary but they cannot be written or presented in an inflammatory manner to inflict a personal attack on the individual or group in question. There is a very moral reason for demanding such regulations: the public should be the ones to make up their own minds concerning the story reported. This would still allow the freedom of the public to make their opinions known, such as via news blogs as are currently in practice. This right of freedom of speech for the general public would not be limited, except in the case of moderators choosing to delete posts perceived to be unsuitable for moral reasons (racism, immature personal attacks, etc.). So far, it all seems as normal as is currently in place in (most of) the western world.

The main differences in the regulations of the press would be that they would not be able to sensationalise events to glorify the details of unpleasant events such as murders, rape, torture, physical attacks or those which are considered to be unpleasant for the population in general to be exposed to. There would simply be a limit on how such stories could be reported. The media would be allowed to report that a certain event had taken place but would not have the freedom to provide as many 'gory details' as they wanted. The reason for the media wanting to do this is simply to gain attention for their corporation. If it can sell newspapers or increase the number of viewers, they will sensationalise these stories as far as they can without stepping over what are currently considered to be the moral guidelines of broadcasting. This decency criterion is one that should be implemented for moral reasons.

There is a reason why this should be considered. Dangers lurk where there are people who have the potential to commit similar crimes. If every possible detail is given of how one person brutally murdered another, it can serve as a source of influence and inspiration. Take, for example, the school/ college shootings in the USA. In recent years, many copycat scenarios have taken place in various schools around the country and on a smaller scale have taken place in other countries. How can we explain why there has been a sudden rise in very much related crimes? Simply because those who had the potential to commit such brutal crimes got their inspiration from the excessive coverage that the media gave. To gain audiences, the media showed as many details as they could, using language in a way that is intended to shock people. Whereas most people are fortunately disgusted by such events, there is the very dangerous minority of people who receive very little positive attention in their lives and have become so resentful of the society in which they live that they like the idea of achieving notoriety for carrying out similar events. Even if they have to kill themselves at the end of their shooting spree, they know their name will be known across the country and even the world. Regardless of it being negative attention, at least they will have become 'famous' for a while and their names will be forever remembered by those families whose relatives were killed.

Therefore, to limit the details given can hopefully reduce the amount of 'copycat' acts as it will not be seen by the press to be as dramatic as it currently is.

This would therefore mean that freedom of speech is somehow limited in the media. Regarding the internet, this would be more difficult to achieve but these regulations would be in place for the official news sites. Any instance of the rules being broken would be subject to fines large enough to act as a serious deterrent for the media companies.

However, it is important to make clear that, in general, the freedom of the press would not be affected significantly. The U.S. Society of Professional Journalists and the International Federation of Journalists, as well as Reporters Without Borders, have wanted to define global ethics and standards in journalism so that "...public enlightenment is the forerunner of justice and the foundation of democracy. The duty of the journalist is to further those ends by seeking truth and providing a fair and comprehensive account of events and issues. Conscientious journalists from all media and specialities strive to serve the public with thoroughness and honesty. Professional integrity is the cornerstone of a journalist's credibility."[1]

Reporters Without Borders takes its inspiration from the 1948 Universal Declaration of Human Rights, which states that everyone has "the right to freedom of opinion and expression" and also the right to "seek, receive and impart" information and ideas "regardless of frontiers."[2]

Morally speaking, there cannot be any disagreement with these words and such principles would be agreed on by a moral government.

Another reason why sensationalist media coverage should be limited is that a lot of the news we see or read is bad news. We get extensive coverage of wars going on all across the world, tensions between governments that might lead to new fighting, and murders and robberies, etc.

It can of course be rightly argued that such events are in the public interest but there are also good things that go on around the world that deserve far more coverage than they currently get. Take the work of Greg Mortensen, for example, and his building of schools in Pakistan and Afghanistan. Or of community-building projects that have the intention of developing the well-being of society.

These types of events have the power to give hope and influence people as well as give them something positive to talk about. It would be recommended to get media corporations to sign an agreement which states that they will allocate a specified percentage of their news stories to more positive events. A number like 50% would not be too much to ask.

As the news is available to everyone and most people get to hear about current events, it should also be seen as a tool by which we can inspire people to become involved in projects that they like the sound of.

Going back to the dilemma of what is in the public interest, actual events that shape our lives and have a real impact on other people around the world are what we should be hearing about, not the personal lives of famous people. This is something that should be regulated as it breaks the Golden Rule. Tabloid newspapers and the 'gutter press' are the most likely culprits of this type of so-called journalism. To report that a famous person has cheated on their spouse or that someone was seen getting drunk in a club is simply an invasion of privacy. It is not difficult to ascertain whether it is in the public right to know or not – put yourself in their position. I don't need to ask you – you wouldn't like it.

It would need to be illegal to pry into people's private lives as long as what they have done is not illegal or affecting the public in any way. This comes back to the notion of decency and developing a moral society. Media corporations are not there to give us something to gossip about; this is not news. The same goes for paparazzi-style photography. It is an invasion of privacy. This was discussed in the 'Fame' chapter in Shaping A Society and simply cannot be permitted under a moral government.

Again, to place a deterrent for such media corporations – if the person has not given their written permission for the media source to print these types of stories or pictures but they were still printed, each time it occurred would incur a substantial fine that would make it not worth their effort to publish such articles.

However, this would still give attention-seeking individuals the right to sign a contract allowing a magazine to print their photos, as in the celebrity magazines. To attempt to prevent this, such publications could also be subject to the higher corporate tax bracket, as what they publish is of no real value to anyone.

Otherwise, there are no other regulations needed that aren't currently in place, but the press has a duty to contribute to the positive development of society, which means they can't be allowed to contribute to the delusional escapism that some people rely upon to take their minds of their own lives.

1. The Code of Ethics - Society of Professional Journalists: www.spj.org/ethicscode.asp

2. Reporters Without Borders: http://en.rsf.org/

Miscellaneous Laws

There are a few other points that I would like to make concerning other aspects of laws and rules that don't require their own chapters. Firstly, it should be made clear that the UDHR can be used as the basis for human rights regarding the law. The relevant articles are as follows:

6 - Everyone has the right to recognition everywhere as a person before the law.

7 - All are equal before the law and are entitled without any discrimination to equal protection of the law. All are entitled to equal protection against any discrimination in violation of this Declaration and against any incitement to such discrimination.

8 - Everyone has the right to an effective remedy by the competent national tribunals for acts violating the fundamental rights granted (them) by the constitution or by law.

9 - No one shall be subjected to arbitrary arrest, detention or exile.

10 - Everyone is entitled in full equality to a fair and public hearing by an independent and impartial tribunal, in the determination of (their) rights and obligations and of any criminal charge against (them).

11 - (1) Everyone charged with a penal offence has the right to be presumed innocent until proved guilty according to law in a public trial at which (they have) had all the guarantees necessary for his defence.

(3) No one shall be held guilty of any penal offence on account of any act or omission which did not constitute a penal offence, under national or international law, at the time when it was committed. Nor shall a heavier penalty be imposed than the one that was applicable at the time the penal offence was committed.

Note - The words in brackets are my alterations as in the UDHR, it usually refers to 'him' or 'his'. This is to make it clear that these rights refer to males and females equally.

These rights, which should be effectively constitutional, have to be followed at all times in a court of law or in the case of arrests.

The main point that I would like to bring up is the practice of lawyers. As there are prosecuting lawyers and defending lawyers, both sides always want to win their particular case. Their reputations and careers are at stake depending on how many cases they win and so it is in their own interests that they win at all costs. The problem there is that even if the defendant is clearly guilty, the defending lawyer will usually try to reduce the sentence or get some of the charges cleared, etc.. Whether this is a case of subverting the course of justice is seen as irrelevant (as long as their strategies are not too ridiculous).

The fundamental and constitutional point is that it cannot be legal for a lawyer to try to get their client off lightly. This often happens in the case of famous people who get their sentences reduced because they have a lot of money and are on TV a lot. This has to be completely outlawed, otherwise the judicial system will be seen a a mockery.

We need deterrents in place that are going to make such lawyers think twice about acting in this way. If the defendant is found guilty, in contrast to the lawyer's attempts to get them cleared, the lawyer would then be liable to their own criminal proceedings. If they are then found guilty of impeding the course of justice, they could lose their job (and the right to work in law again) and possibly be sentenced to prison, depending on the level that they were judged to have been acting against the truth and the law.

Mobile phone usage in vehicles

This needs to be addressed as, in recent years, it has become a problem, which has led to many accidents on the roads, causing both injuries and deaths. The problems are what the penalties should be and actually enforcing them.

First of all, it is right to say that it should be illegal to use a mobile phone while driving or riding any motorised vehicle. It affects one's concentration greatly, this has already been established.

In 2003, the University of Utah's psychology department did and interesting study to compare the effects of alcohol and of using a mobile phone while driving. The two groups of subjects (totalling 120) were tested on their total numbers of accidents, braking reaction times, braking force, speed and their distance from the car in front, in a driving simulation scenario.

The results were interesting: those under the influence of alcohol had no accidents while 10 of those speaking on the phone did. The braking reaction time was better for the drunk drivers than the phone users (888msec v 1022msec). The braking force was greater for the drinkers (69.% v 55.2%). Their average speed was practically the same (52.8mph v 53.2mph) and the following distance was better for the phone users (28.5m v the drinkers' 26.5m).

After controlling for driving difficulty and time on task, the study concluded that mobile phone drivers exhibited greater impairment than intoxicated drivers.[1]

In the UK, currently, there is a small monetary fine of £60 if one is caught using a hand-held phone while driving as well as having three points on the driving licence. Other countries like Portugal have a complete ban on mobile phone use while driving, but I can tell you from experience that as the law is largely ignored by the police, you are likely to see a driver holding a phone to their ear in about every third car that goes past.

The deterrent needs to be a lot tougher when we are talking about an act or irresponsibility that can cause deaths. £60 isn't going to be a huge dent in the pockets of many people in the UK, but £300 is going to make more people think twice and decide to pull over to the side of the road if they want to answer their phones. And if they caught for a second time, they could lose their licence for a month. Now that would not be worth risking for most people, especially if they need to drive to work every day. A third time could see a penalty of losing the licence for a year.

But it's not enough to say that these deterrents would do the job. The law needs to be enforced. If people know that they are unlikely to get caught, they will do what they want. It could be seen as too much of a burden for the police to be stationed on all busy road junctions, but we could use volunteers, who would need to be registered and licensed to have the authority to stop these guilty drivers. There could even be commission given to the volunteers, depending on how many guilty drivers they stop. It's a shame to say it, but when someone has something to gain from doing a certain activity, they are more likely to do it well.

Internet Laws

The internet is a difficult thing to regulate as its international status makes it difficult to put laws into place internationally. There needs to be a move for greater protection of under age users, further to what it already in place: parental control programs can be used to make certain sites inaccessible to under 18s, known as content-control software (or web filtering software) although there are methods to bypass these, such as searching in another language or using alternative protocols such as ftp or https. Content-control software is not only used by parents but also in workplaces and universities to restrict the types of sites that may be visited (workplaces understandably don't like their employees spending their work time playing games or hanging out on social network sites).

A more important aspect to try to address is protecting children from accessing adult content. As it is easy to visit many pornographic sites (e.g. by just clicking on the button that says "I am over 18"), I would propose a method of age identification. Normally, this would be easy to bypass but if these ID systems were seen to be as valuable as credit cards, where obviously you wouldn't want anyone else to know your details, people would be more protective of them. These would therefore have to be very stringent and traceable by authorities for people to want to keep them secret.

For example, if an adult had to use their ID to access all sites that are deemed to be adult-only content with their own special code number, it would need to be one that couldn't be hacked easily. They would have to enter their real name and PIN in the same way as one does for a credit card, although these would not be usable for payments, only for identification. In the case of hacking, there could be a system that traces the IP address of computers that used it. The user could set a list of IP addresses that they use (for example if they use their home desktop computer and their laptop from different locations) and if their PIN was detected from another IP address, they would be alerted and action could be taken to try to trace who was illegally using it. This could also put their own blocks on other IP addresses if their PIN was set to be only valid from the locations that they set.

I can understand that people may have their reservations about this idea being invulnerable to hacking, but in general, the credit card system works well, even though there is some fraud that still happens.

Another more secure way of protecting one's ID comes from a online banking device used by most major banks. When one has entered their details, a numerical code is given. The user then inserts their card into their own electronic device that is like when you pay on your bank card in shops, enters the given numbers and then the device gives you another code that is generated by the first one. This new code is then entered into the website's identification system to verify that it is the correct user. Or a system whereby one is asked to enter specific digits taken from one's personal table of numbers when the program asks you to enter the number located at specified coordinate.

As banks use these types of verification systems already, it would not be difficult to determine which is the most effective and the simplest and quickest for the users.

To reduce the annoyance of entering your ID codes for every website, there could be a setting for the user that is logged on to set the details once so that they are remembered and they don't need to keep doing it.

Of course, people would only be able to have such ID cards as these from their 18th birthday. All adult-content websites would need to use this system by international law and we could take great steps to protecting our children from becoming exposed to content that they are too immature to see.

There would need to be a guarantee that no personal information will be recorded and there will be no traceable activity which would infringe upon the rights of privacy.

File sharing

Another controversial issue on the internet is the illegal downloading of files such as music and films. Politicians have been very aggressive with trying to implement punishments for people who download songs with the intention of selling them or merely for downloading them for free. The problem is the disgust that people have expressed with regard to the amounts of the fines: The UK's Digital Economy Bill has introduced fines of up to £50,000 for criminal offences relating to copyright infringement as well as the users having their ISPs slowed down or even suspended.[2] When you put this against the £60 fine for endangering people's lives by driving whilst talking on a hand-held mobile phone, there is no way that such high amounts can be justified.

It is of course justified to try to protect the rights of musicians and other related people working in the music industry but there needs to be a compromise reached that people are going to respect. For example, the sales of new albums and singles mostly take place in the first one or two years, maybe continuing after subsequent releases that prompt people to buy previous releases. If it was decided that music is only saleable for the first five years after its original release, then became public domain and could be downloaded and shared for free, the incomes of recording artists would not be significantly affected and hopefully, the public would think it was fair to operate in this way. There doesn't need to be such severe monetary fines or punishments in place for people who download a few albums within this five-year period. A fine of £50 per album could be implemented with an upper limit of £500 for more than ten albums. It is highly unlikely that most people could afford to pay £50,000 fines and just because the musicians are not earning the money they would have done if the person had bought the album, it doesn't mean that they are 'losing' that money.

This 'five years until it becomes public domain' would give the public the freedom to download older material and it has the potential to change the mindset of people who then think it is acceptable to have to pay for the two or three albums released that are still within the five year limit. Not that it would not be legal for anyone other than those who own the rights to the music to sell anything that became public domain. As it would be freely available anyway, there would be no market for that but it is a point that needs to be clarified.

Record company executives may still argue that they can't re-release songs or albums as they would already be in the public domain. That, however, is not really an argument as re-releasing music is just a way of making more money; in the case of the music of an artist who has died or artists that no longer have the publishing rights to their own songs, the people who count would not be affected. Record companies could still re-release material with new packaging and so on but if the songs had been previously released, the public could make their own choices about buying them or obtaining them for free.

The same rules could apply to the film and TV industries: they are going to make most of their sales in the first five years of release – through cinema ticket sales and DVDs. After that, the content would become public domain with the same limitations of the music as described above.

We always have to look at both sides of the argument when there is a controversial topic to be resolved. A give-and-take procedure is needed if we are going to get agreement from both sides.

1. Strayer, David; Drews, Frank; Crouch, Dennis (2003). "Fatal Distraction? A Comparison of the Cell-Phone Driver and The Drunk Driver" (PDF). University of Utah Department of Psychology.
www.psych.utah.edu/AppliedCognitionLab/DrivingAssessment2003.pdf

2. Digital Economy Bill Copyright Factsheet November 2009
http://interactive.bis.gov.uk/digitalbritain/2009/11/copyright/

Section 4: Forming a Government

The Voting System

There are various voting systems in use around the world by which candidates are elected to positions of political power. The reason why there are different systems is that there has been debate over which is the fairest one to use.

At a basic level, the 'first past the post' system sounds the fairest: whoever wins the most votes gets elected. However, it is more complicated than that as countries typically divide the nation into its constituencies or states, which have a differing amount of influence depending on the population size of each constituency. Say, for example, constituency A has 50,000 people but constituency B has 5,000 people. Whichever political party won the majority or the most votes in A would be worth more than that of B, simply because it has 10 times the population. It would win more seats in the government because of this difference.

When a country is made up of over a hundred constituencies, this means that things could actually turn out to be very unfair. In the UK general election in 2005, Labour won 55% of the seats with only 35% of the votes because of this anomaly in the voting system.

So what would be fairer? Ian Stewart, writing for the New Scientist magazine in May 2010 found out that no current system is completely fair. Take the plurality system whereby voters rank the candidates in order of their preference. This, on the surface, sounds fairer as they don't just vote for one candidate but rank all of them in order. However, the mathematician Donald Saari showed that again, there is more to it than that. If 15 people are asked to rank their favourite drinks (M)ilk, (W)ine and (B)eer, it could turn out that 6 rank them M-W-B, 5 rank them B-W-M and 4 rank them W-B-M. Under the plurality system used in the UK, Canada and India, only the first choices would be eligible. In this example, milk would have won even though the other voters ranked milk as their least favourite. Also, the non-alcoholic drink would be the winner even though alcoholic drinks accounted for the majority of votes when combined. There would always be room for argument about its fairness when trying to select one overall winner.[1]

In the light of the 2010 UK general election, where a coalition had to be formed when no individual party won the majority of votes or the required number of seats to win outright, there was the suggestion that the alternative or preferential voting system would be better. This is used in the Australian House of Representatives and in some US cities.

To apply this to the above example, even though wine only won 4 first places, it won 11 second places so would get the greatest share of the vote, despite milk and beer gaining more first choices.

In the political realm, this could mean that the ordinarily third choice party would actually win the election because the voters who prefer the two main parties would prefer the smaller party to get in rather than the main rivals. It doesn't seem quite right that the overall second choice party should be the one that runs the government.

Proportional representation is thought to steer clear of such paradoxes entirely. This is when a party is awarded a number of parliamentary seats in direct proportion to the number of people who voted for it. The problem that it has is that it implies that there will be large, multi-representative constituencies which means that there is a great deal of division rather than having one overall constituency (as is used in Israel). The outcome of this in practice is that a coalition is more likely to be formed under this voting system, however, in theory, a fair and open-minded coalition of all parties would be better so that all representatives would be able to put forward their proposals and be listened to without prejudice against which party they represent. But in the current political times, this is only theory as the divisive nature of political parties will always be biased in this way. Favoured parties and those people with more influence due to their connections are more likely to get their proposals considered and taken on.

As Stewart concludes, there is no perfect system in place and it is unlikely that one would be able to be formulated where it is mathematically free of problems and delivers an accurate allocation of representatives all across a country.

So what should we do? Use the system that is the best of a bad bunch? Have people voting for political candidates who have been selected for us and whom they don't believe will deliver the actions that the general public actually need?

We are in a position where we don't have complete trust in the politicians that represent us. Positions of power are susceptible to hidden agendas and corruption. As has been stated, just because a political candidate 'says' they will address such and such an issue doesn't mean that they will do anything significant to bring about positive change.

The other big problem with the mathematical aspect of voting systems is that they are always looking to elect one person, leaving all other candidates out of the office where decisions are made. One person (or the team that they work with) is far less likely to come up with solutions that will attempt to make things fair for everyone. They know what they want to develop and they have the personal connections whereby they want to make things work for their friends, whose interests they will often put before those of the general public.

From this, we can see that simply voting for people is where the big problem lies. We can't trust our own species to be honest with us. But there is a way around this, that can be enforced by parliamentary law.

Instead of voting for people that we don't know, we should vote for policies that elected representatives have to attempt to deliver, regardless of their political party. When the policies have been proposed, adapted where necessary, and fine-tuned so that the majority agree with them, they would then form the basis of the work that has to take place in each constituency.

This is a step towards removing hidden agendas and corruption as the representatives have no choice but to follow the policies that the majority has decided it wants in place. They will have no real freedom to change what they have to accomplish, although depending on many circumstances like the specific needs of the local area, the types of industry in place and the level of unemployment, the action plans will need to be adaptable to some degree, providing that they still adhere to the principles stated in the policy in question.

Of course, this proposal doesn't mean that all corruption would disappear overnight. However, the people in a constituency can see for themselves if action plans are being followed effectively and the transparency that is necessary regarding the allocation of funds can identify why there might be discrepancies and they will have access to the records of accountability of the funds.

If it is decided that a representative is guilty of fraud, deceit, theft or any other aspect of corruption, they would be removed from office and be subject to prosecution in a court of law.

In the run-up to the 2010 UK elections, the website "Vote For Policies" was created for just this reason. With an ingenious way of finding out what people really want to happen, rather than who they would vote for, visitors would read through policies on nine major areas, such as health, education, immigration, etc. and would select the policies that they agreed with the most but would not know which party had proposed them.

This is far more democratic as it means that even if people agreed with the X party on some of their policies but not others, they would not have to just go along with those which they disagree with in the event of their winning the election. Instead, the elected representatives would have to carry out the set of policies that had been amalgamated from potentially all the parties' policies.

The results of the election ended with a coalition being formed between the Conservative and Liberal Democrat parties, replacing Labour in the position of government. But on the above website, after nearly 300,000 completed surveys as of June 2010, the party that would have gained the most votes was the Green Party with 23.66%. (2) In reality, the Green Party gained one seat in the houses of parliament.

By contrast, the Conservative Party gained 15.64%, the Lib Dems 17.83% and Labour 20.35%, so according to this political experiment, the third and fourth placed parties got to form a government.

When looking at the individual policies and their votes, the Conservatives only won in one area – Europe. Labour won in three areas, the Lib Dems two and the Green Party three.

This was a very interesting experiment that showed that even though people voted for the main three parties in the actual elections, if they had focused on the policies, their voting would have been extremely different which would of course have profound implications on how the country would be governed if policies were elected rather than people.

Therefore, I would propose that the best system of voting is the policy vote. It represents a democratic coalition whereby no party is likely to gain overall control, but this not what is not important anyway. The people don't know who they really want in power as there is no real level of trust in politicians these days; we have been consistently let down by whichever party is in the seat of power but the people do know what they want to happen. Irrespective of which party proposed it, the policy that is the most popular should be the one that is put in place.

However, we do still have a problem in that six parties (that were represented on the above website) are not likely to lead to a winning vote of over 50% (none of the policies or parties gained so much – the highest vote was for the Green Party's education policy with 35.49%). So we still have similar problems to the plurality system. How can this be resolved?

Well, whereas people cannot be merged with other people until they become as we want them, just as we would not get desirable results by mixing milk, wine and beer depending on how relatively popular they are, we can merge ideas to reach a compromise.

It is very unlikely that the various policies will be completely unique – there will be commonalities. This is the first way that we can reach a compromise; by finding those principles that are in common between the most popular ones. Those policies which should be considered are those which add up to more than 50% of the votes, otherwise it would be practically impossible to form a coherent coalition of policies from all six (in this case, in other countries it could be even more). For example, regarding education, the Green Party's policy (gaining 35.49%) would need to be refined with the Conservative's second place policy which gained 19.67% as these two add up to more than 55%.

From this, the two sets of policies would be examined to find what they have in common, how they are significantly different and how the smaller anomalies can be fine-tuned. If it takes the policies of three parties (or more) to be examined, then that is simply how it has to be. In this example, if it was proving difficult to find a compromise on a certain issue in education, the Green Party would be able to use their majority-vote factor to have the final say on what should be implemented.

When this process has been completed, the new policy can be put in place as a compromise that the general public have already shown their agreement with in the original voting. It would then be presented to the public so that they can debate it and decide if it is a fair compromise and as long as it doesn't differ too greatly and there is no opposition to the new version of it, it would become the policy that each constituency would have to follow and then adapt depending on its particular circumstances.

This system of voting effectively leaves separate political parties redundant as their overall set of policies are not what counts. The policy vote is far more democratic as the public are getting more of a say as to what will be done rather than who will get to be a member of parliament, simply because of the party that they represent. Additionally, different parties will have their policies selected to be the ones that are put forward for the compromise, so in the UK, the Greens and Conservatives might be the parties behind the education policy, but Labour, the Lib Dems and the Conservatives' policies would form the grounds of the policy compromise for immigration.

As this could be seen as a radical change to the voting system, it would be imperative that the public is provided with debates so that they can fully understand how it work. There would need to be pros and cons argued so that it would be democratically agreed upon for the new system of voting and hence, the new system of government.

This would, of course, be able to be done prior to a general election so that if the public agreed with it, it would then be implemented for the new era of government that it would bring about.

1. Electoral Dysfunction. Ian Stewart. New Scientist, May 2010.
2. Vote For Policies www.voteforpolicies.org.uk

The Formation of a Government

Political Parties and Opposition

"Government is nothing more than a national association; and the object of this association is the good of all, as well individually as collectively." Thomas Paine, Rights of Man (p.136)

To begin, we need to look at how political parties are formed and supported. In non-democratic societies there is generally only one (permitted) party and any opposition to that party can lead to punishment in various forms, such as imprisonment, torture, exile and execution. In democratic countries, there are usually multiple parties that are in a constant struggle to gain the majority's vote and to undermine their opposition. In many western countries we see established parties that are seen as the only realistic options. In the United Kingdom the Conservative party has historically fought against the Labour Party with minor threats from what is currently the Liberal Democrat party who have enough influence to have their voices heard but are perhaps never seen as being enough of a threat (until recently when the Liberal Democrats joined a coalition with the Conservatives to for a government) to encroach on the territory of the first two mentioned. In the United States of America there are fewer alternatives to the Republicans and Democrats that would be taken seriously by the people, or whose voices will be heard.

The power to be heard from these parties all depends on one thing – money. Political campaigns cost money and depending on who their friends are, they usually get enough backing from the party donations to be able to be seen as a powerful force. In return, those donating groups or individuals are highly likely to be rewarded and as the donators are often company executives or other 'people in high places'; they will be treated very leniently by the parties with whom they are connected, sometimes resulting in relaxed laws which would otherwise be implemented fully to those who are not connected to the companies or political parties. Hence, you scratch my back and I'll scratch yours.

I did, however, mention that this is what happens in 'democratic' countries. Here is our first problem. Whether a party claims to be democratic or more specifically, socialist, accepting money from their rich and therefore influential and powerful peers results in an enormous divide between the rich and the poor. We are still left with ruling classes. They may counter it by stating that the people have freedom of speech and freedom of the press (which has come under scrutiny for not being completely true but it has to be said that it is true to a degree) but even though the voices of the general public can be heard, they are not necessarily listened to. What happens is any public pressure to consider an issue may be taken on board but the outcome of it will ultimately depend on what the politicians and their rich friends want and would either benefit or suffer from. Under such systems of government, we are left with an extremely flawed version of democracy where the ruling class exercises control over the masses, between whom there is a divide so great that if you are at the poorer end, you are likely to have so few opportunities to succeed in life or unlikely to have your voice heard by anyone outside your circle of acquaintances. Democracy in this case is a nice sounding label but it is not correctly used.

So would the answer be to make it illegal to accept donations from the rich supporters? Making something illegal is never going to stop it happening. Those involved will always find a way to continue their donations undercover, whether it is an example of corruption or not. How about heavy penalties for those who make illegal payments? We must remember that the donors are likely to be extremely rich and to enforce a monetary penalty is probably not going to dent their profits even marginally. A prison sentence then? We have heard of rich businessmen going to prison for corruption charges but we don't get to see how they are treated when they are inside That is assuming that they are actually inside. Don't forget that they have friends in high places (meaning immoral, exploitative individuals who will certainly make it so that they will not have to suffer).

In a moral government, it would a kind of mixture of the two described systems. One party that still involves the others in the decision-making and working under purely democratic principles.

How could this work? Consider this: opposing political parties continuously slander one another simply because they are the opposition. In the Houses of Parliament in the United Kingdom, for example, it is irrelevant whether the opposition agrees or disagrees with the ruling party's policies or proposals, they simply feel they have to undermine the rulers simply because they are not on the same side. Power, greed, stubbornness, control. A lot of human behaviour is fundamentally flawed in that some people always want more power, more influence, more attention and more control. This is prevalent in the political system. Undermining the opposition is done with the intention of making themselves gain popularity with the public. Any little detail will be emphasised to try to gain the upper hand. It is very rare indeed that the opposition will look at the ruler's decisions and simply offer suggestions to improve them. The very process of discussions in parliament is little more than childish squabbles and bullying. To counteract this, a moral government is a one party system where the head of state is a variant of the presidential system. This was seen in the analysis of the voting system where it is irrelevant which party one is a member of as it is the policies that count.

This doesn't mean that it would be forbidden for any other political parties to exist, as this would infringe upon the right to freedom of speech. What it means is there should be no need for anyone to oppose the moralist party as, for one thing, opinions and proposals should be listened to from anyone who chooses to come forward with them, knowing that as long as they have a moral basis they will be considered, and for another, nobody should feel they are in opposition because if they do, their own morals are likely to be questionable.

The criteria of a moral government

How can we make it so that people – the general public and all politicians – would support the moral government? There are certain criteria to be met to ensure that this could be so.

Trust - We cannot rely on a government to resolve the problems of human conflicts as a government is made up of a relatively small number of people and human conflicts encompass everyone living within any given country. The responsibility is with the citizens, each and every one of them, to make a concerted effort to not react negatively to those at fault, to not criticize or look for revenge for an action that has left us disadvantaged in some way. The effort has to be one of forgiveness and peaceful offerings of help and support. It is important to remember at this point the Golden Rule – Do to others what you would like them to do to you. If you were at fault and caused a problem to someone, you would not want them to react angrily to you, to report you or to enact revenge upon you. When a person has a fault, this does not mean that the person *is* the fault. Outside influences will have caused them to behave in negative ways but they can be helped, they can reduce the amount or the impact of their faults. But they can only begin to see that it would be beneficial to themselves if other people don't label them as inherently bad. To offer a helping hand works wonders in starting to improve other people's behaviour. If they see that they are still being accepted and not rejected by a few people or society in general, they will have faith in themselves and with those who show their desire to help them. They will feel welcome in the community and the society as a whole if other people make it clear that by working together we can form a happier and more stable, more trusting society.

In theory, it may be difficult to understand that this type of behaviour will bring about peace but in the case of Gandhi's strivings, he was able to bring about equality for the Indian people in South Africa who, when he lived there were, treated as second class citizens who had very limited rights and he also, with the help and dedication of his followers in India, brought an end to rule of the British Empire, without ever raising a hand or delivering a cross word.

He saw violence as being a sign of the weak. To react to an attack, verbal or physical, is easy but to offer tolerance and no resistance is a real act of bravery and strength. We cannot live without each other but we must make a greater effort to live with each other in harmony.

To be able to make a start with achieving this goal, a level of trust needs to be built within a society. This is something that has to come initially from the government, for if the people don't feel that they can trust the government to deliver what it promises to deliver, there is no hope for forming a peaceful and integrated society. In terms of how democratic a government is (and therefore how trustworthy), the western governments are generally seen as the most developed in the world at the current time. However, there is certainly no overwhelming level of trust that the people would give to the governments of the UK, USA and many others. There may be a certain level of stability in these countries but the level of trust is another thing.

1

The Nordic (economic) model , which is followed in Finland, Sweden and Denmark (and to a lesser degree in Norway and Iceland) is one that is founded on trust. In these countries, and the Netherlands, there is a higher level of trust in the governments than in most other countries. It is stated that "a high level of trust is also associated with low corruption, which is essential for confidence in authorities". (The Nordic Model p.39)

When this trust is lacking from the people, they know that corruption is being conducted to some degree and therefore if the government is doing it, the people also need to take part in it in order to get what they feel they deserve because they won't believe that the government is going to provide good enough conditions for them. This is, of course, a recipe for failure which will lead to the collapse of a society. In this case, people will always feel that there is a barrier between the government and themselves, where the government rules the majority, decides for them what they can and can't do without any real consultation with the citizens and there will not be a bond of trust or a significant level of respect from the people towards the government.

To be able to feel trust for the government, the people have to know that their rights are respected and are met by those who govern them. The Universal Declaration of Human Rights (UDHR) is followed by many countries (notably not by the USA, see Noam Chomsky's [2] "Rogue States"). Any government worth its salt would appreciate the need for these rights and follow them diligently if they want the public to feel it can be trusted. Of course, this would mean that the UDHR should be referred to whenever it is felt that there has been a violation of these rights by any person or organisation in the country. Chomsky sees the USA as being relativistic in its approach to the UDHR, meaning that the various administrations of the twentieth century agree to follow those articles that won't cause any discomfort to the individuals that control the government in their quest for world domination. Those articles that would empower the average person are looked on with scorn and rejection, which is why the US administrations have not yet ratified the UDHR to date. The same is true of the Convention on the Rights of the Child. Along with the government-less Somalia, only the USA has disagreed to follow this charter. And yet, the people of the USA don't feel particularly distrustful of their governments, but why not? This is where propaganda comes into force; deceiving the public and enforcing the notion of pride that they should feel for their country is fundamental to cover the lies that the people who are being implicitly repressed are told.

The hypothetical government would never deceive its people. It would need to be completely transparent as to its policies and actions and be subject to analysis by anyone in not only the country but the world if it is going to be able to build up a sense of trust and respect from the people. The people need to be able to believe that they are as much of the government as those who fulfil the roles of managing the issues, problems and putting into place on a national scale the actions that the people will gain from as a society. There ought to be no real distinction between the government representatives and the citizens. This does not mean that that's how it should 'appear' to be but how it should actually be. After all, the people who form the government are still people. It is not that they should be seen as having positions of power but positions of responsibility to democratically propose laws and policies with their departments, who then put them forward to the public to debate and analyse to ensure that there are no hidden issues or agendas from the government. Once the true moral perspectives on the issues have been identified with no opinions that will favour a certain 'group' of people more, or will be to the detriment of the environment, the problems will work themselves out. A compromise and an agreement will be reached in a truly democratic sense.

Accountability – It is all too common for politicians to deliver promises in an election campaign and then for those words to mysteriously disappear from memory. These kinds of promises are usually ones that are straight out of the politicians' manual of stock phrases: "We are going to tackle crime", "We are going to create more jobs", "We are going to strengthen the economy". How many times have we heard phrases like this but felt that, after a few years, nothing seems to have changed? The ways that such phrases have been backed up are, again, with stock explanations that usually don't point to any specific actions. Therefore, politicians are generally unaccountable for their promises. If they don't deliver, well never mind, they are still in the positions of power and there's little that can be done about it. At least until the next election.

This is an example of corruption – it is lies and deceit that are spoken with the sole aim of winning the votes.

However, when a new political party wins an election, it is often difficult for them to deliver their promises straight away. Sometimes, for any real progress to develop it can take more than a year. But this doesn't mean that progress cannot be seen to be made. If projects and policies are implemented and progress starts to happen, then the public would be able to judge for themselves if the new party in power is appearing to stick to its words.

If, on the other hand, the promises are not seen to be worked on, even after the first year of office, questions need to be asked by the ministers or representatives, as well as by the general public.

The vote of no-confidence is a useful tool for having the power to remove an official from their position. It currently works in various ways around the world. If, for example, the government is seen to be failing to deliver any results and that it is failing the people, the opposing party might put forward a vote of no-confidence. If the parliament votes no-confidence, then there are two options for the government: to either resign or seek a parliamentary dissolution and call for a general election. This, however, is rare. The United Kingdom has had prime ministers defeated by votes of no-confidence eleven times, which is the highest number in the world. In France, it happened once in 1962 (Georges Pompidou), and once in New Zealand (Thomas MacKenzie) way back in 1912.

In the hypothetical parliament, a vote of no-confidence would definitely be permitted. As the parliament would be structured so that all ministers have equal opportunity to discuss and propose matters, rather than having separate parties, this unified parliament would be able to put forward a motion of no-confidence for any other member, including the leader.

But where does the public come into all of this? The parliamentary representatives would have to be accountable to the public. If there was growing opposition to certain members of parliament and their actions or lack of, the public would be able to demonstrate (either in the streets or by internet votes) to have the representative in question voted on by the parliament. As described above, should the representative lose the vote, they would have to resign from office. In the case of the leader losing the vote of confidence, there could be a call for a general election, if it was decided that the public were dissatisfied with the government on the whole.

Types of political systems

It cannot be objectively argued that any political system to date has succeeded for the benefit of the absolute majority. There are too many forms of government to begin to analyse the merits and deficits of each type but we can look at a general outline of some of the more commonly used forms of government in world history.

Dictatorships, which are ruled by a single leader who has the last word on any aspect of the country have been arguably the worst types of government in terms of human rights and human development. It is usually only the case that a select few of the dictator's cohorts will gain any notable level of life stability through income and relative freedom. Dictatorships are generally found to be favouring certain groups of people over others, where those undesired groups may suffer many forms of torture, and murder or genocide.

Communist states have often been ruled in the form of dictatorships but that aside, have never lived up to the original intentions of Marx and Engels' "The Communist Manifesto" but have claimed to follow the principles whereby they have actually abused the ideology to attempt to justify the imprisonment, forced labour and again, genocide of its own people if they show any signs that they do not support the communist government.

Monarchies, both autocratic and constitutional have, of course, been in effect on a large scale over the centuries and have similarly, in the case of autocratic monarchies, usually been more concerned for the welfare of the monarchies' families and acquaintances than for the general public. Constitutional monarchies have had less of a direct influence on the governing of a country as they are often used primarily as a head of state whereby the political actions have been the responsibility of the ruling political parties.

The typical alternative to a monarchy is a republic, where there can be both a president and a prime minister. A republic may follow a constitutional law, such as the USA, where the political decisions are supposed to reflect what is written in the constitution. This limits how progressive a country can be due to its dependency on the constitution but it can be seen to be effectively democratic if it forms its policies relevant to the educated opinions and beliefs of its people.

A republic is more likely to be parliamentary, which gives it more freedom to change laws if certain circumstances suggest that a law is not adequate in some way. There is currently a large number of parliamentary republics active in the world. Theoretically, this would be more in line with providing a society with well thought out laws that can be adapted to meet the needs of the country while still allowing enough scope for a sensible amount of personal freedom. However, despite there being a large number of parliamentary republics in the developed world, there is a vast difference between the standards of living, income and civil liberties between these countries.

Therefore, it is not as simple as saying that one particular system is the most effective. Countries that are seen to have higher standards of living may be republics or monarchies, constitutional or parliamentary. So how can different political systems be as effective as others yet be have such a range between those countries that follow the same (general) principles?

This is where the quality of leadership comes into the equation.

The idea of a leader, president, prime minister, or monarch leads to ideas of overall power and control. Even those leaders who claim not to want to be seen as having ultimate control are still guilty of it to an extent as they are the ones to make the final decisions on laws and policies. The question is how the decision is arrived at. It is fundamental to a nation that the people's views are listened to and properly considered. Up until recently, without the ability to let people have their say with such immediacy as posting on the internet or emailing news channels, this has been a practical difficulty which until the 1990s could be excused due to the lack of resources.

However, this is not the case any more. In more developed countries, the amount of access to the internet and email as well as mobile phones has increased dramatically and in such countries where these are available, there is no excuse for not knowing what the public thinks.

An effective leadership may propose an idea where a law may need to be brought into effect or changed in some way. At this point, it can be put forward to the public so that they can deliberate it and offer alternative takes on it so that the most effective conclusion can be arrived at. Once this has happened, with the involvement of the public and the value that is placed on their opinions, we can say that is has been done democratically. Of course, it doesn't mean that it can only be the leaders or politicians who can propose ideas to improve the country, ideas can come from the public in the first place.

This can be done by setting up governmental forums for debate online which would need to be monitored for practical purposes so that people aren't overloading them with irrelevant posts. A simple method of users voting to remove posts or ban troublemakers can be implemented to help the forum run as smooth as possibly.

A parliament would also be a recommended way of arriving at satisfactory conclusions. These are of course already in place in many countries although they are not necessarily effective. The hypothetical government would always aim to be inclusive of all so that there is no need to have political parties but all members of parliament would be able to discuss issues and fine tune laws and policies which would be available to watch on television, especially for those who don't have the internet but wish to be involved in the process. People would also be invited to phone in with their own suggestions or to send emails which could then be put forward to the representatives for their consideration.

By acting in this way, the people will feel that their views matter and that they can have a say in how the country develops. The hypothetical government would also be subject to criticism if the public felt that they were still ignoring them and acting in their own interests.

1. The Nordic Model - www.etla.fi/files/
   1892_the_nordic_model_complete.pdf

2. Rogue States, Noam Chomsky. Pluto Press

Positions of Responsibility

The Head of State

In countries where the head of state is not the leading political authority (e.g. a monarch or a president), there seems to be little reason for having a separate person in such a position. The head of state should be the political leader as this person is the one who has the authority to have the final say on implementation of laws and policies in the role of a coordinator, rather than the role of the top of the hierarchy. It is having the role of ultimate responsibility for the development and stability of a country and its relations with the rest of the world.

The concept of monarchies is very primitive and has no real value in modern society as, in the western world, there is no monarch who has overall political power. Monarchs' roles are effectively to be puppets who show up at certain events and receive certain high-profile visitors from abroad. The cost of maintaining a monarchy when they don't give anything substantial to the country does not justify their position and are redundant in the current times. Please refer to the next chapter for a more detailed analysis of the monarchical system.

Therefore, the term for the head of state under a moral government would be the president. This encompasses both the roles of those systems where there is a president/ monarch and a prime minister.

Despite having ultimate responsibility, the president would not have absolute power, as already discussed, and would not be allowed to veto or influence political decisions as democracy would need to be seen to be the driving force in this case.

The president, also being the leader of the party would be able to choose the departmental ministers (from the already existing party members prior to an election) depending on who is thought to be likely to be the most effective to manage a department.

The president would serve a term of office for four years as, for many reasons, it can take time to implement strategies and there needs to be this scope for policies to have an effect. Unlike in the USA but like in the UK, the president would be able to serve indefinitely if the public continued to vote for this person and wanted them to stay in the role.

Government Ministers

Government ministers would only work in the departments that affect the management of the whole country and would not also be local representatives (who will be discussed in the next section). The reason for this is that they would need to be able to dedicate their time to general matters and would have the overall responsibility of ensuring that their department is working effectively. They would still represent the individual constituencies that make up the country and liaise with the local representatives to work on finding solutions to form fundamental principles that every constituency would work from.

These government ministers would lead the team that makes up their department and would also have to be open to suggestions from members of other parties who may still have seats in parliament if they have been elected from some constituencies. This is to emphasise that everyone who has a valid suggestion would be taken seriously, have the potential to contribute democratically to decision making and effectively part of the overall coalition of the house of parliament.

As this cabinet of ministers would be the second highest level in the political hierarchy, they would also need to be evaluated independently to ensure that corruption is not taking place.

The Government Evaluation Committee (GEC)

The GEC would be an independent institution (but still funded by the government) to investigate the activities of the members of parliament. No member of this committee will be eligible for a position in government. The GEC will be kept informed of all meetings, decisions and actions of the ministers to keep a check on their performance and any irregularities.

The GEC will have full access to the departments' budgets to investigate how the money is being spent. Whereas, ideally, the GEC should be seen to be unnecessary, we don't live in an ideal world and if there was no independent committee in place, corruption would still have the potential to take place.

The GEC would effectively be in place for the public's interests so that they feel that any hidden activities that might not ordinarily be known publicly would still be monitored and acted upon accordingly.

If any evaluations made by the GEC are deemed to be biased towards or against a representative, the government ministers will be able to publicly investigate the disputed matters with the authority with the potential to remove a GEC member from their position.

Local Representatives

These are the people who are elected by the public to govern their local constituency. They are the ones whose job it is to implement the policies agreed upon as described in the *Voting System* section. Being the third level in the hierarchy and the last official one, this is who the public would be able to contact regarding specific issues in their community or with suggestions for alterations to policies or laws which the local representatives can forward to the government ministers.

Should a member of another political party win the seat in the general election, they would still be required to follow the policies agreed on by the majority of the public and not have the freedom to govern as they wish as this would have the potential of a very inconsistent country. As described previously, certain issues would need adaptation to suit the needs of a constituency and the public would then be the ones to raise any concerns they have over the validity of these adaptations.

As local representatives would still need to be elected by the public, if it is the case that no candidate wins an overall majority (over 50% of the votes in the constituency) they would need to share the position with the next highest vote winning candidate to form a partnership. If they have very different views and don't relate to each other well, they have to remember that if they are judged to work together ineffectively, the public living in that constituency will be able to vote them out using the system of no-confidence so it would be worth their while to confront their differences if they wish to secure their positions.

The Public

As it has already been made clear, the public would be considered to have a part to play in the government of themselves. The knowledge that the people can also have input into how how things are being run is to give them a sense of purpose, for them to feel more trusting of those in official positions and to feel that they can contribute to society instead of being told what to do and what's going to happen. The public's opinions and suggestions should not only be seen as valid but as being welcomed, considered and implemented if they are looked upon favourably.

To achieve this aspect of being seen favourably, there would need to be monthly meetings with the local representative for the public to listen to analyses of progress so far and what still needs to be improved and for them to offer their views. This is the kind of connection that the public needs (if they wish to) to show that they are involved with their own development. Local issues can have their solutions found in this way far more effectively.

If the constituency is too large for everyone who wishes to attend these meetings to fit into the hall, volunteers can be selected to represent their smaller communities who can then organise smaller meetings for the people of the neighbourhood prior to the meetings with the local representative, at which the issues and suggestions can then be put forward.

This set-up would help to strengthen the community spirit and help people to feel like they are part of the whole process, not just the consumers that are fuelling the current capitalist system for a few to benefit from.

Monarchy

As there are still many countries in the world that have monarchies, it is important to question the relevance of them, considering that they cost a great deal to the taxpayers. In the UK, the cost of the monarchy has been around £40 million a year. The monarchy's official website attempts to show the value for money by stating that this is the equivalent to 69p per person per year.[1] However, it is stated that this is the cost for the taxpayers but the figure is actually divided between the total population of the UK, currently standing at around 62 million. What is not mentioned is that this would actually be the cost for every single person in the country, not every tax-paying person. It is unreasonable to say that every new-born baby pays 69p to the royal family, as well as the unemployed and the retired. In fact, as the national statistics online website states that as of October 2010, 29.13 million people were employed in the UK,[2] this changes the cost to the taxpayers to around £1.38, which is twice the cost that the monarchy claims. It still not may seem like a lot, but this distortion of the facts is certainly questionable.

In terms of what all this money is used for, the monarchy's official website states that things like "the cost of property maintenance, and of utilities, telephones and related services, at: Buckingham Palace, St. James's Palace, Clarence House", etc., etc.; "the cost of communication and information services in connection with official royal functions and engagements in England and Scotland", "official royal travel by air and rail", which is almost 3,000 visits each year, £4.67 million for such things as administration of honours, maintenance of the Palace of Holyroodhouse (£2.25 million in 2003), state visits, etc.

Additionally, Prince Philip is awarded £359,000 a year from the civil list, the Duke of York receives £249,000 and there are countless other members of the royal family receiving six figure sums annually.

But what entitles these people to receive such vast amounts of money when public funds are being cut and public sector workers are being made redundant? What does a royal family actually do for its country? Of course, the queen is the head of state, but what does that actually mean? She is not the head of the government, she doesn't make laws but only approves of what the parliament puts forward to her to sign in order to make them official. What we need to ask is what the royal family actually does for the benefit of the nation. They travel and meet people, hold formal events for thousands of people. They attend their own ceremonies that celebrate the fact that they are the family that has established itself as the monarchy and that cannot be entered unless by marriage. The fact that it is hereditary means that any member that is born into the family is automatically given the right to be maintained by the taxpayers and they do not have to earn the right from anything other than carrying out 'royal duties'. No member of the royal family has been democratically chosen or elected. They are simply there because historically, they decided to be.

Thomas Paine, in his book Rights of Man, asked what monarchy actually is: "Is it a thing, or is it a name, or is it a fraud? Is it a 'contrivance of human wisdom,' or of human craft to obtain money from a nation under specious pretences? Is it a thing necessary to a nation?"[3], p.77) He goes on to say "That civil government is necessary, all civilized nations will agree; but civil government is republican government." (p.78) By this he meant that it is the government's responsibility to organise and manage a nation and there is no need for a hereditary family to exist when it has no real input into such matters. Paine explained that those who work as representatives of the nation have been elected for their merits, as in their knowledge and talents, but we can't say the same for someone just because they have been born into a specific family. He argued that to accept the monarchy and believe they are useful for the nation, "We must shut our eyes against reason, we must basely degrade our understanding, not to see the folly of what is called monarchy." (p.122)

This is a very important perspective to have when deciding if something is in a nation's interests. Should we remain ignorant because a family creates its own importance and derives its money from every taxpayer without their consent? Should we celebrate them because they live in palaces, wear fancy clothes and travel around the world meeting people but not making any real contribution to the state of affairs? Or should we use reason and think whether such a system has any value and is worth the expense?

If a family wishes to maintain its position of self-declaration as head of state, it should pay for itself. It has no right to demand that poorer people pay for it, because if this was seen to be justified, any family could declare itself to be paid for by the public indefinitely at a great expense. Quite clearly, the general public would not agree to such a situation and from this reasoning, I find it hard to see how a royal family can be justified as meaningful and useful to a nation. Monarchy "is the popery of government; a thing kept up to amuse the ignorant, and quiet them into taxes." (Paine, p.124)

1. www.monarchy.net/costMonarchy.htm
2. www.statistics.gov.uk/cci/nugget.asp?id=12
3. Rights of Man, Thomas Paine. Dover Publications.

The Constitution

The constitution is the foundation of a government, which establishes the rules and principles of an autonomous political entity. It defines the fundamental political principles and establishes the structure, procedures, powers and duties of the government. It also guarantees certain rights to its people. All government officials on both a national and local level are bound to adhering to the statements of the constitution and it is the intention that the citizens will adhere to them as well.

In the hypothetical government, the constitution is based fundamentally on a moral level to give the greatest benefits, freedoms and quality of life to every citizen which must take into account the effect the environment, both nationally and internationally.

It would take the form of a codified constitution, meaning that a single document contains every constitutional law in the state, so that all the information is contained and there are no unwritten sources or sources to be found in any other documents.

A codified constitution also has the status over being more powerful than statute law (regular laws that command or prohibit something); in that if there is a discrepancy between statute laws and the constitution, the statute law can be revoked as being unconstitutional.

Sometimes, however, such discrepancies can lead to the agreement that the constitution needs amending. It is rare for this to happen as the constitution is meant to be seen as almost written in stone; a supreme law and that which ultimately defines the country that it is devised for. This entrenchment can be exemplified by the US constitution, which, to be amended, would need to go through a rigorous process and the new amendments would go through a special body of officials who would vote on it. These kinds of entrenched constitutions are the most common kind in place around the world.

Interestingly enough, despite its historical influence and power, the United Kingdom does not have a codified constitution and is one of only three countries in the world to exist in this way (Israel and New Zealand being the other two). Instead it is based on a variety of documents, unwritten laws, customs and traditions. It can be felt that this is a more flexible system for amendments but it can also be seen as being too ambiguous to be effective, in terms of how to know if a law is cohesive with the underlying principles when there is nothing specific in place. This is an example of a constitution that is not entrenched or codified.

The ideal constitution would be proposed by the government and put forward for discussion by the general public. Once agreements have been democratically reached, it would be codified to make sure that the citizens and anything else that is covered by it would always have this protection.

A constitution is divided in a number of areas. These differ from country to country but the most common sections are as follows:

The preamble – the introduction to make clear the overall purpose of the constitution.

Sovereignty – to state that the constitution has power of a certain defined region (the nation or relevant region). In many cases this means that the constitution and laws are set for the entire country. In other cases, such as in Spain, power is devolved more to regional governments, giving them autonomy in certain areas such as economy.

An example of this section, based on the UDHR, would be as follows:

(This country) is indivisible, secular, democratic and social. It ensures the equality of all citizens before the law, irrespective of origin, race, religion, gender, language, opinion, property, birth or other status. Before the law, all people will therefore be treated solely as people and shall not be defined or perceived by any other classification.

The form of government describes the rights and obligations of the government. As stated in this section, it would explain that the government would have the responsibility for proposing the policy for the nation in a democratic way. It would state that the president would have the authority to have the final decision on laws and policies but that the policies, or elements of, would have the potential to come from the citizens, go through the local representatives, then through the government ministers until they were finalised by the president.

The executive power section would explain that the president is bound by the constitution and does not have the authority to override the majority's agreed decisions. The president is accountable for all actions and decisions and is not exempt from legal proceedings in the same way that would apply to any citizen of the country.

The president may hold office for a fixed term of four years, after which they would be eligible to stand for office as many times as they wish to, unless they have been found guilty of conducting illegal activities. In this case, the person would not be eligible to stand for office at any point in the future.

The parliament would be defined as set out in the section of Positions of Responsibility. It would be emphasised that all elected representatives would have an equal status in the parliament and have the scope to put forward proposals and suggestions to improving the conditions to ensure that no citizens would be at risk for the reasons of profit. No policy would be allowed to exist if it was going to be to the detriment to the environment or if it was going to exploit money from the citizens. Additionally, no perceived group of people would be treated more favourably than others and policies can only be implemented if they were seen as being of benefit to everyone.

The parliament would be an open forum where all ideas would be considered if they were seen to be valid but if a motion was attempted to be put through that would marginalise certain groups or favour others, their position as a government minister would be subject to investigation, with the possibility of their removal from office.

The rights of the citizens would include that all people would be given equal opportunities and supported to be able to achieve a state of well-being. All people would have an equal status and have the same obligations.

Many articles from the UDHR could be taken on in their complete form for this section:

3: Everyone has the right to life, liberty and security of person.

4: No one shall be held in slavery or servitude; slavery and the slave trade shall be prohibited in all their forms.

5: No one shall be subjected to torture or to cruel, inhuman or degrading treatment or punishment.

6: Everyone has the right to recognition everywhere as a person before the law.

7: All are equal before the law and are entitled without any discrimination to equal protection of the law. All are entitled to equal protection against any discrimination in violation of this Declaration and against any incitement to such discrimination.

8: Everyone has the right to an effective remedy by the competent national tribunals for acts violating the fundamental rights granted him by the constitution or by law.

9: No one shall be subjected to arbitrary arrest, detention or exile.

10: Everyone is entitled in full equality to a fair and public hearing by an independent and impartial tribunal, in the determination of his rights and obligations and of any criminal charge against him.

(There are many others which could be incorporated similarly, but as this is not intended to be exhaustive, I will leave it to the reader to examine the full list of the UDHR).

The judiciary is included to give a clear understanding of how the judicial system is to operate. It does not give a list of laws, as they are prone to change over time, but states that the judicial system interprets the law and applies it to each case brought before the courts.

The judiciary is effectively a programmable machine that has to function according to the rules that it has been supplied with; therefore, it does not make the laws, which is the job of the government (with the input from the citizens in a true democracy).

Any constitution that is already codified and in practice should, for the reasons of true morality, freedoms and democracy, be examined and if necessary, subject to amendments. Whereas it would be too much to attempt to analyse various constitutions from around the world, one article that I would very strongly recommend should be amended is the right to keep and bear arms. A few countries have this right in place in their constitutions (although the details vary regarding specifically what is allowed and what is not). Those countries which are the most liberal about gun ownership, stating that it is legal to keep a gun at home providing the owner has a licence for it are Cuba, Mexico, North Korea, countries that follow Sharia (Islamic Law), Spain, the USA (for reasons of self-defence), Finland (although the guns have to be inoperable or kept separately from ammunition), and Switzerland, where the firearms have to be kept by certain people (those who have received military training) or the citizens, who must register their ownership with the police.

I have previously discussed this issue but must just reiterate that if people are allowed to keep guns, other people who know that many people have relatively east access to guns are understandably going to be somewhat afraid of armed attack and respond by purchasing a gun to protect themselves. It is an eternal cycle, which is enforced by the neurosis of never really knowing if strangers are carrying a gun, so it's better to get one, just in case.

To avoid the dictatorial aspect of proposing a constitution (which would also take up many, many pages), the final chapter will be to provide thought and debate over what should be included in a democratic and moral constitution.

Conclusion

The Moralist Manifesto

Considering that by now, the reader will have a good understanding of the principles that would be necessary or recommended for a truly successful society, I will conclude with a summary of what has been detailed in this book. The main points proposed are what can be seen as the manifesto for Moralism.

This differs from electoral campaigns where politicians' words are usually either not worth the time it took to say them or if they are put in writing, are not considered to be what they feel that resolutely have to stick to. This manifesto needs to be made clear that a Moralist party would have to be seen to rigorously follow the statements set out, as a country and its laws would be bound by a similar constitution.

There need to be separate sections for what the government will pledge to do and be bound by. The government's role needs to be stated, along with how the country as a whole must operate and what the specific rights of the citizens are. Within these, some issues are related to the environment outside of human society so there doesn't need to be a separate section for the environment as the manifesto dictates how people in various positions must act.

The government will:

- Aim to understand the reasons for social problems, establish the root cause and act morally to find the best solutions to overcome them.
- Not recognise any system of class, caste or other perceived social groups, and will only strive to provide opportunities for everyone.
- Operate in a secular manner and will not be pressured by religious beliefs when reaching its decisions. However, it is willing to take into account moral perspectives that may be written in religious texts if they are considered to be appropriate.
- Strive to help communities to develop, focusing on the integration of everyone relevant for their economic development and greater social cohesion.
- Listen to suggestions and proposals for projects from the citizens. If they are judged to have a moral basis and the likelihood of success, they will be considered and potentially

implemented.

- Protect the citizens from exploitation in the following ways:
  - By not allowing monetary exploitation where the goods or services paid for will be of detriment to the citizens, for example, health-wise or financially.
  - By promoting and enforcing democracy in the workplace via unions that follow defined principles with the aim of reaching compromises from both sides.
  - By giving the citizens of a specified community the right to decide on whether they want certain investments or developments in their community. The democratic vote of the citizens will be the deciding factor.
  - By supporting local banks for the citizens to save their money and to promote those banks' investments into their respective communities.
  - By regulating banks so that they are prohibited from giving loans or selling products to people who are unlikely to be able to repay them.
  - By regulating the advertising and marketing industries to not allow the sale of placebo products or those which have no independent scientific evidence that they are effective.

- Promote creativity in the community to help the citizens achieve a greater sense of well-being.
- Promote multicultural harmony through actions and events to increase interpersonal bonds, an understanding of multicultural traditions, and encourage citizens to be aware of the rights needs and interests of everyone.
- Develop relations with other nations to achieve greater harmony, equality and fair trade and support them to develop where it is moral and practical to do so.
- Not invade, or declare war, on any other nation.
- Maintain a government-controlled military, only for the purpose of national defence.
- Promote the ongoing development of education, which will be freely available to every child resident in the country between the ages of 3 and 18.
- Support a national health system to provide basic health treatment for all citizens.

- Promote a resilient agricultural system and keep the level of food and drink imports to a minimum.
- Promote and support good parenting skills to help people to understand the needs of children and provide better for them, through support groups where necessary.
- Put a greater emphasis on creativity and support people to explore their interests to improve their level of happiness and fulfilment.
- Be committed to developing renewable energy and gradually decreasing the country's reliance on fossil fuels.
- Regulate industry to reduce as far as possible the over-production of products that leads to unnecessary waste and pollution for the environment.
- Support industry to change their fuel sources to renewable energy by allowing to invest without having to pay interest on necessary loans.
- Encourage a change in lifestyle in a way that people will be less dependent on appliances and vehicles that use non-renewable energy by inspiring people to take part in more communal, and where possible, energetic, activities.
- Regulate the food industry to encourage people to buy healthier products. The value added tax on unhealthy foods, when agreed on by a government supported, but independent committee, will increase to attempt to make healthier options more of a sensible choice for the citizens.
- Give workers the priority to reclaim their previous place of work in the case of its closure, through reaching agreements to gradually pay off outstanding costs on the premises. Workers will be supported to become effective managers of their own new businesses to promote the acquisition of their own destiny.
- Support individuals and small businesses to create their own employment on a cooperative level.
- Regulate the banking sector to prohibit the freedom of setting interest rates on loans to customers and businesses.
- Work under a structured immigration action plan to integrate and develop officially permitted immigrants and integrate them into society. They will have equal status with the citizens of the country. The number of immigrants allowed into the country has to be limited, depending on the resources to support them, such as housing and available work.
- Evaluate and adapt laws where necessary to provide fairness in the interests of the citizens and the environment.

- Promote systems of community resilience to ensure good management of resources and businesses that will focus on cooperativism and eliminating competition, with the intention of achieving a well-balanced community that is interdependent.
- Give more autonomy to local governments to take into account their individual needs concerning the citizens and the environment, while still working under the principles of Moralism.
- Promote physical activity to help maintain a good level of fitness and health for its citizens.
- Regulate the pharmaceutical industry to make treatments more financially viable for all citizens.

(This country) will:

- Accept all religions on the basis that they do not have the intention of causing disadvantage to other people or incite hatred between themselves and/ or other religious groups.
- Encourage the citizens to seek their own truth regarding their spiritual beliefs, to investigate evidence and arrive at their own conclusions.
- Put the well-being of everyone at the forefront regarding actions and decisions about development and investments. Well-being will always have the precedence over monetary gain.
- Not allow the abuse or exploitation of animals for human entertainment. If the animals are concluded to be less happy than if they were in their natural environment, they will not be permitted to be kept in that way.
- Respect the environment and only allow exploitation of resources if it is sustainable and the natural environment can be and will be restored to its natural state, as closely as possible.
- Follow the principles of permaculture and improve the conditions of the environment.
- Provide welfare for its citizens in the case of unemployment and support projects to develop new skills and interests with the intention of helping the citizens to find or create their own work.
- Not allow the ownership of any arms, such as guns, unless they are licensed and kept in a designated building. The possession of arms in the home is strictly prohibited. No live ammunition will be permitted for use outside the agriculture sector, the

military and the police.

- Implement a pension system for the retired population, based on obligatory contributions from workers and supplemented by mandatory contributions from high earning citizens and businesses in the case of general workers' contributions not meeting the annual budgets of the pension system.
- Operate a penal system that is focused on the rehabilitation of those convicted, to help them integrate as developed members of society whilst serving their sentences and upon their release.

The citizens will be:

- Covered by the rights set out in the Universal Declaration of Human Rights.
- Eligible to vote, drive, smoke, have sexual intercourse, marry and be of a legally recognised age to consider themselves adults who are responsible for themselves at the age of 18.
- Exempt from military service and it will be their right to refuse to take part in military action with no justification required.
- Able to make the decision to decide on their own euthanasia following the criteria set out in the country's legal documentation regarding this law.
- Eligible to obtain an abortion as long as it is not medically considered a danger to their own life and within the time limit of the first 20 weeks of pregnancy, providing that it has been considered safe by a registered medical official.
- Given equal opportunities to achieve a level of personal and communal well-being.
- Encouraged to integrate fully into the community on all levels.
- Encouraged to explore their creativity and find meaningful employment based on it wherever possible.
- Protected from exploitation by individuals or businesses.
- Encouraged to take control of their own destiny and not be impeded if there is no moral reason to limit their opportunities.
- Supported to find suitable accommodation within the range of their budget and will be supported, not punished, if they fall into financial difficulties.
- Encouraged to collaborate with their fellow residents to favour harmonious, cooperative relationships over competitive rivalry.

There are practical and realistic ways that we can improve the level of well-being for everyone and develop countries so that they are more cooperative. The only way forward is to develop harmony, equality and fairness and to emphasise the importance of peace, acceptance and the understanding that we all share the world together. We rely on successful interdependence of our own species and other species that have the right to exist and flourish in the environment, for which our responsibilities and morals are imperative.

44302385R00239

Made in the USA
Charleston, SC
21 July 2015